Annual Reports

Horace Mann

This work has been selected by scholars as being culturally important, and is part of the knowledge base of civilization as we know it. This work was reproduced from the original artifact, and remains as true to the original work as possible. Therefore, you will see the original copyright references, library stamps (as most of these works have been housed in our most important libraries around the world), and other notations in the work.

This work is in the public domain in the United States of America, and possibly other nations. Within the United States, you may freely copy and distribute this work, as no entity (individual or corporate) has a copyright on the body of the work.

As a reproduction of a historical artifact, this work may contain missing or blurred pages, poor pictures, errant marks, etc. Scholars believe, and we concur, that this work is important enough to be preserved, reproduced, and made generally available to the public. We appreciate your support of the preservation process, and thank you for being an important part of keeping this knowledge alive and relevant.

ANNUAL REPORTS

OF THE

SECRETARY OF THE BOARD OF EDUCATION
OF MASSACHUSETTS FOR THE
YEARS 1845–1848

AND ORATION DELIVERED BEFORE THE AUTHORITIES
OF THE CITY OF BOSTON, JULY 4, 1842

BY

HORACE MANN

BOSTON 1891
LEE AND SHEPARD PUBLISHERS
10 MILK STREET NEXT "THE OLD SOUTH MEETING-HOUSE"
NEW YORK CHAS. T. DILLINGHAM
718 AND 720 BROADWAY

CONTENTS.

                                                                                                   PAGE

NINTH REPORT, FOR 1845 1

    Increasing interest in, and profound importance of, public education, 1. Spirit that should animate the common schools, and duties of the State towards them, 3. School motives and school vices, 17. Regard for moral excellence paramount, 17. The teacher's heart must be in his work, 23. Obedience should be secured through affection and respect, not by fear, 28. Government of the school, 36; expulsion deprecated, 41. Evils of imperfect recitations, 43; of shirking lessons, 46; of deception, 47. The prevention of whispering, 59. Truancy, 72. Knowledge should be made interesting, 75. Fear, ambition, emulation, must be used sparingly, 82. Final examinations, 89. Inductive method of instruction, 95.

TENTH REPORT, FOR 1846 105

    Origin of the common-school system of Massachusetts, 105. Historical arguments for its validity, 113. Its fundamental sanction the trusteeship of the Commonwealth for future generations, 115.

ELEVENTH REPORT, FOR 1847 141

    The power of the common schools to redeem the State from social vices and crimes, 141. Circular letter of inquiry, 151; replies. 161. Conditions necessary to success, 174; I. The cardinal principles of the New England system, 175; II. High qualifications of teachers, 177; III. The regular attendance of all children. 195. Recapitulation, 212. Universality of education, 218.

TWELFTH REPORT, FOR 1848 222

    The capacity of the common-school system to improve the pecuniary condition. and elevate the intellectual, moral, and religious character, of the Commonwealth, 222. Physical education, 233. Intellectual education as a means of removing poverty and securing abundance, 245. Political education, 268. Moral education, 283. Religious education, 292. Vindication from the charge of a purpose to exclude religion and the Bible from the schools, 297.

ORATION DELIVERED BEFORE THE AUTHORITIES OF THE CITY OF BOSTON, JULY 4, 1842 341

Duty to posterity, 342. Intelligence and virtue necessary for a republic, 346. Responsibility of voters, 351. Dangers of ignorance and vice, 354. Capability of man for self-government, 355. Duty of wealthy and educated citizens, 360. Necessity of universal education, 362. National illiteracy, 367. Dangers from privileged classes, 376. Inadequacy of schools, 382. State education, 385. Political crimes, 389.

REPORT FOR 1845.

GENTLEMEN, —

... THE extraordinary facts exhibited in my last Report, respecting the manner of apportioning school-money among the districts, have turned public attention to that important subject.* Those facts have already induced some towns to make very material modifications in the manner of distributing their money; and they promise to do the same thing in many more. The great doctrine which it is desirable to maintain, and to carry out, in reference to this subject, is, *equality of school-privileges for all the children of the town, whether they belong to a poor district or a rich one, a small district or a large one.*

A general interest has been awakened in some towns upon which a deep sleep had fallen before. During no year, since my original appointment, have my advice and assistance been so frequently requested respecting the best methods of arranging and improving our school-system.

Nor is the movement confined to our own Commonwealth. Several States in the south and west seem to be awaking from their lethargy, and inquiring into the detail of means necessary to be adopted for the general education of their people. Within the space of a single month, during the last autumn, I received inquiries from a dozen distinguished men, belonging to a single State, respecting the organic structure of our system, its general

---

* The details of this unequal distribution have not been republished, as they are not of present interest.

administration, and its internal arrangements and management. In the mean time, the great State of New York, by means of her county superintendents, her State Normal School, and otherwise, is carrying forward the work of popular education more rapidly than any other State in the Union, or any country in the world. Within the last year, the State of Rhode Island has entirely renovated her school-system. Under the auspices of that distinguished and able friend of common schools, Henry Barnard, Esq., she is preparing to take her place among the foremost of the States. Within the last few weeks also, the State of Vermont has re-organized her school-system, by passing a law which provides for the appointment of town, *county*, and State superintendents, prescribing the course of duty of each class of officers in regard to the examination of teachers, the visitation of schools, and the general administration of the system.

These indubitable evidences of progress are not only a reward for past exertions, but an incentive to future efforts. But let not complacency in successes already obtained tempt to the relaxation of a single fibre in our endeavors for future advancement. What has been gained must be converted into means for further acquisition. The faithful steward, being intrusted with five talents, therewith gets other five talents.

Our common schools are a system of unsurpassable grandeur and efficiency. Their influences reach, with more or less directness and intensity, all the children belonging to the State, — children who are soon to be the State. They act upon these children at the most impressible period of their existence, — imparting qualities of mind and heart which will be magnified by diffusion, and deepened by time, until they will be evolved into national character, — into weal or woe, into renown or ignominy, — and, at last, will stamp their ineffaceable seal upon our history. The natural philosopher looks at the silky envelopment which an insect has woven for itself; he marks its structure; he recognizes the laws of life which are silently at work within it; and he knows that, in a few days or weeks, that covering will burst, and from it will be evolved a thing of beauty and vivacity, lovely in the eyes of all, or an agent of destruction, fit to be a minister in executing God's vengeance against an offending people. With a profounder insight into the laws of development and growth, and with an eye that embraces an ampler field of time in its vision, the philosopher of humanity looks at the institutions which are moulding the youthful capacities of a nation; he calculates their energy and direction; and he is then able to foresee and to foretell, that, if its course be not changed, the coming generation will be blessed with the rewards of parental forecast, or afflicted with the retributions of parental neglect. Happy are they, who, knowing on what conditions God has made the welfare of nations to depend, observe and perform them with fidelity.

Improvement in schoolhouse architecture — including in the phrase all comfortable and ample accommodations for the schools — is only an improvement in the perishing body in which they dwell. A more perfect organization of the schools themselves, by a wisely-graduated classification of schools and scholars, and by the assignment of such territorial limits as will best combine individual convenience with associated strength, is only an endowment of that perishing body with a superior mechanism of organs and limbs. The more bounteous pecuniary liberality with which our schools, from year to year, are maintained, is only an addition to the nutriment by which the same body is fed, giving enlargement and energy to its capabilities, whether of good or of evil, and empowering it to move onward more swiftly in its course, whether that course is leading to prosperity or to ruin.

The great, the all-important, the only important question still remains: By what spirit are our schools animated? Do they cultivate the higher faculties in the nature of childhood, — its conscience, its benevolence, a reverence for whatever is true and sacred? or are they only developing, upon a grander scale, the lower instincts and selfish tendencies of the race, — the desires which prompt men to seek, and the powers which enable them to secure, sensual ends, — wealth, luxury, preferment, —

irrespective of the well-being of others? Knowing, as we do, that the foundations of national greatness can be laid only in the industry, the integrity, and the spiritual elevation of the people, are we equally sure that our schools are forming the character of the rising generation upon the everlasting principles of duty and humanity? or, on the other hand, are they only stimulating the powers which lead to a base pride of intellect, which prompt to the ostentation instead of the reality of virtue, and which give augury that life is to be spent only in selfish competitions between those who should be brethren? Above all others, must the children of a republic be fitted for society as well as for themselves. As each citizen is to participate in the power of governing others, it is an essential preliminary that he should be imbued with a feeling for the wants, and a sense of the rights, of those whom he is to govern; because the power of governing others, if guided by no higher motive than our own gratification, is the distinctive attribute of oppression; an attribute whose nature and whose wickedness are the same, whether exercised by one who calls himself a republican, or by one born an irresponsible despot. In a government like ours, each individual must think of the welfare of the State, as well as of the welfare of his own family, and, therefore, of the children of others as well as his own. It becomes, then, a momentous question, whether the children in our schools are educated in reference to themselves and their private interests only, or with a regard to the great social duties and prerogatives that await them in after-life. Are they so educated, that, when they grow up, they will make better philanthropists and Christians, or only grander savages? For, however loftily the intellect of man may have been gifted, however skilfully it may have been trained, if it be not guided by a sense of justice, a love of mankind, and a devotion to duty, its possessor is only a more splendid, as he is a more dangerous, barbarian.

We have had admirable essays and lectures on the subject of morality in our schools. In perusing the reports of school-committees from year to year, nothing has given me so much pleasure as the prominence which they have assigned to the subject of moral education, and the sincerity, the earnestness, and the persistence with which they have vindicated its claims to be regarded as an indispensable part of all common-school instruction. Considered as general speculation, nothing could be better; and yet no one will deny that the want of a corresponding action on this subject still beclouds the prospects of the schools, and ofttimes causes us to tremble for the fate of those who are passing through them. Practically, the duty of cultivating the moral nature of childhood has been neglected, and is still neglected. Profound ethical treatises are written for the guidance of men, after the habits and passions of ninety-nine in every hundred of those men have become too deep-rooted and inveterate to be removed by secondary causes. Volumes are published on the nicest questions of casuistry, — questions which probably will never arise in the experience of more than one in a thousand of the community, — while specific directions and practical aids in regard to the training of children in those every-day domestic and social duties on which their own welfare and the happiness of society depend are comparatively unknown. How shall this great desideratum be supplied? How shall the rising generation be brought under purer moral influences, by way of guaranty and suretyship, that, when they become men, they will surpass their predecessors, both in the soundness of their speculations and in the rectitude of their practice? Were children born with perfect natures, we might expect that they would gradually purify themselves from the vices and corruptions which are now almost enforced upon them by the examples of the world. But the same nature by which the parents sunk into error and sin pre-adapts the children to follow in the course of ancestral degeneracy. Still, are there not moral means for the renovation of mankind which have never yet been applied? Are there not resources whose vastness and richness have not yet been explored? Of all neglected and forgotten duties, in all ages of the world, the spiritual culture of children has been most neglected and forgotten. In all things else, art and science have triumphed. In all things else, principles have been investigated, and instruments devised and constructed, to apply those principles in practice. The tree has been taken in the germ, and its growth fashioned to the wants or the tastes of man. By the skill of the cultivator, the wild grain and the wild fruit have been taken in their seed, and have had their dwarfishness expanded into luxuriance, and their bitter and sometimes poisonous qualities ameliorated into richness of flavor and nutrition. The wild animal, and even the beast of prey, if domesticated when young, and from the lair, have been tamed and trained to the service of man, — the wild horse and the buffalo changed into the most valuable of domestic animals, and the prowling wolf into the faithful dog. But man has not yet applied his highest wisdom and care to the young of his own species. They have been comparatively neglected until their passions had taken deep root, and their ductile feelings had hardened into the iron inflexibility of habit; and then how often have the mightiest agencies of human power and terror been expended upon them in vain! Governments do not see the future criminal or pauper in the neglected child, and therefore they sit calmly by, until roused from their stupor by the cry of hunger or the spectacle of crime. Then they erect the alms-house, the prison, and the gibbet, to arrest or mitigate the evils which timely caution might have prevented. The courts and the ministers of justice sit by until the petty delinquencies of youth glare out in the enormities of adult crime; and then they doom to the prison or the gallows those enemies to society, who, under wise and well-applied influences, might have been supports and ornaments of the social fabric. For sixteen centuries, the anointed ministers of the gospel of Christ were generally regardless of the condition of youth. And the same remark holds true in regard to the last two centuries, with the exception of three or four only of all the Christian nations; and by far the greater part, even of these, must be excepted from the exception. The messengers of Him who took little children in his arms and blessed them have suffered juvenile waywardness or perversity to mature into adult incorrigibleness and impenitency; and then they have invoked the aid of Heaven to subdue that ferociousness of the passions which even a worldly foresight would have checked. How often has Heaven turned a deaf ear to their prayers, as if to rebuke the neglect and the blindness which had given occasion for them! Who will deny, that, if one tithe of the talent and culture which have been expended in legislative halls, in defining offences, and in devising and denouncing punishments for them; or of the study and knowledge which have been spent in judicial courts, in trying and in sentencing criminals; or of the eloquence and the piety which have preached repentance and the remission of sins to adult men and women, — had been consecrated to the instruction and training of the young, the civilization of mankind would have been adorned by virtues and charities and Christian graces to which it is now a stranger?

What an appalling fact it is to every contemplative mind, that even wars and famines and pestilences — terrible calamities as they are acknowledged to be — have been welcomed as blessings and mercies, because they swept away, by thousands and tens of thousands, the pests which ignorance and guilt had accumulated! But the efficiency or sufficiency of these comprehensive remedies is daily diminishing. A large class of men seem to have lost that moral sense by which the liberty and life of innocent men are regarded as of more value than the liberty and life of criminals. There is not a government in Christendom which is not growing weaker every day, so far as its strength lies in an appeal to physical force. The criminal code of most nations is daily shorn of some of its terrors. Where, as with us, the concurrence of so many minds is a prerequisite, the conviction of the guilty is often a matter of difficulty; and every guilty man who escapes is a missionary, going through society, and preaching the immunity of guilt wherever he goes. War will never again be waged to disburden the crowded prisons, or to relieve the weary executioner. The arts of civilization have so multiplied the harvests of the earth, that a general famine will not again lend its aid to free the community of its surplus members. Society at large has emerged from that barbarian and semi-barbarian state where pestilence formerly had its birth, and committed its ravages. These great outlets and sluice-ways, which, in former times, relieved nations of the dregs and refuse of their population, being now closed, whatever want or crime we engender, or suffer to exist, we must live with. If improvidence begets hunger, that hunger will break into our garners. If animal instincts are suffered to grow into licentious passions, those passions will find their way to our most secret chambers. We have no armed guard which can save our warehouses, our market-places, and our depositories of silver and gold, from spoliation by the hands of a mob. When the perjured witness or the forsworn juryman invades the temple of justice, the evil becomes too subtle for the police to seize. It is beyond legislative or judicial or executive power to redeem the sanctuaries of religion from hypocrisy and uncharitableness. In a word, the freedom of our institutions gives full play to all the passions of the human heart. The objects which excite and inflame those passions abound; and, as a fact, nearly or quite universal, there is intelligence sufficient to point out some sure way, lawful or unlawful, by which those passions can be gratified. Whatever children, then, we suffer to grow up amongst us, we must live with as men; and our children must be their contemporaries. They are to be our copartners in the relations of life, our equals at the polls, our rulers in legislative halls; the awarders of justice in our courts. However intolerable at home, they cannot be banished to any foreign land; however worthless, they will not be sent to die in camps, or to be slain in battle; however flagitious, but few of them will be sequestered from society by imprisonment, or doomed to expiate their offences with their lives.

In the history of the world, that period which opened with

the war of the American Revolution, and with the adoption of the Constitution of the United States, forms a new era. Those events, it is true, did not change human nature; but they placed that nature in circumstances so different from any it had ever before occupied, that we must expect a new series of developments in human character and conduct. Theoretically, and, to a great extent, practically, the nation passed at once, from being governed by others, to self-government. Hereditary misrule was abolished; but power and opportunity for personal misrule were given in its stead. In the hour of exultation at the achievement of liberty, it was not considered that the evils of license may be more formidable than the evils of oppression, because a man may sink himself to a profounder depth of degradation than it is in the power of any other mortal to sink him, and because the slave of the vilest tyrant is less debased than the thrall of his own passions. Restraints of physical force were cast off; but no adequate measures were taken to supply their place with the restraints of moral force. In the absence of the latter, the former, degrading as they are, are still desirable, — as a strait-jacket for the maniac is better than the liberty by which he would inflict wounds or death upon himself. The question now arises, — and it is a question on whose decision the worth or worthlessness of our free institutions is suspended, — whether some more powerful agency cannot be put in requisition to impart a higher moral tone to the public mind; to enthrone the great ideas of justice, truth, benevolence, and reverence, in the breasts of the people, and give them a more authoritative sway over conduct than they have ever yet possessed. Of course, so great an object can be reached only by gradual approaches. Revolutions which change only the surface of society can be effected in a day; but revolutions working down among the primordial elements of human character, taking away ascendency from faculties which have long had control over the conduct of men, and transferring it to faculties which have long been in subjection, — such revolutions cannot be accomplished by one convulsive effort, though every fibre in the nation should be strained to the endeavor. Time is an essential element in their consummation; nor can they be effected without an extensive apparatus of means, efficiently worked. Yet such revolutions have taken place, — as when nations emerged from the barbarian into the classic and chivalrous or romantic ages, or when they passed from these into the commercial and philosophic periods. By a brief retrospect of the condition of the more civilized nations of ancient and of modern times, it can be easily shown that such a change has already taken place on the subject of education itself. It is the mission of our age to carry this cause one step farther onward in its progress of development.

Among the ancients, physical education was deemed of paramount importance. A preparation of the masses for war was the grand, the almost exclusive, object of national concern. War being carried on, and battles decided, mainly by muscular strength and agility; by the distance and accuracy with which the javelin could be hurled, or the vigor and dexterity with which the falchion could be wielded, — the desire of physical celerity and force predominated among men. It was not the cultivation of the great heart of the nation, it was not even the development of the intellect of the masses, but it was the invigoration of the frame, the growth and the strengthening of the limbs, that constituted the object of national policy and ambition. Bodily hardihood, the power of physical endurance, the ability to make long marches unfatigued, and to fight hand-to-hand, for the longest period, unterrified, were the qualities which won the spoils and the plaudits of victory, and kindled to enthusiasm the aspirations of the emulous youth. Who can fail to see that the tendency of all this was, not only to weaken the intellectual nature, and to narrow its range of action, but to degrade and demoralize the spiritual affections? The man was sacrificed to the animal; his soul was deemed of less value than his sinews. As the nobler qualities of his nature sunk to the level of brute force, it happened, naturally, that the horse became as valuable as his rider; and the elephant that went out to battle was of more consequence than the dozen warriors whom he bore in the tower upon his back. During the middle ages, and until the introduction of fire-arms, — which, to a very great extent, neutralized the inequalities of physical strength, — the great barbarian idea, that the body of man is the only part of him worth cultivating, retained unquestioned ascendency in regard to the masses of the people. The soul was not consciously excluded from culture; for it was not sufficiently thought of, as the object of culture, to raise the question. Even down to the present century, the rulers and aristocracy of England have always encouraged athletic sports among the people — wrestling, running, leaping, boxing — as a part of the national policy, because, as it was said, these exercises tended to invigorate the *breed*, and thus to make better soldiers and sailors; the very language which was used betraying the sentiment, that it was the animal, and not the spiritual, part of man which was the object of national concern. Nor even in our own times, nor in our own country, have philosophy and Christianity dispelled this fatal idea, — an idea which is proper to the savage and the heathen only, and which we have inherited from them. In all the nations of Europe, the regulations of military schools in regard to training the body for vigor and robustness, and the capability of endurance, are entirely different from those of the classical, medical, legal, or theological schools; and in the military academy of our own government, at West Point, the cadets are inured to exposure, and their bodies hardened by camp-duty; while in our colleges and higher schools there are no regulations which have the health of the student for their object. On the contrary, so far as the body is concerned, the latter classes of institutions provide for all the natural tendencies to ease and inactivity as carefully as though paleness and languor, muscular enervation and debility, were held to be constituents in national beauty.

The introduction of the Baconian philosophy wrought a great revolution in the education of mankind. Since that epoch, the cultivation of the intellect has received more general attention than ever before; and, just in proportion as the intellect has been developed, it has seen more clearly and appreciated more fully the advantages of its own development. In Prussia and a few of the smaller States of Continental Europe, the action of the intellect, for reasons too obvious to be mentioned, has taken more of a speculative turn. In Great Britain, it has been turned more towards practical or utilitarian objects; and, in the United States, it has been pre-eminently so turned. The immense natural resources of our country would have stimulated to activity a less enterprising and a less energetic race than the Anglo-Saxon. But such glittering prizes, placed within reach of such fervid natures and such capacious desires, turned every man into a competitor and an aspirant. The exuberance that overspread the almost interminable valleys of the West drew forth hosts of colonists to gather their varied harvests. The tide of emigration rolled on, and it still continues to roll, with a volume and a celerity never before known in any part of the world, or in any period of history. Unlike all other nations, we have had no fixed, but a rapidly-advancing frontier. The geographical information of yesterday has become obsolete to-day. The outposts of civilization have moved forward with such gigantic strides, that their marches are reckoned, not by leagues, but by degrees of longitude; and cities containing thirty or fifty thousand souls have sprung up before the relics of the primeval forests had decayed on the soil they had so lately shaded. In the space of half a century, vast wildernesses have been organized into Territories, and these Territories erected into States, to take their place in the great family of the confederacy, and to be heard by their representatives in the council-halls of the nation. But scarcely had the immigrant and the adventurer surveyed the richness of vegetation which covered the surface of the earth, before they discovered an equal vastness of mineral wealth beneath it, — wealth which had been laid up, of old, in subterranean chambers, no man yet knows how capacious. Thus every man, however poor his parentage, became the heir-apparent of a rich inheritance. And while millions were thus appropriating fortunes to themselves out of the great treasure-house of the West, other millions on the Atlantic seaboard, with equal enterprise and equal avidity, were amassing the means of refinement and luxury. In one section, where Nature had adapted the soil to the production of new and valuable staples, the planter seized the opportunity, — literally a golden one, — and soon filled the markets of the world with some of the cheapest and the most indispensable necessaries of life. In another section, foreign commerce invited attention; and the hardy and fearless inhabitants went forth to the uttermost parts of the earth in quest of gain. They drew wealth from the bosom of every ocean that spans the globe; they visited every country, and searched out every port on its circumference, where wind and water could carry them, and brought home, for sustenance or for superfluity, the natural and artificial productions of every people and of every zone. Meantime, science and invention applied themselves to the mechanic arts. They found that Nature, in all her recesses, had hidden stores of power, surpassing the accumulated strength of the whole human race, though all its vigor could be concentrated in a single arm. They found that whoever would rightly apply to Nature, by a performance of the true scientific and mechanical conditions, for the privilege of using her agencies, should forthwith be invested with a power such as no Babylonian or Egyptian king, with all his myriads of slaves, could ever command. With the aid of a little hand-machinery, at the beginning, water and steam have been taught to construct machines; and out of their matchless perfection, when guided by a few intelligent minds, have come the endless variety, the prodigality and the cheapness, of modern manufactures. In the Northern States, too, one universal habit of personal industry, not confined to the middle-aged and the vigorous alone, but enlisting the services of all, — the old, the young, the decrepit, the bed-ridden, each according to his strength, — has never ceased to coin labor into gold; and from the confluence of these numberless streams, though individually small, the great ocean of common comfort and competence has been unfailingly replenished.

Gathered together from these numerous and prolific sources, individual opulence has increased; and the sum total or valuation of the nation's capital has doubled and redoubled with a rapidity to which the history of every other nation that has ever existed must acknowledge itself to be a stranger. This easy accumulation of wealth has inflamed the laudable desire of competence into a culpable ambition for superfluous riches. To convert natural resources into the means of voluptuous enjoyments, to turn mineral wealth into metallic currency, to invent more productive machinery, to open new channels of intercommunication between the States, and to lengthen the prodigious inventory of capital invested in commerce, has spurred the energies and quickened the talent of a people, every one of whom is at liberty to choose his own employment, and to change it, when chosen, for any other that promises to be more lucrative.

Nor is this the only side on which hope has been stimulated and ambition aroused. Others of the most craving instincts of human nature have been called into fervid activity. Political ambition, the love of power, — whether it consists in the base passion of exercising authority over the will of others, or in the more expansive and generous desire of occupying a conspicuous place among our fellows by their consent, — these motives have acted upon a strong natural instinct in the hearts of all. The chief magistrate and the legislators of the nation, the chief magistrate and the legislators of the States, the numerous county, town, parochial, and district officers, are, with but few exceptions, elective; and therefore the possession of all such offices implies the confidence and the regard, of a majority at least, of their respective constituencies. So, too, of a great proportion of the militia offices. In addition to all these, there are voluntary, civil, social, philanthropic, and corporate organizations, each presided over, and its affairs administered, by officers of its own election. Probably there are, at the present hour, in the United States, as many persons holding offices, bestowed upon them by the votes of others, and therefore indicative of some degree of respect and estimation, as existed through all the centuries of the Roman Republic when its dominion was co-extensive with the known world. Doubtless there are more such elective offices at this time, among the twenty millions of this country, than among the two hundred millions of Europe, and far more than in all the world besides. Many of these offices are sources of emolument as well as of power, and hence they present to competitors the double motive of a desire of gain and a love of approbation. If most of these innumerable fountains of honor are too small to slake the thirst of aspirants, they are sufficient to excite it. They create desires that are often unappeasable, — desires that embroil towns, states, and the nation itself, in the fiercest contentions of party.

Now, it is too obvious to need remark, that the main tendency of institutions and of a state of society like those here depicted is to cultivate the intellect and to inflame the passions, rather than to teach humility and lowliness to the heart. Our civil and social condition holds out splendid rewards for the competitions of talent, rather than motives for the practice of virtue. It sharpens the perceptive faculties in comparing different objects of desire, it exercises the judgment in arranging means for the production of ends, it gives a grasp of thought and a power of combination which nothing else could so effectively impart; but, on the other hand, it tends not merely to the neglect of the moral nature, but to an invasion of its rights, to a disregard of its laws, and, in cases of conflict, to the silencing of its remonstrances and the denial of its sovereignty.

And has not experience proved what reason might have predicted? Within the last half-century, has not speculation, to a fearful extent, taken the place of honest industry? Has not the glare of wealth so dazzled the public eye as often to blind it to the fraudulent means by which the wealth itself had been procured? Have not men been honored for the offices of dignity and patronage they have held, rather than for the everduring qualities of probity, fidelity, and intelligence, which alone are meritorious considerations for places of honor and power? In the moral price-current of the nation, has not intellect been rising, while virtue has been sinking, in value? Though the nation as a nation, and a very great majority of the States composing it, have performed all their pecuniary obligations, and preserved their reputation unsullied; yet have there not been great communities, acting through legislators whom they themselves had chosen, that have been guilty of such enormous breaches of plighted faith as would cause the expulsion of a robber from his brotherhood of bandits?

And who will say, even of the most favored portions of our country, that their advancement in moral excellence, in probity, in purity, and in the practical exemplification of the virtues of a Christian life, has kept pace with their progress in outward conveniences and embellishments? Can virtue recount as many triumphs in the moral world as intellect has won in the material? Can our advances towards perfection in the cultivation of private and domestic virtues, and in the feeling of brotherhood and kindness towards all the members of our households, bear comparison with the improvements in our dwellings, our furniture, or our equipages? Have our charities for the poor, the debased, the ignorant, been multiplied in proportion to our revenues? Have we subdued low vices, low indulgences, and selfish feelings? and have we fertilized the waste places in the human heart as extensively as we have converted the wilderness into plenteous harvest-fields, or enlisted the running waters in our service? In fine, have the mightier and swifter agencies which we have created or applied in the material world any parallel, in new spiritual instrumentalities, by which truth can be more rapidly diffused, by which the high places of iniquity can be brought low, or its crooked ways made straight?

Must it not be acknowledged, that, morally speaking, we stand in arrears to the age in which we live? and must not some new measures be adopted, by which, as philanthropists and Christians, we can redeem our forfeited obligations?

While, then, the legislator continues to denounce his penalties against such wicked desires as break out into actual transgression, and while the judge continues to punish the small portion of offences that can be proved in court, the friends of education must do whatever can be done to diminish the terrible necessity of the penal law and the judicial condemnation.

In view of these considerations, I propose to speak, in the residue of this Report, of *School-motives*, and of some means for avoiding and extirpating *School-vices*.

SCHOOL-MOTIVES AND SCHOOL-VICES.

In the order of events, the first thing which demands attention is the choice of school-committee-men. We need school-committee-men who will scrutinize as diligently the moral character of the proposed teacher, and his ability to impart moral instruction, as they do his literary attainments and his ability to impart knowledge. This official prerequisite in every member of our school-committees is not only necessary on account of the general influence which his character will exert upon children, but on account of the particular duties the law requires him to perform. How would consistency be outraged, what a brand would be affixed by the general verdict of the community upon the character of a town which should elect as school-committee-men, to decide upon the literary qualifications of the instructors of their children, those who could neither read nor write! And yet is it not obvious that an immoral man is as little qualified to pronounce upon moral character as an illiterate man is to decide upon the sufficiency of literary qualifications?

The *general* exemption of the teachers of Massachusetts from immoral habits is a fact to which the committees cheerfully and confidently testify; and it is one which my acquaintance with them enables me to confirm. But freedom from actual vice is not sufficient. In the character of one who is to train up children, a positive determination towards good, evinced by his life as well as by his language, is an essential attribute. No talent can atone for want of principle, no brilliancy of genius compensate for one stain upon the character. The perceptions of a teacher between right and wrong should be as unclouded by interest or passion as the lot of humanity will allow; and his conscience should be trained to an affinity for truth, and an abhorrence of falsehood, as quick and as sure as the elective attractions and repulsions of chemistry. Knowledge is power, talent is power; but they are powers which may be enlisted on the side of evil as well as of good. Nature bestows talent, living among men confers some knowledge, and mere instinct is sufficient to make known to the appetites and passions their related objects; and, therefore, unless a moral sovereign and lawgiver be enthroned in the breast, whose eye can watch and whose arm can defend, these appetites and passions will be to all the sanctuaries of liberty, of reputation, of life, and of chastity, what wolves are to the sheepfold. If talent were sufficient, why are not the greatest men the best men also? If knowledge were sufficient, why does it not always become the handmaid of virtue? or why does much learning ever make men mad? Not nearer to the day of its destruction is a community without knowledge than a community which relies upon knowledge *alone* as sufficient to preserve it. According to the present constitution of the human mind, and of the world in which we are placed, knowledge is a necessity in the pursuit of happiness; but morality is a preliminary necessity, elder-born and eternal. We can conceive of a state of existence where we could be happy without knowledge; but it is not in the power of any human imagination to picture to itself a form of life where we could be happy without virtue.

Generally speaking, I believe there is a commendable desire, on the part of teachers, to impart moral instruction; but there are obstacles in the way of doing it; and, for various causes, the ability or the opportunity does not equal the exigencies of the case. Some of these causes I proceed to notice.

The manner in which school-examinations have heretofore been conducted has tended to make the moral progress of the children secondary to their literary attainments.

Perhaps there is something in the nature of the case conducing to a result so lamentable; if so, it should be sedulously guarded against by a preventive foresight. The scholars are ambitious to win the approval of the committee; but in what way are they to satisfy the committee that they deserve this approval? Let us glance, for a moment, at the course of proceedings as it usually takes place in some of the best of our schools. The committee visit the school soon after its commencement, as they are required to do by law. Their object is to ascertain the condition of the school, as it stands at the time, in regard to the studies pursued. For this purpose, the classes are called upon to spell, and the percentage of misspelled words is noted; to read, and the facility and intelligence with which they read are attended to; to exhibit their writing-books, and the neatness and legibility of their hand-writing are observed; to answer questions in geography and grammar; to work sums or draw maps upon the black-board: and their proficiency and accuracy in these several studies are noted down, at least in the memory, if not in a book. Occasionally, during the term, a committee-man may call in to watch the progress of the school; but, at its close, a more formal and thorough examination is made necessary, both by the law of the land and by public expectation. The committee appear; the classes again spell; and the diminution in the percentage of errors, as compared with what it was at the opening of the school, is recorded. They read, and define words; and the more living and natural expression of the voice, the greater ease and elegance in the elocutionary part of the exercise, together with their enlarged understanding of the scope and drift of the piece selected, and their ability to explain its historical, biographical, or scientific allusions, — all these are susceptible, to some extent, of a numerical notation, and can be reported to persons not present at the exercise. The classes are called to the black-board, and, by a swift process, the answers to difficult arithmetical questions are evolved; or, on requiring a map of a particular country to be drawn, a miniature representation of it, with its boundaries, its mountains, its rivers, and its cities, starts into being before their eyes. Indeed, if the class be large, and has been competently trained, then, by assigning a different part of the globe to each member of it, in ten minutes a very respectable atlas of the world will be depicted upon the walls of the schoolroom, to the honor of the pupils and the delight of all spectators. The committee and the parents participate in the general joy, and both teachers and scholars receive the meed of praise. The teacher wins or confirms an enviable reputation; the district solicits his acceptance of the school for another term; other districts hear of his success, and become competitors for his services; and, as a natural consequence of the competition, he obtains both increased honor and emolument.

But suppose, at the time when the school began, low, perverse, and ungentlemanly habits and manners prevailed among the pupils, which the teacher, by the dignity and impressiveness of his own example, and by the energy and kindness of his expostulations, has extirpated, and has substituted decency and propriety and manliness for them. Suppose profaneness polluted the lips of the children, and he has made them see the beauty and the truth of the saying, that a Christian should be afraid to swear, and a gentleman should be ashamed to. Suppose falsehood overt; or falsehood in some of its thousand forms of equivocation, deception, or suppression, had cankered the vitals of the school, and threatened to consume all the honesty and ingenuousness of the young heart, but the teacher has made it a loathing and an abomination, and has inspired his school with some adequate conception of the moral beauty and the moral necessity of truth. Suppose a love of parents, of brothers and sisters, and a compassion for the poor and the unfortunate, have been warmed into being, and nourished into strength, in bosoms where they did not exist before. Suppose a reciprocation of kind offices among schoolmates has been substituted for alienation or hostility, or that some ancient and long-descended feud has been harmonized by his pacific counsels. Every school of children, as much as every community of men, has a public opinion, which, though an unwritten, is a self-executing law among the pupils, and descends from one school-generation to another: suppose this public opinion of the school has been brought over from the side of insubordination to voluntary acquiescence, and from trickery to open dealing; suppose all or any of these blessed results to have been effected by the teacher: how are they to be brought forward for exhibition at the closing examination of the school? No general answers to general questions, no volubility in the rehearsal of moral precepts, can display them. They cannot be exhibited on the black-board, but they are graven upon the heart. They cannot be recorded in the school-register, but they are written in the Book of Life. All attempts at display, indeed, will refute and corrupt the whole: for there is no more offensive vice than the ostentation of virtue; and the most disgusting of all hypocrisies is a humility ambitious of display. True virtue is lowly and retiring, and finds its highest gratifications in its inward and silent delights; but the moment that a sentiment of pride, on account of its supposed possession, is consciously allowed, or an impulse to boastfulness indulged, then virtue falls from its high and pure estate, and can no longer be numbered with the angels of light.

And yet is not such a change, or any thing approximating to such a change, in the moral character and conduct of scholars, as I have here attempted to describe, worth infinitely more than if the teacher, by a miracle of art, could transfer into their minds all the knowledge of all the philosophers who have ever lived?

Now, an unhappy consequence of the prevalent course of

things is, that the teacher who withdraws some part of his time and attention from the intellectual training of his pupils, and devotes it to their moral culture, may be unable to exhibit so great a degree of proficiency in the studies pursued at the end of a short term, or even of a single year, as one who forgets the existence of a moral nature in his charge, and devotes himself exclusively to their intellectual progress. Whatever time the faithful moral teacher spends in cherishing sentiments of honor, truth, generosity, and magnanimity, the unfaithful one will spend in polishing and perfecting the recitations in grammar, geography, or some other study. The former will use no motive, however efficacious, if its ultimate tendencies are injurious; the latter will make all motives equally welcome, provided they conduce to his immediate end. The object of the one teacher is remote, consisting in the welfare of the children in after-life; that of the other is immediate, consisting in the reputation, and the pecuniary value of the reputation, that will redound to himself at the end of his engagement. And hence it clearly follows, that if the committee attend only, or attend mainly, to the proficiency made by the children in their accustomed studies, then a direct and palpable temptation is held out to the teacher to attend only, or to attend mainly, to this inferior part of his duty; because, by so doing, he will win a higher degree of success and a higher reputation for skill, his future services will be in greater demand, and he will not only enjoy his fame as fame, but be able also to coin it into money. Here, then, there seems to be a disastrous alliance of worldly motives; and they unite to weigh down the teacher who aspires to lofty and noble views in the discharge of his duty.

Is not a change in this part of our school-system imperatively demanded? Is not here a point where positive improvement may forthwith begin? Ought it not to become an axiom and a proverb, that no amount of mere knowledge in a school shall ever be accepted as an equivalent for an uninstructed conscience; but, on the other hand, that the formation of good habits shall be an acceptable apology for inferiority in attainments? Let committees, then, look vigilantly; let them inquire anxiously, day by day, into the effect produced by the teacher upon the conduct, the manners, the disposition of his pupils; and let censure rather than commendation be awarded to the teacher who has carried forward his pupils ever so rapidly in mere knowledge, if he has neglected the culture of the affections, or purchased proficiency in school-studies by means which put the moral nature in jeopardy. How unworthy the sacred office of a teacher, if he incites his pupils to effort, only by displaying before them a brilliant prospect of worldly honors and distinctions, or the power and the pride of wealth, while he neglects to cherish the love of man in their bosoms, or to display before them daily the evidences of the goodness and the wisdom of God! I care not how promptly the classes may respond in the schoolroom, if I hear profaneness or obscenity in the play-ground. I care not how many text-books they have mastered, if they have not mastered the passions of jealousy and strife and uncharitableness. It is not indispensable to the happiness of children that they should know the length of all the great rivers, or the height of all the great mountains, upon the globe; but it is indispensable to their happiness that they should love one another, and do as they would be done unto. A life spent in obscurity and supported by daily toil may be full of blessings; but no worldly honors however high, or wealth however boundless, can atone for one dereliction from duty in acquiring them.

But the great agent in carrying the benign work of reform into our schools must be the teacher himself. No fulness in the qualifications of others can be the supplement of any material deficiency in him.

Essential requisites in a teacher's character are a love of children and a love of his work. He must not be a hireling. It is right that he should have a regard for his compensation; but, his compensation being provided for, it should be forgotten. To exclude the feeling of monotony and irksomeness, he must look upon his work as ever a new one; for such it really is. The school-teacher is not, as it sometimes seems to be supposed, placed upon a perpetually-revolving wheel, and carried through a daily or yearly round of the same labors and duties. Such a view of his office is essentially a low and false one. What if he does turn over the leaves of the same book from day to day, and hear the same lessons recited from year to year? What if he is required to explain the same principles, and to reiterate the same illustrations, until his path in the accustomed exercises of the school-room is as worn and beaten as the one by which, morning and night, he travels to and from it? Still, in the truest and highest sense, his labor is always a new one; *because the subject upon which he operates is constantly changing.* Every day he is developing new faculties, or carrying forward the old through new stages of their course. Though the books which he uses, and the instructions which he imparts, may be the same, yet his real work consists in his taking up class after class, and conducting them onward through new portions of their progress. The charge committed to his care is weak, ignorant, immature, and constitutionally subject to error. He imparts vigor; he supplies knowledge; he ripens judgment; he establishes principle; and he then sends them on their way to fulfil the great duties of earth, and to be more and more prepared for another life. But, so soon as he has fulfilled his duty to one company of the ever onward-moving procession of young life, another company steps in to occupy the place of the former. Their need of guidance, their capacities of improvement, are as great as those which have gone before them. They, too, are bound on the same perilous journey of life, and for the same goal of an immortal existence. He is to guide their steps aright: he is to see, that, before they pass from under his hands, they have some adequate conception of the great objects at which they are to aim, of the glorious destiny at which they may arrive; and that they are endued with the energy and the perseverance which will make their triumph certain. As soon as this labor is done to one company, he bids them a hasty farewell, that he may turn with glad welcome to hail another, more lately arrived upon the confines of existence, who ask his guidance as they are crossing the narrow isthmus of time, on their way to eternity. Such is the teacher's duty,—to welcome each new group, to prepare them for the journey of life, and to speed them on their way; and again to welcome, to prepare, and to speed: and, I repeat it, it is, and forever must be, a new work, while new beings emerge into existence, to receive benefit and blessing from him, to be rescued from what is wrong, to be consecrated to what is right. No teacher, therefore, who regards his duties in the light of reason and religion, can look upon them as repulsive or monotonous or irksome. The angel that unlocks the gate of heaven might as well become weary of the service, though, with every opening of the door, a new spirit is ushered into the mansions of bliss.

Let the teacher, then, who cannot draw exhaustless energies from a contemplation of the nature of his calling; let the teacher whose heart is not exhilarated as he looks round upon the groups of children committed to his care; let the teacher who can ever consciously speak of the "tedium of schoolkeeping," or the "irksome task of instruction," either renovate his spirit, or abandon his occupation. The repining teacher may be useful in some other sphere: he may be fit to work upon the perishable materials of wood or iron or stone; but he is unfit to work upon the imperishable mind.

The teacher should enter the schoolroom as the friend and benefactor of his scholars. He is supposed to possess more knowledge than they, by the utmost diligence and stretch of faculty, can receive from him; but yet no fact is more certain, or law more universal, than that they will make no valuable and abiding acquisition without their own consent and co-operation. The teacher can neither transfuse knowledge by any process of decanting, nor inject it by any force, into the mind of a child; but the law of the relation subsisting between them is, that he must have the child's conscious assent and concurrence before he can impart it. He cannot impart, unless the child consents to receive. What, then, is the state of mind most receptive of knowledge, and most co-operative in acquiring it? Surely, it is a state of confidence, of trustfulness, of respect, of affection. Hence it follows that the first great duty of a teacher is to awaken these sentiments in the breasts of his pupils. For this end, he can do more the first half-day he enters the schoolroom than in any week afterwards. But if a teacher presents himself before his pupils with a haughty or a contemptuous air, if he introduces himself by beginning to speak of *his* power and *his* authority, he will soon create the occasion for using them. The pupils themselves are first to be prepared,—to be put into an apt condition for the work that is to follow. If we take a survey of any department of nature or of art, illustrations and analogies will crowd upon the mind in confirmation of the universal truth, that, if we would exert an influence upon any object, we must first bring it into a condition receptive of that influence. Does not the farmer break up the soil, and open it to the sun, before he commits the seed to its bosom in expectation of a harvest? Have not celebrated artists owed their fame as much to the careful preparation of their materials as to the skill with which they afterwards combined them? By the softening agencies of fire or steam, the mechanic overcomes the rigidity or inflexibleness of his materials, before he attempts to mould or bend them to his purpose; yet the chemical changes effected by heat, through the innermost particles of the bar of iron which the smith wishes to fashion anew upon his anvil, are not deeper or more transmuting than the spiritual changes wrought upon the inmost emotions of a child's soul by a demeanor of dignity, and by looks and tones of affection, on the part of the teacher. When the all-bountiful Giver of the seasons wills to overspread our hemisphere with vegetable beauty and luxuriance, he does not scatter abroad his treasures of snow and of hail, nor bind the rivers in the death-like embraces of frost; but he causes the sun to draw near, and the genial rain to descend; he scatters the infinite drops of dew over the earth, and summons the warming winds from the chambers of the south. Whatever is to be done, whether in the works of Nature or of Art, the material which is to be wrought upon must first be adapted to the work.

All teachers look upon books and apparatus as indispensable to the highest progress of a school; and hence the sending of a child to school with a demand that he should be taught, but without the common instrumentalities for teaching him, they justly regard as a Pharaoh-like requisition. Yet how much more indispensable are a desire and a purpose to learn, in the breast of a child, than a book in his hand! A spelling-book, a geography, and so forth, are very desirable; but a disposition to use them is indispensable. Parents must supply the books; but teachers — with the help of the parents where they can have it, and, as far as possible, without that help where they cannot have it — must supply the disposition. Let this be done, and we may safely affirm that the laws of Nature are not more certain, than that the child will learn; for it is a law of Nature that he will.[*]

[*] In the number of "The Bibliotheca Sacra" for February, 1846, pp. 110-11, we find the following observations from the pen of the Rev. Noah Porter, Jr., of Springfield, Mass. They are so valuable in themselves, and tend so strongly to fortify the views we have expressed, that we cannot forbear to copy them.

"You cannot drive a boy to study. Least of all can you drive study into him. The attention must itself awake and pant with eagerness for knowledge. The affections must lay hold of it with a grasp that nothing can unlock; and the man must appropriate it, turning it into the very substance of the mind. You cannot force open the attention as you must the jaw that is locked, nor bind on enthusiasm, nor infuse the results that come, if they come at all, from the personal activity of the scholar. The appliances of masters and text-books and illustrations and rules and supervision, and the most perfect system of gradations, one and all of them, are in vain, unless you can find or make a generous enthusiasm and a wakeful spirit. Still less at college will the scholar carry forward the work, however well begun at school, unless, with his growing capacity to labor and to learn, there grow likewise the desire to labor and to learn. Still less, after he leaves the university, will there be the overmastering desire to be the thorough and finished man, unless there be an iron energy and a burning enthusiasm. To success in acquiring, then, there is needed a strong and active spirit. Indeed, without it, study becomes a mechanical process, books overmaster the mind that should master them, the love of learning is a morbid habit, an unnatural craving, and the highest attainments of scholarship are as useless and as unnatural as a monstrous lion, or a heart that palpitates when it should beat."

If securing the good will of scholars is preliminary to their attainment of *knowledge*, far more important is it to the cultivation of their *moral sentiments* and to the growth of *good habits*. It is an invariable law of Nature in regard to the young mind, that the affections are developed before the judgment. How woful and desolate would be the condition of a child, if it could never love its mother until it had arrived at an age capable of mastering such a process of reasoning as should convince it that she was deserving of its love! Happily, this law of instinctive love prevails until an age when the reasoning powers can be developed, and the conscience enlightened. Then, and not till then, can a child make his affections intelligently obedient to his duties. All the circumstances and conditions, therefore, which attend the first introduction of a teacher to his pupils, should conciliate regard, and predispose to a mutual good understanding.

Is it not too obvious to need exposition, that the principles of duty can be superinduced upon a state of affection and sympathy more easily than upon one of antipathy and distrust? Is it not so self-evident as to make the idea of confirmation absurd, that a teacher who possesses the love and confidence of his pupils will reclaim them from error, or establish them in good principles, more readily than if he were obliged to break through a rampart of hostile feelings, and carry the citadel of the judgment and conscience by assault, and thus to found his ultimate authority upon the right of conquest, instead of having the gates thrown open to him with welcome and gratulation, and being received and hailed as a friend and deliverer? Every pupil who loves his teacher will feel that love soliciting him to obedience, just as certainly as every true disciple finds the love of Christ " constraining " him to good works. Every teacher animated by the spirit which is alone worthy of a teacher will enter into possession of his school, " not by constraint, but willingly; not for filthy lucre, but of a ready mind; " not as being a " lord " over his pupils, but as being an " ensample " to them.

The idea that there are two antagonist powers in the schoolroom, each struggling for mastery over the other, — like the rival houses of York and Lancaster, contending for the English throne, — will be as fatal to the prosperity of a school as is a civil war to the prosperity of a country. But primary and essential is the idea, that there is one sacred, all-pervading law, to which teacher and pupil are alike subject, — the law of duty and affection. All the rules of the schoolroom are but corollaries or consequences from this paramount law. If the authority and power of a teacher are not offensively set forth, they will rarely be questioned. If instead of flattering a despicable pride by a proclamation of his own supremacy, if instead of arrogating sovereignty to his own personal will, all his words and actions proceed upon the supposition that there is one serene and majestic power to which all are alike bound to render allegiance and to pay homage, — a law by which the judge is to be judged, and the ruler ruled, — and, above all, if the teacher shows himself to be a living and shining example of the doctrine he inculcates, the number of pupils will be few indeed who will ever bring the question of authority to a practical issue. When have soldiers ever undergone such privation of the necessaries of life as when their commander was known to stint himself to the same meagre allowance? When have they ever performed such forced marches as when they saw their leader moving in the van of the column? or made so valorous an assault as when they saw his plume waving at the head of the charge? Or, to draw examples from the highest source, does not the apostle say that the *goodness* of God leadeth us to repentance? and the Saviour's emblem was that of a true shepherd, who does not *drive*, but *leads* forth his flock. However it may be with sheep, we know, that, with children as with men, the difference is unimaginably great between *leading* and *driving*.

It was intimated above, that, if the proper influences constantly radiate from the teacher and pervade the schoolroom, the cases of insurgency against him will be rare. Such cases, however, may occur; and, when they do occur, they suggest their own remedy. If the talent and skill of the teacher are not sufficient to arouse the indolence or restrain the waywardness of the pupil; if his commanding dignity and benevolence cannot change perverseness into docility, or melt down obstinacy into submission; in fine, if the teacher's mind cannot overmaster the pupil's mind in its then present condition, and if the teacher's heart be not of such superior moral power as to overcome, and assimilate to itself, the heart of the pupil, — there is still one resource left: the teacher's physical power *is* superior to the pupil's physical power (for the teacher has a legal right to summon all necessary assistance to his aid); and, with this superiority, he must begin the work of reform. Order must be maintained: this is the primal law. The superiority of the heart; the superiority of the head; the superiority of the arm, — this is the order of the means to secure an observance of the law. As soon as possible, however, the teacher must ascend from the low superiority of muscular force to the higher and spiritual ones; and he must forever cultivate the higher, that they may the sooner supersede the lower.

I think one cannot have been long accustomed to visiting schools, without being able to determine almost at a glance, on entering a schoolroom, what the relation is which exists between the teacher and his scholars. If as soon as the teacher turns his back upon the scholars, in order to approach and to salute his guests, the whole muscular system of the school seems to snap the fetters in which it had been bound, and to break out into mischievous activity, but as soon as the teacher reverts his face all is again subdued and hushed into deathlike stillness; if, as the teacher moves about among his scholars and gives his directions, they exhibit a deference that almost runs into timidity, but, as soon as he has passed by, they make grimaces behind him, or fillip spit-balls at his back; if, as he turns from time to time towards different parts of the room, that portion of the school which is under his eye is constrainedly quiet and submissive, while that portion which he does not see starts out into a hundred disorders, as wild beasts rush forth when the light of day is withdrawn, — if such be the general aspect of the school, then an intelligent spectator becomes as certain at the end of five minutes as he would be at the end of a week that the teacher holds his place only by the law of force. But, on the other hand, if the scholars seem almost unconscious of the teacher's presence; if they are unobservant in what part of the room he stands, or in which direction he may be looking; if he can step out at the door to speak to a visitor, or into a recitation-room to inspect a class, and remain absent for five or ten minutes without there being any buzz or whirring in the schoolroom, — then one may feel the delightful assurance that such a school is under the sway of a serene and majestic authority, — the authority of the great law of duty and love. I have seen many schools of each class in Massachusetts; and I feel warranted in saying, that, in point of numbers, the latter class is rapidly gaining upon the former.

There is a small class of schools intermediate between the two above described, where the teacher, through a false ambition of having it said that he can govern by moral suasion, or through fear of losing his place, or from some equally unworthy motive, seeks to govern without resort to corporal punishment, but still has not the skill that can interest children in their studies, nor the spiritual ascendency that can control their waywardness. But no low motive can ever perform the office of a high one. The laws of Nature will not be circumvented. High influences without can only come from high principles within. If a teacher would govern by intellectual and moral power, he must possess intellectual and moral power; and no spurious or counterfeit similitudes of them can borrow or steal their efficacy. There is great beauty in the Romish superstition, that the moment consecrated water *is sold* it is desecrated. It loses its quality of holiness by the unhallowed motive that transfers it. The spirit of the sentiment applies to the present case. The teacher who would govern by the law of love must have faith in the law of love. In the absence of this, he will be compelled to resort to coaxing or wheedling or hiring children to be good, which is like the sin of laying a false offering upon the altar of the Lord.

Immediately on opening a school, an important question arises as to the expediency or inexpediency of promulgating a code of laws for its government. It is the practice of some teachers to announce orally, during the first day or half-day of the school, the rules whose observance they shall require, and whose infraction they shall punish. Others prepare written statutes, sanctioned by specific penalties, which they post up in some conspicuous place in the schoolroom, so as to give a warning to transgressors, and to provide themselves with a ready answer should the plea of ignorance be urged by any offender. Other teachers anticipate the commission of no offence, but wait until one occurs before they expound its demerits or prescribe its consequences.

It seems to me that very serious objections lie against the promulgation of a code of laws, either oral or written, in advance or at the commencement of the school. If this be done, the scholars instantly adopt the well-known principle of legal construction, that what is not included is excluded; and hence that every thing is permitted which is not prohibited. But as he is a bad citizen who has no higher rule of action than the law of the land, so *is* he a bad scholar who has no other restraint against wrong-doing than the prohibitions of the teacher. No code ever framed by the ingenuity of man, however voluminous or detailed it may have been, ever enumerated a tithe of the acts which an enlightened conscience will condemn; and no language was ever so exact and perspicuous as to be proof against sophistry and tergiversation. The jurisdiction of the conscience is infinitely more comprehensive than that of the statute-book. *Is it right?* and not, *Is it written?* is the question to be propounded in the forum of conscience. Each scholar brings a conscience to school. If it has not been previously enlightened on any given point of duty, then there is no punishable blame in the breach of that duty; if it has been previously enlightened, then the tribunal is already open before which the culprit should be arraigned.

Besides, as most of our schools consist of scholars differing very much from each other in regard to age and intelligence, the rules applicable to one portion of them may be very unsuitable to another; and yet, if relaxed or suspended in one case, the idea of their permanency and immutability will be destroyed, and with that all their moral efficacy ceases. So there may be cases where peculiar circumstances will take an action out of the spirit of a rule, while they leave it within the letter. Suppose, for instance, in consideration of the many mischiefs which follow in the train of whispering and other modes of communication between scholars, they are peremptorily and altogether forbidden; and suppose that, the next day, a child exhibits symptoms of extreme distress, or of fainting, or is exposed to some danger which requires instant warning, shall the general rule be observed at the expense of any consequences? or, if violated, shall it be punished?

Doubtless, too, it has happened, and not very unfrequently, that the idea of the offence was originally suggested by the prohibition; and thus the law has led to its own infraction, as, with ignorant and superstitious persons, predictions often procure their own fulfilment.*

But there is a great variety of duties to be performed in a schoolroom, as well as of offences to be avoided. Would it not be more appropriate to go into a detail of these duties, and expound their reasons and their rewards, rather than to set forth an array of offences with their penalties? And are there no methods by which the teacher can commend the duties beforehand to the good-will of the scholars; ingratiate them, as

* The story of the Catholic priest and the hostler is not inapposite. When a hostler had finished making confession of his sins, the priest inquired of him if he had ever greased the teeth of his customers' horses to prevent them from eating their oats. The hostler not only replied in the negative, but said he had never heard of such a thing. The next time he went to the confessional, the first offence which he had to acknowledge was, that he had been greasing the teeth of his customers' horses.

it were, into the mind of the school, and thus exclude much that is bad by a pre-occupancy of the ground with what is good? I would commend a course by which not only have some excellent schools sustained their character for excellence, but by which some indifferent schools have been made excellent. It is that of employing the first hour, or perhaps more, of the first day of a term, in a familiar and colloquial exposition of the objects of the school, and the means which it is indispensable to observe for the accomplishment of those objects. Certainly all the older children, in all schools above the rank of the primary, are capable of understanding something, both of the advantages and the pleasures of knowledge; of the connection between present conduct and future respectability; of the different emotions which arise in the mind after the performance of a good and of an evil action, and of the inherent tendencies both of virtuous and of vicious habits to accelerate their course towards happiness or misery. Excepting the comparatively few cases of implicit faith, a child will not be deterred from wrong, unless he sees it to be wrong, any more than he will shrink back from a precipice from whose brink he is about to step, if ignorant of its existence. If the moral precipice were made as visible as the natural can be, might we not hope that fewer victims would be precipitated into the abyss of ruin?

A vast deal of the success of a school depends upon the first impression made by the teacher upon it. And by a well-conducted conversation with the scholars at its commencement, and before any prejudices against its requirements have sprung up, or any temptations to disobedience have been presented, the good-will of many, to say the least, may be propitiated. There are some points, indeed, absolutely essential to the prosperity of a school, respecting which the teacher is in the hands of the scholars, — wholly dependent upon their co-operation, — such as the punctuality and regularity of their attendance, and, not unfrequently, their being provided with text-books and other instruments of learning. And, in regard to other points falling more directly within the teacher's control, his only hope of reaching the highest success depends upon securing their assistance. A few hours, therefore, at the beginning of a school, and an occasional one afterwards, as the age and capacities of the scholars may require, may be most beneficially spent in a familiar exposition of the great purposes for which the school has been opened, and of the means and observances by which alone its highest prosperity can be secured. A teacher can hardly enter a school of children, collected from various families, and subjected to various home-influences, without finding some, at least, who have an essentially false view of the object for which they have attended. He must throw light forward to show them the true nature of that object. Among the topics introduced by him, in his first friendly discourse to the youthful group collected around him, may be the duty of cultivating the spirit of honor, and of kindness to each other; a desire for each other's improvement as well as for their own; and a determination generously to assist their companions in improving the advantages of the school. Let him deprecate the meanness that would try to put off blame upon another for the sake of shielding one's self; that would even risk the concealment of a fault for which another might be unjustly blamed or suspected; that would triumph in any success which would give pain to the innocent; and let him fill their bosoms with a noble scorn of deception and falsehood. Let him make his company of hearers perceive that knowledge should only be trusted to those who will use it conscientiously; and this he can do by a graphical description of some immoral great man, who has used power and knowledge for selfish and wicked purposes. Let him convince them that he intends to bring into the schoolroom none but the highest motives, and that it is alike *their* duty and interest to bring into the schoolroom none but the highest motives. Let more or less of these topics be introduced again, — particularly on the accession of new members to the school, and before time has been allowed them for practising or inventing any adroit measures of defiance or deception. If new children, when they come into a school, find its tone a high one, and its habits generous and manly, they will, almost invariably, be assimilated to the prevalent sentiment. Extraordinary cases of perversity may, indeed, occur; but if the new pupils see that the *denizens* of the school make it a matter of honor to govern themselves, instead of being governed by a set of arbitrary rules; if they see such confidence existing between teacher and pupils, that each is ready to trust the other, and that the interests of both sides are the same, instead of clashing like those of enemies, — they will be ashamed to stand out as exceptions, as ugly, misshapen creatures, in a company where all others are beautiful.

One of the highest and most valuable objects to which the influences of a school can be made conducive consists in training our children to self-government. The doctrine of no-government, even if all forms of violence did not meet the first day to celebrate its introduction by a jubilee, would forfeit all the power that originates in concert and union. So tremendous, too, are the evils of anarchy and lawlessness, that a government by mere force, however arbitrary and cruel, has been held preferable to no-government. But self-government, self-control, a voluntary compliance with the laws of reason and duty, have been justly considered as the highest point of excellence attainable by a human being. No one, however, can consciously obey the laws of reason and duty until he understands them: hence the preliminary necessity of their being clearly explained, of their being made to stand out, broad, lofty, and as conspicuous as a mountain against a clear sky. There may be blind obedience without a knowledge of the law, but only of the will of the lawgiver; but the first step towards rational obedience is a knowledge of the rule to be obeyed, and of the reasons on which it is founded.

The above doctrine acquires extraordinary force in view of our political institutions, founded, as they are, upon the great idea of the capacity of man for self-government, — an idea so long denounced by the State as treasonable, and by the Church as heretical. In order that men may be prepared for self-government, their apprenticeship must commence in childhood. The great moral attribute of self-government cannot be born and matured in a day; and, if school-children are not trained to it, we only prepare ourselves for disappointment if we expect it from grown men. Everybody acknowledges the justness of the declaration, that a foreign people, born and bred and dwarfed under the despotisms of the Old World, cannot be transformed into the full stature of American citizens merely by a voyage across the Atlantic, or by subscribing the oath of naturalization. If they retain the servility in which they have been trained, some self-appointed lord or priest on this side of the water will succeed to the authority of the master whom they have left behind them. If, on the other hand, they identify liberty with an absence from restraint and an immunity from punishment, then they are liable to become intoxicated and delirious with the highly-stimulating properties of the air of freedom; and thus, in either case, they remain unfitted, until they have become morally acclimated to our institutions, to exercise the rights of a freeman. But can it make any substantial difference whether a man is suddenly translated into all the independence and prerogatives of an American citizen, from the bondage of an Irish lord or an English manufacturer, or from the equally rigorous bondage of a parent, guardian, or school-teacher? He who has been a serf until the day before he is twenty-one years of age cannot be an independent citizen the day after; and it makes no difference whether he has been a serf in Austria or in America. As the fitting apprenticeship for despotism consists in being trained to despotism, so the fitting apprenticeship for self-government consists in being trained to self-government; and the law of force and authority is as appropriate a preparation for the subjects of an arbitrary power as liberty and self-imposed law are for developing and maturing those sentiments of self-respect, of honor, and of dignity, which belong to a truly republican citizen. Were we hereafter to govern irresponsibly, then our being forced to yield implicit obedience to an irresponsible governor would prepare us to play the tyrant in our turn; but if we are to govern by virtue of a law which embraces all, which overlays all, which includes the governor as well as the governed, then lessons of obedience should be inculcated upon childhood in reference to that sacred law. If there are no two things wider asunder than freedom and slavery, then must the course of training which fits children for these two opposite conditions of life be as diverse as the points to which they lead. Now, for the high purpose of training an American child to become an American citizen, — a constituent part of a self-governing people, — is it not obvious that, in all cases, the law by which he is to be bound should be made intelligible to him? and, as soon as his capacity will permit, that the reasons on which it is founded should be made as intelligible as the law itself?

This view of the subject does not trench one hair's-breadth upon the great doctrine of order and subordination. It only contests the claim to arbitrary power on the one side, and its correlative, blind submission, on the other: it discards these as substitutes for moral power and voluntary obedience, and there it stops. The great question is, to whom or to what the obedience or subordination is due. It is primarily due to the law, — to the law written upon the heart, — to the law of God. The teacher is the representative and the interpreter of that law. He is clothed with power to punish its violations; but this comprehends only the smallest part of his duty. As far as possible, he is to prevent violations of it by rectifying that state of mind out of which violations come. Nor is it enough that the law be obeyed. As far as possible, he is to see that it is obeyed from right motives. As a moral act, blind obedience is without value. As a moral act, also, obedience through fear is without value; and not only so, but, as soon as the fear is removed, the restrained impulses will break out, and demand the arrears of indulgence as a long-delayed debt. To prevent misunderstanding, however, I wish to define the term "fear," as here used. It is here used to signify a dread of bodily pain or injury, or of personal loss. In reference to the Divine Being, the term is used in a widely different sense. That fear of the Lord which "is the beginning of wisdom" includes the emotion of awe and reverence. It is not a servile, but a filial fear. It is a sentiment which an enlightened conscience can never experience towards an unworthy object; and which, therefore, an unworthy object can never inspire. But the mere dread of personal harm, as the consequence of wrong-doing, is not *curative*: it is not *restorative*. It may warn, it may arrest, it may check, the outward commission of wrong; and its use for these purposes, to any extent which circumstances may require, is legitimate. But, with the prevention of wrong, its functions end. Though it may make an offender cease to do ill, it can never, by its own efficacy, make him love to do well; as poison may arrest a disease, though it cannot restore a patient to health. By suppressing outbreaks, by restraining waywardness, fear may prepare the way for the introduction of higher motives of action; but, if the aid of these higher motives be not then invoked, the ground of justification for using the fear is taken away. A reform in character may be begun by fear; but, if it ends in fear, it will prove to be no reform. When the spendthrift finds he is approaching the last dollar of his patrimony, and gaunt hunger and want begin to stare him in the face, he is admonished to desist; and, under the terror of these impending evils, he arrests his course of riot and dissipation. But this terror does not inspire him with the least love of temperance and industry. A habit of diligence and sobriety must come, if it comes at all, from the working of other motives within him. Without the restraint of higher motives, should another inheritance unexpectedly descend to him, he would return to his "wallowing in the mire." The bond-servants of fear always do as little as they can; because they do nothing for the love of the thing done, but only to avoid some painful consequences if it be not done. Work, whether of the hand or of the mind, which is not performed from a love of it, is never performed with that zest or alacrity which the love of it inspires. An external act of duty may be done; but it is done, not from a willing, but from a repugnant, not from a dutiful, but from a rebellious heart. The mind will disown what the hand performs; while each movement and each moment will deepen disgust towards it. This is so clear, even to the intellect, that some of the more sagacious slave-drivers at the South are substituting motives of personal-profit, of appetite, and the love of tawdriness, for the scourge. They have been led to this, not from compassion, but from cupidity. They find the sum total of profits at the end of the year to be greater under the use of pleasurable motives than under the use of painful ones. Formerly (and, to a great extent, even at present) they used the motive of bodily fear and smart,— the motive by which the tyrant maintains his power, by which the savage enforces obedience to his will, by which the brute secures its prey. But the eyes of some of them have been opened to see the neighboring motives, as they lie arranged along the great scale, from the brutish to the angelic; and they now avail themselves of the love of appetite, the love of approbation, the desire of being bedizened with gaudy colors, and so forth, as more efficient agencies than pain. Doubtless the quantity of their work will be increased, and its quality improved, as their masters ascend higher and higher in the scale of motive-powers. Teachers should be children of light, and they should not permit the children of Mammon to be wiser in their generation than they. It should never be forgotten that the highest duty of a teacher is to produce the greatest quantity and the purest quality of moral action.

Fear, then, is no more to be proscribed from the teacher's list of motives than arsenic and henbane from the *materia medica* of the physician; but the teacher or parent who uses nothing but fear commits a far greater error than the physician who uses nothing but poison. Let all wise and good men unite their efforts so to improve both the moral and the physical health of the community, as gradually and regularly to diminish, and finally to supersede, the necessity of either.

The maxim embodied in the law of the land, and sustained by the good sense of all communities, that the teacher stands *in loco parentis*, that is, in the parent's place or stead, has been a thousand times repeated. By virtue of this relation, he is authorized to do, for all the purposes within his jurisdiction, what the parent might rightfully do under like circumstances. But he stands in the parent's place, for love as well as for power, for duty as well as for authority. If a father has any right to punish a child whose reason he has never attempted to enlighten, whose conscience he has never sought to develop, it is a right founded upon the previous commission, on his part, of the highest wrong. If preventives and milder remedies have not been used to avert the ultimate necessity of violent applications, then the parent, in regard to every offence which demands the application of violence, is an accessory before the fact, a suborner to the crime, and justly incurs the largest share of its guilt. If the rights of the teacher as to the exercise of power are commensurate with the rights of the parent, so are the teacher's duties also, in regard to the motives from which he acts, commensurate with parental duties.

A question connected with this subject has been often discussed; and the practice is different in different parts of the State. It is, whether refractory and disobedient scholars should be dismissed from the school, or retained in it and subdued. If a teacher stands in the place of the parent, why should he dismiss any scholar from his school (unless temporarily), any more than a parent should expel a child from his household? There is no Botany Bay to which such a child can be banished. Instead of crossing the ocean to another hemisphere, he remains at home. For all purposes of evil, he continues in the midst of the very children from among whom he was cast out; and, when he associates with them out of school, there is no one present to abate or neutralize his pernicious influences. If the expelled pupil be driven from the district where he belongs into another, in order to prevent his contaminations at home, what better can be expected from the people of the place to which he is sent than a reciprocation of the deed, by their sending one of their outcasts to supply his place, and thus opening a commerce of evil upon free-trade principles? Nothing is gained while the evil purpose remains in the heart. Reformation is the great desideratum; and can any lover of his country hesitate between the alternatives of forcible subjugation and victorious contumacy? In extreme cases, however, the school-committee have an undoubted *legal right* to expel a scholar from school.

But, in those cases where the dangerousness of the symptoms will no longer permit delay, there is an immense difference in the modes of treating a malady. We know that a mere pretender to medical or surgical knowledge will aggravate the puncture of a pin into a mortification, fatal to life; while, by anodyne and restorative, the skilful practitioner will cure the gangrene itself. So, in the case of a distempered will, it may be inflamed and exasperated, by fiery and passionate appliances, into incorrigibleness and misanthropy; or, on the other hand, it may be restored to soundness and docility by reproofs or chastisements administered in wisdom and love.

But after the school has commenced, when classes have been formed, and the routine of exercises begun, it is then that opportunities, without number and without end, will present themselves for inspiring sentiments and cultivating habits of order, of decorum, of honor, of justice, and of truth; or, on the other hand, of engendering a brood of base and dissocial feelings,—unkindness, evasion, hypocrisy, dishonesty, and falsehood. Nay, the teacher may be entirely honest and sincere himself; and yet, from having his mind too intently and exclusively fixed upon the intellectual progress of his pupils, he may be regardless of the moral impulses which secure that progress, and of the emotions which attend it. Every true teacher will consider the train of *feeling*, not less than the train of *thought*, which is evolved by the exercises of the schoolroom.

Here opens a most important and difficult subject. So far as I know, it has never been comprehensively or minutely treated by any writer. It is impossible for me to do it justice. I enter upon it with undissembled diffidence; yet such is its intrinsic importance, and so often, when visiting schools, have I seen exemplifications of wrong where I was sure the teacher intended only what was right, that I can no longer forbear to attempt an elucidation of its merits. May others be led to investigate and expound it, until it assumes a prominence and commands an attention corresponding to its magnitude!

After the provisional classification of a school, the first business ordinarily consists in setting lessons and hearing recitations. In all schools having any claim to respectability, imperfect recitations incur some unpleasant consequences. In some, it is only a forfeiture of the teacher's approval; in some, it is a record of failure; in some, after a fixed number of failures, it is corporal punishment, the infliction of which cancels the old score, and opens the books for a new account. In all decent schools, an imperfect recitation is a thing which the pupils deprecate; but the means of preventing it, or of avoiding the appearance of it, are various.

In the first place, the teacher can insure any number of imperfect recitations by giving too long or too difficult lessons, — lessons beyond the ability of the scholars to learn; and thus a mere mistake in judgment, on the part of the teacher, may lead to discouragement or fraud on the part of the pupils. Lessons should be such that they can be competently mastered by all the scholars in the class, unless in cases of remarkable dulness. Some of the less forward or less bright may require a little extra assistance, which should be freely rendered to them; but, if there be any members of the class who cannot make themselves tolerably well acquainted with the lessons, they should be removed to a lower class. Habitually to break down at a recitation has a most disastrous influence on the character of a child. It depresses the spirits, takes away all the animation and strength derived from hope, and utterly destroys the *ideal* of intellectual accuracy, which is next in importance to moral accuracy, — on which, indeed, moral accuracy often depends. It is still worse when the whole class fails. Shame never belongs to multitudes. It is a feeling which arises when we contrast our own deficiency or misconduct with the opposite qualities in others; but where all are equally deficient, or equally wrong, there is no opportunity for such a contrast. Common deficiency at the recitation begets a mingled feeling of contempt for the study, and recklessness of reputation, which is fatal to all advancement. It may begin by merely disheartening the pupil; but it will soon become disgust towards the study, and aversion from the teacher. Few things are of more baneful tendency than to have a scholar or a class leave the recitation-stand, after a half-hour of blundering and darkness, with no sense of shame or regret at the dishonor. Few things are of more evil augury than for children to become so inured, by frequency, to having marks of discredit entered against their names, that they grow indifferent and callous to a recorded censure. Such children lose all that delicacy of feeling, that fine sensitiveness to honor, which are strong outposts of virtuous principle. Day after day, to have a dishonorable mark set upon the body, or the hand, or *on the name*, without any feeling of regret, or effort at amendment, is as deplorable for a boy or a girl as it would be for a man or a woman to receive, without shame and without compunction, a tenth or a twentieth sentence to the house of correction or jail. The former, indeed, foretokens the latter.

But suppose the character of the lesson to be rightly adjusted to the capacity of the learner, still a brood of temptations lurk around. In the first place, there is the device of getting one part of the lesson better than the rest, under the expectation of being questioned on that part. How often has this been done! In some of the studies, it is to be forestalled and excluded by the method, before described, of putting each question to the whole class, waiting a sufficient time for each pupil to think out the answer in his own mind, and then calling upon some one by name to answer it. The naming of the scholar to give the answer should be in no set order, but promiscuous. This method especially applies to grammar, to oral spelling, to oral recitations in geography, and to mental arithmetic. In written arithmetic, a question for solution may be propounded, and one pupil required to state the first step in the process, and then another pupil in another part of the class the second step, and so on, until the explanation is completed. Where there is, as there should be in every schoolroom, a sufficient extent of blackboard to allow the whole class to stand before it at once, a separate question may be given to each member of the class, to be wrought upon it. Occasionally, when the solution is half completed, the pupils may be transposed, and each one required to examine and complete his neighbor's work.

Such are some of the methods — to be constantly varied and interchanged — by which the temptation to deal treacherously with the lesson may be met and defeated. And yet the teacher should make no avowal that he entertains suspicions against any individual, and designs to baffle his plans for deception. He uses these means only for banishing temptation where it exists, and for shutting the door against it where its invasion is threatened. Temptation may be analyzed into two elements, — desire and opportunity. Take away the desire, and the opportunity can work no harm; take away the opportunity, and the desire is baffled. The former course is the better, when it can be taken; but here the latter is recommended as one of the means of accomplishing the former.

It sometimes happens that scholars experiment upon the numbers, or terms, of an arithmetical question. In proportion, for instance, if they have no knowledge of the principle which should guide them, they may try the effect of multiplying two of the numbers together, and dividing the product by the third; but, if that does not yield the right answer, they may transpose the order, and try again; and in the end, having exhausted all the errors, they will obtain the truth. But it is only by a comparison of their result with the answer in the book that they will know that they have arrived at the truth. They will not know on what principle the true answer was obtained; and, on attempting a solution of the next question, they will be as ignorant as ever, and be again obliged to go through with the same experimental process. In order to prevent this appeal to chance, instead of an appeal to principle, the class may be occasionally required to lay aside their slates, and to work out all the questions contained in a lesson *on paper*. Here they will not be able to obliterate what they have done, as they can do on the slate; and, therefore, the teacher, by a single glance of the eye, can see the track which the mind has made, whether straight or circuitous, in its search after the answer. He will also see the mechanical correctness with which each step may have been performed.

Frequent reviews, by carrying the pupils a second time over the ground they have traversed, will be another means of determining whether they have left any part of it unexplored.

Devices or excuses to escape the lesson altogether, when the pupil is conscious of not having faithfully learned it, are an aggravated form of the evil above mentioned; and it should be guarded against by an examination of the absentee upon the omitted lesson at another time.

I fear that this *slurring* or *shirking* of the lesson is sometimes regarded in no other light than as a clog upon the progress of the pupil, or as an abatement from the success of the coming examination. The substance of the argument often used as a warning against this species of misconduct is, that whoever leaves a lesson of his course unmastered, leaves an enemy in ambush behind him, — an enemy who will, at some day, rise up to molest his peace, and perhaps to defeat his most cherished hopes. But, though this is a legitimate consideration, yet the subject has relations far more important. It is not so much the lesson which is omitted, as the wrongful act which is committed. The knowledge that is lost is an insignificant matter compared with the trickish habit that is gained. The avoidance of the lesson has deprived the intellect of so much exercise, and, therefore, has prevented whatever of strength that exercise would have given; but the means by which the lesson was avoided have given exercise and strength to motives of deception and fraud. Herein lies the lamentable character of the deed. It is only a misfortune to be ignorant, but it is an unspeakable calamity to be dishonest. However vigilantly the teacher may look after the intelligence of his charge, he should use a thousand times more vigilance in preserving their integrity. Limited attainments are not incompatible with a high degree of happiness; but every immoral act diminishes the capacity for happiness for ever and ever.

Another means of avoiding study — and, I am sorry to say, I have found no little evidence of its existence — is, after procuring some fellow-pupil or other person to perform the work which the teacher has assigned, to present the work, thus performed by another, as the product of one's own labor. The intellectual loss and injury of such a course are great. It leaves the mind unexercised, when it was one of the principal objects of the lesson to exercise it. It also disqualifies the pupil more and more for mastering subsequent lessons. A scholar who did not get his lessons last week through indolence may be unable to get them this week through incapacity, and next week he may give them up in despair. But the most deplorable quality of such conduct is, that it is an *acted* falsehood; and, as subsequent lessons are mastered with so much more difficulty after the omission of preceding ones, the power of the temptation increases in a geometrical ratio at each succeeding step.

The cases above referred to are generally those where assistance is obtained out of school; but the prompting of a fellow-pupil in school, and during the recitation, comes under the same general head, and incurs the like mischievous consequences. To guard against the latter species of misconduct, the teacher should be all eye and all ear. He should be so familiar with the lesson that he can devote his whole attention to the class, instead of occupying the time in preparing himself, by looking at his book, to hear the successive answers. His eye should be on them on their account, and not on his book on his own account. To guard the pupil against taking fraudulent measures out of school, he should instruct as faithfully in regard to the object of the lesson as in regard to the lesson itself. The attention of the pupil should be forever turned towards the state of his own mind. Have the lesson, the fact, the principle, the scientific relation, been reproduced within himself? Are they recorded on the tables of his intellect? Are they so clearly and enduringly written there, that if the slate and blackboard were broken to fragments, if the book were to be consumed, he would still possess them as his own, ineffaceably inscribed on the mind? Is the lesson so luminously recorded in his memory, that he can see it there in the darkness of midnight, and revive it in the solitude of the desert? Every pupil should be made to see, that to transfer or to copy an answer or a process from a text-book to his own slate or paper, or to take it from another's dictation, is valueless in the way of acquisition, of improvement; that it is, in its nature, the veriest task-work or tread-mill service ever performed. He should be made to see that he might as well learn the art of swimming by getting another boy to swim for him; that he might as well increase his stature and strength by employing another to eat his meals; or that he might as well expect to gain wealth by forfeiting all his daily earnings to the more industrious. Perhaps the most appropriate punishment, in cases where a punishment is deemed advisable, for stealing the solution of a sum from a book, or for transferring it from another's slate, or for borrowing another's composition instead of writing one, would be to make the offender copy off figures in logarithms, or the letters of some algebraic process, about which he knows nothing, or to transcribe passages in the French or Latin language. This would be a parallel to his own " vain knowledge," and would show him how pleasant it is to feed upon the east wind.

But the forfeiture of privileges and of knowledge which the

pupil incurs by such a course as is above described is not the principal evil. It is not a loss of utility merely, but it is a departure from honor and honesty. Why should not the scholar who now cheats his teacher in the recitation-room cheat his master in his work when he becomes an apprentice or a clerk, and his customers in their utensils or their goods when he becomes a mechanic or a merchant? All great robbers began by stealing small things; and the foulest assassins and murderers commenced their career by inflicting petty injuries.

I fear the little departures from rectitude and truth which sometimes pervade a school, or are practised by particular members of it, are not regarded in their true light, — as seminal principles or germs, which, if not eradicated, will grow up to maturity, and bear the fatal fruit of falsehoods, perjuries, and frauds. How narrow the range of a school-child's thoughts, compared with the vast compass and combinations of an adult mind! how slow the mental operations of the former, compared with the celerity with which the latter passes from premises to conclusions, and from means to ends! The child is obliged to commence his calculations with visible and tangible units, and for a long time he moves feebly and totteringly forward, constantly seeking the support of another's hand; yet what vast and complicated schemes the same mind, in its maturity, will project! When we thus witness the capacity of growth and expansion with which the intellect is endowed, why should we doubt that the appetites and propensities have at least an equal power of expansion and activity? Nay, is it not conceded in every system of mental philosophy ever promulgated, that the appetites and desires are endowed with an ardor and a vehemence to which the intellect is a stranger; and that the passions, if unregulated and unchastened, rush to extremes infinitely more wide and more ruinous than the understanding can ever reach? Why then, when we find the mind which was once so feeble, now capable of concerting vast plans for wealth, for ambition, or other forms of personal aggrandizement, — why should we doubt that the little tricks and prevarications of the schoolroom may grow up into fraudulent bankruptcies, or stupendous peculations and embezzlements? States and empires are no more to the man than the toys of the nursery to the infant; why, then, should not corruption in politics, and hypocrisy in religion, grow out of the artifices and pretexts of the playground? If we would enjoy an immunity from the latter, we must suppress the former. How much easier and safer to crush the brittle egg than to kill the coiling serpent!

The act of furnishing arithmetical solutions, or translations in the classics, to a fellow-pupil before recitation, or of prompting him during it, is to be treated as a wrong in the giver as well as in the receiver. Yet always, or nearly so, the subject presents itself in a different light to children, and generally, I believe, even to mature minds. It is commonly regarded as an act of kindness — as a social pleasure, if not a social duty — to give, to one who wants, what we, without any loss, can spare. Shall a pupil who has neglected his lesson until the hour of recitation approaches be subjected to punishment, when we can supply his deficiencies in ten minutes, and save him from harm? Shall a friend and classmate, who has suffered the time of probation to pass by unimproved, — shall he be subjected to mortification, if not to rebuke or chastisement, when we, merely by a whisper in his ear, can save his feelings, his character, and perhaps his skin? Such is the aspect in which the subject presents itself to most minds, especially to the minds of school-children. So, to the natural eye, the earth appears to be flat. But what do we do as soon as the child arrives at a proper age for understanding its true shape? Do we not spend time, use apparatus, and give explanations, again and again, until the natural error of the senses is corrected? And why should not as much time be spent in correcting those moral errors into which all children naturally if not necessarily fall? No reason can be assigned, unless it be the infinitely false one, that moral culture is less important than intellectual. The first impressions of children on this whole subject of prompting answers, and of supplying solutions, can easily be shown to be illusory and false. The true question goes far deeper than the scholar's appearance at the recitation. The recitation is only a means to an end. In itself, it is valueless. The only question of any importance is, What is the state of the pupil's mind? Does that which he writes down upon his slate, or speaks with his tongue, come from his understanding? or does it only come mechanically from his fingers, or from his lips, by the dictation of another, and not from his own mind? The pupil who submits himself to the ordeal of a recitation, like a witness in court, is under a moral obligation to make true answers, *from his own knowledge*, to whatever questions may be propounded to him; and is that pupil an honest one, who, under such an obligation, gives either the work or the answer of another as his own? If the deficiencies of others are to be recorded, or if there is a competition for places or medals or parts, and one pupil escapes a mark, or gains a credit, by indirect means, is it fair towards his fellows, or doing as he would be done by? If two children collude together, and agree to help each other, by private signs or otherwise, during the recitation, ought we to be surprised if, afterwards, they agree to run up stocks in the market, in order to cheat innocent purchasers? Besides, where is the iniquity to stop? If one pupil may be assisted or prompted once, why may not all go to the same extent? This, however, would reduce the whole to their original equality; for, if all take the liberty to cheat once, they stand in the same relative position as at first. He, therefore, who means to get a dishonest advantage over his fellows must now cheat twice in order to gain his end; and so on indefinitely. If the grocer adulterates his sugar and his flour to the amount of ten per cent of its value, and the purchaser pays him ten per cent of counterfeit coin or bills, neither is a gainer in money, while both are sufferers in morals. So it is with children who cheat each other and their teacher at the recitation. Now, is not the moral spirit with which the lesson is studied and recited of as much consequence as the knowledge it confers? And, if so, ought not the teacher to spend as much time on the former as on the latter? I exhort teachers and committee-men to ask themselves the question, whether this is done.

The hour of recitation is the hour of reckoning; the place of recitation is the place for weighing and gauging the amount of acquisition made by the pupils. Emphatically, therefore, it is a place for fair-dealing, for truth, for uprightness towards the teacher, and for equity between fellow-pupils. Any deception there is like the use of false balances; and the teacher should no more wink or connive at it, however anxious he may be that his school should appear well, than he should instruct his scholars how they may use false weights or measures in their traffic with men.

I think the nature of a recitation can be so unfolded and explained to all, excepting, perhaps, the lowest class of minds, and that the recitation itself can be so conducted, as to save it from the frauds to which it now gives birth. Invested with the associations of honor and good faith, it may be made to assume something of a sacred character. I have known scholars who would not give an answer with which a prompter had supplied them, any more than they would receive stolen goods, or pass counterfeit money. The inherent absurdity of one pupil's getting a lesson for another may be made so obvious and glaring, even by a moderate degree of ability to a moderate capacity of understanding, as to excite contempt or abhorrence for it. The objects of a child's studying are usefulness, respectability, eminence, happiness. These objects are reached through the acquisition of knowledge, and through an increase of mental activity and energy. But each child's mind must grow for itself as much as each child's body must grow for itself. I may as well be warmed by another man's putting on my garments as be improved by another man's getting my lessons. If a child is idle, or squanders away his time, he, in his own proper person, must suffer for it. No friend can bear the burden of his future ignorance or imbecility. One person may as well bear another's toothache, or transfer another's consumption to his own lungs. Nor does the fraud bring any profit to the defrauder. Suppose the children, instead of gathering the richer treasures of knowledge, were only gathering gold-dust, which, day by day, should be brought to the scales, that the amount of their gains might be ascertained. Would any sluggard become richer by concealing a worthless pebble in his heap? Would not the assayer detect the fraud, and expose both it and its author? and would not every one who supplied, or who only assisted in supplying, the spurious substance, be justly regarded as an accomplice in the guilty act? Time is the Great Assayer, and will surely expose the folly and the ignorance of all those who cheat at the recitation, and impose upon the teacher the semblance of knowledge for its reality.

I fear that too much value is ordinarily attached to the recitation. I fear it is often regarded as an object, and not as an instrument; as the goal, and not as the path that leads to it. The daily routine of exercises, and the examinations of the school-committee, may cause all the forces of the school to converge to this point. When such is the case, the pupils, especially the ambitious ones, will devote themselves to the words of their lesson rather than to its meaning; they will aim at readiness and volubility rather than at depth and discrimination; they will confine themselves within the author's train of thought, instead of taking discursive views, tracing analogies, and sending the mind out to the right and left in quest of materials for confirmation or for questioning, from all collateral and related topics. So, too, under such a mistaken view of the object of a recitation, the pupils will be tempted, when it is over, to discharge the subject from their minds, that they may make room for the next exercise. All this is delusive. It grasps at the shadow, but misses the substance. To exhibit to the teacher the state of the pupil's mind is the true object of the recitation, so that whatever is right may be fastened there securely and forever; so that deficiencies may be supplied; and so that whatever is erroneous may be rectified or obliterated before the impression is deepened beyond effacing. If the arrangements and the general spirit of the school are such as to make the pupils desire a brilliant recitation only, then they are tempted to manage adroitly to conceal their ignorance in order to escape degradation, and to gain a credit upon the teacher's books. But such a course will redound to their own discredit, and will entail enduring degradation upon the moral sense.

Closely akin to the above subject is the use of keys in mathematical studies. To avoid cumbrous enumeration, I shall refer to *arithmetical* keys only, although the remarks on this topic will apply to algebra as well as to arithmetic. In our old arithmetical text-books, the answers were regularly appended to the questions, each to each. The complaint of the pupil who studied the old arithmetics in the old way was, " I cannot get the answer." He did not say he could not understand the principle; but the answer, as given in the book, was the thing he sought for. By observing the denomination in which it was expressed, and the number of places of figures which it contained, he could conjecture the process by which it might be reached. The pupil thus made an illicit use of the answer itself as a means of obtaining it. This was obviously preposterous. The answer was the unknown quantity which was to be obtained from known data on known principles. But, as soon as the answer was included among the known data, the pupil might arrive at it by repeated experiments, although each time he should proceed on unknown principles. The knowledge of the answer beforehand, therefore, became, to some extent, a substitute for such a knowledge of principles as would command the true answer, not only in the given case, but in all analogous cases. Had it been the only object to arrive at the answer contained in the book, then any additions, subtractions, multiplications, and divisions which would secure that end, would be sufficient; and the result would be equally satisfactory, whether the answer contained in the book should be correct or erroneous. Now, it is obvious that there is no more legitimate exercise of the power of calculation in such a procedure than there is of true piety in those contrivances of the Japanese, where, by turning a crank, they wind off a long scroll of written prayers from one cylinder on to another. The arithmetical faculty is as little employed in the one case as the heart is in the other.

To obviate this difficulty, arithmetics were prepared containing the questions only. But lest the teacher should not be able, for want of time, or for some other reason, to determine the correctness or incorrectness of the answers as they should be found by the pupil, the author prepared a second book, — a book for the answers, as well as a book for the questions. This second book is called a " Key." Both questions and answers are numbered so as to correspond. According to the theory, the key is to be used only by the teacher. It is a labor-saving instrument, designed to supersede the necessity of the teacher's looking over each sum. But it being known to the scholars that there is a key, containing not only the answers, but solutions or partial solutions of the most difficult questions, a grievous temptation is presented to them to get it and use it. So far as this is done, it defeats the very object of separating the answers from the questions, and makes the increased cost of two books over one a gratuitous expense. But what is infinitely more to be deprecated than any cost, or any diminution in intellectual attainments, is the moral delinquency which is involved in the act of using the key clandestinely. If the use of keys be prohibited, they must be obtained surreptitiously, and examined by stealth. The key itself must be kept in some secret place, where the teacher will not be likely to discover it. Hence a system of frauds. The purchasing of a book; the selection of a covert place for its concealment; the stealthy step or look by which it is examined; the transfer of the answers, perhaps upon a piece of paper, to be carried privately about the person; the plans laid to satisfy or circumvent the teacher, should he make any inquiry into the subject; and, finally, the presence of the pupil at the recitation, with the questions all correctly solved, but with a lie visible to himself lying at the bottom of every solution, — all this planned and consummated deception it is indeed fearful to contemplate. It is a practical training of the young heart to iniquity. Each commendation obtained under such circumstances is a reward for past deception, and a lure to its repetition in future. Why should not the child who does this, and who, perhaps, is not reprehended for doing it, if done when the committee or visitors are present, — why, when the opportunity comes, should he not overreach his neighbor in making a bargain, or put two votes into the ballot-box to secure the election of his favorite candidate, or defraud the post-office and the custom-house? And how much is the virulence of the temptation increased when prizes are offered to the foremost pupils! when, perhaps, badges of honor are bestowed upon the successful competitors, and their names are brought forward with *éclat* in reports, or proclaimed to the world through newspapers, while a proportionate degradation awaits the unsuccessful! — and all this is made to depend upon the marks of credit or discredit received at the end of the recitations.

What the world is seen to regard with honor, ambitious children will, of course, strive to obtain; and, when intellectual attainments take precedence of moral qualities, how cruelly will they be tempted to sacrifice the latter to the former! In foreign universities, where a subscription to creeds is a prerequisite to the honors and emoluments of professorships and presidencies, do we not know that men, for the sake of a conspicuous and lucrative station, will subscribe to theological dogmas, and articles of church government, which their souls abhor? For such bold treason against God and man, they were prepared in childhood, by slight and gradually-increasing deviations from truth and duty, under temptations whose force they could not be expected to resist. Is it not the worst form of sacrilege to invade the unsophisticated consciences of children with temptations to evil, before which it is almost certain they will fall?

For years past, I have made particular inquiries of teachers and others on this subject. I have endeavored to ascertain to what extent keys are allowed or forbidden in our schools; and also whether they are used, although forbidden. I am satisfied that a startling amount of deception is practised; and that not a few of our children are learning those arts in school, which, we have reason to fear, will be matured in after-life into flagrant immorality and turpitude.

In some cases, it has been discovered that a class owned a single key in common, which was passed round privately among them. In some, the sons of a family go to one school, and the daughters to another; and although, in one of the schools, keys are strictly prohibited, yet in the other they are openly allowed, or, at least, they are not forbidden; so that all the children have equal access to them. I believe it would be far better than that things should continue in their present condition, that all restriction in the use of keys should be removed (in which case it would, of course, be better to return to the old system of inserting the answer with the question in the text-book); but the only effectual remedy, while such helps are prepared and are accessible, is to cultivate the moral feelings of the pupils to such a high tone as will make them disdain and abhor those acts of deception by which one pupil obtains an advantage over another, or by which the pupils succeed in deceiving the teacher. It is fervently to be hoped that teachers will look more carefully into this subject than they have been accustomed to do. Better that we should go back to counting on the ten fingers, *and remain there*, than that the learners of arithmetic should imbibe the spirit by which they will hereafter make fraudulent invoices or false entries in the books of banks, or of the government.

It might prove a preventive to the fraudulent use of keys, and save children from some of the temptations which now spring from the use of them, if teachers would make it a frequent practice to dictate original questions from their own minds. However great the pupil's proficiency may be, a competent teacher could easily frame questions equivalent and analogous to those contained in the book; and the impossibility, in such cases, of getting at the answer by the use of a key, would preclude the thought and prevent the desire of doing so. Is not this in consonance with the spirit of the prayer,— at once so religious and so philosophical, — that we may not be led into temptation? The only objection that can be made to the preparation of questions by teachers is, that they may not have time to examine the solutions, and decide upon their correctness; and must, therefore, submit to the necessity of taking questions where the answers are at hand. But surely, to an accomplished teacher, it can be the work of but a few moments to look over even a long demonstration, and to determine whether the successive steps have been correctly taken. As to what may be regarded as the mechanical part of the solution, — the addition, subtraction, multiplication, and division, — he has no need to trouble himself with that. He knows the nature of the question he has given; he perceives, in the twinkling of an eye, what the necessary steps are to arrive at a correct result; and a single glance from point to point, even in an extended process, is sufficient to show him whether the correct course, or one of several correct courses, has been pursued. As to the rudimental parts, he may, occasionally at least, set some of the younger classes to examine them. They will be able to detect errors, if any exist, in the work of the older pupils; and the older pupils, mortified at being exposed by the younger, will be incited to greater care.

In advanced Prussian schools, where arithmetic was so remarkably well taught and learned (though, if it were well taught, it is almost tautology to say it was well learned), instead of an octavo volume, or a series of duodecimos, imposing burdensome expenses upon the parents, I generally found arithmetical text-books which did not contain more than fifty or sixty pages, — mere skeletons, — and yet amply sufficient for the use of the schools. Probably nineteen-twentieths, if not forty-nine fiftieths, of the questions were supplied extemporaneously by the teacher from his own mind. Under such a system, no temptations to idleness, and no provocations to fraud, could enter in, to weaken the intellect and to deprave the morals.

Children should also be encouraged to frame questions for themselves, for their own working; and, within certain limits, to frame questions for each other. In some parts of arithmetic, such an exercise would be of great utility, as it would help them to understand more thoroughly the nature, the number, and the relation of the terms necessary to form a practical question. Preparing questions would fasten more securely in the mind the principles for their solution.

I leave this topic with the expression of an intense desire that those who use, as well as those who prepare, mathematical text-books, will take into consideration the moral tendencies as well as the intellectual bearings of the methods they adopt, and of the works they publish. If each day's addition to arithmetical knowledge is to be a subtraction from the authority of conscience, it would be better that such days should never dawn.

I have sometimes found the preservation of good order in schools, and especially the prevention of whispering, attempted by means which seem to me to incur great moral and social hazards. In some schools, a pupil caught in an act of delinquency is made to take a place upon the platform, or other elevated site in the schoolroom, and there to watch for other delinquents. When he detects any one of his schoolmates in a violation of any of the rules of the school, he is expected to announce the name of the offender and the offence. If not contradicted, or although contradicted, yet if confirmed, he is absolved, and returns to his seat; and the new culprit succeeds to the post and the office of sentinel. Here *he* is expected to remain, until, in his turn, he can obtain his discharge by successfully inculpating another. Such a watchman is usually called a monitor; but his real office is that of a spy. If indolent, he may prefer the post to one which obliges him to study. He stands guard under no responsibility. If he sees one of his friends about to commit an offence, he can overlook it, or even connive at it, by turning away, so as to afford an opportunity for its commission. I have seen such an overseer violating, with those immediately around him, the very rules which he was stationed there to enforce. If, however, he entertains any grudge against a schoolmate, he may there find an opportunity to indulge it.

I think the practice here described has an injurious influence, both upon the school and upon the sentinel himself, whose only qualification to watch others consists in his own offence. It obviously tempts to concealment, which is unfaithfulness; and to partiality, which is injustice. The old proverb, "Set a rogue to catch a rogue," needs, even for the public safety, some additional direction by which the public may be guarded against the collusion of the two rogues when they come to understand each other. At best, the proverb is founded on a low principle; and it inculcates no lesson of wisdom or benevolence in regard to the reformation of either party.

Some teachers adopt the above plan, but include another element of danger in it. If the original culprit does not succeed in detecting a fellow-pupil in some offence, he receives a punishment. If he discovers another, and that other a third, and so on, until the session of the school is closed, the punishment falls upon the last. Now, to escape punishment by subjecting another to punishment, brings into active exercise the most unkind and dissocial propensities of human nature. It makes our welfare or our immunity depend upon another's wrong-doing. It connects our escape from suffering with another's subjection to it. It makes it for our immediate interest that an offence should be committed; and thus tempts us to rejoice at the error or the misconduct of our neighbor, instead of obeying the commandment to love him as ourselves. Is this a Christian relation in which to place children in regard to each other? Suppose it had been so ordained by the Creator, that one man could escape from his wounds or diseases only by touching the person of another, and thus transferring them to him; how few Samaritans would be found who would suspend the journey or the business of life that they might heal their neighbor! and would not such a law turn the world into Levites, who would pass by on the other side of the way? In the end, such a law would be ruinous even to those for whose benefit it was devised; since it would make it the interest of all to inflict mutual harm. When one drowning man attempts to save himself by grasping another, the consequence almost invariably is, that both go to the bottom. I trust that all teachers, who, either through example or inadvertence, have been led to adopt the course whose evils are here exposed, will adandon, and never resume it.

Whispering is very justly and almost universally considered to be one of the greatest mischiefs that can infest a schoolroom. In small schools, consisting either of very large or of very young scholars, it occasions less inconvenience; but in large schools, especially if composed of scholars of all ages, it is a very serious annoyance, and energetic teachers usually strive to suppress it. In a room containing sixty scholars, if each should whisper only one-sixtieth part of the hour, — not an inordinate allowance, if whispering be permitted at all, — it would be sufficient to make the buzz perpetual. The mischief of whispering, however, is by no means confined to the noise it makes. If one be allowed to whisper, another must be allowed to listen; and it is too much to expect that the neighbors of the parties will be indifferent hearers or spectators of what is going on around them. Sometimes, too, a plan or a joke started in one corner will be telegraphed round the room almost with the rapidity of a lighted train of gunpowder. The course of thought of the whole school will thus be interrupted; and, though the act of whispering may occupy but half a minute, it may occasion the loss of several minutes to each pupil.

But, objectionable as is the practice of whispering in schools, some means are used for avoiding it which seem to me to be far more so. In some schools, all whispering is prohibited under sanctions more or less severe; while the teacher, conscious of his own inability to detect all offenders, and discarding the practice by which the guilty are set to watch for the guilty, establishes another rule, by which the offenders are required to report their own offences. At the close of each day, or half-day, the roll is called, and each pupil is required, when his name is announced, to confess the number of breaches, if any, which he has committed.

One of the objections to this mode of prevention is, that it hazards the commission of a greater offence in order to avert a less one. To prevent whispering, it tempts to falsehood. Now, though whispering is mischievous, yet who, considerately, would suppress a thousand cases of it at the expense of one lie? Consider the force of the temptation. At the appointed time, the teacher calls upon the pupils to declare whether any violation of the rule has been committed by them. He calls upon them to plead guilty or not guilty. To acknowledge that they are guilty is a public avowal of wrong-doing; and, if the feelings are not blunted, must always incur some mortification. A penalty or forfeiture of some kind — such as noting the case in a record-book, or reporting it to the parents, or, at least, the teacher's disapproval — must be attached to the act, or the whole will soon degenerate into a farce. Under these circumstances, the pupil is called upon to avow a breach of duty. He is to do that publicly, which involves some degree of shame; he is to do that voluntarily, which requires some moral courage; and he is to do that promptly, which demands such a vigorous impulsion of conscientiousness as belongs to comparatively few. On the other hand, by silence, or by a moment's delay, — during which he may perhaps be debating within himself what course to take, — the occasion will pass by, and immunity from outward censure be secured. Is not this a snare to conscience? Is not this leading children into temptation, — a grievous temptation? Does it not, in fact, lead two persons — perhaps even more than two — into temptation? for, if one pupil has whispered, he must have whispered *to* another, — generally to a friend sitting at the same desk. For the friend to betray the offender may wear the aspect of unkindness. Besides, to betray a fellow-pupil, is held, whether justly or not, — according to the moral code of the college and the schoolroom, — to deserve great odium. Perhaps both have offended, and therefore stand in equal need of each other's forbearance.

There is one aspect belonging to the course above described, which it is peculiarly painful to contemplate, — that of a child debating with himself, either before the commission of an offence, or when called upon to confess it, respecting the chances of his escape; and making the commission of the offence in the first instance, or the denial of it in the second, depend upon the balance of probabilities in favor of detection or of exemption. A falser condition of mind cannot be conceived. Probably the fiend who tempts to crime by the hope or promise of concealment outnumbers all his fellow-fiends in the retinue of his victims. A wrong consciously perpetrated by the heart is neither made greater by exposure, nor less by impunity. The question which Conscience puts respecting a guilty act is, not whether it is known or unknown, but whether it has been done; and, before her awful tribunal, the judgment is the same, whether it is concealed by darkness and silence from the eyes and ears of all created beings, or whether all the stars of the firmament have arranged themselves, for the revelation and the condemnation of the deed, into a language of everlasting and unquenchable light.

Now, I can conceive of a school — I think I have seen such schools — where the moral sense of the pupils has been so enlightened and trained, that it would be safe to put a question of the kind above supposed, without jeoparding the integrity of the pupils. But how much more frequently, in the present state of our schools as to morals, would the solicitations to wrong be an overmatch for fidelity to truth, and thus begin a habit of falsehood, or confirm one already begun, which, before the end of life, by the confluence of hundreds of little streams into one deep current of corruption, would prove the ruin of the tempted! As a guardian of the morals of youth, and especially of their veracity, — that central point of morals, — no teacher should allow his own convenience, or his pride in the appearance of the record of his school, or his fear of incurring the displeasure of any pupil, or the parent of any pupil, for one moment to weigh down the scale against the perpetration, or even the imminent danger of the perpetration, of an untruth. The love of truth is a primal element in moral character. Truth is the cement of society. Without it, all friendships, partnerships, communities themselves, would be dissolved. Without some degree of mutual confidence, no two men, whether virtuous or vicious, could look each other in the face for a minute. Complete distrust at all points would segregate each individual of the race from all the rest; and, like an unbalanced centrifugal force, would impel each to fly away, and to seek some vacant part of the universe for his solitary abode.

There is a natural adaptation between the love of intellectual and the love of moral truth to confirm and strengthen each other. One should never be set in opposition to the other. Circumstances should never be so arranged, that the pursuit of an intellectual good may conflict with that of a moral one. Not antagonists, but co-laborers for the happiness of man, the teacher should unite and marry them into an inseparable union, and thus lay an imperishable foundation for the virtues and duties of life.

In regard to the prevention of whispering in school, the following important questions arise; and I do not see how they can be answered in the negative: If it be practicable to train a school to such a high point of principle and of honorable feeling, that its members will promptly acknowledge the transgression of a rule, may not the same members be so trained as not to be guilty of the transgression itself? Or, if children cannot be deterred from whispering by the reasonableness of the requisition, are they not likely to be guilty of falsehood under the pressure of so violent a temptation? And, finally, does not falsehood surpass whispering as an offence, too much to allow us to secure our schools from the inconvenience of the latter by incurring a serious hazard of the baseness of the former?

The chances of success in preventing whispering by an exercise of vigilance on the part of the teacher will be increased or diminished by the number and ages of the scholars, and by the good or ill construction of the seats in the schoolroom. The smaller the school, other things being equal, the more easy to banish this invader of its quiet, — not easier in the ratio of the diminished number merely; but, to express it mathematically, the ease is as the square of the diminution. Any school, however, may be considered as only of a moderate or medium size, if the number of the teachers is fitly proportioned to the number of the scholars.

The construction of the schoolroom bears directly upon this subject. The old-fashioned schoolhouses, with seats on three, and sometimes on four sides of the schoolroom, — leaving only a space on one side, unoccupied by seats, sufficient for a door, — could not have been more ingeniously contrived to invite disobedience and trickery had the Genius of Deception been the architect. In such a room, one-half the children, at least, were always without the range of the teacher's eye, and so within the sphere of temptation. Where circumstances had been so skilfully contrived to entice them into transgression, who can wonder that they so often became its victims? Even schoolhouse architecture has a palpable connection with moral culture.

Various remedies have been suggested for the prevention of whispering in school, besides the extreme one of corporal punishment in any of its forms.

Occupation is one of the most effectual. While each scholar has employment on his own account, he has neither time nor inducement to trespass upon his neighbor. This is the case for two reasons. His own occupation precludes the desire of communicating with his fellow; and the occupation of his fellow will repel approaches, should he be tempted to make them.

The privation of some customary privilege — such as being kept within doors at recess — is another expedient. If a single act of communication in school, occupying but half a minute, causes a forfeiture of a five-minutes' privilege of communication at recess, then the balance of advantage is so obviously on the side of self-restraint as to become a powerful motive for abstaining. Such a forfeiture for such an offence seems unobjectionable; but, in all cases where it is inflicted, the offender should have a recess by himself at another time: for the recess is demanded by the laws of health; and the teacher's punishments should never endanger health.

Recognizing the strong natural desire of all children to communicate with each other, and the inherent difficulty of repressing such an inborn and powerful impulse, some teachers adopt the expedient of an intermediate recess; or rather a suspension of the exercises of the schoolroom, for a period of five minutes, at prescribed times, in each half-day's session. During this suspension, the pupils are allowed to rise, to walk about, and to converse, and thus to give vent to their pent-up desires for muscular action and for social communication. This may be allowed twice during each half-day, — once before and once after the customary recess at the middle of the session. Of course, it becomes less necessary as the scholars are older.

But, from my own observation and experience, I am led to believe that all methods for preventing communication between scholars in school, however skilfully devised or energetically executed they may be, will prove inadequate to the intended purpose, unless they include another element, — the assent and co-operation of the scholars themselves. The natural propensity to speak, the inborn social instinct to make known our thoughts and feelings to our fellow-men, is so vigorous, that it requires the most powerful motives of fear, of interest, or of duty, to smother them. In infancy, it is as vain to command a child to stifle the expression of its desires and emotions as to command the gushing waters of a fountain to cease from their uprising. Later in life, though the inward propulsion of feeling, seeking some form of outward expression, may be regulated, yet it cannot, even then, be wholly suppressed. Probably no two animals of any kind were ever together for two minutes, — unless asleep, or profoundly absorbed in something else, — without some transmission, by looks or signs, of sympathy or aversion. With the human species, if the lips are sealed, the fingers will be made the medium of communication; if the hands are confined, the eye will become the subtle messenger of thought. But the voice is the natural sign-maker, and therefore it is through the voice that the will acts most promptly and energetically. In prisons, where the inmates work in companies, but under a rigorous prohibition, sanctioned by terrible penalties, against intercommunication, either by word or gesture, cases have occurred where the tortured spirit within would give vent to its natural instinct by a tremendous shriek or yell, and then submit to a flagellation, with patience, as an expiation of the offence.

In this, therefore, as in all other cases, whether pertaining to the government or to the proficiency of a school, the teacher's best resources — the only allies he can enlist, who will, in all cases, secure him the victory — are the pupils themselves. No threats, no forfeitures, no fear, no pain, though the teacher should summon these to his aid in formidable hosts, will ever expel whispering from school, unless superadded thereto is the scholars' consent. I have witnessed proofs of the truth of this assertion too numerous to be contested. In schools where authority and superior physical power were mainly relied on, I have witnessed cases of transgression, even while the teacher was assuring me of the sufficiency of his own sovereign command to prevent them. But, if the pupils have confidence in their teacher, — if they respect his talents and his attainments, and are constantly drawn towards him by the attractions of a filial affection, — their co-operation can be obtained, and that will prove all-sufficient. Indeed, if only every other scholar — that is, if no more than one-half of the school — should unite in placing a ban upon the practice, it would be suppressed; for, as a scholar will rarely if ever be whispered to without his own permission, it follows, that, if every other scholar should join the league of abstinence, the other half would be debarred from addressing them, and thus an interdict would be placed even upon willing transgressors.

It is hardly necessary to observe, that, under the generic term whispering, I here include all forms of illicit communication, whether carried on through the medium of the voice, the finger-language, writing on paper or on a slate, marking words or letters in a book so as to make a sentence, or by any other of the ingenious devices which fear and fraud have contrived. Their object is the same, and their mischief is the same. They all train the mind to base and unmanly artifices, for which no amount of knowledge is any equivalent, — artifices which only confer more formidable powers of mischief upon the highly-developed intellect.

Perhaps no other combination of circumstances pertaining to a school furnishes so favorable an opportunity as the one under consideration for the inculcation of self-denial, and for habituating the pupils to its practice. Self-denial is not so much a pre-eminent virtue as it is the parent of all the virtues. To be able to resist the present solicitations of passion or of appetite, in consideration of a future good; to be able to postpone or to forego immediate gratification, in obedience to a principle of duty; to be able, in the solitude of a desert or in the darkness of midnight, when no human eye can see us, when no obstacle or bar, save the eternal law of right, comes between the object of our unlawful desire and our enjoyment of it; to be able, under such circumstances, not only to abstain, but to feel that our resolution would be no stronger though all the universe were gathered around us in a circle, of which we were the luminous centre, — this may be justly regarded as the acme of moral power and grandeur. How vast the distance between this moral altitude and the low region of weakness, of temptation, and of peril, in which the child is born! But just in proportion to this distance are the reward and the glory of the teacher who leads the young spirit onward in its sublime ascension to the heights of virtue.

The very scheme and constitution of human nature demonstrate that we have as deep an interest in any portion of futurity — hour for hour, and day for day — as in the same portion of time now passing; for the simple but decisive and perfectly intelligible reason, that future time *is to be* present time. Indeed, our personal interest preponderates in favor of that portion of time which lies beyond us, rather than in favor of that now present; because the current of our life widens and deepens as it advances; and because new capacities and sources of happiness and of misery are perpetually pouring in their confluent streams to increase the volume of our future existence, and thus making that existence more desirable for enjoyment, or more terrible for suffering. We know, too, that the present not only has its concomitants of weal or woe, but that it will modify and color all that is to come after it. To the eye of reason and conscience, therefore, the stages of being through which we are hereafter to pass have as close a relation to ourselves, to our identity, as those through which we are now passing. It is the eye of sense only which magnifies the near, but sees the distant in the diminished proportions of perspective; as has been strikingly illustrated in the saying, that a straw placed near the eye seems as large as an oak of a hundred years in the distance. But the difficulty is, that, with a spiritual nature perpetually existent, we have appetites and desires that demand immediate gratification; and, to give plausibility to their demands, it is also true that those appetites and desires must, to a certain extent, be gratified, or our temporal existence would cease. The teacher, then, should put the future visibly into the scale, that it may counterbalance the present. For this purpose, the connection between the present and the future must be explained, — the tendency of habits, whether good or evil, to increase in velocity and momentum; the tendency of all indulged desires and thoughts to redouble their strength, and their control over the will; the danger, therefore, of uttering a profane word, of venturing upon the terrible experiment of a falsehood, of dissimulation, of envy, of unkindness, of disobedience. The competent teacher adopts this method in regard to all the studies pursued in his school. He shows the relation between what is present and visible, and what is distant and unseen. Physical geography can never be learned, unless the child is first led to form adequate conceptions of *space*, where he can assign locality to objects, and give arrangement to all the facts he learns. History can never be learned, unless the learner has adequate conceptions of past *time*, — of successive centuries, along whose years and decades he can distribute and arrange the events which history brings under his notice. So the duty and the utility of self-denial can never be adequately enforced or appreciated, unless the future be opened, and the relations of passing events to the fortunes of after-life be exhibited. Why, then, should so great a proportion of the school-hours be spent upon studies, and so small a proportion upon motives? Why should the reputation and the patronage of schools depend more upon what the scholars *know* than upon how they *act?* Why should the public inquire more frequently respecting the school or the college where a *great* man has been educated than respecting the influences under which a *good* man has been trained? In the vast majority of our schools throughout the length and breadth of the land, are not the laws of orthoepy more carefully taught than the laws of justice and equity between man and man? Is the duty of forgiveness as much insisted on as the rules of grammar? Are the elementary ideas of right and wrong as laboriously explained as the elements of arithmetic? or are the mighty results of good or evil principles, as they are evolved in society, in the affairs of government, and in the intercourse of nations with each other, as perseveringly expounded as are the higher combinations of arithmetical numbers? Are not errors in text-books, or even in the language of visitors, sometimes brought forward with care and exposed with vanity, while obscene carvings, or emblems of pollution, around the premises, or on the walls of the schoolroom itself, are suffered to remain unmolested? These frightful inconsistencies must be terminated. Their continuance is suicide. Self-preservation as well as religion demands a change. Neglect moral and Christian culture in the schoolroom, and if the exchange is shaken by stupendous frauds, if perjuries invade the tribunals of justice, if hypocrisy and intolerance are installed in the sanctuaries of religion, if political profligacy reigns in the council-halls of the nation, and sends its streams of corruption through all the channels of government, we shall reap only as we have sown.

There are some schools in Massachusetts, and the number is increasing, where, without invading the conscientious rights or scruples of a single denomination, social and Christian principles have been so wisely acted on by the teacher, have been so clearly and convincingly brought down and brought home to the minds of the pupils, that not only whispering, but other sources of disorder and misconduct, has been almost entirely banished from the schoolroom. Cases have occurred where, voluntarily, without solicitation, the older and more influential scholars have signed a pledge, obligating themselves to abstain from particular school-offences, and to use their influence to induce others to practise the like abstinence. How high the point of self-respect and of principle which the pupils have reached, when such a measure emanates spontaneously from them! How greatly is the power of acquisition promoted when the power of self-control is enthroned in the breast! And how far-reaching and decisive in its influences upon after-life is a successful resolution in childhood to seek counsel of duty, and to abide by its decisions! Blessed is the fortune of those children who are led by wise and benignant hands to some moral eminence, where they can survey the path that will conduct them to happiness, and are inspired with the motives which will prompt them to pursue it! *

* As a specimen of the utter oblivion into which a love of intellectual acuteness and skill may throw the moral relations of a subject, I quote the following question from a modern arithmetic: —

The vice of truantship is to be regarded under the same moral aspects. The truant, it is true, loses privileges which can never be recovered; because no revolution of the wheel of time ever brings back an hour that has been wasted. By foregoing his opportunity of acquiring knowledge, the truant forfeits at least a portion of his chances for future usefulness and success in life; and he also forfeits those enduring satisfactions which are the rewards of intellectual culture. Loitering by the wayside but for a single day, or deviating into illicit paths but for a single hour, he allows those who were behind him to pass by, and to seize upon the advantages or the honors, which, by the use of diligence, he might rightfully have made his own. He enrolls himself with the most wasteful of all prodigals, — those who are prodigal of time. But the positive good which is lost is trifling compared with the positive evil which is incurred. Every act of truantship is a twofold falsehood. It is a falsehood committed against the parent who sends, and against the teacher who expects. Worse than either of these, it is a violation of the culprit's own sense of duty. To waste the seed-time, and to consume the seed from which a rich harvest might be reaped, does but condemn the fields of after-life to barrenness; but the pretence, the equivocation, the deceit, and occasionally the downright lie, and, what is worst of all, the perpetual holding of the mind in an active lying state, — that is, in a state ready to lie, — these strew thickly those tares of vice over the fields of youth whose harvest will be ruin. It is

---

" A sea-captain on a voyage had a crew of thirty men, half of whom were blacks. Being becalmed on the passage for a long time, their provisions began to fail; and the captain became satisfied, that, unless the number of men was greatly diminished, all would perish of hunger before they reached any friendly port. He therefore proposed to the sailors that they should stand in a row on deck, and that every ninth man should be thrown overboard until one-half of the crew were thus destroyed. To this they all agreed. How should they stand *to save the whites?* "

Doubtless this question was prepared by the author, and has been laboriously studied by thousands of pupils, without any distinct contemplation of the fiendish injustice and fraud which it involves, but only with admiration for the ingenuity which originated, and for the talent that can solve it; and yet the idea which the question has lodged in the mind may become the parent of a fraud as base if not as appalling as its prototype.

not, then, the squandering of school-privileges which gives to this offence its most malignant type; it is not the loss of money expended for books and for tuition; it is not the indignity offered to the teacher: but it is the positive wrong, self-inflicted upon the pupil's own moral nature; it is that struggle between his own illicit desires and his sense of duty, in which the former are victorious; it is the stratagem, and the putting of the mind into a frame to invent stratagems, in order to secure impunity or to avoid suspicion, — it is this inward training of the soul to the contemplation and the devices of iniquity, which gives to the evil its magnitude and frightfulness. But is it so regarded by those parents who never visit the school from the beginning to the end of the term, in order to examine the teacher's register, or to learn, by personal inquiry, whether their children have been delinquent? Is it so regarded by any teacher who records absences, half-day after half-day, without ever visiting the parents to know whether the absence is necessary or fraudulent? Is it so regarded either by parents or teachers, who, when the offence is detected, inflict chastisement upon the offender as the penalty of his misconduct, but take no other measures to reach the secret workings of his mind, and there to rectify the springs of action themselves?

In rural districts, where the population is sparse, cases of truantship are of rare occurrence. In cities and large towns, and especially in manufacturing villages, the offence is not unfrequent. Various devices are resorted to for its successful commission. In most schools, no written excuse for absence or tardiness is required, and therefore a truant has only to fabricate some excuse for being late or absent; and the teacher too often dismisses the subject without further inquiry. When written excuses are required, parents often give one without date, which the pupil will keep as long as he dares, — perhaps for several days, — and then present it. Sometimes a child is necessarily detained at home for half an hour after the commencement of the school; and, having obtained an excuse from his parent without any specification as to time, he plays truant for the greater part of the session, and then goes in and presents it. Or the parent sends written word that he wishes his child to return home before the school is done, without specifying how long before; and an hour or two of playtime is gained by obtaining dismission too early. Instances have occurred where a child has had the wickedness to forge an excuse, and present it as genuine. But if the *child* will forge his father's name to an excuse, in order to get an hour of play, ought we to be surprised if the same child, when grown to manhood, should commit the crime of forgery to obtain the means of criminal indulgence? Is it a vain apprehension that a child, thus false to his own interests and to the claims of duty, will be false to all the interests and duties which may afterwards be committed to his keeping? If we think we foresee, in the remarkable answers of a school-boy, — remarkable only because so little is expected at so early an age, — proofs of the power and the splendor that shall aggrandize and adorn the future man, why may not we foresee, in these juvenile offences which are so lightly passed over, proofs of those enormous misdeeds which afterwards shall bring distress upon a family, a community, or a country? With pleasure it is admitted, that there are cases of reformation, — cases where the evil that was betokened by a youth of error is averted by repentance, and followed by a life of uprightness. On the other hand, also, it must be conceded that there are instances where all the hopes that were cherished by a childhood of innocence have been blasted by a manhood of profligacy. But, on both sides, these cases are exceptions to the general rule; and they are no further to be recognized as grounds of action, than as they admonish us never to sink into the inaction of over-confidence in regard to the good, nor into the hopelessness of despair in regard to the bad. A venerable clergyman belonging to the State, always watchful of the condition of youth, and regarding the conduct of the child as foretokening the character of the man, has informed me that he taught school for many years in the town where he was afterwards settled as a minister; that it was his practice, while in school, to keep a detailed record of the diligence, proficiency, and moral deportment of his pupils, which record he has preserved; and now, on recurring to this school-diary, he finds, with but few exceptions, that it would answer very well as an index, or table of contents, for the acted volume of their subsequent lives. There is one vice, indeed, or rather a prolific parent of all vices, which disturbs this great law of probabilities, and often falsifies the indications given by an exemplary youth of an honorable old age. It is the vice of intemperance. This vice is a horrid alchemy, which transmutes every thing good into evil; and not merely changing affinities, but, corrupting the very elements on which it works, renders it impossible ever afterwards to restore them to their pristine strength and purity. It is the theological opposite of regeneration; for it depraves depravity itself.

In the new register-book which has been prepared by the Board, and which will be in the schools the ensuing summer term, provision is made for the entry of each pupil's name. If the teacher performs his duty in keeping the register, as it is to be presumed he will, then every parent, on visiting the school, can learn by mere inspection whether his child is charged on the book with more cases of tardiness or absence than have been authorized; and, by a vigilant use of this check, the vice of truantship may be generally extirpated.

The question, By what motives shall children be incited to study? opens a vast and most interesting field of inquiry. That the human mind was pre-adapted by its benevolent Creator for the acquisition of knowledge and the exercise of reason, is not merely an inference drawn from the wisdom and goodness of God, but it is ocularly demonstrated by the constitution of our nature. It is not merely what we should expect, but what we actually see. Before the human lungs are brought into the world, how admirably are they prepared for the air that is to surround and to fill them! Not only are the lungs tubular and vesicular, in the highest degree, for the reception of the air, but the air has a property which the blood must imbibe, or it would perish in five minutes; and, further, the blood has a property which it must cast out through the lungs into the air, or again it would perish in five minutes from another cause. What need has the unborn child of that exquisite mechanism, the eye; of the iris, invested with power to enlarge or diminish itself by a spontaneous movement; of its crystalline lens, and of its different humors, to cause the rays of light to converge; of the finely-wrought net-work of the retina, spread at the true focal distance over its interior surface; of the wonderful nerve that lies behind it, holding mysterious communication with the secret chambers of the brain; and of the solid masonry of bones, which is built up as a wall of protection around it? This marvellous contrivance is prepared in reference to the sun,—an object almost a hundred millions of miles distant from it; it is prepared in reference to sidereal systems, lying at incomputable distances from our system; and He who, in the beginning, created the greater and lesser lights of the firmament, and who now selects and arranges the subtlest particles of matter for the formation of the human eye, established of old the relations between them, and pre-adapted their powers and their properties to each other. How curiously has the Creator fashioned the mechanism of the ear! He has planted it so deeply and securely within the protecting walls of the cranium, that it needs no bars or portals to defend it from external encroachments; he has made it to stand forever open, — by night as well as by day, and whether sleeping or waking, — so that there is scarcely a natural agent of harm that can approach us, without warning us of its coming. With what a delicate equilibrium is its tympanum balanced!— vibrating at the buzz of an insect's wing, or at the tread of an insect's foot, yet able to bear uninjured the ocean's roar, or the thunder's crash; and it is made to delight in all the variety of sweet sounds that lie between these far-distant extremes. And so of all the other senses. Is it not intuitively obvious that they were designed to bring us into communication and relationship with the infinitely-varied objects of the world around us; with the food and drinks which nourish and sustain us; with the solid substances that shelter, and the textile ones that clothe us; with the various races of animals over which "dominion" has been given us; with the dry land which abideth in its place, and with the waters which make their perpetual circuit from the mountains and hills into the rivers, from the rivers into the sea, from the sea into the clouds, and from the clouds to the mountains and hills and rivers again?

Nor is utility the only purpose of those beautiful relations which exist between ourselves and the external world. The goodness of God is as pervading as his power, and hence he has everywhere intermingled pleasure with advantage. Golden threads are thickly interspersed in every web which Nature has woven. How conspicuous is this truth in regard to the property of color! Most of the other properties of matter seem to have a primary reference to utility. The inflexibility of stone, and the elasticity of steel; the combustibility of wood, and the relative incombustibility of the metals; the hardness of flint, and the softness of wool and silk, — seem primarily designed for use rather than for pleasure; and so of innumerable other objects. But what profit can the cold utilitarian extort from all the variegation and changeful beauties of color? The rainbow, the orient sun, the evening clouds, the plumage of birds, the flower-strewn fields, the hues of the blossoming spring, and of the foliage of autumn, joyful in its death, — these add no gold to his coffers, nor acres to his lands, nor fruit to his garners. Yet this beautiful property of matter is spread upon the surface of all things, as if to attract our attention to them, and to win our regards for them, not only before, but after, the age of reflection; and no other property is at once so universal and so varied as this. In almost every instance, the gracious Author of this property of matter, and of our capacity to perceive it, has made it pleasurable; and probably no child ever consciously looked, even for the thousandth time, upon the moon, or a sun-illumined cloud, or stream, or lake, without an emotion of joy.

Such is the relation which our *senses* bear to the external universe.

And, in the second place, the faculties by which we reason stand in the same relation to the perceptive powers, and to the images or notions of things which they collect, as the perceptive powers themselves do to the objects of the external world. Through the senses we collect notions, more or less accurately and extensively, of the boundless variety of things that constitutes the world around us, — of all that is great or small, high or low, solid or fluid, cold or hot, moving or motionless, odorous or inodorous, savory or vapid, hard or soft, loud or low, and so forth; but all this knowledge of properties would be of no more service to us than to the beasts of the field or the fowls of the air, did not the illuminating reason preside over them, discerning the relations between them, disentangling consequences by referring each effect to its cause, and, out of new arrangements and combinations, educing new uses to increase the physical comforts and the spiritual elevation of mankind. It is only by the safer light of reason, indeed, that we rectify the mistakes into which the senses would inevitably and constantly lead us. To the senses, the earth and sun are flat: reason declares them to be spheres. If we ask the senses, they affirm that the earth is thousands of times larger than the sun; if we consult the reason, we are assured that the sun would contain within its circumference more than thirteen hundred thousand globes, each as large as the earth. The senses declare that the earth is stationary, and that the sun revolves around it every day; but reason gives stability to the sun, and a diurnal revolution to the earth. So, from the beginning of life, reason rectifies the errors of the senses; and, without its aid, we should be in a world of illusions, each one leading us astray. Reason also teaches us to discover those things which are too remote and too minute for the senses ever to reach, — the magnificent bodies and distances of astronomy, and the imperceptibly minute atoms and motions of chemistry. Who, then, let me again ask, can doubt that the great Author of our reason designed that it should be used, and that it should be developed and cultivated in order to be used? As the senses were created to receive images or perceptions of things belonging to the external world; so the reason was created to work upon those images or perceptions when received, to correct and modify and assort them, to discover the *insensible* qualities they possess, and to penetrate to the laws they obey. Hence it is obvious, from our very constitution, that the Deity meant that the science of optics should be *understood*, as much as that the sensation of light should be *felt;* that the atmosphere should be analyzed into its different ingredients, and the properties of each ingredient determined, as much as that the atmosphere itself should be breathed; and that the laws of life and health should be discovered, as much as that we should desire to live.

And in all these exercises of the reason upon the crude materials of knowledge, not less than in the acquisition of the knowledge itself, there is pleasure. Nature has not constituted this portion of the mind upon the principles of utility alone, but upon the principles of utility and pleasure combined. How intensely have all the great intellectual luminaries of the world loved the sciences in which they labored! and who has ever *understandingly* surveyed any part of the creation of God, without being thrilled with delight?

Is not the course of Nature, then, — which is a lesson given by the Creator himself, — full of instruction and wisdom in regard to the school-motives which should be brought to bear upon children? First, in order to win attention, the objects of knowledge should be made attractive, as Nature, by bestowing upon her objects the pleasing qualities of form and color, of motion and sound, makes them attractive. As the powers of perception precede the powers of reasoning, in the order of development, the sensible qualities of things should first be presented to the learner. Afterwards, and when the reasoning powers are developed, the profounder relations that exist between things, and the laws by which they are governed, should be unfolded to the reason in the same manner in which the sensible properties had been exhibited to the senses. In this clear light of Nature, too, we see where language should come in. Words are but the signs of things, not only useless, but burdensome and pernicious, without a knowledge of the things themselves. For all mankind, the course of Nature is, *things*, and then their *names*. For a year, and not unfrequently for two years, after a child's birth, the Deity forbids to it, withholds from it, the use of language. At that period of life, so cumbrous and uncertain an instrument as language would confuse and bewilder the mind, and divert it from the perception of qualities to signs. Yet, during that time, how much does a child learn respecting the properties and distances and relative positions of the objects about him! What more stupendous folly, then, can be conceived, than to teach children to read, without seeing that they understand what they read; to teach them the pauses and emphases and cadences which are designed to aid the intellect, and the modulation and tones which are expressive of the passions, while they themselves receive but little more conscious intelligence or emotion from the lesson than do the benches on which they sit! Still worse is it if coarse and harsh appliances are used as substitutes for those true and genuine sources of interest which are thus withheld.

But, notwithstanding this original adaptation of the faculties for acquiring and using knowledge, it must be conceded that there are cases in actual life where the natural tendency of the mind to become acquainted with the things around it has been marred, and sometimes almost obliterated. As the stomach, with its instinctive longings for healthful food, may be so abused as to loathe the most appropriate nourishment; so the mind, with its inborn love of knowledge, — which seems to be not merely an attraction for knowledge, but a repulsion from ignorance, — may be so abused as to look with disgust at what it should have longed for. And this is not unfrequently done, by parental ignorance or perversity, before the child passes into the hands of the professional teacher. In such a case, the teacher may appear to do a vast deal more by stimulating the verbal memory of the child, and by giving him the show instead of the substance of knowledge, than if he should strive to re-animate the apparently dead powers of acquisition and of thought. Yet the latter should be done, at whatever seeming delay; and the faithful teacher will do it, irrespective of the consequences to his own reputation. It is only the unfaithful teacher who will adopt the course which will make the child appear best at the end of the term, irrespective of his permanent welfare.

It was the opinion of Pestalozzi, — that wisest of schoolmasters, — that the children's want of interest in their studies, in his day, was almost universally referable to a want of skill in those who had charge of them. "There are scarcely any circumstances," he says, "in which a want of application in children does not proceed from a want of interest; and there are perhaps none under which a want of interest does not originate in the mode of treatment adopted by the teacher. I would go so far as to lay it down as a rule, that whenever children are inattentive, and apparently take no interest in a lesson, the teacher should always first look to himself for a reason." Undoubtedly, in expressing this opinion, Pestalozzi must have referred to permanent teachers only, and not to such as keep the same school only for a few weeks, or for a single term; and in many cases, certainly, the parents as well as the teacher should be included in the stricture. Yet, if any person had a right to say this, it was Pestalozzi; for, however stubborn or stupid children had ever been found to be under other masters, they became docile and improving under him. But every teacher cannot become what Pestalozzi was, with his extraordinary natural endowments, and with his life of experience, any more than every man can become what Lord Bacon or Sir Isaac Newton or Dr. Franklin was. What, then, shall be done by such teachers as we have, and are glad to employ? Shall they not, as far as possible, imitate him, and, by pursuing similar means, approximate to similar results? Shall they not, as he did, determine what they will *not do*, as well as what they will do? "The motive of fear," says he, "should not be made a stimulus to exertion. It will destroy interest, and will speedily create disgust. The *interest* in study is the first thing which a teacher should endeavor to excite and keep alive." And again, speaking of that class of children who are subjected to a mere "mechanical training," and who, therefore, need some collateral stimulus to spur them on to study, he says, "The common motive by which such a system acts on those whose indolence it has conquered is *fear*. The very highest to which it can aspire, in those whose sensibility is excited, is *ambition*.

"It is obvious," he continues, "that such a system can calculate only on the lower selfishness of man. To that least amiable or estimable part of the human character, it is, and always has been, indebted for its best success. Upon the better feelings of man it turns a deaf ear.

"How is it, then, that motives leading to a course of action which is looked upon as mean and despicable, or at best as doubtful, when it occurs in life, — how is it that motives of that description are thought honorable in education? Why should that bias be given to the mind in a school, which, to gain the respect or the affection of others, an individual must first of all strive to unlearn? — a bias to which every candid mind is a stranger.

"I do not wish to speak harshly of ambition, or to reject it altogether as a motive. There is, to be sure, a noble ambition, — dignified by its object, and distinguished by a deep and transcendent interest in that object. But if we consider the sort of ambition commonly proposed to the school-boy; if we analyze ' what stuff 'tis made of, whereof it is born,' — we shall find that it has nothing to do with the interest taken in the object of study; that such an interest frequently does not exist; and that, owing to its being blended with that vilest and meanest of motives, — with *fear*, — it is by no means raised by the wish to give pleasure to those who propose it; for a teacher who proceeds on a system in which fear and ambition are the principal agents must give up his claim to the esteem or affection of his pupils.

"Motives, like fear or inordinate ambition, may stimulate to exertion, intellectual or physical; but they cannot warm the heart. There is not in them that life which makes the heart of youth heave with delight of knowledge, with the honest consciousness of talent, with the honorable wish for distinction, with the kindly glow of genuine feeling. Such motives are inadequate in their source, and inefficient in their application; for they are nothing to the heart, and ' out of the heart are the issues of life.' "

In remarking upon school-motives, the use of emulation as an incentive to study cannot be overlooked; and yet I mean to abstain, on this occasion, from touching upon the debatable ground which it covers. To discuss the subject fully would require, not a paragraph merely, but a treatise. In regard to the general question, — the expediency of a system of means to excite emulation between scholars, — there are distinguished advocates on both sides; but it will be my endeavor, at the present time, only to elucidate some points, respecting which there is, so far as I know, an entire unanimity of abstract opinion, though with no inconsiderable diversity in practice.

May we not expect the assent of all intelligent men to the doctrine, that it is the teacher's duty to effect the greatest *general* proficiency of his pupils? It is not the remarkable progress of a few scholars, while others remain in a stationary condition, or are even retrograding, that is desirable or allowable. The spirit of all our institutions coincides herein with the spirit of humanity and religion; all enforcing the duty of succoring the destitute, of instructing the ignorant, of elevating the lowly. As it would be a violation of the soundest principles of political economy to make the rich richer, and the poor poorer; so it would transgress the plainest dictates of republican duty and Christian ethics to give knowledge to the learned at the expense of suffering the ignorant to remain in their ignorance. To present this idea with arithmetical precision, let us suppose, that, in a class of twenty children in one school, the improvement of ten of them shall be equal to 5 each, or 50 in all; and that of the other ten shall be nothing: so that 50 shall represent the improvement of the whole class. In another school, suppose a class of the same number, but an improvement of $2\frac{1}{2}$ for each of the whole. As in the former case, *fifty* will be the product; and who will not acknowledge that the greatest good has been accomplished in the latter instance? Who will deny that the teacher in the latter case has accomplished a far nobler object than in the former?

When schools are very large, and it is the custom of the committee to examine only the first class, or, perhaps, only a part of the first class, the temptation to carry forward those who are to be examined, even at the expense of neglecting the residue, is peculiarly strong; and it needs all the guards of an active conscience in the teacher, and a vigilant superintendence in the committee, to prevent it.

As a spur to emulation, it is not an unfrequent practice to make a record, at the end of each recitation, of the number of mistakes which each scholar may have made. In the great majority of instances, so far as I have witnessed, this record is made without any reference to the quality of the mistake committed. Yet can any thing be more unjust than to recognize no difference between a mistake *in fact* and a mistake *in principle?* In arithmetic, for instance, one scholar, with his mind intently fixed upon the principle according to which his problem is to be wrought, makes a mistake in subtracting or dividing, and fails, therefore, of arriving at the true answer. Another, regardless of principle, performs the mechanical part of his work correctly, but proceeds upon such an erroneous hypothesis as will insure error in every question which comes under the same head or rule. In geography, one makes a mistake of a few hundreds in the census of a great city; another does not perceive that there is any connection between the great slopes of a continent and the course of its rivers. In history, one has forgotten the date of an unimportant event; another makes Gen. Washington a Frenchman. Yet in these cases, or such as these, the mistakes are reckoned *numerically;* no difference being made between a mistake which a wise man might have committed and one which stigmatizes its author as a dunce. To estimate the demerit of mistakes by number, instead of quality, is as rude a way as it would be, in the transactions of the bank or the market-place, to receive and pay all the various coins of our common currency by tale, instead of weight and fineness.

Again: will it not be conceded by all that the degree of emulation is excessive which induces scholars to study for *recitation* rather than for *knowledge?* The difference between the two modes is great, and it diffuses its consequences over all the future life. To learn for the purpose of repeating or reciting what is learned at the end of an hour, or of a few hours, supposes a state of mind entirely different from that which is necessary in order to learn the same thing with a view of treasuring it up in the mind to be remembered forever. The mind approaches, surveys, and grasps the subject, in these two cases, by modes wholly unlike. If a thing is to be remembered only for an hour, there are many auxiliary helps, which are useless, and even pernicious, if the object be to insure its retention for life. The order in which the lesson stands upon the pages of the text-book; the sequence of paragraphs or sections; the accident of a principle's being stated at the top or the bottom of a page, on its right hand or on its left; the fact that a place in the lesson has been rendered conspicuous to the eye by a proper name or a date, — all these and many other accidental associations may be temporary helps, though they are permanent obstructions. They are like the tricks and devices of the professors of mnemonics, who, in ten lessons, will teach their classes the greatest quantity of things, which, however, are like records made upon the beach whence the tide has receded, to be washed away by its refluent wave. The pupil who studies for recitation merely, is tempted, all the while, to use the *artificial* memory: the pupil who studies for knowledge will use the *philosophic* memory only. Knowledge acquired by the artificial method remains only while the arbitrary associations on which it is founded remain; but knowledge acquired by a perception of philosophic relations, being inwrought into the very structure and constitution of the mind, will be perpetuated until the happening of such a catastrophe as shall shatter to pieces the mind itself; and, even then, it will be seen shining among the fragments. Who ever heard of a great philosopher or jurist or mathematician, — a Franklin, a Marshall, or a Bowditch, — whose vast sequences of thought were linked together only by the brittle chain of an artificial memory? Among the graduates of those institutions of learning where emulation is one of the main incentives to study, is it the general rule that the scholars who obtain the highest honors of the class achieve a corresponding rank in society? On the other hand, is it not a fact that the exceptions to the contrary rule hardly amount to a respectable number?

Not only is the state of the mind different while studying and while reciting, if the only or the main object be to make a brilliant recitation, but there is a still greater difference after the recitation than before it. If superior rank at recitation be the object, then, as soon as that superiority is obtained, the spring of desire and of effort for that occasion relaxes. The pupil knows that the record, "perfect," set against his name, will stand, whatever fading-out of the lesson there may be from his mind. He dismisses, therefore, all thought of the last lesson, and concentrates his energies upon the next; and this becomes his history from day to day. Instead of spending an extra hour or half-hour in collateral reading, for the purpose of fortifying and expanding the views contained in the text-book, he spends it for increasing the volubility, or polishing the style, of the recitation. But, to the pupil who studies for the sake of understanding and retaining the subject-matter of the lesson, the recitation is only one of the early stages in the progress of his investigations. As he goes abroad, and views the works of nature and of art, he revives and applies the principles he has learned, until they become so familiar, that they rise spontaneously in the mind on every related occasion. If he reads any thing in a book or a newspaper, or hears any thing in conversation, involving the same principles, or explicable by them, the principles become consciously present to his reflection, until frequent repetition, seconded by the ready welcome they always receive, domiciliates them in the mind, and enfranchises them as members of the household of thought.

The spirit of the above remarks applies to all cases of studying for *review* as well as to studying for *recitation*.

Now, that I may avoid, on this occasion, all points of controversy in regard to the use of emulation in schools, I desire only to commend the following rule of practice to teachers: If they perceive that the use of emulation as a motive-power tends to increase the bulk and showiness of acquisition rather than to improve its quality; if it leads pupils to cultivate a memory for words rather than an understanding of things; and if it be found that the knowledge acquired through its instrumentality is short-lived, because it has been acquired for the temporary purpose of the recitation or examination rather than for usefulness in after-life, — if teachers find all or any of these mischiefs resulting from the use of such a motive, they should restrict it within such limits as will effectually avoid them.

But the most serious objection which can be urged against this agency is of a moral character. I suppose no one will deny that emulation *may* be plied to such a degree of intensity as to incur moral hazards and delinquencies. Addressing each teacher on his own ground, whatever that may be, I would, with deference, submit to him the following considerations: If the object of a pupil be to learn; if he compares himself with himself, which may be called self-emulation, and asks whether he knows more to-day than he did yesterday, or has acquired more during the current term or year than he did during the corresponding part of the last term or year; if he has some elevated object before him, which he desires to reach, and rejoices in his progress towards it, — all this seems not only lawful, but laudable. But if the pupil rejoices, not because he has acquired so much knowledge, but because, in acquiring so much, he has excelled another, and therefore would have grieved, even though he had made still greater acquisitions than he has, if another had surpassed him; if he indulges a feeling of exultation, not because he has shone, but because he has *out*-shone a rival; if he yields to the temptation of disparaging a competitor whom he would not have disparaged but for the competition, and is not as prompt to defend or justify him as though the rivalship did not exist between them; if he enjoys his own triumph with a keener zest because of the mortification of a fellow-aspirant, — in all and in each of these cases, I suppose it will be admitted by every one, that the law of Christian, and even of heathen, morality is violated. Bishop Butler defines emulation to be " the desire and hope of equality with or superiority over others with whom we compare ourselves;" and he then adds, " To desire the attainment of this equality or superiority by the particular means of others being brought down to our own level, or below it, is, I think, the distinct notion of envy." Abstaining, then, from all discussion of the general question, I would still say, that wherever teachers perceive the above-described consequences, or any of them, to be produced by emulation, they should be admonished that it has gone too far.

It is obvious that the question respecting the propriety or the impropriety, the justifiableness or the unjustifiableness, of using emulation as an incentive to intellectual progress, will be decided in different ways by different persons, according to the relative rank which they respectively assign to mental as distinguished from moral qualities. Whether talent be admired above virtue, or virtue above talent, the weaker affection will be sacrificed to the stronger, just as certainly as a parent, whose bark is in danger of sinking, will throw his treasures overboard to save his first-born, if the first-born be nearer to his heart than his treasures. So, if a teacher desires that his pupil should be a great man rather than a good one; or that he should acquire wealth rather than esteem; or that he should master the Latin and Greek languages rather than rule his own spirit; or attain to high official preferment rather than love the Lord his God with all his heart, and his neighbor as himself, — then he will goad him on by the deep-driven spur of emulation, or any other motive, until he outstrips his fellows, at whatever peril to his moral nature. But if, on the other hand, the teacher esteems the greatness of humility above the greatness of ambition; if he prefers mediocrity, or even obscurity, with uprightness and independence of soul, to princely fortune or regal power without them; if, in fine, he would see his pupil dispensing blessings along the lowliest walks of life rather than blazing athwart the sky with a useless splendor, — then he will forego the brilliant recitation, the talented essay, the annual prize, the college honor, rather than win them by any incentive which jeopards honor, veracity, or benevolence. But while there is such a *practical* diversity of opinion in regard to what constitutes the highest destination of our nature, even in a worldly point of view, we cannot expect a general concurrence of opinion as to the influences under which the youthful character should be formed. Those who are intent upon ends which are so different can hardly agree as to means. A discussion, however, of these unsettled questions, in a spirit of kindness and candor, may lead to a convergence, if not to a coincidence, of opinion.

Having spoken of the temptations that encompass our children in regard both to the manner and the motive of their studies and recitations, I wish to add a few remarks in regard to the final examinations of the schools.

From the moment when the school is opened, it ought to be understood that each day is equally a day of preparation for the closing visit of the committee. It ought to be understood that every absence and every tardiness, every instance of idleness and of inattention, is so much of time or of effort withdrawn from that preparation. At all times, by every means, in every form, the expectation is to be extinguished, the idea is to be annihilated, that especial preparation, as the school draws towards its close, on a few pages or a few lessons, can atone for or conceal any want of studiousness or of regularity as the term advances. Every pupil should be made clearly to see, and deeply to feel, that his fortune is in his own hands; that the responsibility of his future appearance rests upon himself; that no arts or devices are to be made use of, either to conceal his ignorance or to display his knowledge; that his mind will be submitted for inspection, not on its bright side only, but on all sides; and that it will be useless for him to expect to shine on that occasion, with only a radiant beam of light thrown across it here and there, while wide intervals of darkness lie between. Above all, will the teacher who wishes to keep the moral character of his scholars pure and stainless beware of encouraging or of tolerating any imposition upon the committee. He will not turn the last few days of the school into seasons of rehearsal for the examination. He will not indicate lessons or pages or questions that are to be specially conned for the occasion. To be guilty of any such artifice, with a view to make the school appear better than it is, is to corrupt the minds of his pupils. To the conscientious teacher, the formation of such a conspiracy, whether tacit or express, between himself and his pupils, will be the abominable thing which his soul hateth. It is true, that strong temptations may beset a teacher, and solicit him to deviate from the course of rectitude by an unfair preparation of his school. All laudable and honorable motives unite with the dictates of self-interest to make him desire the approval of the committee, and of his employers generally; and, what is more, such fraudulent preparations have not been uncommon in former times, so that precedent can be pleaded for them. It is well known, that, a few years ago, some teachers used *to cast the parts*, among their scholars, as much as they were ever cast in a play. The scholars committed the portions assigned them to memory. The committee and parents attended, and listened, with apparent delight, to recitations which proceeded with such volubility, that answers were often given before the questions were put. And, when the day was over, all parties — teacher, committee, parents, and children — congratulated each other upon the success and brilliancy of the farce. Were such a course so common as to be understood to mean nothing, much of its mischief would be taken away. But, at the present day, it is not so. Universally, an examination is now understood to be an *assaying* of the value of the school. All, therefore, who are now guilty of any counterfeiting of the image and superscription of knowledge, like other counterfeiters, conceal it if they can. Hence, any one who ventures upon such a course now is a teacher of evil, and not of good. Standing before his charge in the sacred character of a moral guide, he guides to immorality. Considering the immaturity of the children, and the deference with which they naturally look up to him, he is not so much the accomplice in a fraud, as the originator and instigator of it. By presenting the alluring side of wrong to unsophisticated minds, he creates, rather than connives at, its commission; and, by one such practical example, he neutralizes a volume of formal moralizing. Few things in a teacher's conduct furnish a more fair or a more certain test of the question, whether he has a lively and sensitive conscience, or has no standard of duty higher than mere conventional rules and observances.

It is in the power of the school-committee to uphold and to perpetuate this loss to the minds and this demoralization of the hearts of pupils, or at once and utterly to annul it. If, when visiting the school for the first time, they announce that they shall themselves conduct the closing examination; that, however much or however little ground the classes may undertake to cultivate, they will be liable to be taken to any part of that ground, to show in what condition they have left it; and that they will be examined on the subject rather than on the book, — if this be done, the pupils will study throughout the whole term with a very different object in their minds from what they would otherwise do. They will perceive at once, that if they devote special attention to a few lessons, or to a few sections, to the neglect of the rest, the neglected portions may be the very ones on which they will be questioned; and that the probability of their being taken up on a less prepared part will be in the ratio of the extent of that part. Such a course, too, will furnish a teacher with one of the most palpable arguments in favor of the steady, persevering application of his pupils.

At the examination, every thing, as far as possible, should be rescued from the dominion of chance. No pupil should feel that he can escape by what is called *good luck*, or suffer by *bad*. Hence examinations by written or printed questions are better than by oral; for, in such case, the question can be put to all; and a comparison of the different answers will be an impartial test of relative attainments. In arithmetic, the identical questions contained in the text-book should not be put, but equivalent ones. As grammar pertains to language, there is a special propriety in requiring answers to be given in writing, in order to determine whether a pupil who can parse glibly, and cite all the rules, can write any better English than one who has never opened a grammatical text-book. When proficiency in hand-writing is made one of the tests or titles for deserving rank or rewards, it is alleged that some children begin their copy-books by writing a few pages in a style inferior to their ability, for the dishonest purpose of appearing to have made more rapid improvement during the term than they really have done. To prevent this, some committees have adopted the expedient of providing themselves with one or more specimen-books for each school, in which all the writers are required to write at the end of the term. This specimen is then compared with the specimens of the preceding year; and the real progress of the writer is determined by the comparison. In this case, no inferior specimen can be prepared as a foil to set off its fellow.

In deprecating the devices and stratagems of the pupils against their teacher, we should be no less earnest in deprecating all devices and stratagems of the teacher against the pupils. There should be no arts to entrap on his side, any more than arts to evade on theirs. He should practise the utmost vigilance; but vigilance is as opposite to circumvention as a friendly visit to ask for an explanation is to eaves-dropping. Let the teacher, then, never descend to sly watchings or insidious questionings; but let his countenance, his manner, and his language bespeak frankness in himself, and confidence in his pupils. The atmosphere between him and them should be sunny and genial, unclouded by suspicion, and unchilled by distrust. Were it always sunlight, there would be no thievish owls nor felon foxes. As like begets like, confidence or unworthy suspicion in the teacher will beget confidence or unworthy suspicion in the school.

It is sometimes tauntingly asked by the opponents of our common-school system, why this boasted institution does not yield more abundant harvests of virtue; why the young men and the young women who come from our public schools are not nobler specimens of whatever is pure in feeling, and exemplary in conduct. I feel no disposition to retort upon such sinister inquirers by asking the question, what they themselves have ever done to elevate these schools to a condition from which purer influences might be expected to flow. But another inquiry will answer their inquiry, and dispel the ominous doubtings which it suggests. Let this startling question then be first answered, What is the relative amount of time and attention devoted to the moral culture of our children in school as compared with that which is devoted to the intellect? Follow the routine exercises of our schools for a single term; or, rather, take a broad survey of the whole course of instruction, from the day when the little child first crosses the threshold of the schoolhouse, to the day when, on the verge of manhood or womanhood, the young man and the young woman bid it farewell to enter upon some of the varied duties of life.

What innumerable lessons have been set! how many recitations have been performed! what a graduated series of books has been read, for the purpose of leading the young mind upward, step by step, along the ascent of knowledge! what questionings, and repetitions of questionings, to the hundredth time! and what reviews, and reviewing of things reviewed! But, on the other hand, how comparatively sterile of instruction has all this course of years been in the duties of children to each other; in the mutual duties of brothers and sisters; in filial duties; in the duties of the talented towards those less highly endowed by Nature; of those who are well-clad towards those who are clad in the homely garb of poverty; of the well-formed towards the deformed, or the sufferers under any physical privation; and, indeed, in that vast range of civil and social duties which awaits each one of them in after-life; and of the duty of love to their heavenly Father, and of obedience to his laws! What has been said against the passions of pride and cupidity, and envy and revenge? What expositions have been made of the inherent detestableness of profaneness and obscenity and falsehood? or of the retinue of calamities that come in the train of intemperance and gaming? Has arithmetic been so taught as to show the folly of buying lottery-tickets as a means of obtaining wealth? In teaching grammar, has a reference to the grammatical blunders and solecisms of the ignorant been accompanied by such humane and benevolent inculcations as will inspire all the learners with a desire to seek out ignorance, and to enlighten it? or have the errors of unavoidable ignorance been so ridiculed and contemned, that all the class will be led to vie with each other in jeering at the unfortunately and innocently ignorant wherever they may meet them? In teaching history, have the criminality of nine-tenths of all the wars ever waged, and the unspeakable sufferings they have inflicted upon mankind, been portrayed? or, on the other hand, have victorious armies and blood-stained conquerors been held up as objects of admiration? Who can rejoice at the proficiency of the children in their studies, if, when the school is dismissed, the older ones gather themselves hastily into some corner to draw a lottery, though it should involve only the value of a knife or a pencil-case? or if the younger ones are seen to leap the fences, and to explore woods and fields, that they may rob birds' nests? or if those of any age trespass upon the neighboring orchards to purloin fruit? Are our children taught in school the duty of restoring lost articles which they may have found? or the infamousness of cheating the post-office by sending concealed letters, or substitutes for letters? or the iniquity of adulterating commodities for sale, or of defrauding in weight or measure? or the cruelty and sinfulness of detraction and slander? Where these things are neglected, the children may be well trained in reading and writing and arithmetic; but they are not trained in the way they should go. Such children may make powerful or crafty or worldly-prosperous men; but they will not become men of unspotted and stainless lives; they are not preparing themselves to do as they would be done by; they are not learning to do justly, to love mercy, and to walk humbly with God.*

There is another fact which deepens and aggravates, to an alarming extent, the evil here spoken of. I refer to the mode often used in imparting even the pittance of moral instruction that is given.

Since the time of Pestalozzi, there has been scarcely any difference of opinion among the leading educators of Europe or America as to the true and philosophical method of instruction. With one consent, their decision is in favor of the *exhibitory, explanatory,* and *inductive* method. This method is the opposite of the *dogmatic.* The latter method consists in

* During the last year, while I was passing by a school, the children came out to take their forenoon recess. They were boys, in appearance, between eight and ten or eleven years of age. As they rushed into the street, one of the largest boys turned, and cried out, "Now let's play robber!" Whereupon he drew a pine dagger from under his coat, seized one of his fellows, and exclaimed, "Your money, or your life!" This scene, thus enacted in sport, was doubtless drawn from some of the novels of the day, whose guilty authors receive the patronage, if not the homage, of society; while the comparatively innocent felon, who only steals a horse or burns a house, is sentenced to the penitentiary. Was that school doing its duty, or building up character after a Christian model?

laying down abstract rules, formulas, or theorems, in a positive, authoritative manner, and requiring the forms of words in which the abstractions are expressed to be committed to memory. Of course, the principle embodied in these forms of words is to be received by the learner whether he understands it or not, and without any inquiry on his part whether it be true or false. But, on the Pestalozzian method, nothing which lies beyond the reach of intuition is asserted without being explained. If a complex idea is affirmed, it is analyzed into its elements: if an abstruse one is introduced, it is illustrated, if practicable, by some sensible object; if not susceptible of illustration by any sensible object, some anecdote or narrative is related, or some combination of circumstances supposed, which will make it intelligible. When the subject-matter will admit, there is an actual exhibition of the thing spoken of. If the thing spoken of cannot be exhibited, there is explanation, founded on the exhibition of some analogous thing. Should the lesson refer to any common or simple substance, a specimen is exhibited, — as in the case of minerals, metals, fruits, manufactures, and so forth. To a child who has never seen a mountain, a hill is made a unit of measure for explaining the mountain's height and extent. So of a brook, to one who has never seen a river; and of a pond, to one who has never seen a lake or an ocean. If a centaur or sphinx or mermaid be referred to, the teacher draws the likeness of one upon the blackboard, or exhibits an engraving. In case of a complex object, as a machine, a ship, a fort, or an Indian pagoda, some miniature model, or, at least, some pictorial representation, is produced, and made the basis, or framework, of the conceptions that are to be founded upon it, or collocated around it. When the thing to be taught is not an object of the senses, but of the mind only, and especially when the thing lies remote from elements, or first principles, this method requires that the learner's mind should be conducted through all the intermediate stages of progress, until it arrives at the point where the complex or abstract idea can be understood; and then, and not till then, that it should be brought forward. In fine, this method requires that individuals should be introduced before species, species before genera, and so forth. But the dogmatic method begins with the most comprehensive generalizations, and runs the risk of the pupil's obtaining any knowledge of particulars afterwards. In the one case, the learner is expected to receive blindly what is dictated to him; while the other method exhibits, explains, illustrates, exemplifies, and educes, and then submits the whole to the learner's intelligence, to be received or discarded.

After this statement of the points of distinction between the Pestalozzian and the dogmatic method, it would be only an illustration of the former were an example of each to be given. Suppose, then, a foreign gentleman should send his son to Boston, under the care of a tutor, in order that he might become acquainted with the city and its vicinity, and learn something of its public works, its institutions, and its distinguished men. According to the dogmatic method, when the strangers should have arrived and taken their lodgings, the tutor would obtain a guide-book for his pupil. In a series of lessons, he would see that the peninsular shape, the territorial extent, the statistics of population, commerce, education, and so forth, were well studied and recited. The boundaries of the city — Charles River on the north, the ocean on the east, and the interior on the south and west — would be learned. The pupil would be taught to name the principal streets, bridges, and railroads, probably in an alphabetical order, until they could be volubly repeated. A directory would be put into his hands, with a mark against the names of the men whose distinction entitled them to a place in his memory. He would be told, that, in the city or its vicinity, there are an Asylum for the Insane, an Institution for the Blind, a Navy Yard, Bunker-hill Monument, Dorchester Heights, Lexington and Concord battle-grounds, and so forth. These facts, and such as these, would be deposited in the memory, reviewed and rehearsed, until they could all be called up at will; and then the parties would re-embark, congratulating themselves that the object of their mission had been successfully accomplished. This is the dogmatic method.

On the other hand, suppose the tutor to instruct his pupil on the exhibitory, explanatory, and inductive plan. For the first lesson, he takes him to the dome of the State House, — the highest point in the metropolis, and one which commands the splendid panorama of the city and its suburbs. There, before a single object is pointed out, before a single glance at the broad and varied scene is allowed, the points of the compass are determined. If the sun be visible, this is done by an observation, consisting of but two elements, — the position of the sun, and the hour of the day. First a general survey is allowed, in order to impress the mind with a general conception of outline and extent. This is in analogy to that summary description of the nature, the advantages, and the pleasures of a study, which a teacher should always give to his class when a new branch is introduced. Then a single class of objects is selected for attention, — suppose it to be the public buildings; and, as the one from whose observatory they are looking is the central point from which the bearings and distances of all the rest are to be estimated, it is first considered. Then the other great public edifices or structures are taken in their order, — the Quincy Market, the public buildings at South Boston, the Blind Institution, the Colleges, the Hospitals, Bunker-hill Monument, the Navy Yard, the lighthouses and forts in the harbor. When the most interesting of this class of objects are completed, — after such reflections and explanations, and, perhaps, pencillings, as may be deemed necessary, — the eye is withdrawn from the whole; the parties retire; and the pupil is required to reproduce from his recollection, in the form of a map, all the objects he has examined, with their apparent distances, positions, and so forth. In succeeding lessons, given from the same elevated point, other objects and neighboring towns are pointed out. Here the telescope is used. The bridges, and the six lines of railroads radiating from the city, towards the south, west, and north, are designated. After every lesson, a map of objects or localities is prepared, both for the purpose of determining the accuracy of the impression carried away, and of deepening it in the mind. After such minuteness of detail as circumstances will allow, the same objects are visited and inspected; and their history, administration, amount of success or causes of failure, and so forth, learned. The streets are learned by passing through them; the schools, by visiting and questioning them; the state of commerce and merchandise, from the wharves, the custom-house, and the depositories; the manufactories, by the amount and the quality of their fabrics; the distinguished men, by introduction, conversation, and personal intimacy; and historical events, not merely by reading the narrative, but by visiting the scenes where they occurred. Such is an inadequate representation of what may be called the Pestalozzian method of instruction. Which of the two methods is most conducive to an understanding of the subject, it is not difficult to decide.

Now, it is but a few years since the dogmatic method was the one almost universally practised in our schools in regard to intellectual instruction. Arithmetic was taught without oral exercises or the blackboard; geography, without globes, maps, or map-drawing; grammar, by the endless repetitions of government and agreement, mood and tense, gender, number, and case, — the children asseverating ten thousand times the remarkable facts that *he* is masculine, *she* feminine, and *it* neuter; that *one* is in the singular number, *two, three, four*, and all the rest, in the plural, and so forth. But such a change has taken place in this respect, that, at the present time, there is not one of our first class of schools where the principles of arithmetic are not explained; where words are not defined, and the meaning of the author paraphrased; poetry turned into prose; maps drawn; orthographical and grammatical exercises *written*; and, generally, the thing itself sought for and understood, instead of a mere babbling from memory of the words in which it is expressed. But, in regard to moral subjects, I fear the dogmatic method still remains,—precepts, rules, abstruse principles, mere formulas of speech,—without specification, without expansion, without illustration, without the living, glowing, inspiring spirit. Suppose, in arithmetical proportion, the teacher should tell the pupil that, "as the first term is to the second, so is the third to the answer," and should there stop. Would the pupil ever know how to work a sum in the rule of three? But the moral lesson, "Do as you would be done unto," is precisely analogous to the arithmetical one, if it stops with the general injunction. The latter needs exemplification, by instances, as much as the former, and would profit as much by it. Yet, under this head in the arithmetic, a hundred examples will be given; under the moral axiom, not one. I cannot see why it is not as absurd to give a moral rule to a child, without examples under it, as it is to give an arithmetical rule, without examples under that; and, if questions pertaining to business are selected in the one case, why should not questions pertaining to duty be selected in the other? Suppose the teacher of a normal school should prescribe, as a rule to the future teachers, "Train up a child in the way he should go," and should there leave them, without giving them any specific instructions as to what that way is, and by what means children can be *trained* — that is, *accustomed* — to walk in it. How easy it would be to make accomplished teachers, if such a precept, comprehensive and perfect as the principle of it is, were all that is necessary! But such a rule requires years of exemplification and practice: it requires years of reading, reflection, and consultation with masters of the art. Under the rule, to do as we would be done unto, a thousand instances, taken from the play-ground, the schoolroom, the domestic fireside, the pleasure-party, the shop, the counting-room, should be given. Under the rule, to love our neighbors as ourselves, the illustrations may be as numerous as all the interests and wants of life. How varied are those rights of property which come within the protection of the command, "Thou shalt not steal;" and those rights of character and of reputation that are embraced within the spirit of the prohibition, "Thou shalt not bear false witness against thy neighbor"! Are these things of less consequence than the frivolous discussions whether *a* and *an* and *the* are articles or adjectives? Are these momentous subjects, with all their finite and infinite bearings, to be postponed in order that we may have time to teach children not to spell *labor* and *honor* with the letter *u*, or *public* and *music* with the letter *k;* or when to reduplicate the final consonants of primitive words, and when not? How can a child be led to love the Lord his God with all his heart, unless, in the first place, he has a heart which has been trained to love what is good; and, in the second place, unless some of those glorious attributes of his Maker which are fitted to excite his love are unfolded to his perceptions? How can a child love God while he knows nothing of him but the name, and has perhaps heard that name spoken more frequently in profaneness or blasphemy than in reverence? Is it of more consequence for a child to know the specks of islands in the Indian or Pacific Oceans than it is to know the reason why he is taught to say that God is good, and that his tender mercies are over all his works? Is it more important that a child should be taught the anomalies of our arbitrary language than that he should be instructed in the beneficence of his heavenly Father, who has created the sun for his warmth and light, and the earth for his dwelling-place; who robes Nature in beautiful colors for the gratification of his eye, and surrounds him with an atmosphere which is an undecaying medium of communication with his friends, and, like a vast instrument of music, is forever ready to be played upon for the delight of his ear; whose skill and power are made known in the formation of his body, and whose bounty in the abundance that sustains it; whose munificence in the bestowment of his faculties, with their adaptations to happiness; and who has given him, in the words and life of the Saviour, a perfect rule and a perfect example? If there be nothing in orthography or etymology or syntax of superior value to an upright life, or better becoming an immortal being than devout feelings towards his Maker, why should the former be allowed to dispossess the latter, and usurp their place?

The natural conscience needs training in order to discern the distinctions between right and wrong, in the same manner that the intellect needs training in regard to addition and subtraction, or substantive and verb, or latitude and longitude, or republics and monarchies. No man, then, has any right to oppose our system of common schools because the children who come from them are not as honest as they are intelligent, and as benevolent as they are sagacious, until our teachers are as competent and as faithful in teaching their pupils humanity and morality, and in training them to the practice of the social virtues, as they are in teaching them the common branches of study, and in training them for the business of life. When the voice of public opinion shall imperatively demand as high a degree of culture for the moral as for the intellectual nature, and teachers shall bestow it, all opposition to our schools will be destroyed; for the opponents themselves will be *reformed* into advocates.

The unexpected length to which this Report has already extended admonishes me to bring it to a close; although, in so doing, I am obliged to omit other and kindred topics, to which I would gladly advert. Instead of generalizing on the subject of morals, or vainly attempting to embellish their inherent beauty and loveliness, I have preferred to set forth in the preceding pages, with some minuteness and detail, the principal dangers to which our children are exposed as they are passing through our schools; and I have endeavored to help the conscientious teacher in the discharge of his duties to those children by setting up a few way-marks and beacons along their perilous path. This, however, is a subject heretofore uninvestigated, so far as I know, by any writer on education. Like other pioneers, I must, doubtless, have made a very imperfect survey of the extensive field I have entered, — all the more imperfect because it is so extensive. But I devoutly hope that what has now been said may prove sufficient to incite others to make more complete explorations, until every precipice and pitfall that besets the pathway of the rising generation in their common pursuit of knowledge may be not only discovered, but surmounted with warning signals too conspicuous to be unnoticed.

Directly and indirectly, the influences of the Board of Education have been the means of increasing, to a great extent, the amount of religious instruction given in our schools. Moral training, or the application of religious principles to the duties of life, should be its inseparable accompaniment. No community can long subsist, unless it has religious principle as the foundation of moral action, nor unless it has moral action as the superstructure of religious principle. Not at present, any more than in the days of the Jewish theocracy, does the strength of a nation consist in the number of its horsemen, or its chariots, or its mighty men of valor, but in those who fear the Lord, and work righteousness.

Travellers inform us, that, in some of the vast deserts of the Eastern continent, the course of the wayfarers across the trackless waste is marked by the bleaching bones of mighty caravans that had perished on their way in traversing the desolate expanse. Spread out upon the arid sands, or heaped in mounds, these relics of the dead give warning of the dangers by which they had been overwhelmed. The pilgrim troop or merchant company, as they pass along, and behold these eloquent memorials of others' fate, are admonished to press on with vigor, that they may reach the place of safety. Even thus, along the track of time, for thousands of years, do historic memorials — like vast monumental piles upon the right hand and upon the left — make known to us the causes of the decline and fall of ancient and of modern republics. They fell through the ignorance and debasement of the people that composed them. But for these, Greece, having revivified her spirit by the genius of Christianity, and turned her Pantheon into a temple of the living and true God, might, to this day, have spread far more than her ancient happiness and splendor over those beautiful regions where now the Mahommedan bears sway; and, but for these, Rome might have adopted the principles of that purer faith which was preached to her by the Apostle to the Gentiles, and saved the world from the thousand years of unspeakable horrors which the dark ages inflicted upon it. Happy will our young Republic be, if, forewarned by the perdition of others, she avoids their fate by avoiding the causes that incurred it.

REPORT FOR 1846.

GENTLEMEN,—

To write a history of popular education in Massachusetts would be a work of great interest, and of little difficulty. Such a history, however, seems not to have been contemplated, and, therefore, would not be warranted, by those resolves of the legislature under which the following pages are prepared. The resolves provide only for " the republication of so much of his (the late Secretary's) Tenth Annual Report, as, with the requisite additions and alterations, will exhibit a just and correct view of the common-school system of Massachusetts, and the provisions of law relating to it.* An adequate idea of this " system," however, can hardly be obtained without a brief reference to its origin, and to those great fundamental principles which its authors and supporters seem rather to have tacitly assumed than to have fully expounded.

The Pilgrim Fathers who colonized Massachusetts Bay made a bolder innovation upon all pre-existing policy and usages than the world had ever known since the commencement of the Christian era. They adopted special and costly means to train up the whole body of the people to industry, to intelligence, to virtue, and to independent thought. The first entry in the public record-book of the town of Boston bears date, " 1634, 7th month, day 1." The records of the public meetings for the residue of that year pertain to those obvious necessities that

---

* The provisions of law are omitted in this volume.

claimed the immediate attention of an infant settlement. But in the transactions of a public meeting, held on the 13th day of April, 1635, the following entry is found: " Likewise it was then generally agreed upon, that our brother Philemon Purmont [or Purment] shall be intreated to become scholemaster for the teaching and nourtering of children with us." Mr. Purmont was not expected to render his services gratuitously. Doubtless he received fees from parents; but the same records show, that a tract of thirty acres of land, at Muddy River, was assigned to him; and this grant, two years afterwards, was publicly confirmed. About the same time, an assignment was made of a " garden plott to Mr. Daniel Maude, schoolemaster, upon the condition of building thereon, if neede be." From this time forward, these golden threads are thickly inwoven in the texture of all the public records of Boston.

It is not unworthy of remark, that a word of beautiful significance, which is found in the first record on the subject of schools ever made on this continent, has now fallen wholly out of use. Mr. Purmont was entreated to become a " scholemaster," not merely for the " teaching," but for the " NOURTERING " of children. If, as is supposed, this word, now obsolete in this connection, implied the disposition and the power on the part of the teacher, as far as such an object can be accomplished by human instrumentality, to warm into birth, to foster into strength, and to advance into precedence and predominance, all kindly sympathies towards men, all elevated thoughts respecting the duties and the destiny of life, and a supreme reverence for the character and attributes of the Creator, then how many teachers have since been employed who have not NOURISHED the children committed to their care!

In 1642, the General Court of the colony, by a public act, enjoined upon the municipal authorities the duty of seeing that *every child* within their respective jurisdictions should be educated. Nor was the education which they contemplated either narrow or superficial. By the terms of the act, the selectmen of every town were required to " have a vigilant eye over their brethren and neighbors, — to see first that none of them shall suffer so much barbarism in any of their families, as not to endeavor to teach, by themselves or others, their children and apprentices, so much learning as may enable them perfectly to read the English tongue, and [obtain a] knowledge of the capital laws; upon penalty of twenty shillings for each neglect therein."

Such was the idea of " barbarism " entertained by the colonists of Massachusetts Bay more than two centuries ago. Tried by this standard, even at the present day, the regions of civilization become exceedingly narrow; and many a man who now blindly glories in the name and in the prerogatives of a republican citizen would, according to the better ideas of the Pilgrim Fathers, be known only as the " barbarian " father of " barbarian " children.

The same act further required that religious instruction should be given to all children; and also "that all parents and masters do breed and bring up their children and apprentices in some honest, lawful calling, labor, or employment, either in husbandry or some other trade profitable for themselves and the Commonwealth, if they will not or can not train them up in learning to fit them for higher employments."

Thus were recognized and embodied in a public statute the highest principles of political economy and of social well-being, the universal education of children, and the prevention of drones or non-producers among men.

By the same statute, the selectmen and magistrates were empowered to take children and servants from the custody of those parents and masters, who, " after admonition," " were still negligent of their duty in the particulars above mentioned," and to bind them out to such masters as they should deem worthy to supply the place of the unnatural parent, — boys until the age of twenty-one, and girls until that of eighteen.

The law of 1642 enjoined universal education; but it did not make education *free*, nor did it impose any penalty upon municipal corporations for neglecting to maintain a school. The spirit of the law, however, worked energetically in the hearts of the people; for in Gov. Winthrop's Journal ("History of New England," vol. ii. p. 215, Savage's edition), under date of 1645, we find the following: "Divers free schools were erected, as at Roxbury (for maintenance whereof every inhabitant bound some house or land for a yearly allowance forever) and at Boston, where they made an order to allow fifty pounds to the master, and an house and thirty pounds to an usher, who should also teach to read and write and cipher, and Indians' children were to be taught freely, and the charge to be by yearly contribution, either by voluntary allowance, or by rate of such as refused, &c.; and this order was confirmed by the General Court. Other towns did the like, providing maintenance by several means."

It is probable, however, that some towns, owing to the sparseness of their population and the scantiness of their resources, found all the moneys in their treasury too little to pay the salary of a master; and surrounded by dangers, as they were, from the ferocity of the aborigines and the inclemency of the climate, believed that not an eye could be spared from watching nor a hand from labor, even for so sacred a purpose as that of instruction; and therefore failed to sustain a school for the teaching and "nourtering" of their children. But, in all these privations and disabilities, the government of the colony saw no adequate excuse for neglecting the one thing needful. They saw and felt, that "if learning were to be buried in the graves of their forefathers, in Church and Commonwealth," then they had escaped from the house of bondage, and swum an ocean, and braved the terrors of the wilderness, in vain. In the year 1647, therefore, a law was passed making the support of schools compulsory, and education both universal and *free*.

By this law, every town containing fifty householders was required to appoint a teacher " to teach all such children as shall resort to him to write and read;" and every town containing one hundred families or householders was required to " set up a grammar school," whose master should be " able to instruct youth so far as they may be fitted for the university."

The penalty for non-compliance with the above requirements was five pounds per annum. In 1671, the penalty was increased to ten pounds per annum; in 1683, to twenty pounds; and in 1718, to thirty pounds for every town containing one hundred and fifty families; to forty pounds for every town containing two hundred families; and so on, *pro rata*, for towns containing two hundred and fifty or three hundred families. The penalty was increased from time to time, to correspond with the increasing wealth of the towns. All forfeitures were appropriated to the maintenance of public schools.[*]

It is common to say that the act of 1647 *laid the foundation* of our present system of free schools; but the truth is, it not only laid the foundation of the present system, but, in some particulars, it laid a far broader foundation than has since been

---

[*] It is well known, that, in the dearth of the precious metals which prevailed among the early settlers of Massachusetts, the colonial and provincial governments made various kinds of grain, — wheat, rye, barley, Indian corn, &c., — with several other commodities, a legal tender in payment of debts, and received them for taxes. In our early legislation and history, these were called "country pay." From time to time, the law determined the value of the bushel, or unit, of each kind of product. On an examination of twenty such determinations of value, made from 1642 to 1694 inclusive, I find that Indian corn was rated at from one shilling and two pence a bushel to three shillings and six pence; and that the average for this whole period was, within a very slight fraction, two shillings and ten pence a bushel.

Allowing six persons to a family, a town of three hundred families would contain a population of eighteen hundred.

To pay a fine of sixty pounds, therefore, to which such a town would be liable by one of the laws above referred to, if paid in Indian corn, at the average of the prices which prevailed from 1642 to 1694, would require four hundred and twenty-three bushels.

The rates of labor, as ordained by the colonial government, show, in a still more striking manner, how heavily the towns were mulcted for neglecting to support schools.

Under date of Sept. 30, 1630, "It is ordered, that laborers shall not take aboue 12d a day for their work and not aboue 6d and meate and drink under paine of 10s; noe master carpenter, mason, joyner or bricklayer, shall take aboue 16d a day for their worke, if they have meate and drink, — and the second sort not aboue 12d a day under payne of 10s both to giuer and receauer."

At these rates, it would take a laborer (having board) four hundred and eighty days to pay a fine of one pound. The penalty imposed upon towns, by the law of 1647, for not maintaining a free school, was five pounds, — equivalent, at the above

built upon, and reared a far higher superstructure than has since been sustained. Modern times have witnessed great improvements in the methods of instruction, and in the motives of discipline; but, in some respects, the ancient foundation has been narrowed, and the ancient superstructure lowered. The term "grammar school," in the old laws, always meant a school where the ancient languages were taught, and where youth could be " fitted for the university." Every town containing one hundred families or householders was required to keep such a school. Were such a law in force at the present time, there are not more than twelve towns in the Commonwealth which would be exempt from its requisitions. But the term " grammar school " has wholly lost its original meaning; and the number of towns and cities which are now required by law to maintain a school where the Greek and Latin languages are taught, and where youth can be fitted for college, does not exceed thirty. The contrast between our ancestors and ourselves in this respect is most humiliating. Their meanness in wealth was more than compensated by their grandeur of soul.

The institution of a free-school system on so broad a basis, and of such ample proportions, appears still more remarkable when we consider the period in the world's history at which it was originated, and the fewness and poverty of the people by whom it was maintained. In 1647, the entire population of the colony of Massachusetts Bay is supposed to have amounted

rate, to the work of a common laborer (with board, but without clothing) for twenty-four hundred days, or all the working days in almost eight years.

Under date of Sept. 3, 1634, it was ordered that " noe person that keepes an ordinary shall take above 6d a meale for a person, and not above 1d for an ale quarte for beare out of meale time vnder the penalty of 10s for eury offence, either of dyet or beare."

In 1654, May 3, the following order was made: " As the countrje is in debt, no stock in the treasury, no meanes at present to raise any, so that workmen cannot be procured to finish the Castle, which yett is necessary forthwith to be done," the several military companies must do it; one division of them by having each of their soldiers labor three days on this fortification, and another by being individually assessed 4s. 6d. Hence it would seem that 4s. 6d. were held to be an equivalent for three days' work on the Castle, and going to and returning from the work. — See *An Historical Account of Massachusetts Currency*, by JOSEPH B. FELT.

only to twenty-one thousand souls. The scattered and feeble settlements were almost buried in the depths of the forest. The external resources of the people were small, their dwellings humble, and their raiment and subsistence scanty and homely. They had no enriching commerce; and the wonderful forces of Nature had not then, as now, become gratuitous producers of every human comfort and luxury. The whole valuation of all the colonial estates, both public and private, would hardly have been equal to the inventory of many a private citizen of the present day. The fierce eye of the savage was nightly seen glaring from the edge of the surrounding wilderness; and no defence or succor, save in their own brave natures, was at hand. Yet it was then, amid all these privations and dangers, that the Pilgrim Fathers conceived the magnificent idea, not only of a universal, but of a free education, for the whole people. To find the time and the means to reduce this grand conception to practice, they stinted themselves, amid all their poverty, to a still scantier pittance; amid all their toils, they imposed upon themselves still more burdensome labors; and, amid all their perils, they braved still greater dangers. Two divine ideas filled their great hearts, — their duty to God and to posterity. For the one, they built the church; for the other, they opened the school. Religion and knowledge, — two attributes of the same glorious and eternal truth, and that truth the only one on which immortal or mortal happiness can be securely founded!

It is impossible for us adequately to conceive the boldness of the measure which aimed at universal education through the establishment of free schools. As a fact, it had no precedent in the world's history; and, as a theory, it could have been refuted and silenced by a more formidable array of argument and experience than was ever marshalled against any other institution of human origin. But time has ratified its soundness. Two centuries of successful operation now proclaim it to be as wise as it was courageous, and as beneficent as it was disinterested. Every community in the civilized world awards it the meed of praise; and states at home, and nations abroad, in the order of their intelligence, are copying the bright example. What we call the enlightened nations of Christendom are approaching, by slow degrees, to the moral elevation which our ancestors reached at a single bound; and the tardy convictions of the one have been assimilating, through a period of two centuries, to the intuitions of the other.

The establishment of free schools was one of those grand mental and moral experiments whose effects could not be developed and made manifest in a single generation. But now, according to the manner in which human life is computed, we are the sixth generation from its founders; and have we not reason to be grateful both to God and man for its unnumbered blessings? The sincerity of our gratitude must be tested by our efforts to perpetuate and to improve what they established. The gratitude of the lips only is an unholy offering.

In surveying our vast country, the rich savannas of the South, and the almost interminable prairies of the West, — that great valley, where, if all the nations of Europe were set down together, they could find ample subsistence, — the ejaculation involuntarily bursts forth, "WHY WERE THEY NOT COLONIZED BY MEN LIKE THE PILGRIM FATHERS?" And as we reflect how different would have been the fortunes of this nation, had those States — already so numerous, and still extending, circle beyond circle — been founded by men of high, heroic, Puritan mould; how different in the eye of a righteous Heaven, how different in the estimation of the wise and good of all contemporary nations, how different in the fortunes of that vast procession of the generations which are yet to rise up over all those wide expanses, and to follow each other to the end of time, — as we reflect upon these things, it seems almost pious to repine at the ways of Providence; resignation becomes laborious, and we are forced to choke down our murmurings at the will of Heaven. Is it the solution of this deep mystery, that our ancestors did as much in their time as it is ever given to one generation of men to accomplish, and have left to us and to our descendants the completion of the glorious work they began?

The alleged ground upon which the founders of our free-school system proceeded, when adopting it, did not embrace the whole argument by which it may be defended and sustained. Their insight was better than their reason. They assumed a ground, indeed, satisfactory and convincing to Protestants; but, at that time, only a small portion of Christendom was Protestant, and even now only a minority of it is so. The very ground on which our free schools were founded, therefore, if it were the only one, would have been a reason, with more than half of Christendom, for their immediate abolition.

In later times, and since the achievement of American independence, the universal and ever-repeated argument in favor of free schools has been, that the general intelligence which they are capable of diffusing, and which can be imparted by no other human instrumentality, is indispensable to the continuance of a republican government. This argument, it is obvious, assumes, as a *postulatum*, the superiority of a republican over all other forms of government; and, as a people, we religiously believe in the soundness both of the assumption and of the argument founded upon it. But if this be all, then a sincere monarchist, or a defender of arbitrary power, or a believer in the divine right of kings, would oppose free schools for the identical reasons we offer in their behalf. A perfect demonstration of our doctrine — that free schools are the only basis of republican institutions — would be the perfection of proof, to his mind, that they should be immediately exterminated.

Admitting, nay, claiming for ourselves, the substantial justness and soundness of the general grounds on which our system was originally established, and has since been maintained, yet it is most obvious, that, unless some broader and more comprehensive principle can be found, the system of free schools will be repudiated by whole nations as impolitic and dangerous;

aud, even among ourselves, all who deny our premises will, of course, set at nought the conclusions to which they lead.

Again: the expediency of free schools is sometimes advocated on grounds of political economy. An educated people is always a more industrious and productive people. Knowledge and abundance sustain to each other the relation of cause and effect. Intelligence is a primary ingredient in the wealth of nations. Where this does not stand at the head of the inventory, the items in a nation's valuation will be few, and the sum at the foot of the column insignificant.

The moralist, too, takes up the argument of the economist. He demonstrates that vice and crime are not only prodigals and spendthrifts of their own, but defrauders and plunderers of the means of others; that they would seize upon all the gains of honest industry, and exhaust the bounties of Heaven itself, without satiating their rapacity for new means of indulgence; and that often, in the history of the world, whole generations might have been trained to industry and virtue by the wealth which one enemy to his race has destroyed.

And yet, notwithstanding these views have been presented a thousand times with irrefutable logic, and with a divine eloquence of truth which it would seem that nothing but combined stolidity and depravity could resist, there is not at the present time, with the exception of the States of New England and a few small communities elsewhere, a country or a state in Christendom which maintains a system of free schools for the education of its children. Even in the State of New York, with all its noble endowments, the schools are not free.[*]

I believe that this amazing dereliction from duty, especially in our own country, originates more in the false notions which men entertain *respecting the nature of their right to property* than in any thing else. In the district-school-meeting, in the town-meeting, in legislative halls, everywhere, the advocates for a

---

[*] By an act of the New-York legislature, passed at its last session, the question whether free schools shall be established throughout the State is to be submitted to the decision of the people, to be determined by ballot, at their primary meetings, during the current year.

more generous education could carry their respective audiences with them in behalf of increased privileges for our children, were it not instinctively foreseen that increased privileges must be followed by increased taxation. Against this obstacle, argument falls dead. The rich man who has no children declares that the exaction of a contribution from him to educate the children of his neighbor is an invasion of his rights of property. The man who has reared and educated a family of children denounces it as a double tax when he is called upon to assist in educating the children of others also; or, if he has reared his own children without educating them, he thinks it peculiarly oppressive to be obliged to do for others what he refrained from doing even for himself. Another, having children, but disdaining to educate them with the common mass, withdraws them from the public school, puts them under what he calls "selecter influences," and then thinks it a grievance to be obliged to support a school which he contemns. Or if these different parties so far yield to the force of traditionary sentiment and usage, and to the public opinion around them, as to consent to do something for the cause, they soon reach the limit of expense at which their admitted obligation or their alleged charity terminates.

It seems not irrelevant, therefore, in this connection, and for the purpose of strengthening the foundation on which our free-school system reposes, to inquire into the nature of a man's right to the property he possesses; and to satisfy ourselves respecting the question, whether any man has such an indefeasible title to his estates, or such an absolute ownership of them, as renders it unjust in the government to assess upon him his share of the expenses of educating the children of the community up to such a point as the nature of the institutions under which he lives, and the well-being of society, require.

I believe in the existence of a great, immortal, immutable principle of natural law, or natural ethics, — a principle antecedent to all human institutions, and incapable of being abrogated by any ordinance of man, — a principle of divine origin, clearly legible in the ways of Providence as those ways are manifested in the order of Nature and in the history of the race, which proves the *absolute right* to an education of every human being that comes into the world; and which, of course, proves the correlative duty of every government to see that the means of that education are provided for all.

In regard to the application of this principle of natural law, — that is, in regard to the extent of the education to be provided for all at the public expense, — some differences of opinion may fairly exist under different political organizations; but, under our republican government, it seems clear that the minimum of this education can never be less than such as is sufficient to qualify each citizen for the civil and social duties he will be called to discharge, — such an education as teaches the individual the great laws of bodily health, as qualifies for the fulfilment of parental duties, as is indispensable for the civil functions of a witness or a juror, as is necessary for the voter in municipal and in national affairs, and, finally, as is requisite for the faithful and conscientious discharge of all those duties which devolve upon the inheritor of a portion of the sovereignty of this great Republic.

The will of God, as conspicuously manifested in the order of Nature, and in the relations which he has established among men, founds the *right* of every child that is born into the world, to such a degree of education as will enable him, and, as far as possible, will predispose him, to perform all domestic, social, civil, and moral duties, upon the same clear ground of natural law and equity as it founds a child's *right*, upon his first coming into the world, to distend his lungs with a portion of the common air, or to open his eyes to the common light, or to receive that shelter, protection, and nourishment, which are necessary to the continuance of his bodily existence. And so far is it from being a wrong or a hardship to demand of the possessors of property their respective shares for the prosecution of this divinely-ordained work, that they themselves are guilty of the most far-reaching injustice when they seek to resist or to evade the contribution. The complainers are the wrong-doers. The cry, "Stop thief!" comes from the thief himself.

To any one who looks beyond the mere surface of things, it is obvious that the primary and natural elements or ingredients of all property consist in the riches of the soil, in the treasures of the sea, in the light and warmth of the sun, in the fertilizing clouds and streams and dews, in the winds, and in the chemical and vegetative agencies of Nature. In the majority of cases, all that we call *property*, all that makes up the valuation or inventory of a nation's capital, was prepared at the creation, and was laid up of old in the capacious storehouses of Nature. For every unit that a man earns by his own toil or skill, he receives hundreds and thousands, without cost and without recompense, from the all-bountiful Giver. A proud mortal, standing in the midst of his luxuriant wheat-fields or cotton-plantations, may arrogantly call them his own; yet what barren wastes would they be, did not Heaven send down upon them its dews and its rains, its warmth and its light, and sustain, for their growth and ripening, the grateful vicissitude of the seasons! It is said that from eighty to ninety per cent of the very substance of some of the great staples of agriculture are not taken from the earth, but are absorbed from the air; so that these productions may more properly be called fruits of the atmosphere than of the soil. Who prepares this elemental wealth? Who scatters it, like a sower, through all the regions of the atmosphere, and sends the richly-freighted winds, as His messengers, to bear to each leaf in the forest, and to each blade in the cultivated field, the nourishment which their infinitely-varied needs demand? Aided by machinery, a single manufacturer performs the labor of hundreds of men. Yet what could he accomplish without the weight of the waters which God causes ceaselessly to flow, or without those gigantic forces which he has given to steam? And how would the commerce of the world be carried on, were it not for those great laws of Nature — of electricity, of condensation, and of rarefaction —

that give birth to the winds, which, in conformity to the will of Heaven, and not in obedience to any power of man, forever traverse the earth, and offer themselves as an unchartered medium for interchanging the products of all the zones? These few references show how vast a proportion of all the wealth which men presumptuously call their own, because they claim to have earned it, is poured into their lap, unasked and unthanked for, by the Being so infinitely gracious in his physical as well as in his moral bestowments.

But for whose subsistence and benefit were these exhaustless treasuries of wealth created? Surely not for any one man, nor for any one generation, but for the subsistence and benefit of the whole race from the beginning to the end of time. They were not created for Adam alone, nor for Noah alone, nor for the first discoverers or colonists who may have found or have peopled any part of the earth's ample domain. No. They were created for the race collectively, but to be possessed and enjoyed in succession, as the generations, one after another, should come into existence, — equal rights, with a successive enjoyment of them. If we consider the earth and the fulness thereof as one great habitation or domain, then each generation, subject to certain modifications for the encouragement of industry and frugality, — which modifications it is not necessary here to specify, — has only a life-lease in them. There are certain reasonable regulations, indeed, in regard to the outgoing and the incoming tenants, — regulations which allow to the outgoing generations a brief control over their property after they are called upon to leave it, and which also allow the incoming generations to anticipate a little their full right of possession. But, subject to these regulations, Nature ordains a perpetual entail and transfer, from one generation to another, of all property in the great, substantive, enduring elements of wealth, — in the soil; in metals and minerals; in precious stones, and in more precious coal and iron and granite; in the waters and winds and sun, — and no one man, nor any one generation of men, has any such title to or ownership in these ingredients and substantials of all wealth, that his right is invaded when a portion of them is taken for the benefit of posterity.

This great principle of natural law may be illustrated by a reference to some of the unstable elements, in regard to which each individual's right of *property* is strongly qualified in relation to his contemporaries, even while he has the acknowledged right of *possession*. Take the streams of water, or the wind, for an example. A stream, as it descends from its sources to its mouth, is successively the property of all those through whose land it passes. My neighbor who lives above me owned it yesterday, while it was passing through his lands; I own it to-day, while it is descending through mine; and the contiguous proprietor below will own it to-morrow, while it is flowing through his, as it passes onward to the next. But the rights of these successive owners are not absolute and unqualified. They are limited by the rights of those who are entitled to the subsequent possession and use. While a stream is passing through my lands, I may not corrupt it, so that it shall be offensive or valueless to the adjoining proprietor below. I may not stop it in its downward course, nor divert it into any other direction, so that it shall leave his channel dry. I may lawfully use it for various purposes, — for agriculture, as in irrigating lands, or watering cattle; for manufactures, as in turning wheels, &c., — but, in all my uses of it, I must pay regard to the rights of my neighbors lower down. So no two proprietors, nor any half-dozen proprietors, by conspiring together, can deprive an owner, who lives below them all, of the ultimate right which he has to the use of the stream in its descending course. We see here, therefore, that a man has certain qualified rights — rights of which he cannot lawfully be divested without his own consent — in a stream of water, before it reaches the limits of his own estate; at which latter point, he may somewhat more emphatically call it his own. And, in this sense, a man who lives at the outlet of a river, on the margin of the ocean, has certain incipient rights in those fountain-sources that well up from the earth at the distance of thousands of miles.

So it is with the ever-moving winds. No man has a *permanent* interest in the breezes that blow by him, and bring healing and refreshment on their wings. Each man has a temporary interest in them. From whatever quarter of the compass they may come, I have a right to use them as they are passing by me; yet that use must always be regulated by the rights of those other participants and co-owners whom they are moving forward to bless. It is not lawful, therefore, for me to corrupt them, — to load them with noxious gases or vapors by which they will prove valueless or detrimental to him, whoever he may be, towards whom they are moving.

In one respect, indeed, the winds illustrate our relative rights and duties even better than the streams. In the latter case, the rights are not only successive, but always in the same order of priority; those of the owner above necessarily preceding those of the owner below: and this order is unchangeable, except by changing the ownership of the land itself to which the rights are appurtenant. In the case of the winds, however, which blow from every quarter of the heavens, I may have the prior right to-day; but, with a change in their direction, my neighbor may have it to-morrow. If, therefore, to-day, when the wind is going from me to him, I should usurp the right to use it to his detriment, to-morrow, when it is coming from him to me, he may inflict retributive usurpation upon me.

The light of the sun, too, is subject to the same benign and equitable regulations. As the waves of this ethereal element pass by me, I have a right to bask in their genial warmth, or to employ their quickening powers; but I have no right, even on my own land, to build up a wall, mountain-high, that shall eclipse the sun to my neighbor's eyes.

Now, all these great principles of natural law which define and limit the rights of neighbors and contemporaries are incorporated into and constitute a part of the civil law of every civilized people; and they are obvious and simple illustrations of the great proprietary laws by which individuals and generations hold their rights in the solid substance of the globe, in the elements that move over its surface, and in the chemical and vital powers with which it is so marvellously endued. As successive owners on a river's bank have equal rights to the waters that flow through their respective domains, subject only to the modification that the proprietors nearer the stream's source must have precedence in the enjoyment of their rights over those lower down, so the rights of all the generations of mankind to the earth itself, to the streams that fertilize it, to the winds that purify it, to the vital principles that animate it, and to the reviving light, are common rights, though subject to similar modifications in regard to the preceding and succeeding generations of men. They did not belong to our ancestors in perpetuity; they do not belong to us in perpetuity; and the right of the next generation in them will be limited and defeasible like ours. As we hold these rights subject to the claims of the next generation, so will they hold them subject to the claims of their immediate successors, and so on to the end of time; and the savage tribes that roam about the headsprings of the Mississippi have as good a right to ordain what use shall be made of its copious waters when in their grand descent across a continent they shall reach the shores of arts and civilization, as any of our predecessors had, or as we ourselves have, to say what shall be done, *in perpetuity*, with the soil, the waters, the winds, the light, and the invisible agencies of Nature, which must be allowed, on all hands, to constitute the primary and indispensable elements of wealth.

Is not the inference irresistible, then, that no man, by whatever means he may have come into possession of his property, has any natural right, any more than he has a moral one, to hold it, or to dispose of it, irrespective of the needs and claims of those, who, in the august processions of the generations, are to be his successors on the stage of existence? Holding his rights subject to their rights, he is bound not to impair the value of their inheritance either by commission or by omission.

Generation after generation proceeds from the creative energy of God. Each one stops for a brief period upon the earth, resting, as it were, only for a night, — like migratory birds upon their passage, — and then leaving it forever to others whose existence is as transitory as its own; and the migratory flocks of water-fowl which sweep across our latitudes in their passage to another clime have as good a right to make a perpetual appropriation, to their own use, of the lands over which they fly, as any one generation has to arrogate perpetual dominion and sovereignty, for its own purposes, over that portion of the earth which it is its fortune to occupy during the brief period of its temporal existence.

Another consideration, bearing upon this arrogant doctrine of absolute ownership or sovereignty, has hardly less force than the one just expounded. We have seen how insignificant a portion of any man's possessions he can claim, in any proper and just sense, *to have earned;* and that, in regard to all the residue, he is only taking his turn in the use of a bounty bestowed, in common, by the Giver of all, upon his ancestors, upon himself, and upon his posterity, — a line of indefinite length, in which he is but a point. But this is not the only deduction to be made from his assumed rights. The *present* wealth of the world has an additional element in it. Much of all that is capable of being earned by man has been earned by our predecessors, and has come down to us in a solid and enduring form. We have not erected all the houses in which we live, nor constructed all the roads on which we travel, nor built all the ships in which we carry on our commerce with the world. We have not reclaimed from the wilderness all the fields whose harvests we now reap; and if we had no precious metals or stones or pearls but such as we ourselves had dug from the mines, or brought up from the bottom of the ocean, our coffers and our caskets would be empty indeed. But, even if this were not so, whence came all the arts and sciences, the discoveries and the inventions, without which, and without a common right to which, the valuation of the property of a whole nation would scarcely equal the inventory of a single man, — without which, indeed, we should now be in a state of barbarism? Whence came a knowledge of agriculture, without which we should have so little to reap? or a knowledge of astronomy, without which we could not traverse the oceans? or a knowledge of chemistry and mechanical philosophy, without which the arts and trades could not exist? Most of all this was found out by those who have gone before us; and some of it has come down to us from a remote antiquity. Surely all these boons and blessings belong as much to posterity as to ourselves. They have not descended to us to be arrested and consumed here, or to be sequestrated from the ages to come. Cato and Archimedes, and Kepler and Newton, and Franklin and Arkwright and Fulton, and all the bright host of benefactors to science and art, did not make or bequeath their discoveries or inventions to benefit any one generation, but to increase the common enjoyments of mankind to the end of time. So of all the great lawgivers and moralists who have improved the civil institutions of the state, who have made it dangerous to be wicked, or, far better than this, have made it hateful to be so. Resources developed and property acquired after all these ages of preparation, after all these facilities and securities, accrue, not to the benefit of the possessor only, but to that of the next and of all succeeding generations.

Surely these considerations limit still more extensively that absolutism of ownership which is so often claimed by the possessors of wealth.

But sometimes the rich farmer, the opulent manufacturer, or the capitalist, when sorely pressed with his natural and moral obligation to contribute a portion of his means for the education of the young, replies, — either in form or in spirit, — " My lands, my machinery, my gold, and my silver, are mine: may I not do what I will with my own?" There is one supposable case, and only one, where this argument would have plausibility. If it were made by an isolated, solitary being, — a being having no relations to a community around him, having no ancestors to whom he had been indebted for ninety-nine parts in every hundred of all he possesses, and expecting to leave no posterity after him, — it might not be easy to answer it. If there were but one family in this Western hemisphere, and only one in the Eastern hemisphere, and these two families bore no civil and social relations to each other, and were to be the first and last of the whole race, it might be difficult, except on very high and almost transcendental grounds, for either one of them to show good cause why the other should contribute to help educate children not his own. And perhaps the force of the appeal for such an object would be still further diminished if the nearest neighbor of a single family upon our planet were as far from the earth as Uranus or Sirius. In self-defence or in selfishness, one might say to the other, "What are your fortunes to me? You can neither benefit nor molest me. Let each of us keep to his own side of the planetary spaces." But is this the relation which any man amongst us sustains to his fellows? In the midst of a populous community to which he is bound by innumerable ties, having had his own fortune and condition almost predetermined and fore-ordained by his predecessors, and being about to exert upon his successors as commanding an influence as has been exerted upon himself, the objector can no longer shrink into his individuality, and disclaim connection and relationship with the world at large. He cannot deny that there are thousands around him on whom he acts, and who are continually re-acting upon him. The earth is much too small, or the race is far too numerous, to allow us to be hermits; and therefore we cannot adopt either the philosophy or the morals of hermits. All have derived benefits from their ancestors, and all are bound, as by an oath, to transmit those benefits, even in an improved condition, to posterity. We may as well attempt to escape from our own personal identity as to shake off the threefold relation which we bear to others, — the relation of an associate with our contemporaries; of a beneficiary of our ancestors; of a guardian to those who, in the sublime order of Providence, are to succeed us. Out of these relations, manifest duties are evolved. The society of which we necessarily constitute a part must be preserved; and, in order to preserve it, we must not look merely to what one individual or one family needs, but to what the whole community needs; not merely to what one generation needs, but to the wants of a succession of generations. To draw conclusions without considering these facts is to leave out the most important part of the premises.

A powerfully corroborating fact remains untouched. Though the earth and the beneficent capabilities with which it is endued belong in common to the race, yet we find that previous and present possessors have laid their hands upon the whole of it,— have left no part of it unclaimed and unappropriated. They have circumnavigated the globe; they have drawn lines across every habitable portion of it, and have partitioned amongst themselves not only its whole area or superficial contents, but have claimed it down to the centre, and up to the concave,— a great inverted pyramid for each proprietor, — so that not an unclaimed rood is left, either in the caverns below or in the aerial spaces above, where a new adventurer upon existence can take unresisted possession. They have entered into a solemn compact with each other for the mutual defence of their respective allotments. They have created legislators and judges and executive officers, who denounce and inflict penalties even to the taking of life; and they have organized armed bands to repel aggression upon their claims. Indeed, so grasping and rapacious have mankind been in this particular, that they have taken more than they could use, more than they could perambulate and survey, more than they could see from the top of the masthead, or from the highest peak of the mountain. There was some limit to their physical power of taking possession, but none to the exorbitancy of their desires. Like robbers, who divide their spoils before they know whether they shall find a victim, men have claimed a continent while still doubtful of its existence, and spread out their title from ocean to ocean before their most adventurous pioneers had ever seen a shore of the realms they coveted. The whole planet, then, having been appropriated, — there being no waste or open lands from which the new generations may be supplied as they come into existence, — have not those generations the strongest conceivable claim upon the present occupants for that which is indispensable to their well-being? They have more than a pre-emptive, they have a possessory, right to some portion of the issues and profits of that general domain, all of which has been thus taken up and appropriated. A denial of this right by the present possessors is a breach of trust, a fraudulent misuse of power given and of confidence implied. On mere principles of political economy, it is folly; on the broader principles of duty and morality, it is embezzlement.

It is not at all in contravention of this view of the subject that the adult portion of society does take, and must take, upon itself the control and management of all existing property until the rising generation has arrived at the age of majority. Nay, one of the objects of their so doing is to preserve the rights of the generation which is still in its minority. Society, to this extent, is only a trustee managing an estate for the benefit of a part-owner, or of one who has a reversionary interest in it. This civil regulation, therefore, made necessary even for the benefit of both present and future possessors, is only in furtherance of the great law under consideration.

Coincident, too, with this great law, but in no manner superseding or invalidating it, is that wonderful provision which the Creator has made for the care of offspring in the affection of their parents. Heaven did not rely merely upon our perceptions of duty towards our children, and our fidelity in its performance. A powerful, all-mastering instinct of love was therefore implanted in the parental, and especially in the maternal breast, to anticipate the idea of duty, and to make duty delightful. Yet the great doctrine founded upon the will of God as made known to us in the natural order and relation of things would still remain the same, though all this beautiful portion of our moral being, whence parental affection springs, were a void and a nonentity. Emphatically would the obligations of society remain the same for all those children who have been bereaved of parents; or who, worse than bereavement, have only monster parents of intemperance or cupidity, or of any other of those forms of vice that seem to suspend or to obliterate the law of love in the parental breast. For these, society is doubly bound to be a parent, and to exercise all that rational care and providence which a wise father would exercise for his own children.

If the previous argument began with sound premises, and has been logically conducted, then it has established this position, — that a vast portion of the present wealth of the world either consists in, or has been immediately derived from, those great natural substances and powers of the earth which were bestowed by the Creator alike on all mankind; or from the discoveries, inventions, labors, and improvements of our ancestors, which were alike designed for the common benefit of all their descendants. The question now arises, *At what time* is this wealth to be transferred from a preceding to a succeeding generation? At what point are the latter to take possession of it, or to derive benefit from it? or at what time are the former to surrender it in their behalf? Is each existing generation, and each individual of an existing generation, to hold fast to his possessions until death relaxes his grasp? or is something of the right to be acknowledged, and something of the benefit to be yielded, beforehand? It seems too obvious for argument, that the latter is the only alternative. If the incoming generation have no rights until the outgoing generation have actually retired, then is every individual that enters the world liable to perish on the day he is born. According to the very constitution of things, each individual must obtain sustenance and succor as soon as his eyes open in quest of light, or his lungs gasp for the first breath of air. His wants cannot be delayed until he himself can supply them. If the demands of his nature are ever to be answered, they must be answered years before he can make any personal provision for them, either by the performance of any labor, or by any exploits of skill. The infant must be fed before he can earn his bread, he must be clothed before he can prepare garments, he must be protected from the elements before he can erect a dwelling; and it is just as clear that he must be instructed before he can engage or reward a tutor. A course contrary to this would be the destruction of the young, that we might rob them of their rightful inheritance. Carried to its extreme, it would be the act of Herod, seeking, in a general massacre, the life of one who was supposed to endanger his power. Here, then, the claims of the succeeding generation, not only upon the affection and the care, but upon the *property*, of the preceding one, attach. God having given to the second generation as full and complete a right to the incomes and profits of the world as he has given to the first, and to the third generation as full and complete a right as he has given to the second, and so on while the world stands, it necessarily follows that children must come into a partial and qualified possession of these rights, by the paramount law of Nature, as soon as they are born. No human enactment can abolish or countervail this paramount and supreme law; and all those positive and often arbitrary enactments of the civil code, by which, for the encouragement of industry and frugality, the possessor of property is permitted to control it for a limited period after his decease, must be construed and executed in subservience to this sovereign and irrepealable ordinance of Nature.

Nor is this transfer always, or even generally, to be made *in kind*, but according to the needs of the recipient. The recognition of this principle is universal. A guardian or trustee may possess lands, while the ward, or owner under the trust, may need money; or the former may have money while the latter need raiment or shelter. The form of the estate must be changed, if need be, and adapted to the wants of the receiver.

The claim of a child, then, to a portion of pre-existent property, begins with the first breath he draws. The new-born infant must have sustenance and shelter and care. If the natural parents are removed, or parental ability fails; in a word, if parents either cannot or will not supply the infant's wants,—

then society at large — the government having assumed to itself the ultimate control of all property — is bound to step in and fill the parent's place. To deny this to any child would be equivalent to a sentence of death, a capital execution of the innocent, — at which every soul shudders. It would be a more cruel form of infanticide than any which is practised in China or in Africa.

But to preserve the animal life of a child only, and there to stop, would be, not the bestowment of a blessing, or the performance of a duty, but the infliction of a fearful curse. A child has interests far higher than those of mere physical existence. Better that the wants of the natural life should be disregarded than that the higher interests of the character should be neglected. If a child has any claim to bread to keep him from perishing, he has a far higher claim to knowledge to preserve him from error and its fearful retinue of calamities. If a child has any claim to shelter to protect him from the destroying elements, he has a far higher claim to be rescued from the infamy and perdition of vice and crime.

All moralists agree, nay, all moralists maintain, that a man is as responsible for his omissions as for his commissions; that he is as guilty of the wrong which he could have prevented, but did not, as for that which his own hand has perpetrated. They, then, who knowingly withhold sustenance from a newborn child, and he dies, are guilty of infanticide. And, by the same reasoning, they who refuse to enlighten the intellect of the rising generation are guilty of degrading the human race. They who refuse to train up children in the way they should go are training up incendiaries and madmen to destroy property and life, and to invade and pollute the sanctuaries of society. In a word, if the mind is as real and substantive a part of human existence as the body, then mental attributes, during the periods of infancy and childhood, demand provision at least as imperatively as bodily appetites. The time when these respective obligations attach corresponds with the periods when the nurture, whether physical or mental, is needed. As the right of sustenance is of equal date with birth, so the right to intellectual and moral training begins at least as early as when children are ordinarily sent to school. At that time, then, by the irrepealable law of Nature, every child succeeds to so much more of the property of the community as is necessary for his education. He is to receive this, not in the form of lands, or of gold and silver, but in the form of knowledge and a training to good habits. This is one of the steps in the transfer of property from a present to a succeeding generation. Human sagacity may be at fault in fixing the amount of property to be transferred, or the time when the transfer should be made, to a dollar or to an hour; but certainly, in a republican government, the obligation of the predecessors, and the right of the successors, extend to and embrace the means of such an amount of education as will prepare each individual to perform all the duties which devolve upon him as a man and a citizen. It may go farther than this point; certainly it cannot fall short of it.

Under our political organization, the places and the processes where this transfer is to be provided for, and its amount determined, are the district-school-meeting, the town-meeting, legislative halls, and conventions for establishing or revising the fundamental laws of the State. If it be not done there, society is false to its high trusts; and any community, whether national or state, that ventures to organize a government, or to administer a government already organized, without making provision for the free education of all its children, dares the certain vengeance of Heaven; and in the squalid forms of poverty and destitution, in the scourges of violence and misrule, in the heart-destroying corruptions of licentiousness and debauchery, and in political profligacy and legalized perfidy, in all the blended and mutually-aggravated crimes of civilization and of barbarism, will be sure to feel the terrible retributions of its delinquency.

I bring my argument on this point, then, to a close; and I present a test of its validity, which, as it seems to me, defies denial or evasion.

In obedience to the laws of God and to the laws of all civilized communities, society is bound to protect the natural life of children; and this natural life cannot be protected without the appropriation and use of a portion of the property which society possesses. We prohibit infanticide under penalty of death. We practise a refinement in this particular. The life of an infant is inviolable, even before he is born; and he who feloniously takes it, even before birth, is as subject to the extreme penalty of the law as though he had struck down manhood in its vigor, or taken away a mother by violence from the sanctuary of home where she blesses her offspring. But why preserve the natural life of a child, why preserve unborn embryos of life, if we do not intend to watch over and to protect them, and to expand their subsequent existence into usefulness and happiness? As individuals, or as an organized community, we have no natural right, we can derive no authority or countenance from reason, we can cite no attribute or purpose of the divine nature, for giving birth to any human being, and then inflicting upon that being the curse of ignorance, of poverty, and of vice, with all their attendant calamities. We are brought, then, to this startling but inevitable alternative, — the natural life of an infant should be extinguished as soon as it is born, or the means should be provided to save that life from being a curse to its possessor; and, therefore, every State is morally bound to enact a code of laws legalizing and enforcing infanticide, or a code of laws establishing free schools.

The three following propositions, then, describe the broad and ever-during foundation on which the common-school system of Massachusetts reposes: —

The successive generations of men, taken collectively, constitute one great commonwealth.

The property of this commonwealth is pledged for the education of all its youth, up to such a point as will save them from poverty and vice, and prepare them for the adequate performance of their social and civil duties.

The successive holders of this property are trustees, bound to the faithful execution of their trust by the most sacred obligations; and embezzlement and pillage from children and descendants have not less of criminality, and have more of meanness, than the same offences when perpetrated against contemporaries.

Recognizing these eternal principles of natural ethics, the Constitution of Massachusetts, — the fundamental law of the State, — after declaring (among other things), in the preamble to the first section of the fifth chapter, that "the encouragement of arts and sciences, and all good literature, tends to the honor of God, the advantage of the Christian religion, and the great benefit of this and the other United States of America," proceeds, in the second section of the same chapter, to set forth the duties of all future legislators and magistrates in the following noble and impressive language: —

"Wisdom and knowledge, as well as virtue, diffused generally among the body of the people, being necessary for the preservation of their rights and liberties; and as these depend on spreading the opportunities and advantages of education in the various parts of the country, and among the different orders of the people, — it shall be the duty of legislatures and magistrates, in all future periods of this Commonwealth, to cherish the interests of literature and the sciences, and all seminaries of them, especially the University of Cambridge, public schools and grammar schools in the towns; to encourage private societies and public institutions, rewards and immunities, for the promotion of agriculture, arts, sciences, commerce, trade, manufactures, and a natural history of the country; to countenance and inculcate the principles of humanity and general benevolence, public and private charity, industry and frugality, honesty and punctuality in their dealings, sincerity, good humor, and all social affections and generous sentiments among the people." — See also Rev. Stat., ch. 23, sect. 7.

Massachusetts is *parental* in her government. More and more, as year after year rolls by, she seeks to substitute prevention for remedy, and rewards for penalties. She strives to make industry the antidote to poverty, and to counterwork the progress of vice and crime by the diffusion of knowledge and the culture of virtuous principles. She seeks not only to mitigate those great physical and mental calamities of which mankind are the sad inheritors, but also to avert those infinitely greater moral calamities which form the disastrous heritage of depraved passions. Hence it has long been her policy to endow or to aid asylums for the cure of disease. She succors and maintains all the poor within her borders, whatever may have been the land of their nativity. She founds and supports hospitals for restoring reason to the insane; and, even for those violators of the law whom she is obliged to sequestrate from society, she provides daily instruction and the ministrations of the gospel at the public charge. To those who, in the order of Nature and Providence, have been bereft of the noble faculties of hearing and of speech, she teaches a new language, and opens their imprisoned minds and hearts to conversation with men and to communion with God; and it hardly transcends the literal truth to say that she gives sight to the blind. For the remnants of those aboriginal tribes, who, for so many ages, roamed over this land without cultivating its soil, or elevating themselves in the scale of being, her annual bounty provides good schools; and when the equal, natural, and constitutional rights of the outcast children of Africa were thought to be invaded, she armed her courts of judicature with power to punish the aggressors. The public highway is not more open and free for every man in the community than is the public schoolhouse for every child; and each parent feels that a free education is as secure a part of the birthright of his offspring as Heaven's bounties of light and air. The State not only commands that the means of education shall be provided for all, but she denounces penalties against all individuals, and all towns and cities, however populous or powerful they may be, that shall presume to stand between her bounty and its recipients. In her righteous code, the interception of knowledge is a crime; and, if parents are unable to supply their children with books, she becomes a parent, and supplies them.

The policy of the State promotes not only secular but religious instruction, yet in such a way as leaves to every individual the right of private judgment and the sacred freedom of conscience.

Public sentiment exceeds and excels the law. Annually, vast sums are given for eleemosynary and charitable purposes, — to promote the cause of temperance, to send the gospel to the heathen, and to diffuse the doctrines of peace, which are the doctrines of the Prince of Peace.

For public, free education alone, including the direct outlay of money and the interest on capital invested, Massachusetts expends annually more than a million of dollars. To support religious institutions for the worship of God and the salvation of men, she annually expends more than another million; and what she gives away in the various forms of charity far exceeds a third sum of equal magnitude. She explores the world for new objects of beneficence; and so deep and common is the feeling which expects and prompts all this, that she is gradually changing and ennobling the definition of a cardinal word in the language of morals, — doing what no king or court with all their authority, nor royal academy with all its sages and literary men, can do: she is changing the meaning of *charity* into *duty*.

For the support of the poor, nine-tenths of whose cost originate with foreigners or come from one prolific vice, whose last convulsive energies she is now struggling to subdue, she annually pays more than three hundred thousand dollars; for the support and improvement of public highways, she pays a much larger sum; and, within the last dozen or fourteen years, she has invested a capital in railroads, within and without the State, of nearly or quite sixty millions of dollars.

Whence come her means to give, with each returning year, more than a million of dollars to public education; more than another million to religion; and more than a third to ameliorate and succor the afflicted and the ignorant at home, and to bless, in distant lands, those who sit in the region and shadow of death? How does she support her poor, maintain her public ways, and contribute such vast sums for purposes of internal improvement, besides maintaining her immense commercial transactions with every zone in the world?

Has she a vast domain? Her whole territory would not make a court-yard of respectable dimensions to stand in front of many of the States and Territories belonging to the Union.

Does she draw revenues from conquered provinces or subjugated realms? She conquers nothing, she subdues nothing, save the great elemental forces of Nature, which God gives freely, whenever and wherever they are asked for in the language of genius and science; and in regard to which no profusion or prodigality to one can diminish the bounty always ready for others.

Does she live by the toil of a race of serfs and vassals whom she holds in personal and hereditary bondage? — by one comprehensive and sovereign act of violence seizing upon both body and soul at once, and superseding the thousand acts of plunder which make up the life of a common robber? Every man who treads her sacred soil is free; all are free alike; and within her borders, for any purpose connected with human slavery, iron will not be welded into a fetter.

Has she rich mines of the precious metals? In all her coffers there is not a drachm of silver or of gold which has not been obtained by the sweat of her brow or the vigor of her brain.

Has she magazines of mineral wealth embedded in the earth? or are her soil and climate so spontaneously exuberant that she reaps luxuriant harvests from uncultivated fields? Alas! the orator has barbed his satire by declaring her only natural productions to be granite and ice.

Whence, then, I again ask, comes her wealth? I do not mean the gorgeous wealth which is displayed in the voluptuous and too often enervating residences of the affluent, but that *golden mean* of property — such as Agur asked for in his perfect prayer — which carries blessings in its train to thousands of householders; which spreads solid comfort and competence through the dwellings of the land; which furnishes the means of instruction, of social pleasures and refinement, to the citizens at large; which saves from the cruel sufferings and the more cruel temptations of penury. The families scattered over her hills and along her valleys have not merely a shelter from the inclemencies of the seasons, but the sanctuary of a home. Not only food, but books, are spread upon their tables. Her commonest houses have the means of hospitality; they have appliances for sickness, and resources laid up against accident and the infirmities of age. Whether in her rural districts or her populous towns, a wandering, native-born beggar is a prodigy; and the twelve millions of dollars deposited in her savings institutions do not more loudly proclaim the frugality and providence of the past than they foretell the competence and enjoyments of the future.

One copious, exhaustless fountain supplies all this abundance. It is education, — the intellectual, moral, and religious education of the people. Having no other mines to work, Massachusetts has mined into the human intellect; and, from its limitless resources, she has won more sustaining and enduring prosperity and happiness than if she had been founded on a stratification of silver and gold, reaching deeper down than geology has yet penetrated. From her high religious convictions, she has learned that great lesson, — *to set a value upon time.* Regarding the faculties as the gift of God, she has felt bound both to use and to improve them. Mingling skill and intelligence with the daily occupations of life, she has made labor honorable; and, as a necessary consequence, idleness is disgraceful. Knowledge has been the ambition of her sons, and she has reverenced and venerated the purity and chastity of her matrons and her daughters. At the hearth-stone, at the family table, and at the family altar, — on all those occasions where the structure of the youthful character is *builded up,* —

these sentiments of love for knowledge, and of reverence for maidenly virtue, have been *builded in;* and there they stand, so wrought and mingled with the fibres of being, that none but God can tell which is Nature, and which is education; which we owe primarily to the grace of Heaven, and which to the co-operating wisdom of the institutions of men. Verily, verily, not as we ought have we obeyed the laws of Jehovah, or imitated the divine example of the Saviour; and yet, for such imperfect obedience and distant imitation as we have rendered, God has showered down manna from the heavens, and opened a rock whence flow living waters to gladden every thirsty place. He who studies the present or the historic character of Massachusetts will see (and he who studies it most profoundly will see most clearly), that whatever of abundance, of intelligence, or of integrity, whatever of character at home or of renown abroad, she may possess, all has been evolved from the enlightened, and, at least, partially Christianized mind, not of a few, but of the great masses, of her people. They are not the result of outward riches or art brought around it, or laminated over it, but of an awakened inward force, working energetically outwards, and fashioning the most intractable circumstances to the dominion of its own desires and resolves; and this force has been awakened, and its unspent energies replenished, more than from all things else, by her common schools.

When we witness the mighty achievements of art, — the locomotive, taking up its burden of a hundred tons, and transporting it for hundreds of miles between the rising and the setting sun; the steamboat, cleaving its rapid way, triumphant over wind and tide; the power-loom, yielding products of greater richness and abundance in a single day than all the inhabitants of Tyre could have manufactured in years; the printing-press, which could have replaced the Alexandrian Library within a week after it was burnt; the lightning, not only domesticated in the laboratories of the useful arts, but employed as a messenger between distant cities; and galleries of beautiful paintings, quickened into life by the sunbeams, — when we see all these marvels of power and of celerity, we are prone to conclude that it is to them we are indebted for the increase of our wealth and for the progress of our society. But were there any statistics to show the aggregate value of all the thrifty and gainful habits of the people at large, the greater productiveness of the educated than of the brutified laborer, the increased power of the intelligent hand, and the broad survey and deep intuition of the intelligent eye; could we see a ledger account of the profits which come from forethought, order, and system, as they preside over all our farms, in all our workshops, and emphatically in all the labors of our households, — we should then know how rapidly their gathered units swell into millions upon millions. The skill that strikes the nail's head instead of the fingers' ends; the care that mends a fence and saves a cornfield, that drives a horseshoe nail and secures both rider and horse, that extinguishes a light and saves a house; the prudence that cuts the coat according to the cloth, that lays by something for a rainy day, and that postpones marriage until reasonably sure of a livelihood; the forethought that sees the end from the beginning, and reaches it by the direct route of an hour instead of the circuitous gropings of a day; the exact remembrance impressed upon childhood to do the errand as it was bidden; and, more than all, the economy of virtue over vice, of restrained over pampered desires, — these things are not set down in the works on political economy; but they have far more to do with the wealth of nations than any laws which aim to regulate the balance of trade, or any speculations on capital and labor, or any of the great achievements of art. That vast variety of ways in which an intelligent people surpass a stupid one, and an exemplary people an immoral one, has infinitely more to do with the well-being of a nation than soil or climate, or even than government itself, excepting so far as government may prove to be the patron of intelligence and virtue.

From her earliest colonial history, the policy of Massachusetts has been to develop the minds of all her people, and to imbue them with the principles of duty. To do this work most effectually, she has begun it with the young. If she would continue to mount higher and higher towards the summit of prosperity, she must continue the means by which her present elevation has been gained. In doing this, she will not only exercise the noblest prerogative of government, but will co-operate with the Almighty in one of his sublimest works.

The Greek rhetorician Longinus quotes from the Mosaic account of the creation what he calls the sublimest passage ever uttered: " God said, Let there be light, and there was light." From the centre of black immensity, effulgence burst forth. Above, beneath, on every side, its radiance streamed out, silent, yet making each spot in the vast concave brighter than the line which the lightning pencils upon the midnight cloud. Darkness fled as the swift beams spread onward and outward in an unending circumfusion of splendor. Onward and outward still they move to this day, glorifying, through wider and wider regions of space, the infinite Author from whose power and beneficence they sprang. But not only in the beginning, when God created the heavens and the earth, did he say, " Let there be light." Whenever a human soul is born into the world, its Creator stands over it, and again pronounces the same sublime words, " Let there be light."

Magnificent, indeed, was the material creation, when, suddenly blazing forth in mid-space, the new-born sun dispelled the darkness of the ancient night: but infinitely more magnificent is it when the human soul rays forth its subtler and swifter beams; when the light of the senses irradiates all outward things, revealing the beauty of their colors, and the exquisite symmetry of their proportions and forms; when the light of reason penetrates to their invisible properties and laws, and displays all those hidden relations that make up all the sciences; when the light of conscience illumines the moral world, separating truth from error, and virtue from vice. The light of the newly-kindled sun, indeed, was glorious. It struck upon all the planets, and waked into existence their myriad capacities of life and joy. As it rebounded from them, and showed their vast orbs all wheeling, circle beyond circle, in their stupendous courses, the sons of God shouted for joy. That light sped onward, beyond Sirius, beyond the Pole-star, beyond Orion and the Pleiades, and is still speeding onward into the abysses of space. But the light of the human soul flies swifter than the light of the sun, and outshines its meridian blaze. It can embrace not only the sun of our system, but all suns, and galaxies of suns: ay, the soul is capable of knowing and of enjoying Him who created the suns themselves; and, when these starry lustres that now glorify the firmament shall wax dim and fade away like a wasted taper, the light of the soul shall still remain; nor time nor cloud, nor any power but its own perversity, shall ever quench its brightness. Again I would say, that, whenever a human soul is born into the world, God stands over it, and pronounces the same sublime fiat, "Let there be light;" and may the time soon come when all human governments shall co-operate with the divine government in carrying this benediction and baptism into fulfilment!

REPORT FOR 1847.

GENTLEMEN, —

. . . THE incontestable progress which the cause of popular education is making in Massachusetts, and in some of the other States of our Union, is a subject for hearty congratulation among ourselves, and for devout gratitude to Heaven. It cannot be denied that the cause has won to itself most able and earnest advocates, who are in no way officially connected with it, but who cherish it from the purest motives of duty and philanthropy. But it happens to this, as to all other good causes, that some of its professed friends have attached themselves to it from collateral, and some from sinister motives. It is equally true that the cause has enemies; although, in this community, there are but few who dare to make open proclamation of their hostility. But opponents are all the more formidable when their opposition is secret. Their measures of counteraction are not the less efficient because they are indirect, and hide their origin under specious pretences. There is a third class, who have no faith in the utility of education. They number it among what they are pleased to call the Utopian schemes of reform with which the age is teeming; and they regard with an ill-concealed suspicion either the honesty of purpose or the soundness of intellect of those who are laboring to uphold its banner, and to bear it forward. There are those also who suspect, in education, the existence of some unknown and mystical power, which, should it once obtain the ascendency, would bear the community onward, they know not whither; and having some *ism* or *ology* of their own, by which, provided all civil institutions, and Nature herself, will succumb to their dictation, they can forthwith extricate the world from all its troubles, and carry it forward in the directest line, and with the swiftest speed, to a millennial goal, they discard an agency whose power they can neither control nor comprehend. And, lastly, there are those who array themselves against education solely from mercenary motives,— because of the one or two mills upon the dollar which its support subtracts from their property.

To meet the opposition and the indifference originating in these and similar prejudgments, the subject of education has been very much " agitated," particularly in the northern portion of our country, within the last dozen years. There can be no hazard in affirming, that far more has been spoken and printed, heard and read, on this theme, within the last twelve years, than ever before, were it all put together, since the settlement of the colonies. The consequence certainly has been a very marked development of the merits of the subject, and a corresponding opening or expansion of the public mind for their recognition. To many sensible men, it has come like a revelation, inspiring hopes for the amelioration of mankind, and for the perpetuity of our institutions, which they had never dreamed of before. There are thousands of persons amongst us, whose once darkened minds have been so quickened with life, and illuminated with wisdom, on this subject, as to beget an intolerable impatience under old imperfections, — a perception of which has made rest impossible, and the pleasures of home uncomfortable, until, within their respective spheres, they had effected a reform.

In order to make this subject more intelligible to the common mind, as well as to conform to broad distinctions which Nature herself has established, it has been considered under a threefold aspect, — first, as embracing the proper care and training of the body, that its health and longevity may be secured; second, as cultivating the faculties by which we perceive, compare, analyze and combine, remember, reason, and perceive natural fitness and the beauty of things, so that we may know more of the world in which we are placed, and of the glorious attributes of its Maker, and so that, by more faithfully harmonizing our conduct with its laws, we may the better enjoy its exquisite adaptations to our welfare; and, thirdly, as fashioning our moral nature into some resemblance to its divine original, — subordinating our propensities to the law of duty, expanding our benevolence into a sentiment of universal brotherhood, and lifting our hearts to the grateful and devout contemplation of God.

In pursuance of these fundamental ideas, it has been shown, by the authority of the highest medical men in the country, that, even in the present imperfect state of physiological science, more than one-half of all the cases of bodily disability and disease, more than one-half of all the pains and expenditures of sickness, more than one-half of all the cases of premature death, — that is, of death under the age of seventy years, — are the consequence of sheer ignorance, not of any irrepealable decree or fatality necessitating their existence, independently of our consent and co-operation, but of our own brutish ignorance of the conditions of health and life to which our bodies have been subjected by their Maker. And I desire, also, to be here understood as not including in this moiety of unnecessary suffering and of untimely death a single one of that extensive class of cases which result from a slavish submission to some tyrannous appetite, — such as intemperance, for instance, — where the knowledge, even if we possessed it, might be overborne in a conflict with the sensual desire: but I mean maladies, pains, and death, which a bad man would be as quick to avoid as a good one; which every sane man would desire to escape from, as he would from blindness or deafness, the gout or the toothache. Even were ignorance, then, to be classed among the greatest luxuries of life, it would be found too costly an indulgence to be borne by an economical people.*

The indispensableness of education to worldly prosperity has also been demonstrated. An ignorant people not only is, but must be, a poor people. They must be destitute of sagacity and providence, and, of course, of competence and comfort. The proof of this does not depend upon the lessons of history, but on the constitution of Nature. No richness of climate, no spontaneous productiveness of soil, no facilities for commerce, no stores of gold or of diamonds garnered in the treasure-chambers of the earth, can confer even worldly prosperity upon an uneducated nation. Such a nation cannot create wealth of itself; and whatever riches may be showered upon it will run to waste. The ignorant pearl-divers do not wear the pearls they win. The diamond-hunters are not ornamented by the gems they find. The miners for silver and gold are not enriched by the precious metals they dig. Those who toil on the most luxuriant soils are not filled with the harvests they gather. All the choicest productions of the earth, whether mineral or vegetable, wherever found or wherever gathered, will, in a short time, as by some secret and resistless attraction, make their way into the hands of the more intelligent. Within the last four centuries, the people of Spain have owned as much silver and gold as all the other nations of Europe put together; yet, at the present time, poor indeed is the people who have less than they. The nation which has produced more of the raw material, and manufactured from it more fine linen, than all contemporary nations, are now the most ragged and squalid in Christendom. Let whoever will sow the seed or gather the fruit, intelligence will consume the banquet.

It must be admitted, indeed, that, when the people composing any particular state or country are compared with each other, the wisest are not always the wealthiest. This natural law, like others, is liable to fluctuations and disturbances from arti-

* See letters of eminent physicians, in my Sixth Annual Report. Also Common-school Journal, vol. v.

ficial and arbitrary institutions. Primogeniture, entail, monopoly, may derange its action; yet even here, as if to add confirmation to the general principle, it is always found that the families of inferior minds who inherit wealth, and the imbecile sovereigns or rulers who inherit power, owe their elevation to the greatness of some ancestor whose mental superiority not only won pre-eminence for himself, but for his descendants also. Where wealth or social position has not been earned or won by the possessors themselves, it is the representative of some ancestral talent whose force is not yet expended.

Who that visited the late Mechanics' Fair in the city of Boston was not bewildered by the number and diversity of the products of inventive genius and skill there exhibited? To the common observer, it was profusion producing confusion. What would be the result and "sum total" of a Mechanics' Fair among a tribe in the interior of Africa, or among the aborigines of our Western wilderness? Hardly more than a stone hatchet, a flint-headed arrow, a stick burned at the end, and sharpened into a spear, and a few yards of tawdry wampum. Yet the variety and richness of the one, compared with the poverty and rudeness of the other, would be but feeble symbols of the relative power and weakness of the minds from which they sprung. And whence came the vast, the wonderful intellectual superiority? It came from the old slate and pencil; the bit of chalk and the bit of board, planed or unplaned; the spelling-book and the reading-book, which have been found in every household through all our borders, from the time of the first rude huts that went up, amid winter and storm, about Plymouth Rock,— which have been the companions and playthings of every nursery, and the business-things of every schoolroom, for more than two centuries, until the children, as if by force of hereditary instinct, seem to look round inquiringly after them almost as soon as they are born. These are the acorns whence the majestic forest has sprung.

If the difference between persons dwelling in the same community, and living side by side, be less striking to the senses, it is not less instructive to the reason. In my Fifth Annual Report, I presented the testimony of some of the most eminent and successful business-men amongst us, proving from business-data, and beyond controversy, that labor becomes more profitable as the laborer is more intelligent; and that the true mint of wealth, the veritable coinage of the country, is not to be found in magnificent government establishments, at Philadelphia or New Orleans, but in the humble schoolhouse.

On the occasion referred to, one of our most sagacious manufacturers declared, not only in accordance with the conclusions of his own reason, but as the result of an actual experiment, that the best cotton-mill in New England, if worked by operatives so low in the scale of intelligence as to be unable to read and write, would never yield the proprietor a profit; that the machinery would soon be worn out, the owner impoverished, and the operatives themselves left penniless. Another witness, for a long time superintendent of many work-people, made the following striking remark: "So confident am I that production is affected by the intellectual and moral condition of help, that, whenever a mill or a room should fail to give the proper amount of work, my first inquiry, after that respecting the condition of the machinery, would be *as to the character of the help;* and, if the deficiency remained any great length of time, I am sure I should find many who had made their marks upon the pay-roll, being unable to write their names; and I should be greatly disappointed, if I did not, upon inquiry, find a portion of them of irregular habits and suspicious character." *

Is it not, in fact, most palpably demonstrable, from a comparison of the nature of man with the powers and properties of the material universe in which he is placed, that he was designed to reach a point of intellectual and moral elevation far higher than any which the most favored people on the earth have yet attained? A material world, active with such invisible energies, and constantly displaying such fitful changes, as

* See Report for 1841, vol. iii., p. 106.

belong to our planet, would be the most cruel prison-house to beings capable of perceiving its aspects, but incapable of understanding its laws. The superiority of our affective and sympathetic faculties over those possessed by the lower orders of creation would only render us so much the more miserable and defenceless, if we had not the faculties of reason and judgment also, by which we are able to bring ourselves into harmony with surrounding circumstances. Without knowledge, our present lives would be far more wretched than those of the brutes which perish; for we should be vulnerable on all sides, capable of suffering the keenest pain, while incapable of avoiding its causes. The revolution of the seasons would inflict want and debasement upon the whole race, if we could not foresee their vicissitudes and provide for their varying necessities. Comets and eclipses are fitted, in their very natures, to shed consternation and dismay upon the hearts of men, until the intellect comes in to explain the sublime order that produces them.*

To the savage, thunder and lightning are tokens of divine wrath; while to the Christian philosopher they are only emphatic and vivid proofs of the greatness and wisdom of God. To the enlightened mind, a tempest or a whirlwind is only a tempest or a whirlwind; but a barbarian dreads them a thou-

* It has been well said, " No eye has ever witnessed the spectacle of a total eclipse of the sun, even when announced with every characteristic of accuracy, without a shudder of awe, a sensation of deep terror, which reason in vain essays to subdue. The chilling and sombre darkness which spreads over Nature; the manifest terror of birds and animals, their instinctive retreat to the abodes of man, as if some awful danger were impending; the horror of the idea of the destruction of the great source of light and life, and the possible dissolution of Nature,— all conspire to render this one of the most terrific scenes that the eye of man has ever witnessed. What, then, must have been the horror which seized every spectator of this awful scene in those ages of the world when profound ignorance of its physical causes existed, and this terrible phenomenon burst suddenly upon the world, unanticipated and unannounced!

"The great Roman historian and annalist has, in a few graphic sentences, depicted the effect of an eclipse of the moon on the devoted legions of Pannonia. These hardy veterans, these iron men, born and bred to battle and to war, cowered before the awful spectacle, marched in agony to their contemned commanders, and implored their forgiveness, and deprecated the wrath of the avenging gods, for their disobedience and insubordination."— *Sidereal Messenger.*

sand times more for the anger of the gods which they denote, and for the evils they portend, than for any actual injuries which they inflict. The auroras of the North, so beautiful to the eye of science, have shaken myriads of hearts with fear. That numerous and various class of phenomena which we call optical illusions are sources of the direst terror to the ignorant, while they gratify a philosophic curiosity with the purest delight. In short, we know that all the wonders and glories which Nature displays in her majestic course are only sources of superstition to those who have not learned her sublime laws, darkening the already darkened mind, debasing the debased, and terrifying the affrighted. It seems impossible that a benevolent Being could have gifted the human race with its high faculties, if he had not provided for and ordained their development and edification. All the other orders of animated Nature are adapted to their condition: but a human soul, quickened by irrepressible impulses of curiosity, subject to the illusions of hope and to the agonies of fear, but with no power to unriddle the mysteries by which it is encompassed; with no power to realize the hopes spontaneously springing up within it, or to emancipate itself from the bondage of fear, — such a soul would be forever the trembling slave of Nature; while Nature would be a tyrant over it, deaf and remorseless. Whatever name might be given to the place of its habitation, it would be a habitation of unquenchable fire.

Knowledge and a highly-developed and highly-trained reason are to the temporal necessities of man what instinct is to the brute. But instinct is complete, perfect, self-active; while knowledge and reason can never reach any adequate height without vigorous self-effort and copious instruction from others. Far better, therefore, would it have been for mankind, had they never been elevated in the scale of existence above the *Simia* tribe, — the ape, the monkey, or the baboon, — than that they should have been endowed with the faculties of memory, of hope, of fear, and of imagination, without an adequate ability to derive wisdom from past experience, and to make provision for future necessities. There is no earthly power but education, which, by supplying these wants, can rescue the human race from sinking as much below the brute creation as they were designed to rise above it.

So, too, if the practice of equity, virtue, and benevolence, were not possible for the race, its condition would be far more deplorable than that of any horde of wild beasts that ever prowled through a wilderness, or hid themselves for ambush in the depths of a jungle. Even tigers and wolves, with all their ferocity, can inflict but a transitory pain upon each other, or upon the weaker races around them. The most ingenious of all the animals have never invented machines to torture those of their own or of an inferior order. The iron boot, the thumbscrew, the rack, the fagot, are dreadful realities in natural history; but the infamy of their invention and their use belongs not to the brute creation. Brutes cannot build ships, and cross oceans, to despoil or enslave a defenceless and kindred race in another hemisphere; nor can they forge any fetters, whether of iron or of law, which shall bind in remorseless bondage, not only the victim himself, but generations of his descendants. Brutes cannot bereave each other of their natural instincts, make the mother forget her young, the mated pair assail each other's lives, or the offspring lay parricidal hands upon its parent by transforming the choicest fruits of the earth into poison, and selling this poison for ignominious gain. The most selfish and ignoble races that ever flew through the air, or swam in the sea, never availed themselves of the accidental possession of power to establish orders of patrician and plebeian, or of lord and commoner, and thus to doom one portion of their number to perform all the toil and bear all the burdens of the tribe, while they themselves monopolized all its leisure and its luxuries. What a spectacle would be presented, if a few individuals of some family of insects, gathering themselves into conclave upon some spire of grass in the middle of a vast plain, or upon some leaf in a boundless forest, should there presume not only to adjudicate upon all the purposes of creation and all the mysteries of eternity, but should denounce imprisonment and torture, the fagot and the scaffold, upon all who would not bow to their authority, and avow assent to their conclusions! There are tribes of the brute creation, it is true, which prey upon other tribes; but it is only for the satisfaction of a physical want, and, when their hunger is appeased, their fierceness subsides: but not in the north, where their rage is whetted by arctic cold, nor in the south, where their blood is fevered by tropical heats, do they ever inflict upon a victim the life-long solitude of a dungeon, or gratuitously burn his body, and heap contempt upon his ashes, for not believing as they believe, or for not acknowledging, as the Great Spirit of the universe, the idol which they may have set up. If, then, I say, it had not been a part of the divine determination, in the creation of our race, that its terrible propensities should be controlled, and its higher susceptibilities advanced into supremacy, zoölogy has yet to discover the species of animals so vile, so wretched, so mutually predaceous, that mankind has not reason to envy them. If posterity is to be what history shows us that nineteen-twentieths of all the preceding world have been, what not less than four-fifths of it now are, then is man not the noblest, but the ignoblest, work of creation; the accursed, and not the favored, of Heaven. Not believing in such a destiny, I believe there is a way to avoid it.

Having proved, then, in former Reports, by the testimony of wise and skilled men, that disease may be supplanted by health, bodily pain by enjoyment, and premature death by length of life, merely by the knowledge and practice of a few great physiological principles, such as every person can easily master before the age of sixteen years; and having also shown, by testimony equally authentic and satisfactory, that intelligence, co-operating with the bounties of Nature, is sufficient to secure comfort and competence to all mankind, — I propose to myself, in the residue of this Report, the still more delightful task of showing, by proofs equally unexceptionable and convincing, that the great body of vices and crimes which now sadden and torment the community may be dislodged, and driven out from amongst us, by such improvements in our present common-school system as we are abundantly able immediately to make.

During the last summer, in order to a clear and full presentation of the subject to those persons whose testimony I wished to obtain, I prepared a circular, setting forth, with as much precision and completeness as possible, certain specific emendations of our present school-system, — only such emendations, however, as we can readily make, — and appealing to the experience and judgment of the persons addressed, to know what would be the results, were the system to be so amended. This circular was sent to teachers highly competent to give evidence on so important a subject, — competent from their science and from their personal experience, from the sobriety of their judgment, and from their freedom from any motive to overstate facts, or to deduce inferences too broad for the premises on which they were founded. In fine, the circular was sent to persons whose elevated character, and whose extended personal acquaintance with the subject-matter on which they testify, place them above denial, cavil, or suspicion.

The circular, and the answers to it, follow : —

CIRCULAR.

To —— ——.

I desire to obtain the opinion of teachers who are both scientific and practical on a subject of great importance to the cause of popular education. Your long experience in school-keeping, the great number of children whom you have had under your care, and your well-earned reputation as an instructor and trainer of youth, prompt me to apply to you for answers to the subjoined inquiries.

My general object is to obtain such an opinion as your experience will authorize you to give respecting the efficiency, in the formation of social and moral character, of a good common-school education, *conducted on the cardinal principles of the New-England systems*. In other words, how much of improvement in the upright conduct and good morals of the community might we reasonably hope and expect, if all our common schools were what they should be, what some of them now are, and what all of them, by means which the public is perfectly able to command, may soon be made to become?

As we look around us, we see that society is infested by vices, both small and great. The value of life is diminished, and even life itself is sometimes made burdensome and odious, by the existence amongst us of pests and nuisances in human form, whom the law forbids us to destroy, and whom, with all our efforts, we are unable wholly to reform. Were we permitted to hunt out and exterminate from society a wicked or mischievous man as we would a prowling wolf from the sheep-fold, or could we apply the sovereign antidote of extinction to a pestilent brood of children whom profligate parents are about to send forth into the world, we might then secure ourselves in a summary manner from present fears and from future annoyance. So, too, if we could arrest the momentum of long habit, or win back to the paths of virtue those, who, by their frequent tread, have worn the highways of vice both smooth and broad, we should then have access to a milder, though a more laborious remedy. But the common sentiments of mankind would revolt at any proposal to prevent all violations of the moral code by extinguishing the life of the violators; and all history and experience afford concurrent proof that the inbred habits of grown men and women — their accustomed trains of thought and of action — are mainly beyond the control of secondary causes. Hence it is, that a great part of the legislation of every state and nation, a vast majority of the decisions of all legal tribunals, and a still larger proportion of all the labors and expenditures of philanthropic and Christian men, have been devoted to the punishment of positive wrong, or to the vain attempt to repair its nameless and numberless mischiefs. Could these wrongs and mischiefs be prevented, our descendants would inherit a new earth.

The *classes* of common offences by which society is vexed and tormented are numerous; but the *individual acts of commission*, under the respective classes, are absolutely incomprehensible, save by the Omniscient.

There is the detestable practice of profane swearing, which is motiveless and gratuitous wickedness. This is a vice which neither gives any property to the poor man, nor any luxury to the rich one. It degrades even the clown to a lower state of vulgarity; and it would render the presence even of the most polished gentleman offensive and disgusting, if it were ever possible for a *gentleman* to be guilty of it.

Though greatly restricted, at the present day, in its destructive agency, and gradually withdrawing itself from the more respectable and intelligent classes to the two extremes of society, — to the luxuriously rich and the self-made poor, — yet the vice of intemperance still exists amongst us. Wherever it invades, it eats out the substance of families; not only consumes the means of educating children, but eradicates also the very disposition to educate them; involves the innocent in the sufferings of the guilty, even torturing them with superadded pangs of shame which the guilty do not feel; and, according to the divinely-ordained laws of our physical being, it visits the iniquities of the fathers upon the children, unto the third and fourth generation, by sowing in their constitution the seeds of inordinate desires.

Below that degree of slander or defamation which the law denounces as punishable, there exists such an amount of censoriousness and detraction as often estranges acquaintances, dissolves friendships, introduces discord into neighborhoods and communities, and sometimes entails hereditary animosities upon families and circles, which might otherwise be blessed by harmony and peace.

Nor can the gross and cowardly offence of lying be omitted from this odious catalogue. This vice includes in its very nature so much of the assassin and the dastard, that it lurks to inflict secret blows, or only ventures abroad when large numbers, bound together by strong ties of passion or of interest, impart mutual confidence and boldness in the prosecution of a common object. Hence a private individual who is known as a liar is detested, scorned, and shunned; while profligate political defamers and sectarian zealots, inspired by a common sentiment of ambition or of intolerance, and keeping themselves in countenance by their numbers and their partisanship, welcome this vice as an ally, and rejoice in the successes obtained by its aid. No patriotism is proof against the rancor of party spirit; no piety or good works, against the rage and blindness of religious bigotry.

In pecuniary transactions, the temptations to overreaching, to exorbitance, and to actual dishonesty, are yielded to with a most lamentable frequency. The buyer takes advantage of the necessities of the seller, and obtains a transfer of his property for a small part of its value; or sometimes, by adroit management and preliminary scheming, he creates the necessity which places the victim within the jaws of his avarice. The seller knowingly overstates the quantity, the quality, or the value of the commodities he sells; and, perhaps, takes advantage of the ignorance or credulity of the purchaser to obtain a price which he knows to be exorbitant and inequitable. The employer often avails himself of the necessities of the employed to obtain his services for less than they are worth; he summons in hunger and cold, and the sufferings of a dependent family, as advisers in helping to make an unrighteous bargain, and as sureties for its performance. Men, without any pecuniary resources which they can call their own, embark in hazardous speculations, where, if the rash adventure should chance to prove successful, they will pocket all the gain; but, should it turn out to be disastrous, their creditors must suffer all the loss.

In some of the commercial countries of Europe, a merchant's insolvency affects his moral character hardly less than his pecuniary credit. If a bankrupt cannot show that his deficiency of means was occasioned by some disaster which he could not control, or by some loss which he could not reasonably be expected to foresee, he forfeits his mercantile standing amongst honorable dealers, and can retrieve his character only by actual proof of returning or of newly-created honesty. A second failure, unexplained and unatoned for, brands with disgrace, and expels not more from the traffic than from the companionship of honorable men.

The above classes of wrong-doing, together with many others of a kindred nature, are regarded by the law as minor offences. Some of them it does not undertake to punish; yet, from their wide-spread prevalence and great frequency, they perhaps inflict as large an aggregate of evil upon society as those of a more heinous and formidable character, but of less frequent occurrence.

In regard to offences of a graver nature, — such as come under the head of crimes or felonies, — the condition of our country compares favorably with that of any other part of Christendom. Especially will this remark appear true if we consider the slight amount of preventive force made use of, in any part of our Union, to deter from actual transgression, and, as a general rule, the lightness of the penal sanctions held up as a terror to evil-doers. Yet that there does exist amongst us an appalling amount of criminality of this deeper dye; that flagrant offences against the rights of property, of person, of reputation, and of life, are perpetrated, — is proved by the records of our criminal courts, and by the mournful procession of convicts and felons whom we see on their way to our penitentiaries and other receptacles prepared for the guilty.

Including all classes of offenders, both the less and the more flagitious, it is undeniable that there exists amongst us a multitude of men, of whom it may be truly said, that it would be better for the community had they never been born, or had they died in childhood, before their propensities for evil had been developed, or before they had gone abroad to disturb the peace of society, and to destroy that sense of security which every honest man is entitled to feel. To thin the ranks of this host of enemies to the welfare of the race, or to cripple the evil energies of those who could not be wholly reclaimed, has been the object of philanthropists and sages from the beginning of time. Their efforts, however, have been expended a million-fold more upon the old than upon the young; and a million-fold more, also, in the way of punishment than of prevention.

Among the republics of ancient times, a few wise and sagacious men did clearly perceive the bearing of education upon character, and, of course, upon innocence and guilt, both personal and public; but among the masses of the people there never existed any settled and operative conviction of this truth: and not a single year can be pointed out in all their long annals, where a majority of those who held the reins of government, and framed the laws of the State, rose to any practical or even theoretic conception of the grand idea, that the vital intelligence or the stupidity, the integrity or the dishonesty, of the people at large, will be measured and bounded by the kind and degree of the education imparted to its children, just as the zones upon the earth's surface are measured and bounded by the amount of sun light which is shed upon them.*

In modern times, this relation of early education to adult character has been more clearly and generally recognized as being, what it truly, to a very great extent, is, a relation between cause and effect. As one means of establishing this truth, many earnest well-wishers of their race have made extensive collections of what are called the "Statistics of Education and Crime." The inmates of large penal establishments have been subjected to a personal examination in order to ascertain whether a greater proportion of them than of the community at large from which they were taken were wholly ignorant of letters. In this investigation, the comparison has been made between those who were able both to read and write, and those who could perform neither or but one of these operations.

I will not dwell here upon the amazing absurdity of any definition of the word "education," whose spirit or whose terms are satisfied by the mere ability to read and write. Reading and writing may be, and, among this class of persons, they usually are, mere mechanical processes: and how such attainments should ever have been dignified by the name of education, or confounded with that noble culture of the soul which pours the noon-day illumination of knowledge upon the midnight darkness of ignorance; which seeks to enthrone the moral faculties over all animal desires and propensities, and to make the entire course of instruction subservient to the great duties of love to God and love to man, — how an absurdity so extravagant, and now so obvious, could ever have been committed, can be explained only by reference to the low and unworthy ideas of education which once prevailed.

The naked capacity to read and write is no more education than a tool is a workman, or a telescope is a La Place or a Le Verrier. To possess the means of education is not the same as to possess the lofty powers and immunities of education, any more than to possess the pen of a poet is to possess a poet's skill and "faculty divine," or than the possession of the gospel is the possession of that liberty wherewith Christ maketh his disciples free; and that reading and writing are only instruments or means to be used in education is a truism now so intuitively obvious as to disdain argument. And hence it is, that of two persons, one of whom can barely write his name or spell out a paragraph in a newspaper, while to the mind of the other the contents of all manuscripts and of all libraries have no more existence than nonentity has to his senses, it would be hazardous to affirm that the chances of the former for a virtuous life are much superior to those of

* Even Marcus Aurelius declared himself satisfied if he could only improve a few persons; and he denied the possibility of establishing Plato's republic.

the latter. Nor do the best authorities dispel all the clouds of doubt which hang over this question. Some writers maintain that crime actually increases in proportion to the diffusion of the rudiments of knowledge, provided the knowledge which is diffused stops with mere rudiments. I think, however, it must be conceded that the preponderance of names and of statistical results does, on the whole, clearly favor the opinion, that crime recedes as knowledge advances; and that, as the full-risen sun enables a traveller to see his path, and to avoid the dangers that beset it, so the first and faintest gleaming of the morning twilight *helps* him to discover his way, and to shun its perils. It must also be remembered, that when great numbers are taken as the basis of comparison, all of whom possess the rudiments of knowledge, it will always happen that some of them will possess more than the rudiments. Hence, taking whole communities together, I believe the legitimate and inevitable conclusion to be, that every advance in knowledge amongst a people is *pro tanto* an invasion of the domain of crime.

For years past, however, although I have carefully scrutinized these so-called "Statistics of Education and Crime," and am convinced that they do establish a distinction between the two classes, — one of which can read and write, while the other can do neither of these things, or but one of them, — in regard to their relative exemption from crime or exposure to it, yet I have never been able to bring myself to present these schedules to our people as an argument in favor of that elevated and ennobling education to which it is their duty to aspire. I have felt, that, by so doing, the argument would be shorn of half its power by the feebleness of the proofs brought to sustain it. It would be like exhibiting a taper to prove the existence of light while surrounded by the sun's effulgence. Our present state of society, the form of government under which we live, the improvable faculties with which we have been endowed by our Maker, and the solemn destiny that awaits us, — all demand vastly more than "a knowledge of the nature and power of letters, and the just method of spelling words," and the mechanical ability to imitate, with a pen, their written or printed signs.

Yet this degrading idea of education, which was first conceived in reference to the ignorant classes of Europe, has been, to some extent, adopted and acted upon in our own country. The last census of the United States, taken by authority of a law of Congress, and in compliance with a provision of the Federal Constitution, proceeded upon this European fallacy. It virtually adopted the old line of distinction between education and ignorance; for it required an enumeration of all persons over twenty years of age who were unable to read and write. The results have been published, and they are now embodied with the permanent statistics of the country. Towns, counties, and states are classed; their condition is mentioned with honor or with opprobrium, according to their relative position above or below this absurd standard of knowledge and culture. It is inevitable that this legislative sanction of such a standard — this naturalization of it, so to speak — should have a most baneful effect in debasing public opinion upon the subject. Facts of an interesting nature are presented, it is true; but their tendency is to rob education of all its noblest attributes.

But though the public mind always tends strongly to conform its modes of thinking to legal definitions, and to subscribe to opinions sanctioned by high authority, yet the common sense of the community, especially in the more educated States of the Union, has outgrown these contracted notions, and has claimed for the word "education" a far ampler and loftier significance. All intelligent thinkers upon this subject now utterly discard and repudiate the idea that reading and writing, with a knowledge of accounts, constitute education. The lowest claim which any intelligent man now prefers in its behalf is, that its domain extends over the threefold nature of man, — over his body, training it by the systematic and intelligent observance of those benign laws which secure health, impart strength, and prolong life; over his intellect, invigorating the mind, replenishing it with knowledge, and cultivating all those tastes which are allied to virtue; and over his moral and religious susceptibilities also, dethroning selfishness, enthroning conscience, leading the affections outward in good-will towards men, and upward in gratitude and reverence to God. In thousands of reports prepared by school-committees, in frequent addresses and lectures delivered on public occasions, in all educational documents emanating from high official sources, and in every work pretending to scientific accuracy, or to any comprehensive outline of the subject, these sacred and majestic attributes have been set forth; and it has been demonstrated, hundreds of times over, that the effect of a sound education of the people must, not accidentally, but necessarily, not occasionally, but always, be to repress the commission of crime, and to promote the diffusion of human happiness; and that to act in conscious defiance or disregard of these truths is treachery to the best interests of our fellow-men, and impiety towards the Author of the moral universe.

But notwithstanding all that has been said, and so well said, as to the moral power of education in reforming the world, there have still been a vagueness and an indefiniteness *in regard to the extent of that power*, which have shorn argument and eloquence of much of their strength. Nowhere have its advocates set forth, distinctly and specifically, *how much* they believe can be accomplished by it. When an alleged improvement is presented to a judicious man, he wishes to know whether, and to what extent, its benefit will exceed its cost. A capitalist will not aid a new enterprise with his money until he is satisfied of the profitableness of the investment; nor will a manufacturer purchase new machinery unless he is convinced that it will do better work in the same time, or equal work in less.

It seems to me that the time is now arrived when the friends of this cause should plant themselves on a more conspicuous position; when, surveying the infinite of wretchedness and crime around them, before which the stoutest heart is appalled, and humanity stands aghast, they should proclaim the power and the prerogatives of education to rescue mankind from their calamities. Founding themselves upon evidence that cannot be disputed, and fortifying their conclusions by the results of personal experience, they should proclaim how far the miseries of men can be alleviated, and how far the dominion of crime can be overthrown, by such a system of education as it is perfectly practicable for every civilized community forthwith to establish; and thus they should awaken the conscience of the public to a sense of its responsibility.

The idea will be more distinctly presented under an inquiry like the following: —

Under the soundest and most vigorous system of education which we can now command, what proportion, or percentage, of all the children who are born, can be made useful and exemplary men, — honest dealers, conscientious jurors, true witnesses, incorruptible voters or magistrates, good parents, good neighbors, good members of society? In other words, with our present knowledge of the art and science of education, and with such new fruit of experience as time may be expected to bear, what proportion, or percentage, of all children, must be pronounced irreclaimable and irredeemable, notwithstanding the most vigorous educational efforts, which, in the present state of society, can be put forth in their behalf? what proportion, or percentage, must become drunkards, profane swearers, detractors, vagabonds, rioters, cheats, thieves, aggressors upon the rights of property, of person, of reputation, or of life; or, in a single phrase, must be guilty of such omissions of right, and commissions of wrong, that it would have been better for the community had they never been born? This is a problem which the course of events has evolved, and which society and the government must meet. If, with such educational means and resources as we can now command, eighty, ninety, ninety-five, or ninety-nine per cent of all children can be made temperate, industrious, frugal, conscientious in all their dealings, prompt to pity and instruct ignorance instead of ridiculing it and taking advantage of it, public-spirited, philanthropic, and observers of all things sacred; if, I say, any given proportion of our children, by human efforts, and by such a divine blessing as the common course of God's providence authorizes us to expect, can be made to possess these qualities, and to act from them, — then, just so far as our posterity shall fall below this practicable exemption from vices and crimes, and just so far as they shall fail to possess these attainable virtues, just so far will those who frame and execute our laws, shape public opinion, and lead public action, *be criminally responsible for the difference.* I can conceive of no moral proposition clearer than this. Society, in its collective capacity, is the possessor of all the knowledge, and the owner of all the property, in existence. Governments have been organized, and are invested with power, to use any needful amount of this property for purposes of education; and, by holding out adequate inducements and remuneration, they can command the services of the highest talent. Here, then, duty, and the means to perform it, come together. The only remaining question is, *How much can be done?* for, in a cause and for a purpose like this, nothing which can actually be done can be guiltlessly omitted. If it is proved, with a reasonable degree of certainty, that ninety-nine, ninety-five, ninety, eighty, or any other given percentage of all children can be rescued from vice and crime, and can be so educated and trained as to become valuable citizens, but the State refuses or declines to do this work, then the State itself becomes a culprit; and, before the great moral Judge who is seated on the throne of the universe, it must stand a spectacle of shame and guilt, like one of its own inferior culprits before its own judicial tribunals.

With these preliminary observations, which seemed to be necessary in order to a full exposition of the object I have in view, I proceed to submit the following specific inquiries, and to request your answer to them: —

1. How many years have you been engaged in school-keeping? and whether in the country, or in populous towns or cities?

2. About how many children have you had under your care? of which sex? and between what ages?

3. Should all our schools be kept by teachers of high intellectual and moral qualifications, and should all the children in the community be brought within these schools for ten months in a year, from the age of four to that of sixteen years, then what proportion, what percentage, of such children as you have had under your care, could, in your opinion, be so educated and trained, that their existence on going out into the world would be a benefit, and not a detriment, an honor, and not a shame, to society? Or, to state the question in a general form, if all children were brought within the salutary and auspicious influences I have here supposed, what percentage of them should you pronounce to be irreclaimable and hopeless? Of course, I do not speak of imbeciles or idiots, but only of rational and accountable beings.

You will perceive, that, in certain respects, I am supposing no change in the present condition of society. I am taking families as they now are, and am allowing all the unfavorable as well as the favorable influences of the old upon the young to continue to operate, at least for a time, as heretofore. Nor do I suppose any sudden or transforming change in co-operative or auxiliary institutions, — such as the Sabbath school, the pulpit, and so forth, — although it is certain that such a state of things as is here outlined would gradually impart new vigor to all that advances the progress of society, while it would impair the force of all that retards it.

On the other hand, however, I am supposing two great changes. I am supposing all our children to be placed under the care of such a class of men and women as we now honor by the appellation of first-class or first-rate teachers, — of such teachers as are able, in the schoolroom, both to teach and to govern; and who, out of the schoolroom, will be animated by a missionary spirit in furthering the objects of their sacred vocation. I have also supposed that *all* the children in the community shall be brought under the forming hands of such teachers, from the age of four to that of sixteen, for ten months in each year.

While, therefore, the above supposition leaves children exposed, in many cases, to the pernicious family and social influences under which they are now suffering, it assumes that all the children, when out of school, shall meet only such children as are enjoying the same high training, the same daily instillation of moral principles, as themselves. My supposition allows a continuance of the same family and adult influences (at least until these shall be supplanted by the better influences of the rising generation, action and re-action hastening results), because these influences are facts which no earthly power can cause to be immediately changed. But I have supposed this noble company of teachers, this length of schools, and this universality of attendance, because these are reforms on the present condition of things, which can be effected without any great delay, — at the farthest, a very few years being an ample allowance for the completion of such a change.

To reduce my third question, then, within its narrowest limits, and to make it as definite and precise as possible, suppose yourself to be stationed as a school-teacher in a place similar to any of those in which you have before labored; suppose yourself, too, to be surrounded by teachers fully as capable and as zealous in all respects as yourself; and suppose, further, that all the children are brought under your care or theirs, as above specified, — that is, for a period of twelve years, or from four to sixteen, and ten months in each year, — and will you then please to declare what proportion, or percentage, of those under your own care, you believe could be turned out the blessing, and not the bane, the honor, and not the scandal, of society? and on what proportion, or percentage, — the complement of the other, — would your experience compel you to pronounce the doom of hopelessness and irreclaimability?

Very truly and sincerely yours,
HORACE MANN.

I extract from the replies to this circular only the specific answers to the circular: —

LETTER FROM JOHN GRISCOM, Esq.

BURLINGTON, N.J., 8 mo. 27th, 1847.

MY ESTEEMED FRIEND,— . . . My belief is, that, under the conditions mentioned in the question, not more than two per cent would be irreclaimable nuisances to society, and that ninety-five per cent would be supporters of the moral welfare of the community in which they resided.

With teachers properly trained in normal schools, and with such a popular disposition towards schools as wise legislation might effect, nineteen-twentieths of the immoralities which afflict society might, I verily believe, be kept under hatches, or eradicated from the soil of our social institutions.

Every step in such a progress renders the next more easy. This is proved not only on the grand scale of comparing country with country, and state with state, but district with its adjacent district, and neighborhood with neighborhood.

Finally, in the predicament last stated in the circular, and supposing the teachers to be imbued with the gospel spirit, I believe there would not be more than *one-half of one per cent* of the children educated, on whom a wise judge would be "compelled to pronounce the doom of hopelessness and irreclaimability."

In nothing which I have advanced has it been my intention to advocate any sectarian instruction in our schools, or any thing adverse to the statutory limits of the Massachusetts school-system. I therefore expressly disavow any intention to recommend truths or doctrines, as part of the moral instruction to be given in public schools, which any believer in the Bible would reasonably deem to be sectarian.

I am, with true esteem, thy friend,

JNO. GRISCOM.

LETTER FROM D. P. PAGE, Esq.

STATE NORMAL SCHOOL, ALBANY, N.Y., Nov. 20, 1847.

HON. HORACE MANN.

Dear Sir,— . . . Could I be connected with a school furnished with all the appliances you name, where all the children should be constant attendants upon my instruction for a succession of years, where all my fellow-teachers should be such as you suppose, and where all the favorable influences described in your circular should surround me and cheer me, even with my moderate abilities as a teacher, I should scarcely expect, after the first generation of children submitted to the experiment, to fail, *in a single case*, to secure the results you have named.

. . . But I should not forgive myself, nor think myself longer fit to be a teacher, if, with all the aids and influences you have supposed, I should fail, in one case in a hundred, to rear up children who, when they should become men, would be "honest dealers, conscientious jurors, true witnesses, incorruptible voters or magistrates, good parents, good neighbors, good members of society;" or, as you express it in another place, who would be "temperate, industrious, frugal, conscientious in all their dealings, prompt to pity and instruct ignorance instead of ridiculing it and taking advantage of it, public-spirited, philanthropic, and observers of all things sacred;" and, negatively, who would *not be* "drunkards, profane swearers, detractors, vagabonds, rioters, cheats, thieves, aggressors upon the rights of property, of person, of reputation, or of life, or guilty of such omissions of right, and commissions of wrong, that it would be better for the community had they never been born."

With sincere regard, your friend,

D. P. PAGE.

LETTER FROM SOLOMON ADAMS, Esq.

BOSTON, Nov. 24, 1847.

HON. HORACE MANN.

My dear Sir, — . . . 1. I have been engaged in this profession twenty-four years; the first five years in the country, the remainder of the time in a city.

2. My whole number of pupils is a little below two thousand. The last nineteen years, my pupils have been females. Previously, both sexes.

If a well-conducted education produces benevolence, justice, truth, patriotism, love to God and love to man, in one case, the same education, in the same circumstances, will produce the same results in all cases. The results for which we look and labor sometimes fail, not because the great law of uniformity is at fault, but by reason of counteracting causes, which may escape our most careful scrutiny. Does the failure impair our confidence in the uniformity of moral causes and effects? The moment this law fails, every cord that binds society together is sundered; society is disintegrated. Every social enactment by which society attempts to regulate its members, every motive by which one man hopes to influence another, assumes this uniformity. It is the hinge on which all social influences turn. Without it, we could not shape moral means to moral ends. To destroy it, to *doubt* it, would be the moral unhingement of society.

In this great law are the teacher's hopes and encouragements. The great outline of the means he is to employ is well defined. It is his province to bring all those moral appliances to bear upon the soul which are suited to lead it into harmony with truth and with God, to train it to the perception and love of truth and goodness. In doing this, the faithful teacher is a co-worker with God, and may confidently look to the Author of all good to give the crowning blessing to his strenuous endeavors. There are those (and I confess myself of the number) who believe and feel that all human endeavors, unaided by an influence from on high, will prove fruitless, so far as the highest wants of the immortal spirit are concerned. Yet those who feel so can tell us of no way in which they are authorized to expect such an influence, and of no way in which it is exerted even by almighty power, except through the instrumentality of truth presented to the mind. There might as well be a conflagration without fire, or a flood without fluid.

I confess I do not see how our different theological views can essentially alter our modes of instruction. We are all to train the young in the way in which they should go, "giving line upon line, precept upon precept, here a little and there a little," waiting for and expecting precious fruit. The fruit may ripen slowly. From day to day, you may not be able to see any progress. This holds true both in moral and intellectual training. But, by comparing distant intervals, progress is perceptible. At length a result comes, which repays all the teacher's labor, and inspires new courage for new efforts. You ask for my own experience. This is my apology for alluding with freedom to myself. Permit me to say, that in very many cases, after laboring long with individuals almost against hope, and sometimes in a manner, too, which I can now see was not always wise, I have never had a case which has not resulted in some good degree according to my wishes. The many kind and voluntary testimonials given, years afterwards, by persons who remembered that they were once my wayward pupils, are among the pleasantest and most cheering incidents of my life. So uniform have been the results, when I have had a fair trial and time enough, that I have unhesitatingly adopted the motto, *Never despair*. Parents and teachers are apt to look for too speedy results from the labors of the latter. The moral nature, like the intellectual and physical, is long and slow in reaching the full maturity of its strength. I was told, a few years since, by a gentleman who knew the history of nearly all my pupils for the first five years of my labor, that not one of them had ever brought reproach upon himself, or mortification upon friends, by a bad life. I cannot now look over the whole list of my pupils, and find one, who had been with me long enough to receive a decided impression, whose life is not honorable and useful. I find them in all the learned professions, and in the various mechanical arts. I find my female pupils scattered as teachers through half the States of the Union, and as the wives and assistants of Christian missionaries in every quarter of the globe.

So far, therefore, as my own experience goes, so far as my knowledge of the experience of others extends, so far as the statistics of crime throw any light on the subject, I should confidently expect that ninety-nine in a hundred, and I think even more, with such means of education as you have supposed, and with such divine favor as we are authorized to expect, would become good members of society, the supporters of order and law, and truth and justice, and all righteousness.

That I may not be misunderstood, allow me to add a few explanatory remarks.

I have no confidence in the reformatory power of education into which moral and religious influences do not enter. I assume, — as any one having the slightest acquaintance with your writings and teachings on this subject knows that you do, — that the three great classes of powers, the physical, intellectual, and moral, shall each receive its proper training; and then I feel authorized to look confidently for that providential blessing which will secure the high results already alluded to. Without such a training, I have no right to expect the blessing of Heaven, or a good result. I do not fulfil the conditions on which such results are promised.

It is to be feared, yea, to be for a lamentation, that comparatively few of teachers, and still fewer of the community, have looked upon a school-education as any thing more than a very limited intellectual training, leaving physical and moral culture to take care of themselves. The school-laws of Massachusetts have always contemplated other attainments and vastly higher ends. Yet it so happens, that that part of the law has been best remembered and acted on which speaks of reading, writing, and the elements of arithmetic. These have been insisted on chiefly with reference to their direct application to the business and traffic of life; as if it were the chief end of man to count coppers, pocket them, and keep them. While the law contemplates these elementary attainments as merely the beginnings and inlets to all the treasures of wisdom, how many have looked upon them as *the education* of the boy and the man!

Very truly your obedient friend and servant,

S. ADAMS.

LETTER FROM REV. JACOB ABBOTT.

NEW-YORK CITY, June 25, 1847.

HON. HORACE MANN.

Dear Sir, — ... 1. I have been engaged in the practical duties of teaching for about ten years, chiefly in private schools in Boston and New York.

2. I have had under my care, for a longer or shorter time, probably nearly eight hundred pupils. They have been of both sexes, and of all ages, from four to twenty-five.

3. If all our schools were under the charge of teachers possessing what I regard as the right intellectual and moral qualifications, and if all the children of the community were brought under the influence of these schools for ten months in the year, I think that the work of training up *the whole community* to intelligence and virtue would soon be accomplished, as completely as any human end can be obtained by human means.

I do not think, however, that, so far as the formation of the habits of virtue in the young is concerned, the accomplishment of the result depends either upon the intellectual powers or attainments of the teacher, or upon the amount of formal moral instructions which he gives his pupils. Knowledge alone has but little tendency to affect the feelings and principles of the heart; and formal moral instructions, except as auxiliaries to other influences, have very little power, according to my experience, over the consciences and characters of the young.

The true power of the teacher in giving to his pupils good characters in future life seems to me to lie in his forming them to *the practice of virtue*, while under his charge, by the influence of *his own personal character and actions*. To do this, however, he must have the right character himself. He must be governed in all that he does by high and honorable principles of action. He must be really benevolent and kind. He must take an honest interest in his pupils, — not merely in their studies and general characters, but in all their childish thoughts and feelings, in the difficulties they encounter, in their temptations and trials, in their sports, in their contentions, in their troubles; in every thing, in fact, that affects them. He must, in a word, feel a strong interest and sympathy for them in the thousand difficulties and discouragements they must encounter in slowly finding their way, with all their ignorance and inexperience, to their place in the complicated and bewildering maze of human life.

A teacher who takes this sort of interest in his pupils will *understand* them and *sympathize* with them in a way which will at once command their kind regard, and give him a powerful, and, in the view of others, a very mysterious, ascendency over their minds. They feel as if he was upon their side, taking their part, as it were, against the difficulties and dangers and troubles which surround them. Thus he becomes one of them, a sharer in their enjoyments, a partaker of their feelings. They come to him with confidence. He plans their amusements, he joins them in conversation, he settles their disputes. They see on what principles he acts; and they *catch*, themselves, the same mode of action from him by a kind of sympathy. They imbibe his sentiments insensibly and spontaneously, not because he enunciates them, or proves them in lectures, but because he exhibits them in living reality in his conversation and conduct. This sort of sympathetic action between heart and heart has far greater influence among all mankind than formal teachings and exhortations. It is the life and spirit of virtue in contradistinction from the letter and the form.

. . . If all the children of this land were under the charge of such teachers for six hours in the day, and ten months in the year, and were to continue under these influences for the usual period of instruction in schools, I do not see why the result would not be, that, in two generations, substantially the whole population would be trained up to virtue, to habits of integrity, fidelity in duty, justice, temperance, and mutual good-will. It seems to me that this effect would take place in all cases, except where extremely unfavorable influences out of school should counteract it; which, I think, would hardly be the case, except in some districts in the more populous cities.

I am, very respectfully, yours,

JACOB ABBOTT.

LETTER FROM F. A. ADAMS, Esq.

ORANGE, N.J., Dec. 11, 1847.

HON. HORACE MANN.

Dear Sir,—. . . I do not hesitate to express the conviction that there is no agency which society can exert, through the government, capable of exerting so great a moral influence for the rising generation as the steady training of the young in the best schools.

In reply to the specific inquiry, in your circular, what proportion of our youth would probably, under the advantages of schooling presupposed in the circular, fail of fulfilling honorably their social and moral obligations in society, I would say, that in the course of my experience, for ten years, in teaching between three and four hundred children, mostly boys, I have been acquainted with not more than two pupils in regard to whom I should not feel a cheerful and strong confidence in the success of the proposed experiment. In regard to these two cases, I should not despair, but should have a strong preponderance of fear, that, under the best influences such as you have supposed, they would still remain wedded to low and mischievous habits. From their peculiar temperament, there was much reason to suppose that a life of steady and hard labor would do for them much, in a moral point of view, which the influences of school could not accomplish.

The class of youth I have had under my care would, in some respects, afford a better than average chance for the success of the experiment, as they, in all cases, have been exempt from the evils of poverty. In other respects, however, this exemption was counterbalanced by habits of self-indulgence, which could not have existed had the pecuniary means been wanting.

I remain, dear sir, with sincere respect and esteem, yours,

F. A. ADAMS.

LETTER FROM E. A. ANDREWS, Esq.

NEW BRITAIN, CONN., Dec. 8, 1847.

HON. HORACE MANN.

Dear Sir,—... In reply to your first and second questions, permit me simply to remark, that I have been connected with the department of education, either as pupil or as teacher, for more than fifty years. I have instructed both in the country and in cities: in the former I have, for the most part, had the charge of only a few select pupils; in the latter, for about twenty years, I was connected with large institutions of instruction. I have no means of determining, with any tolerable approach to accuracy, the whole number of my pupils, nor the proportion of each sex.

I do not hesitate to express my conviction, that such an education as your question supposes, continued for so long a period as twelve years, and including all the children of the community, would remove a very large portion of the evils with which society is now burdened. I need not say, that I would be far from attributing so important results to any system of merely intellectual training, or even to the most perfect combination of intellectual, physical, and moral discipline, to the exclusion of that which is strictly religious. Such a qualification of my meaning might have been necessary, on account of the limited sense in which the word "education" is often used, had not the necessity been removed by the express terms of the conditions annexed to the question in your circular.

It may indeed be feared that society is not yet fully prepared to put forth the effort necessary to accomplish so desirable a result; but I cannot believe that the time is very remote when its attainment will be considered an object of paramount importance. It cannot be that the millions of intelligent men found in this and in other Christian countries can much longer permit their feelings to be enlisted, and the resources of the communities to which they belong to be employed, in promoting objects of far inferior value, while the advantages of a good system of general education are, in so great a degree, overlooked. If, as I fully believe, it is in the power of the people of any State, by means so simple as your question supposes, and so completely in their own power as these obviously are, so to change the whole face of society in a single generation that scarcely one or two per cent of really incorrigible members shall be found in it, it cannot be that so great a good will continue to be neglected, and the means for its attainment unemployed.

In forming our estimate of the probability of so important a result as I have supposed, it must not be forgotten, that, simple as are the means now proposed for its attainment, they have never been employed, so far as I know, in any extended community whose experience is on record. In Scotland, and of late in Prussia, a considerable approximation has been made towards reaching the supposed conditions, and with benefits, it is believed, fully corresponding with the degree of perfection of their respective systems. The common schools of New England, which have done so much to elevate her character, have still fallen immeasurably short of the conditions supposed. With all their acknowledged defects, however, the instances, I believe, are few, in which those who have been trained in them, from childhood to the close of the period usually allotted to education in these schools, have afterwards, on mingling with the world, proved to be incorrigibly vicious, a burden rather than a benefit to society. The records of our criminal courts and the doors of our penitentiaries have seldom been opened to those who, in childhood, had been in regular daily attendance for ten or twelve years upon the exercises of our common schools, however imperfect these schools may have been in their organization, and notwithstanding all the evil influences of uneducated associates to which the pupils have been exposed when out of school. The cell of the convict has, on the contrary, been almost uniformly occupied by those who have enjoyed few of the benefits of our common schools; and even the tenants of our poorhouses, it is believed, have, in most instances, belonged to the same unfortunate class.

Very truly yours,

E. A. ANDREWS.

LETTER FROM ROGER S. HOWARD, Esq.

THETFORD, VT., Sept. 1, 1847

HON. HORACE MANN.

Dear Sir, — . . . Judging from what I have seen and do know, if the conditions you have mentioned were strictly complied with; if the attendance of the scholars could be as universal, constant, and long-continued as you have stated; if the teachers were men of those high intellectual and moral qualities, — apt to teach, and devoted to their work, and favored with that blessing which the word and providence of God teach us always to expect on our honest, earnest, and well-directed efforts in so good a cause,

— on these conditions, and under these circumstances, I do not hesitate to express the opinion, that the failures need not be, would not be, one per cent. Else what is the meaning of that explicit declaration of the Bible, "Train up a child in the way he should go; and, when he is old, he will not depart from it"?

I am aware that the opinion I have expressed above may by some be considered extravagant. But I have not formed or expressed it without deliberation. During all my experience as a teacher, I have never known the scholar, whom, if brought within the reach of these salutary and auspicious influences for the length of time named, I should now be willing to believe, or dare to pronounce, utterly hopeless and irreclaimable. I do not mean to say that I never failed. But I do say, that in some of the most difficult and desperate cases I have ever met with, as a teacher, the result of direct, special, and persevering effort, was such as to create the conviction, that with more zeal, patience, and perseverance, and especially with the favoring influences above alluded to, success would have been certain and complete. And this conviction became more settled and strong the longer I continued to teach.

The power of a truly enlightened and Christian system of common-school education is but little understood and appreciated. When parents shall begin to feel, as they ought, its importance; when the community generally shall be willing to make the necessary efforts and sacrifices; and when teachers of the requisite literary qualifications, and of high moral aims, shall enter upon the work with a martyr's zeal, conscious that every day they are making deathless impressions upon immortal minds, — then shall we see, as I believe, results which will greatly surpass the highest expectations of the most ardent and enthusiastic advocates of popular education.

But I am occupying more space than I intended, and will only add that I am, dear sir,

Very respectfully and truly yours,

ROGER S. HOWARD.

LETTER FROM MISS CATHERINE E. BEECHER.

BRATTLEBOROUGH, Aug. 20, 1847.

HON. HORACE MANN.

Dear Sir, — In reference to the questions you propose, I would reply, that I have been engaged, directly and personally, as a teacher, about fifteen years, in Hartford, Conn., and Cincinnati, O. I have had a few classes of quite young children under my care for the purpose of making some practical educational experiments; but most of my pupils, in age, have ranged from twelve to twenty. I have had pupils from every State in the Union; and, though I have no precise records, I think the number cannot be less than a thousand.

I have ever considered *intellectual* culture as subordinate to the main end of education, which is the formation of that character which Jesus Christ teaches to be indispensable to the *eternal* well-being of our race. Excepting the few classes of young children before named, my efforts have been directed to measures for reforming bad and supplying good habits and principles in minds already more or less developed by education. And this I consider a much more difficult work than the right training of minds as yet uninjured by pernicious influences.

In reference to the work of reforming miseducated minds, I have found that the noblest-constructed minds, when greatly mismanaged, are most liable to become the worst; while, at the same time, they most readily yield to reformatory measures: so that, as a general rule, with exceptions, of course, I should expect to do the most good to the worst class of pupils, and, in some cases, to make finer characters from this class than from those who, possessing less excitable temperaments, have not fallen so far.

I would also remark, that, in the results I should anticipate in the case to be supposed hereafter, my *chief* hope of success would rest on the *proper* application of those truths and motives which distinguish the *teachings of Jesus Christ* from what is called "*natural religion;*" and by modes of presentation more simple and practical than I have ever seen fully adopted, or than I ever adopted myself when a practical teacher.

With these preliminaries, which I hope will be carefully pondered, and borne in mind as indispensable, I will now suppose that it could be so arranged, that in a given place, containing from ten to fifteen thousand inhabitants, in any part of our country where I ever resided, *all* the children at the age of four shall be placed, six hours a day, for twelve years, under the care of teachers having the same views that I have, and having received that course of training for their office that any State in this Union can secure to the teachers of its children. Let it be so arranged, that all these children shall remain till sixteen under these teachers, and also that they shall spend their lives in this city; and I have no hesitation in saying, I do not believe that *one*, no, *not a single one*, would fail of proving a respectable and prosperous member of society: nay, more, I believe every one would, at the close of life, find admission into the world of endless peace and love. I say this solemnly, deliberately, and with the full belief that I am upheld by such imperfect experimental trials as I have made, or seen made by others; but, more than this, that I am sustained by the authority of Heaven, which sets forth this grand palladium of education, — "*Train up a child in the way he should go ; and, when he is old, he will not depart from it."*

This sacred maxim surely presents the divine *imprimatur* to the doctrine that *all* children can be trained up in the way they should go, and that, when so trained, they will not depart from it. Nor does it imply that education *alone* will secure eternal life, without supernatural assistance ; but it points to the true method of securing this indispensable aid.

In this view of the case, I can command no language strong enough to express my infinite longings that my countrymen, who, as legislators, have the control of the institutions, the laws, and the wealth of our *physically* prosperous nation, should be brought to see that they now have in their hands the power of securing to *every* child in the coming generation a life of virtue and usefulness here, and an eternity of perfected bliss hereafter. How, then, can I express or imagine the awful responsibility which rests upon them, and which hereafter they must bear before the great Judge of nations, if they suffer the present state of things to go on, bearing, as it does, thousands and hundreds of thousands of helpless children in our country to hopeless and irretrievable ruin ?

Respectfully yours,
C. E. BEECHER.

P. S. — All I anticipate, as stated in my communication, may come to pass without any departure from your statutory regulations in regard to religious instruction, *as I understand these statutes*, and as I suppose them to be understood by the great body of those who formed them, and of those who are bound by them.   C. E. B.

The above answers are not choice specimens selected from among many ; they are all I have received : and every person to whom the circular was sent was pleased to answer it. From conversations held at different times with many other teachers, I believe the *amount* of testimony might have been very much increased, though no confirmation can be needed of its *authority*. The witnesses here introduced certainly possess all the requisites to entitle them to implicit credence. Their character for honor and veracity repels the idea of distrust. Years of experience in different places, and the training of children in great numbers, qualify them, in point of knowledge, to speak with authority ; and they are exempt from any imaginable bias to warp or to color the truth.

From time immemorial, it has been customary for parliaments and other legislative bodies to commit important practical subjects to committees, and, through their instrumentality, to obtain the testimony of learned and skilled men on the matter of inquiry. Sometimes witnesses are heard at the bar of the House, — that is, before the legislative body by whom the inquiry was instituted. Now, I have desired in the present case to introduce testimony of such credibility and cogency, that no legislative committee could report against it, and no legislative body could act against it, without incurring an historic odium, either for want of intelligence or want of integrity.

So, too, by the rules of the "common law," all questions of fact are decided by the intervention of a jury. In ancient times, when the character of juries was very different from what it now is, they sometimes gave a corrupt verdict, — that is, a verdict so contradictory to evidence as to be of itself proof that they had discarded the testimony adduced, and been governed by some dishonest motive in their own breasts. A jury convicted of this offence was said to be "*attainted:*" its members were punished by a fine, and rendered infamous ever after. It was my intention, in the present case, to introduce evidence of such authority and directness, as, if submitted to a jury and rejected by them, would, under the ancient law referred to, subject them to the penalties of an "*attaint.*"

There is one quality or characteristic common to all the witnesses whose testimony is above introduced, which, as it seems to me, I am not only justified in stating, but which it would be inexcusable to withhold. All of them, without exception, are well-known believers in a theological creed, one of whose fundamental articles is *the depravity of the natural heart*. They hold, in a literal sense and with regard to all mankind, that the innate affections or dispositions of the soul are "not subject to the law of God, neither indeed can be," until another influence, emanating from the Godhead, and equal in itself to an act of creation, shall have renewed them. With this private belief of the witnesses, of course, neither the Board of Education, nor any man or body of men, have aught to do, — unless, indeed, it be to affirm their right to hold it, in common with every other man's right either to agree with them or to dissent from them. But, as bearing upon the point under consideration, the fact is most important : it adds great cogency to their testimony, and invests it, as it were, with a compulsory power. For if those who believe that the human heart is by nature alienated from God, that its innate relation to the Holy One is that of natural repulsion, and not of natural attraction, nor even of neutrality, — if they, from their own experience in the education of youth, believe that our common-school system, under certain practicable modifications, can rear up a generation of men who will practise towards their fellow-men whatsoever things are true, honest, just, pure, lovely, and of good report, — then, surely, a rational community can need no additional evidence or motive to impel it to the work of reform. And all those, if such there are, who believe that moral evil comes from the abuse or misuse of powers in themselves good, and not from any inborn and original predilection for wrong, may well take courage, and may tender their heartiest co-operation in furthering an enterprise, which, even under fundamental postulates the most adverse, promises results so glorious. If they who believe that there is a principle of evil in the human soul, lying back of consciousness, incorporated as an original element into its constitution, beginning to be when the spirit itself began to be, and growing with it through all the primordial stages of its growth, — which, indeed, belongs to the ante-natal period of every descendant of Adam as much as spottedness belongs to an unborn leopard before it has a skin, or venom to an unhatched cockatrice before it has a sting, — if those who believe this do nevertheless believe that our common-school system, with certain practicable modifications, can send out redeeming and transforming influences which shall expel ninety-nine hundredths of all the vices and crimes under which society now mourns and agonizes, then those who dissent from the belief that the natural heart is thus organically intractable and perverse will be all the more ready to proclaim the ameliorating power of education, and will all the more earnestly labor for its diffusion. And the crowning beauty of the whole is, that Christian men of every faith may cordially unite in carrying forward the work of reform, however various may be their opinions as to the cause which has made that work necessary; just as all good citizens may unite in extinguishing a conflagration, though there may be a hundred conflicting opinions as to the means or the men that kindled it. In short, it may be difficult to determine which class will act under the more conscience-moving motives, — those who hold to a total depravity or corruption of the human heart, but still believe it can be emancipated from worldly vices and crimes by such instrumentalities as we can readily command; or those who hold that heart to be naturally capable of good as well as evil, and who therefore believe, not only that a still larger proportion of the race can be rescued from the dominion of wrong-doing, but that a consummation so glorious can be reached at a still earlier period, and with a less expenditure of effort.

But this divine result of staying the desolating torrent of practical iniquity by drying up its fountain-head in the bosoms of the young is promised only on the antecedence or performance of certain prescribed conditions. These conditions are the three following: —

1. That the public schools shall be conducted *on the cardinal principles of the present New-England systems.*

2. That they shall all be taught, for a period of ten months in each year, by persons of high intellectual and moral qualifications; or, in other words, that all the teachers shall be equal in capacity and in character to those whom we now call first-class or first rate teachers. And,

3. That all the children in the Commonwealth shall attend school regularly — that is, for the ten months each year during which they are kept — from the age of four to that of sixteen years.

As it is on the performance of these conditions that the renovation of society is predicated, it is, of course, necessary to show that they are practicable conditions. I therefore proceed to consider, and, as I trust, to establish, their practicability.

I. The first condition — namely, that the schools shall be conducted on the cardinal principles of the New-England systems — is already satisfied. The Massachusetts school-system represents favorably the systems of all the New-England States. Not one of them has an element of prosperity or of permanence, of security against decay within, or the invasion of its rights from without, which ours does not possess. Our law requires that a school shall be sustained in every town in the State, — even the smallest and the poorest not being excepted; and that this school shall be as open and free to all the children as the light of day or the air of heaven. No child is met on the threshold of the schoolhouse-door, to be asked for money, or whether his parents are native or foreign, whether or not they pay a tax, or what is their faith. The schoolhouse is common property. All about it are enclosures and hedges, indicating private ownership, and forbidding intrusion; but here is a spot which even rapacity dares not lay its finger upon. The most avaricious would as soon think of monopolizing the summer cloud, as it comes floating up from the west to shed its treasures upon the thirsty earth, as of monopolizing these fountains of knowledge. Public opinion — that sovereign in representative governments — is in harmony with the law. Not unfrequently there is some private opposition, and occasionally it avows itself, and assumes an attitude of hostility; but perseverance on the part of the friends of progress always subdues it, and the success of their measures eventually shames it out of existence.

The law requires all public schools to be kept by a teacher whose literary and moral qualifications have been examined and approved by a committee chosen for the purpose by the people themselves. Not less than the six following branches of knowledge are to be taught in every town; namely, orthography, reading, writing, English grammar, geography and arithmetic. The teaching of "good behavior," which includes all the courtesies of life and all the minor morals, is also expressly enjoined. These peremptory requisitions are the *minimum*, but not the *maximum*. Any town may enlarge the course of studies to be pursued in its schools as much as it may choose, even to the preparation of young men for the university, or for any branch of educated labor. It may also bestow an equivalent education upon the other sex. The law also contains a further provision (subject, however, to be set aside by the *express* vote of a district or town), that, in every school of more than fifty scholars in regular attendance, an assistant teacher shall be employed. Although there is no statutory provision to this effect in any other of the New-England States, yet the good sense of the community everywhere advocates this rule.

Nor are the needs of the intellect alone provided for. In prescribing the education to be given to the moral nature, the law grows more earnest and impressive. Its beautiful and deep-toned language is, "It shall be the duty of the president, professors, and tutors of the University at Cambridge, and of the several colleges, and of all preceptors and teachers of academies, and all other instructors of youth, to exert their best endeavors to impress on the minds of children and youth committed to their care and instruction the principles of piety, justice, and a sacred regard to truth, love to their country, humanity, and universal benevolence, sobriety, industry, and frugality, chastity, moderation, and temperance, and those other virtues which are the ornament of human society, and the basis upon which a republican constitution is founded; and it shall be the duty of such instructors to endeavor to lead their pupils, as their ages and capacities will admit, into a clear understanding of the tendency of the above-mentioned virtues to preserve and perfect a republican constitution, and secure the blessings of liberty, as well as to promote their future happiness, and also to point out to them the evil tendency of the opposite vices." But lest any individual, or body of individuals, forgetful of the divine precept to do unto others as they would be done unto, should seize upon this statutory injunction, or upon some part of it, as a pretext for turning the schools into proselytizing institutions, the law rears a barrier against all sectarian encroachments. That which is "calculated to favor the tenets of any particular sect of Christians" is excluded from the schools. The use of the Bible in schools is not expressly enjoined by the law, but both its letter and its spirit are in consonance with that use; and, as a matter of fact, I suppose there is not, at the present time, a single town in the Commonwealth in whose schools it is not read. Whoever, therefore, believes in the Sacred Scriptures, has his belief, in form and in spirit, in the schools; and his children read and hear *the words themselves* which contain it. The administration of this law is intrusted to the local authorities in the respective towns. By introducing the Bible, they introduce what all its believers hold to be the rule of faith and practice; and although, by excluding theological systems of human origin, they may exclude a peculiarity which one denomination believes to be true, they do but exclude what other denominations believe to be erroneous. Such is the present policy of our law for including what all Christians hold to be right, and for excluding what all, excepting some one party, hold to be wrong.

If it be the tendency of all parties and sects to fasten the mind upon what is peculiar to each, and to withdraw it from what is common to all, these provisions of the law counterwork that tendency. They turn the mind towards that which produces harmony, while they withdraw it from sources of discord; and thus, through the medium of our schools, that song which ushered in the Christian era — "Peace on earth and good-will to men" — may be taken up and continued through the ages.

The first condition, then, not only *may be*, but actually *is*, complied with in the school-system of Massachusetts, as now established and administered.

II. The second condition requires that all our schools shall be kept, for ten months in each year, by persons of high intellectual and moral qualifications, — by persons equal in capacity and in character to those whom we now call first-class or first-rate teachers.

This condition supposes two things, which, as yet, we are very far from having attained. The question is, Are they attainable?

In regard to teachers, it supposes such an improvement as shall advance all those who are now behind what we call the front rank, until they shall come upon a line with it. Of course, if this be done, some will be found in advance of this line; for it never can happen with regard to all the members of any profession, that they will stand precisely abreast. It supposes, also, that all our schools shall be kept for ten months each year.

The questions, then, for consideration under this head, are two; namely: —

1. Is there, in the community at large, sufficient natural endowment or capacity, from which, by appropriate training and cultivation, the requisite number of teachers, possessing the supposed qualifications, can be prepared? And,

2. Can the towns and the State, separately or as copartners, bear the expense of maintaining the required class of teachers for the required length of time?

Is not the first question answered in the affirmative by observation and experience? For the last two generations, with exceptions comparatively few, all the eminent men of our State, whether men of letters, physicians, lawyers, clergymen, legislators, or judges, have taught school, more or less, during the early part of their lives. Now, it is no disparagement to say, respecting those who constitute at present our best class of teachers, that they are not superior in endowments or natural capacity, in industry, or in versatility of genius, to a vast number of their predecessors, who, having labored for a limited period in this field, at length abandoned it in quest of some other occupation, truly known to be more lucrative, and falsely supposed to be more honorable. It is no unauthorized assumption, then, to say, that great numbers of those who left the employment of school-keeping for something deemed to be more eligible, would, had they continued in it, have won the honor of standing in the foremost rank of this noble profession.

In the second place, to prove that there is no lack of natural talent in existence from which to form the supposed class of teachers, I may refer to the general history and experience of mankind in all other departments of human effort. No new calling has ever reached such an elevation as to insure honor and emolument to its professors, which has not, without delay, attracted to itself an adequate number of followers. Witness the intrinsically odious profession of arms, — a profession so odious, that those have been held worthy of especial reward who resisted the natural love of ease, and instincts of self-preservation, to encounter its hardships and perils. So, also, has it been in regard to commerce and the useful arts. And in those truly dignified and honorable professions, — the legal and clerical, — where mind is the object to be acted upon, as well as the agent to act, the supply has generally exceeded the demand. Now, could the business of education take its stand in public estimation by the side of the most honorable and lucrative callings in life, we are authorized by all the experience of mankind to conclude that it would soon cluster around itself an amount of talent, erudition, and genius, at least equal to what has ever adorned any other avocation among civilized men.

But, independently of personal knowledge and of historic experience, may not a conclusive argument in support of the general position be drawn from the energy and versatility with which, as we all know, Nature has gifted the minds of her children? In the variety and strength of the capacities belonging to the race, there must be the means or instruments by which Providence can accomplish every good work. Somewhere in each generation, the powers exist by which the generation that is to succeed it may be advanced another stage along the radiant pathway of improvement. But in the whole of the past history of the world, no generation has yet existed, whose faculties have not, to a very great extent, lain dormant, — to say nothing of the perversion of those which have been developed. But our free institutions cherish growth. The future, with us, is not to be measured by the past. The mind of the masses, which for so many ages had been crippled, and fettered after it was crippled, is here unbound. Under the stimulus applied to native vigor, talent and genius start up as naturally as vegetation in the spring. The desire of bettering one's condition springs from a universal instinct in the human mind. With us, every man sees that the gratification of this desire is within his reach. Including the lifetime of a single generation, — that is, within the last forty or fifty years, — there is not a school-district in Massachusetts, however obscure, which has shown any interest in the character of its schools, that has not sent out one or more men who have become conspicuous in some of the honorable positions of society. They are found throughout the Union, wherever enterprise or talent is rewarded. Those districts, and, still more, those towns, where common schools have been an object of special regard, have sent forth many such men. While visiting different parts of the State for the last ten years, facts, in sufficient numbers to make a most interesting and instructive book, have come to my knowledge. showing that those districts and towns, where special pains have been exerted and special liberality bestowed in behalf of common schools, have supplied a proportion of all the distinguished men of the vicinity, corresponding with the superior excellence of the early education afforded them. So, on the other hand, neglectful towns and districts have been comparatively barren of eminent men. The great ears of corn will not grow on sandhills. Great men will not spring up in an atmosphere void of intellectual nutrition. Nature observes a law in this respect, in regard to her spiritual as well as her physical productions. Now, although something has been done in Massachusetts for the culture and expansion of the common mind, yet indefinitely more may be done. Even were it admitted, therefore, that the State had not been able in past times to supply the requisite number of teachers of the highest grade, it would by no means follow that she could not do so in future.

The intrinsically noble profession of teaching has, most unfortunately, been surrounded by an atmosphere of repulsion rather than of attraction. Young men of talent are generally determined by two things in selecting an employment for life. The first of these is the natural tendency of the mind, — its predisposition towards one pursuit rather than towards another. In this way, Nature often predetermines what a man shall do; and, to make her purpose inevitable, she kneads it, as it were, into the stamina of his existence. She does not content herself with standing before his will, soliciting or tempting him to a particular course, but she stands behind the will, guiding and propelling it; so that from birth he seems to be projected towards his object like a well-aimed arrow to its mark. Those in whom the love of beautiful forms, colors, and proportions, predominates, are naturally won to the cultivation of the fine arts, or to some branch of the useful arts most congenial to the fine. Those who have a great fondness for botany and chemistry, and to whom physiological inquiries are especially grateful, become physicians. Persons enamoured of forensic contests, roused by their excitements, and panting for the *éclat* which their victories confer, betake themselves to the study of the law, and become advocates. The clerical profession is composed of men whose minds are deeply imbued and penetrated with the religious sentiment, and who ponder profoundly and devoutly upon the solemn concerns of an hereafter.* This constitutional or moral affinity for one sphere of employment rather than for another predetermines many minds in choosing the object of their pursuit for life. It is like the elective attractions of the chemist, existing beforehand, and only awaiting the contiguity of the related substances to make their secret affinities manifest.

---

* This general remark must be taken with the exception of a few of the very worst men which any age ever produces. These become members of the clerical profession, because, under the mask of its sanctity, they hope to practise their iniquities with impunity.

But this natural tendency is often subjected to a disturbing or modifying force; and it yields to this force the more readily as it is itself less intense and dominant. All minds have a desire, more or less energetic, for pleasure, for wealth, for honor, or for some of that assemblage of rewards which obtains such willing allegiance from mankind. Hence the internal, inborn impulse is often diverted from the specific object to which it naturally points, and is lured away to another object, which, from some collateral or adventitious reason, promises a readier gratification.

There is also a class of minds of vigorous and varied capacities, which stand nearly balanced between different pursuits, and which, therefore, may be turned, by slight circumstances, in any one of many directions. They are like fountains of water rising on a table-land, whose channels may be so cut as to cover either of its slopes with fertility.

Now, the qualities which predispose their possessor to become the companion, guide, and teacher of children, are good sense, lively religious sensibilities, practical, unaffected benevolence, a genuine sympathy with the young, and that sunny, genial temperament which always sees its own cheerfulness reflected from the ever-open mirror of a child's face. The slightest exercise of good sense makes it apparent that any one year of childhood will exert a more decisive control over future destiny than any ten years afterwards. The religious and benevolent elements seize instinctively upon the promise made to those who train up children in the way they should go. The love of children casts a pleasing illusion over the mind in regard to every thing they do, — if, indeed, it be an illusion, and not a truth above the reach of the intellect, — elevating their puerile sports into dignity, hailing each step in their progress as though it were some grand discovery in science, and grieving over their youthful wanderings or backslidings with as deep a sorrow as is felt for the turpitude of a full-grown man, or for the heaven-defying sins of a nation. So that genial, joyous, ever-smiling temperament, which sees only rainbows where others see clouds, and which is delighted by the reflection of itself when coming from one child's face, will never tire of its labors when the same charming image perpetually comes back from the multiplying glasses of group after group of happy children, — ever-varying, but always beautiful.

Now, I think we have abundant reason to believe that a sufficient number of persons, bearing from the hand of Nature this distinctive image and superscription of a school-teacher, are born into the world with every generation. But the misfortune is, that when they arrive at years of discretion, and begin to survey the various fields of labor that lie open before them, they find that the noblest of them all, and the one, too, for which they have the greatest natural predilection, is neither honored by distinction nor rewarded by emolument. They see, that, if they enter it, many of their colleagues and associates will be persons with whom they have no congeniality of feeling, and who occupy a far less elevated position in the social scale than that to which their own aspirations point. If they go through the whole country, and question every man, they cannot find a single public-school teacher who has acquired wealth by the longest and the most devoted life of labor. They cannot find one who has been promoted to the presidency of a college, or to a professorship in it; nor one who has been elected or appointed to fill any distinguished civil station. Hence, in most cases, the adventitious circumstances which surround the object of their preference repel them from it. Or, if they enter the profession, it is only for a brief period, and for some collateral purpose; and, when their temporary end is gained, they sink it still lower by their avowed or well-understood reasons for abandoning it. Such is the literal history of hundreds and of thousands who have shone or are now shining in other walks of life, but who would have shone with beams more far creative of human happiness had they not been struck from the sphere for which Nature pre-adapted them.

Look at the average rate of wages paid to teachers in some of the pattern States of the Union. In Maine, it is $15.40 per month to males, and $4.80 to females. In New Hampshire, it is $13.50 per month to males, and $5.65 to females. In Vermont, it is $12.00 per month to males, and $4.75 to females. In Connecticut, it is $16.00 per month to males, and $6.50 to females. In New York, it is $14.96 per month to males, and $6.69 to females. In Pennsylvania, it is $17.02 per month to males, and 10.09 to females. In Ohio, it is $15.42 per month to males, and $8.73 to females. In Indiana, it is $12.00 per month to males, and $6.00 to females. In Michigan, it is $12.71 per month for males, and $5.36 for females. Even in Massachusetts, it is only $24.51 per month to males, and $8.07 to females. All this is exclusive of board; but let it be compared with what is paid to cashiers of banks, to secretaries of insurance-companies, to engineers upon railroads, to superintendents in factories, to custom-house officers, navy agents, and so forth, and so forth, and it will then be seen what pecuniary temptations there are on every side, drawing enterprising and talented young men from the ranks of the teacher's profession.

Nor does the social estimation accorded to teachers much surpass the pecuniary value set upon their services. The nature of their calling debars them, almost universally, from political honors, which, throughout our whole country, have a factitious value so much above their real worth. Without entire faithlessness to their trust, they cannot engage in trade or commercial speculations. Modes of education have heretofore been so imperfect, that I do not know a single instance where a teacher has been transferred from his school to any of those departments of educated labor in which such liberal salaries are now given. And thus it is, that the profession at large, while it enjoys but a measured degree of public respect, seems shut out from all the paths that lead to fortune or to fame. No worldly prize is held up before it; and, in the present condition of mankind, how few there are who will work exclusively for the immortal reward! It supposes the possession only of very low faculties, to derive pleasure from singing the praises of a martyr; but to be the martyr one's self requires very high ones.

Hence it is, as was before said, that when the aspiring and highly-endowed youth of our country arrive at years of discretion, and begin to survey the varied employments which lie spread out before them, they find that the noblest of them all presents the fewest external attractions. Those whose natural or acquired ambition seeks for wealth, go into trade. The mechanical genius applies himself to the useful arts. The politically ambitious connect themselves with some one of those classes from which public officers are usually selected. Medicine attracts those who have the peculiar combination of tastes congenial to it. Those who ponder most upon the ways of God to men, minister in sacred things. Who, then, are left to fill the most important position known to social life? A few remain, whose natural tendencies in this direction are too vehement to be resisted or diverted; a somewhat larger number, who have no strong predilection for one sphere of exertion rather than for another, and to whom, under the circumstances peculiar to each, school-keeping is as eligible as any other employment: but many, very many, the great majority, engage in it, not for its own sake, but only to make it subservient to some ulterior object, or — with humiliation it is said — perhaps only to escape from manual labor.

The profession of school-keeping, then, as a profession, has never had an equal chance with its competitors. On the one hand, it has been resorted to by great numbers, whose only object was to make a little money out of it, and then abandon it; and, on the other, its true disciples, those who might have been and should have been its leaders and priesthood, have been lured and seduced away from it by all the more splendid prizes of life.

Even though, therefore, the profession of school-keeping has not been crowded by learned and able men, devoting their energies and their lives to its beneficent labors, this fact wholly fails to prove that Nature does not produce, with each generation, a sufficient number of fit persons, who, under an equitable distribution or apportionment of honors and rewards for meritorious services, would be found pre-adapted for school-keeping, in the same way that Newton was for mathematics, or Pope for poetry, or Franklin for the infallibility of his common sense. Indeed, the proportion of good teachers whom we now have, notwithstanding all their discouragements against entering, and their seducements for leaving, the profession, seem demonstrative of the contrary.

Thus far, the argument has proceeded upon the basis that the required number of teachers, possessing the high grade of qualifications supposed, must equal the present number, such as these are. But it is almost too obvious to need mentioning, that if the qualifications of teachers were to be so greatly enhanced, and the term of the schools so materially lengthened, as is proposed, teaching would then really become a profession, and the same teachers would keep school through the year. Instead, therefore, of changing from male teachers in the winter to females in the summer, back again to males in the winter, and so on alternately, — the children of each school suffering under a new step-father or a new step-mother each half-year, — they would enjoy the vastly-improved system of continuous training under the same hands. This would diminish, by almost one-half, the required number of teachers for our schools; the poorer half would be discarded, the better half retained. Surely, under these circumstances, if a sufficient number of the very highest class of teachers could not be found, it would not be owing to any parsimony of Nature in withholding the endowments, but to our unpardonable niggardliness in not cultivating and employing them.

Feeling now authorized to assume that the first proposition has been satisfactorily established, it only remains to be considered, under this head, whether the community at large — the towns separately, or the towns and the State by joint contributions — can afford to make such compensation as shall attract to this field of labor the high order of teachers supposed, and shall requite them generously for their services.

To induce persons of the highest order of talent to become teachers, and to deter good teachers from abandoning the profession, its emoluments must bear some close analogy to those which the same persons could command in other employments. The case, too, as presented in the circular, and upon which the evidence has been obtained, supposes the schools to continue for ten months in each year. Although in many large towns the schools are now kept more than this portion of the year, yet their average length for the whole State is but eight months. The increased expense, then, both of the longer term and of the more liberal compensation, must be provided for. Can the community sustain this expense?

Let us suppose, for a moment, that ninety-nine per cent of our whole community should be temperate, honest, industrious, frugal people, — conscientious in feeling, and exemplary in conduct, — is it not certain that two grand pecuniary consequences would immediately follow; namely, a vast gain in productive power, and a vast saving in the criminal destruction and loss of property? Either of these sources of gain would more than defray the increased expenses of the system, which, according to the evidence I have obtained, would insure both. The current expenses last year, for the education of all the children in the State between the ages of four and sixteen, was $3.14, on an average, for each one. Look into the police courts of our cities in the morning, and especially on Monday morning, when the ghastly array of drunkards is marched in for trial. A case may not occupy ten minutes; and yet the fine, costs, and expenses would educate two children, for a year, in our public schools, at the present rate, or one child at double the present rate. The expenses incurred in punishing the smallest theft that is committed exceed the present cost of educating a child in our schools for a year. A knave who proposes to obtain goods by false pretences will hardly aim at making less than a thousand dollars by his speculation. There are more than one hundred and fifty towns in Massachusetts, — that is, about half the whole number in the State, — in each of which the annual appropriation for all its schools is less than one thousand dollars. A burglar or highway robber will seldom peril his life without the prospect of a prize which would educate five hundred or a thousand children for a year. An incendiary exhibits fire-works at an expense which would educate all the children of many a school-district in the State, from the age of four to that of sixteen; while the only reward he expects is that of stealing a few garments or trinkets during the conflagration. In a single city in the State, consisting of sixteen or seventeen thousand inhabitants, it was estimated by a most respectable and intelligent committee, that the cost of alcoholic drinks during the last year far exceeded the combined cost of all the schools and all the churches in it, although, for both religion and education, it is a highly liberal city. The police expenses alone of the city of New York are about half a million a year. But all these are but a part of the sluice-ways through which the hard-earned wealth of the people is wasted. What shall be said of those stock-swindlings and bank-failures whose capitals of hundreds of thousands of dollars are embezzled in " fair business transactions; " whose vaults, sworn to be full of specie or bullion, remind one, on inspection, not merely of a pecuniary, but of a philosophical, vacuum? what of those epidemic speculations in land (often Fairy-land, though void of both beauty and poetry), where fortunes change hands as rapidly as if dependent upon the throw of a gambler's dice? and what of those enormous peculations by government defaulters, where more money is ingulfed by one stupendous fraud than Massachusetts expends for the education of all her children in a year? All this devastation and loss the public bears with marvellous, with most criminal composure. The people at large stand by the wreck-covered shore, where so many millions are dashed in pieces and sunk, and seem not to recognize the destruction; and, what is infinitely worse, there are those who rejoice in the howl of the tempest and the shrieks of the sufferers, because they can grow rich by plundering only here and there a fragment of property from the dead or the defenceless. By charity, by direct taxes, by paying twenty or thirty per cent more for every article or necessary of life than it is equitably worth, by bad debts, by the occasional and involuntary contribution of a pocket-book, a watch, a horse, a carriage, a ship, or a cargo, to which the robber and the barrator help themselves by paying premiums for insurance, and in a hundred other ways, the honest and industrious part of the people not only support themselves, but supply the mighty current of wealth that goes to destruction through these flood-gates of iniquity. The people do not yet seem to see that all the cost of legislating against criminals; of judges and prosecuting officers, of jurors and witnesses, to convict them; of building houses of correction and jails and penitentiaries for restraining and punishing them, — is not a hundredth part of the grand total of expenditure incurred by private and social immoralities and crimes. The people do not yet seem to see that the intelligence and the morality which education can impart is that beneficent kind of insurance, which, by preventing losses, obviates the necessity of indemnifying for them; thus saving both premium and risk. What is ingulfed in the vortex of crime in each generation would build a palace of more than Oriental splendor in every school-district in the land, would endow it with a library beyond the ability of a life-time to read, would supply it with apparatus and laboratories for the illustration of every study and the exemplification of every art, and munificently requite the services of a teacher worthy to preside in such a sanctuary of intelligence and virtue.

But the prevention of all that havoc of worldly goods which is caused by vice transfers only one item from the loss to the profit side of the account. Were all idle, intemperate, predatory men to become industrious, sober, and honest, they would add vast sums to the inventory of the nation's wealth, instead of subtracting from it. Let any person take a single town, village, or neighborhood, and look at its inhabitants individually, with the question in his mind, how many of them are producers, and how many are non-producers, — that is, how many, either by the labor of the body or the labor of the mind, add value and dignity to life, and how many barely support themselves, — and I think he will often be surprised at the smallness of the number by whose talent and industry the storehouses of the earth are mainly filled, and all the complicated business of society is principally managed. Could we convert into coworkers for the benefit of mankind all those physical and spiritual powers of usefulness which are now antagonists or neutrals, the gain would be incalculable.

Add the above two items together, — namely, the saving of what the vicious now squander or destroy, and the wealth, which, as virtuous men, they would amass, — and the only difficulty presented would be to find in what manner so vast an amount could be beneficially disposed of.

But it is not to be disguised, whatever reforms may be instituted, that the cost of crime cannot, at once, be prevented. For a season, therefore, and until the expenses of education shall arrest and supersede the expenses of guilt, both must be borne. I wish to state the difficulty without extenuation. The question, then, is, Can both be temporarily borne?

The appropriations for which the towns voluntarily taxed themselves last year for the current expenses of the schools — that is, for the wages and board of teachers, and for fuel — were $662,870.57. Adding the income of the surplus revenue, when appropriated for the support of schools, it was $670,628.-13. The valuation of the State I suppose to be not less than $450,000,000. Last year's tax, therefore, for the current expenses of the schools, was less than one mill and a half on the dollar, — less than one mill and a half on a thousand mills. Taking the average of the State, then, no man was obliged to pay more than one six hundred and sixty-sixth part of his property for this purpose; or, rather, such would have been the case had there been no poll-tax, — had the whole tax been levied upon property alone. At this rate, it would take six hundred and sixty-six years for all the property of the State to be *once* devoted to this purpose. And does not the portion of our worldly interests which is dependent upon public schools bear a greater ratio to the whole of those interests than one to six hundred and sixty-six? I need not argue this point; for who, out of an insane asylum, or even of the *curable* classes in it, will question the fact? Who will say that the importance of this interest, as compared with all the earthly interests of mankind, is not indefinitely greater than this? Who will say, that, to secure so precious an end as the diffusion of almost universal intelligence and virtue, and the suppression, with an equal degree of universality, of ignorance and vice, it would not be expedient to do as the Bishop of Landaff once proposed that the British nation should do, in an eventful crisis of its affairs, — vote away, by acclamation, one-half of all the wealth of the kingdom? But there is no need of carrying our feelings or our reason to this pitch of exaltation. There is no need of any signal or unwonted sacrifice. There is no need of a devotion of life, as is done in battle. There is no need of perilling fortunes, as is done every day in trade. There is no need that any man in the community should lose one day from his life, or an hour from his sleep, or a comfort from his wardrobe or his table. Three times more than is now expended — that is, four and a half mills on every thousand mills of the property of the State, or only one part in two hundred and twenty-two, instead of one in six hundred and sixty-six — would defray every expense, and insure the result. Regarded merely as a commercial transaction, — a pecuniary enterprise, whose elements are dollars and cents alone, — there is not an intelligent capitalist in the State who would not, on the evidence here adduced, assume the whole of it, and pay a bonus for the privilege. When the State was convinced of the lucrativeness or general expediency of a railroad from Worcester to its western border, it bound itself, at a word, to the amount of five millions of dollars; and I suppose it to be now the opinion of every intelligent man in the Commonwealth, that, when the day of payment shall arrive, the road itself, in addition to all the collateral advantages which it will have conferred, will have paid for itself, and will then forever remain, not merely a monument of wisdom, but a reward for sagacity. Yet what is a railroad, though it does cut down the mountains and lift up the valleys, compared with an all-embracing agency of social and moral reform which shall abase the pride of power, and elevate the lowliness of misfortune? And those facilities for travel which supersede the tediousness of former journeyings and the labor of transportation — what are they, when compared with the prevention of that "lamentation, mourning, and woe" which come from the perpetration of crime? When the city of Boston was convinced of the necessity of having a supply of pure water from abroad for the use of its inhabitants, it voted three millions of dollars to obtain it; and he would be a bold man who would now propose a repeal of the ordinance, though all past expenditures could be refunded. Yet all the school-houses in Boston, which it has erected during the present century, are not worth a fourth part of this sum. For the supply of water, the city of New York lately incurred an expenditure of thirteen millions of dollars. Admitting, as I most cheerfully do, that the use of water pertains to the moral as well as to the ceremonial law, yet our cities have pollutions which water can never wash away, — defilements which the baptism of a moral and Christian education alone can remove. There is not an appetite that allies man to the brutes, nor a passion for vain display which makes him more contemptible than any part of the irrational creation, which does not cost the country more, every year, than such a system of schools as would, according to the evidence I have exhibited, redeem it, almost entirely, from its follies and its guilt. Consider a single factitious habit of our people, which no one will pretend adds any degree to the health, or length to the life, or decency to the manners, of the nation: I mean the smoking of tobacco. It is said, on good authority, that the *annual* expenditure in the country for the support of this habit is ten millions of dollars; and if we reflect that this sum, averaged upon all the people, would be only half a dollar apiece, the estimate seems by no means extravagant. Yet this is far more than is paid to the teachers of all the public schools in the whole United States.

Were nations to embark in the cause of education for the redemption of mankind, as they have in that of war for their destruction, the darkest chapters in the history of earthly calamities would soon be brought to a close. But, where units have been grudged for education, millions have been lavished for war. While, for the one purpose, mankind have refused to part with superfluities, for the other they have not only impoverished themselves, but levied burdensome taxes upon posterity. The vast national debts of Europe originated in war; and, but for that scourge of mankind, they never would have existed. The amount of money now owed by the different European nations, is said, on good authority, to be $6,387,000,000. Of this inconceivable sum, the share of Great Britain is about $4,000,000,000 (in round numbers, 800,000,000 pounds sterling); of France, $780,000,000; of Russia and Austria, $300,000,000 each; of Prussia, $100,000,000; and the debts of the minor powers increase this sum to $6,387,000,000. The national debt of Great Britain now amounts to more than $140 for every man, woman, and child in the three kingdoms. Allowing six persons to each family, it will average more than $850 to every household, — a sum which would be deemed by thousands and tens of thousands of families in that country to be a handsome competence, nay, wealth itself, if it were owing *to* instead of *from* them.

It is estimated, that, during the twenty-two years preceding the general peace of 1815, the unimaginable sum of 6,250,000,000 pounds sterling, or $30,000,000,000, had been expended in war by nations calling themselves *Christian*, — an amount of wealth many fold greater than has ever been expended, for the same purpose, by all the nations on the globe whom we call *savage*, since the commencement of the Christian era. The earth itself could not be pawned for so vast a sum as this, were there any pawn-broker's office which would accept such a pledge. Were it to be set up at auction, in the presence of fierce competitors for the purchase, it would not sell for enough to pay its war-bills for a single century. The war-estimates of the British Government, even for the current year of peace, are $85,000,000; and the annual interest on the national debt incurred by war is at least $120,000,000 more, or more than $200,000,000 for a common, and, on the whole, a very favorable year. Well might Christ, in the Beatitudes, pronounce his emphatic benediction upon the "peace-makers."

We have emulated, in this country, the same gigantic scale of expenditure for the same purpose. Since the organization of the Federal Government, in 1789, the expense of our military and naval establishments and equipments, in round numbers, is $700,000,000. Two of our ships of the line have cost more than $2,000,000. The value of the arms accumulated at one time at the Arsenal in Springfield, in this State, was $2,000,000. The Military Academy at West Point has cost more than $4,000,000. In our town-meetings, and in our school-district-meetings, wealthy and substantial men oppose the grant of $15 for a school-library, and of $30 for both library and apparatus; while at West Point they spend $50 in a single lesson at target-firing; and the government keeps a hundred horses, and grooms and blacksmiths to take care of them, as an indispensable part of the *apparatus* of the academy. The pupils at our normal schools, who are preparing to become teachers, must maintain themselves: the cadets at the academy receive $28 a month, during their entire term, as a compensation for being educated at the public expense. Adding bounties and pensions to wages and rations, I suppose the cost of a common foot-soldier in the army cannot be less than $250 a year. The average cost of female teachers for the public schools of Massachusetts last year was only $13.60 a month, inclusive of board, or at a rate which would give $163.20 for the year; but the average length of the schools was but eight months: so that the cost of *two* common soldiers is nearly that of *five* female teachers. The annual salary of a colonel of dragoons in the United-States army is $2,206; of a brigadier-general, $2,958; of a major-general, $4,512; that of a captain of a ship of the line, when in service, $4,500; and, even when off duty, it is $2,500. There are but seven towns in Massachusetts where any teacher of a public school receives so high a salary as $1,000; and, in four of these towns, one teacher only receives this sum.

Had my purpose been simply to show the pecuniary ability of the people at large to give the most generous compensation to such a company of accomplished, high-minded, noble teachers as would lift the race, at once, out of the pit of vice and ignorance and superstition as safely and as tenderly as a mother bears her infant in her arms, — had my purpose been merely to show this pecuniary ability, then I have already said too much. But my design was, not merely to carry conviction to the minds of those who would contest this fact, but to make the denial of it ridiculous.

III. But the consummation of this reformatory work is not promised, except upon the performance of a third condition, — namely, that all the children in the State between the ages of four and sixteen years shall be brought into school for ten months in each year. In other words, while the schools are kept, the attendance of all the children upon them, with one or two exceptions to be hereafter noticed, must be regular.

Since the keeping of registers in our schools has made known the enormous amount of absences from them, there is but one subject which has excited greater alarm, or given rise to louder complaints. Teachers complain of this absence, because, while it increases their labors, it diminishes their success; indeed, it makes entire success an impossibility. Parents who do send their children regularly to school complain of it, because the tardy and the occasional comers are a dead weight upon the progress of those who are uniformly present and prompt. Committees complain of it, in behalf of the towns which they represent, because it lowers the general standard of intelligence among the people; and because, taken on an average for the whole State, it incurs a total loss of from one-third to one-half of all the money which is annually levied by taxation for the support of schools. Men of wealth who have no children to send to school, or who for any reason send none, complain of it, because, though they may be willing to be taxed for the education of all, yet they are not willing to be taxed to have their money taken and thrown away. They think it, and with good reason too, to be an intolerable hardship to be first confronted with the argument that they are bound to secure the general intelligence and morality of the people through the instrumentality of schools, and when they have acknowledged the validity of this argument, and cheerfully paid their money, to have the very men who so argued and so claimed turn upon them, and say, "We are still at liberty to throw your money away by keeping our children at home; and, though you must keep the school regularly for us, we have a right to use it irregularly, or not at all, as we please." Thus the delinquents, where they owe apology and repentance, retort with indignity, and persevere in injustice.

I cannot believe that our people will always, or even long, submit to this enormous abuse, now made known to them by well-authenticated documents. For an economical people, who form political parties on the subject of expenditures by the government, and make "retrenchment" a watch-word; for a people whose legislature sometimes debates for days together whether the salary of an officer shall be a few hundred dollars more or less, — to continue to throw away, as was done last year, more than $200,000 on account of voluntary, gratuitous, and, in most cases, wanton absences from school, is not credible. For a people who are sufficiently proud, to say the least, of their general intelligence, and who are sincerely anxious to perpetuate and improve their moral character, to be willing to forfeit one-third part of all the blessings of their free-school system, without any necessity, or any plausible pretext, is not to be believed. This great evil must be dealt with according to its magnitude. Violent diseases demand energetic remedies. It would be as unwise in a State as in an individual to allow its precautions to diminish while its dangers increase; to sleep more quietly as peril becomes more imminent. When we know that a malady is dangerous, and that a remedy is at hand, wisdom dictates its speedy application.

I propose, then, to consider the objections that may possibly be urged to the regular attendance of all our children upon school for ten months in each year, from the age of four to that of sixteen years. I believe them to be by no means insurmountable; nay, that their formidableness will wholly disappear if subjected to a candid examination.

1. It may be said that there is a class of parents amongst us who depend partially upon the labor of their children for the support of their families, and who are too poor to forego the earnings of these children for ten months in the year, and for twelve years of their minority.

With regard to a portion of the class of parents referred to, this suggestion would have a foundation in fact; with regard to another portion of them, it would have no such foundation. It is well known that a class of parents exists amongst us, who work their children that they may themselves be idle; who coin the health, the capacities, and the future welfare, of their own offspring into money, which money, when gained, is not expended for the necessaries or the comforts of life, but is wasted upon appetites that brutify or demonize their possessor. The objections of this class against permitting their children to be educated at the public expense are not legitimate. It would be infinitely better for them, for their families, and for the public, if they were cut off from these means of sinful indulgence. It would improve their condition still further, if they were obliged to be industrious, even though coerced to labor by the goads of hunger and cold. The best of all conditions for them would be, that they should themselves labor for the support of their children at school, where those intellectual and virtuous habits would be formed, and that filial piety inculcated, which would lead the children, in after-years, to return to the parents, with a generous requital, the favors they had received.

There is, doubtless, another portion of this general class, with whom the alleged necessity for their children's earnings as a part of the means for family support is no pretence. The number or age of the family, sickness, misfortune, or other cause, may render this or some other resource indispensable to the procurement of the necessaries and decencies of life. I would not underrate the number or the necessities of this class of persons; they have claims upon our warmest sympathies: but I have reason to believe that the class itself is not a very large one. Where the heads of the family enjoy good health; where they may have the assistance of their children, who are of an age able to render it, for several hours each day, for one or two entire half-days each week, and for two months uninterruptedly each year, — the circumstances must be peculiar where industry and frugality, with such favors as the honest and praiseworthy poor may always count upon from their better-conditioned neighbors, will not supply the means of a comfortable subsistence.

Still, cases of necessity do and will exist; and, where the need is not supplied by individual charity, there is no other alternative but to do it at the public expense. This would introduce no new principle into our legislation. It would be only a moderate but highly beneficial extension of an existing one. Our laws now provide for physical destitution, whatever may be its cause; and they enjoin upon school-committees the duty of furnishing all needful school-books, at the expense of their respective towns, to all children whose parents are unable to procure them.

The question then arises, What degree of destitution — and there is no propriety in restricting this to physical destitution — makes it expedient for a wise government to interfere, and afford relief? "Poor-laws," as we understand the term, are of modern origin. They were not only unknown to all barbarous nations, but to most Christian and civilized ones until a recent period. In England, they date from the reign of Elizabeth. In Scotland, although in a small class of extreme cases legal relief may have been rendered, yet "poor-laws" can hardly be said ever to have had an effective existence in that country. In Ireland, they were unknown until recently. In this country, they are almost coeval with our colonial settlements.

But there neither is, nor ever has been, any legal standard of poverty. The degree of destitution which shall entitle the sufferer to relief is not a fixed quantity, like the statutory length of a yard, or the Winchester bushel. The general notions of men as to what constitutes poverty range between wide extremes, according to their prevalent style of living, their enlightenment, and their benevolence. It is said, that when the present king of France heard that the income of the Jewish banker in London amounted only to some hundreds of dollars each hour, he expressed his deep grief at learning that he was so poor. With us, he who can command a comfortable shelter, decent clothes, and a sufficient supply of wholesome food, for himself and family, excites no special commiseration for his poverty; while there are places upon the earth where a potato a day is considered an independent fortune. Now, between these extremes, what shall the true definition of poverty be?

So the line which divides poverty from competence is not a stationary but a movable one. The laws themselves change; and the same law, on a question like this, will be made to speak a very different language under different administrators. In favor of the militia, or of the country's defence, our law exempts from attachment, execution, and distress, whether for debt or for taxes, the uniform, arms, ammunition, and accoutrements which officers, non-commissioned officers, and privates, are required to possess. In favor of the common sentiments of humanity, our law exempts also from attachment and execution not only wearing apparel, but a great variety of articles of household furniture, — bedsteads, beds, bedding, an iron stove, fuel, and other commodities, to the value of fifty dollars; also a cow, six sheep, one swine, and two tons of hay; also the tools and implements used by a debtor in his trade, not exceeding fifty dollars in value; and also rights of burial, and tombs used as repositories for the dead. Our legislation on this subject has been humanely progressive, as may be seen by reference to statutes 1805, ch. 100; 1813, ch. 172; 1822, ch. 93, § 8; 1832, ch. 58; 1838, ch. 145, &c. In a neighboring State, by a late law, a portion of the debtor's homestead is also brought within the same rule. In favor of learning and religion, all school-books and Bibles used in the family are also exempted from attachment and execution for debt: and, as was before said, all school-children destitute of school-books are first supplied with them at the public expense; and, where the parents are unable to reimburse the cost, the supply is gratuitous. Massachusetts has, from time to time, founded and endowed hospitals for the insane; and she makes annual and liberal appropriations for the education of the blind and the deaf and dumb. She is now engaged in erecting a noble institution for the reformation of juvenile delinquents; and a commission instituted by her is inquiring, at the present time, into the condition of idiots, — which unfortunate, repulsive, and hitherto outcast portion of the community, it is not to be doubted, she will soon gather together, and, in imitation of the noble examples set by France, Switzerland, and Prussia, will educate to cleanliness, to decency, and to no inconsiderable degree of positive enjoyment and usefulness. Each one, too, of all these great movements, when carried out into execution, has proved economical as well as philanthropic and Christian. What striking results, in proof of this, are exhibited by the statistics of the State Lunatic Hospital at Worcester! According to the last report of that institution which Dr. Woodward made, the average expense of twenty-four old cases — taking the first twenty-four on the list, and not selecting them, or taking them at random — was $1,945.83 each; and their aggregate expense, $46,700: while the average expense of the same number of recent cases, taking the last on the list who were discharged cured, was $41.53 each; and their aggregate expense, $996.75: so that the whole expense of *twenty-four* recent cases was but about one-half as much as of *one* old one. That hospital already has far more than paid for itself by the saving it has effected; because, without it, all the new cases would have been old ones. I present these economical aspects of the subject, by no means because I deem them to be the most important, but because, all over the world, there is a large class of persons with whom the pecuniary argument is the most persuasive and eloquent, and who will be induced to lend their services in aid of great social ameliorations only when they find that humanity is economy, and that "godliness" is "great gain" in a worldly sense. They will then enlist for the sake of the "great gain," though quite indifferent as to the other quality. When I have been asked by persons from the fertile and exuberant regions of our own country, or from transatlantic nations, how it is, that, with our ungenerous soil and ungenial clime, we are pecuniarily able to support these various and costly establishments, my answer has been, that we are able *because we do support them.*

But the question recurs, What is poverty? What is that straitness of circumstances, which, for educational purposes, would require a wise and profound statesman, and, of course, the State itself, to interpose, and to supply those means for the education of the child which the parent is unable to render? It being proved, if all our children were to be brought under the benignant influences of such teachers as the State can supply, from the age of four years to that of sixteen, and for ten months in each year, that ninety-nine in every hundred of them can be rescued from uncharitableness, from falsehood, from intemperance, from cupidity, licentiousness, violence, and fraud, and reared to the performance of all the duties, and to the practice of all the kindnesses and courtesies, of domestic and social life;

made promoters of the common weal, instead of subtracters from it, — this being proved, I respectfully and with deference submit to the Board, and, 'through them, to the legislature, and to my fellow-citizens at large, that *every man is* POOR, *in an educational sense, who cannot both spare and equip his children for school for the entire period above specified;* and that, while he remains thus poor, it is not only the dictate of generosity and Christianity, but it is the wisest policy and profoundest statesmanship too, to supply from the public treasury — municipal or state, or both — whatever means may be wanted to make certain so glorious an end. These principles and this practice the divine doctrines of Christianity have always pointed at, and a progressive civilization has now brought us into proximity to them. How is it that we can call a man *poor* because his body is cold, and not because his highest sympathies and affections have been frozen up within him, in one polar and perpetual winter, from his birth? Hunger does not stint the growth of the body half so much as ignorance dwarfs the capacities of the mind. No wound upon the limbs, or gangrene of vital organs, is a thousandth part so terrible as those maladies of the soul that jeopard its highest happiness, and defeat the end for which it was created. And infinitely aggravated is the case where children are the sufferers; where moral distempers are inflicted upon them by parents, or are inherited by them from ancestors; where they are born into an atmosphere saturated with the infection of crime; where vice obtrudes itself upon every sense, and presses inward, through every pore, to be imbibed and copied, just as the common air forces itself into the nostrils to be breathed; and where, in their early imitative transgressions, they are no more consciously guilty than in the heaving of their lungs in an act of respiration.

Were a ship, in mid-ocean, to be overtaken by a storm, to be dismantled, dismasted, and reduced to an unmanageable hulk, and while its crew were famishing, and in momentary danger of foundering, were another ship to pass within hail, but to refuse all succor and deliverance, should we not justly regard the deed as an enormous atrocity? But what moral difference does it make whether we pass by our perishing "neighbor" on the sea or on the dry land? The pitfalls of perdition on shore are deeper and far more terrible, and are inhabited by direr monsters, than any ocean-caves. Now, it is the children of the man who, through sickness or other misfortune, has not the means fully and thoroughly to educate them for the duties of life, who represent this perishing and foundering crew; and the man who has superfluities, or even an independency of means, but refuses to aid in giving these children an education sufficient for all the common responsibilities of life, — *he* is the hardened mariner who sails recklessly by, and sees the helpless sufferers ingulfed in the wake of his own proud vessel.

On this point, then, are we not authorized to conclude, in the first place, that the cases are comparatively few where parents cannot afford to forego the earnings of their children, and to send them to school for the length of time and with the regularity proposed? and, in the second place, were the cases of destitution far more numerous than they are, that there is still an abundance of means, as well as an obvious duty, on the part of the public, to supply all deficiencies? Assuming the value of all the property in the State to be four hundred and fifty millions of dollars, the simple interest upon it alone, at six per cent, and without any addition from earnings, is twenty-seven millions annually. The industrial statistics of the State show that its income, from all its occupations and trades, is more than a hundred millions of dollars annually; and even this does not include improvements upon its wharves, bridges, roads, or lands. Must such a State pare and clip and scrimp, and dole out its means with a niggardly hand, when unfolding the mortal and the immortal capacities of its children?

2. But though the means for supporting the schools are abundant, and though the earnings of children, as a part of the family's daily livelihood, may be forborne in one class of cases, and made up in the other, a further question still remains, —

Can the State itself afford to forego these juveniles services? Can the machinery be operated, the shoes bound, the types set, the errands and "chores" done, and the door-bells tended, if all children under sixteen years of age are withdrawn from the performance of these kinds of service for ten months each year? Minors, under sixteen, are let out to corporations to be employed in manufacturing establishments; they are taken into the families of the wealthy and forehanded as under-servants; a few are employed as errand-boys in the offices and shops of cities; and, in several of the lighter handicrafts, they are put to regular labor. There are no exact data by which to determine the number of children so employed in the State. Compared with the whole number of children in it between the ages of four and sixteen, I suppose it to be inconsiderable; so inconsiderable, indeed, that, if their services in these employments were henceforth to be wholly discontinued, it would subtract hardly an appreciable fraction from the aggregate products of our labor and machinery. A highly-intelligent gentleman, who has been engaged in manufacturing business for many years, informs me that the company with which he is associated now employs 3,119 persons, — namely, 2,571 in five cotton-mills, 450 in two machine-shops, and 98 in one woollen-mill. In the cotton-mills, 346 persons are employed who are under sixteen years of age, — equal to thirteen per cent. In the machine-shops, there are none. In the woollen-mill, there are six, or six per cent. The average for the whole is about eleven per cent. He adds, "I am of the opinion that this statement may be taken as a fair representation, in regard to age, of the persons in these several employments. Very few are under fifteen. . . . This class of labor is not profitable to the employer, and, except in particular cases, is only employed from motives of charity. From my recollection of the labor required in print-works" [he was formerly extensively engaged in printing calicoes], "I am inclined to think the proportion of persons under sixteen is not greater than the average in the mills and shops before mentioned."

Here, then, is a statement, worthy of implicit reliance, respecting the largest branch of labor in which those children are employed, who, on the proposed reformatory plan, would be sent to school. Can a substitute be found for this juvenile labor?

In the first place, if that class of parents who now coin into money their children's highest capacities for usefulness and enjoyment, that they themselves may live in idleness and intemperance, were peremptorily deprived of this source of gain, they could perform a portion of the labor now exacted of the children; or, if not capable of performing this particular kind of labor, they could at least do some other work, and thus set free a class of persons who could perform it.

In the second place, manufacturers could employ, at a slightly-enhanced price, a few more adults, or more persons over the age of sixteen. I trust that no liberal-minded manufacturer would object to employing older help, at the present time, on the plea of non-remunerating returns.

But, thirdly, — a consideration of more significance than all the rest, — the children who had enjoyed such a school development and training as we are now supposing would go into the mills, after the completion of their educational course, with physical and intellectual ability to help, and with a moral inability to harm, which, of itself, would far more than compensate for all the loss of their previous absence. Take any manufacturer whose mind has ever wandered, even by chance, to a contemplation of the only true sources and securities of wealth, and what would he not give to have all his operatives transformed at once into men and women of high intelligence and unswerving morality? to have them become so faithful and honest, that they would always turn out the greatest quantity and the best quality of work, without the trouble and expense of watching and weighing and counting and superintending? that they would be as careful of his machinery as though it were their own? that they would never ask or accept more in payment than their just due? that they would always consult their employer's interest, and never sacrifice it from motives of personal ease or gain or ill-will?

I have been told by one of our most careful and successful manufacturers, that, on substituting in one of his cotton-mills a better for a poorer educated class of operatives, he was enabled to add twelve or fifteen per cent to the speed of his machinery, without any increase of damage or danger from the acceleration. Here there was a direct gain of twelve or fifteen per cent, — a larger percentage than that of the supposed whole number of children under sixteen years of age in all our factories. And this gain was effected, too, without any additional investment of capital, or any increased expense for board. The gain from improved morals would far exceed that from increased intelligence. On the whole, then, if all children under sixteen years of age were withdrawn from the factories for ten months of each year in order to be sent to school, there is reason to believe that the aggregate amount of the fabrics produced by the mills would not be diminished even a yard.

The above considerations have special reference to children employed in factories. I have selected this department of labor, because I suppose that at least as many children under sixteen are let out to service in factories as in all other branches of business taken together. The same views, with inconsiderable modifications, will apply to all others. It will be seen at a glance, therefore, that the contemplated diversion of children from manual labor to mental and moral pursuits will not be such as to impair the industrial resources of the State, or to diminish the marketable value of its products.

But there is one remark which applies alike to all these classes of employers. They use the services of children not their own. Now, it must be conceded, that there exists a well-grounded reluctance, on the part of free governments, to any such interference with parental relations as is not made necessary by the nature of the government itself, or by the criminal conduct or culpable neglect of the parents. But those who employ other men's children for their own profit cannot intrench themselves behind the sacredness of parental rights. Their object is their own personal gain, — a lawful and laudable object, it is true, when pursued by justifiable means, but one which cannot sanction for a moment the infliction of a positive injury upon any child, or the deprivation of any privilege essential either to his well-being, or to the permanence and prosperity of the republic. The republic, indeed, if true to itself, can never allow any of its members to do what will redound to its own injury; and, where no parental title can be alleged, the assertion of any right over the labor of children has as little foundation in natural justice or equity as the tyrant's claim to the toil of his vassals. How can any man, having any claim to the character, I will not say of a Christian or a philanthropist, but to the vastly lower one of a patriot, use the services of a child in his household, his shop, his office, or his mill, when he knows that he does it at the sacrifice, to say the least, of that child's highest earthly interests? How can any man seek to enlarge his own gains, or to pamper his own luxurious habits, by taking the bread of intellectual and moral life from the children around him?

I can anticipate but one objection more, having the aspect of plausibility. It may be said, that although the schools should be kept for the proposed length of time by teachers ennobled with all the intellectual and moral attributes contemplated, yet there are persons capable, like brutes, of bringing children into the world, but impervious to those moral considerations which should impel them to train up those children in the way they should go; and that, in regard to this class of parents, some coercive measures will be necessary to secure the attendance of their children at school. I admit this. But is coercion a new idea in a community where there are houses of correction and jails and state-prisons and the gallows? Surely, bolts and bars, granite walls, and strangulating hemp, are strange emblems of the voluntary principle. Massachusetts has, at the present moment, about two thousand persons under lock and key, nineteen-twentieths of whom, had they been blessed with a good common-school education, would, according to the testimony I have adduced, be now useful and exemplary citizens, — building up, instead of tearing down, the fabric of public welfare. With a population of between eight hundred thousand and nine hundred thousand, she has at least five thousand police-officers and magistrates, armed with power to seize and restrain, and bring to trial and punishment, any transgressors of those laws which she has paid many other thousands for enacting. Does it not argue, then, a perversion of intellect, or an obliquity of the moral sense, to contend that a child, for the purpose of being blessed by the influences of a good school, cannot be taken from a parent who is preparing him to become at least a private, if not an officer, in the great army of malefactors; while it is conceded, that by and by, when this same child becomes a parent, he may then be taken from *his* children, imprisoned, put to hard labor, or put to death? So far as force is concerned, so far as any supposed invasion of private rights is concerned, does not the greater contain the less a thousand times over? If the State can send a sheriff's *posse* to take a man from his own bed at midnight, and carry him to jail, to trial, and to execution, does it require a greater extension, or a bolder use, of its prerogatives, for the same State to send a kind moral guardian to take a child from the temptations of the street, or from the haunts of wickedness, and bring him within the benign influences of a good school?

Should it be said, that, in the case of the adult offender, there has been a forfeiture of civil rights by some overt act of violation, while in the case of the child the violation is prospective only, I reply, that nothing is more common than to arrest and imprison men on probable suspicion merely; nothing is more common than to hold men to bail in sums proportioned to the suspected offence; and when a man gives proof that he intends to do a wrong, and is only awaiting a favorable opportunity to execute his intention, nothing is more common than to put him under bonds for his good behavior. Every child who is not receiving a good education comes at least within these latter categories. He is an object of violent suspicion. The presumption is strong that he will not make a good citizen; that, in some form or other, he will get his living out of the earnings of his fellow-men, or offend against their welfare. If the Commonwealth, then, has a right to imprison an adult, or hold him to bail on suspicion, or to bind him over to keep the peace and be of good behavior, has it not an equal, nay, a superior right, to demand guaranties for the child's appearance upon the stage of manhood, there to answer to the great duties that shall be required of him as a citizen? — and a good education is surely better security than any bail-bond that ever was executed. Has not the State a right to bind each child to his good behavior by imparting to him the instruction, and by instilling into his mind the principles, of virtue and religion, by which he shall be twice-bound or doubly-fastened (for such is the etymological meaning of the word " religion ") to perform, with intelligence and uprightness, his social and political duties when he becomes a man?

Nor is our legislation without numerous precedents in favor of securing education, even at the expense of coercive measures. These precedents are scattered along our annals from the earliest periods of our colonial existence. The colonial law of 1642, after premising that " forasmuch as the good education of children is of singular behoof and benefit to any commonwealth," ordered " that the selectmen of every town . . . shall have a vigilant eye over their brethren and neighbors, to see, first, that none of them shall suffer so much barbarism in any of their families as not to endeavor to teach, by themselves or others, their children and apprentices so much learning as may enable them perfectly to read the English tongue, and knowledge of the capital laws;" and it imposed upon parents what in those times was a heavy penalty for neglect.

By the law of 1671, the selectmen were again required to see that all children and youth " be taught to read perfectly the English tongue, have knowledge in the capital laws," &c.

So the laws of the Plymouth Colony, after setting forth that "whereas many Parents & Masters, either through an over-respect to their own occasions and business, or not duely considering the good of their Children & Servants, have too much neglected their duty in their Education, whilest they are young & capable of Learning," proceeded to make substantially the same requirements as were made by the above-cited provisions in the laws of the Massachusetts Bay Colony; and then declared, that if any parents or masters, after warning and admonition, should still remain negligent in their duty, " whereby Children & Servants may be in danger to grow Barberous, Rude, or Stubborn, & so prove Pests instead of Blessings to the Country," then " a fine of ten shillings shall be levied upon the goods of such negligent Parent or Master." If, after three months subsequent to the levying of this fine, " no due care shall be taken & continued for the Education of such children & apprentices," then a fine of twenty shillings was to be levied. "And Lastly, if, in three months after that, there be no Reformation of the said neglect, then the Select-men, with the help of two Magistrates, shall take such children & servants from them [the parents], & place them with some Masters for years, (boyes till they come to twenty-one, and girls eighteen years of age), which will more strictly educate and govern them, according to the rules of the Order."

Nor were the above enactments a dead letter. The earlier judicial and municipal records show, that, when the natural parent broke from the ties of consanguinity and duty by neglecting the education of his children, the law interfered, and provided a civil parent for them.

Modern legislation, it is true, has greatly relaxed the stringency of these provisions. No adequate substitute is to be found for them in our present educational code; and already neglected childhood is avenging itself upon society by its manhood of crime, — not unfrequently by its precocity in crime long before the years of manhood have been reached.

Compulsory enactments, however, still attest that all the

spirit of our ancestors is not yet gone. Our laws provide, in various cases, that minor children may be bound out to service, — males to the age of twenty-one years, and females to the age of eighteen years; but, in all cases, it is to be stipulated in the contract that they shall be taught to "read, write, and cipher." "Stubborn children" may be committed to the house of correction. Children in the city of Boston, under the age of sixteen years, whose "parents are dead, or, if living, do, from vice or any other cause, neglect to provide suitable employment for or to exercise salutary control over" them, may be sent by the court to the house of reformation. By the late act establishing the State Reform School, male convicts under sixteen years of age may be sent to this school from any part of the Commonwealth, to be there "instructed in piety and morality, and in such branches of useful knowledge as shall be adapted to their age and capacity." The inmates may be bound out; but, in executing this part of their duty, the trustees "shall have scrupulous regard to the religious and moral character of those to whom they are to be bound, to the end that they may secure to the boys the benefit of a good example and wholesome instruction, and the sure means of improvement in virtue and knowledge, and thus the opportunity of becoming intelligent, moral, useful, and happy citizens of the Commonwealth." Manufacturers, and overseers in manufacturing establishments, are prohibited, under a penalty, from employing any child in their factories under fifteen years of age who has not attended some day-school for a specified portion of the year within which he may be so employed; and they are also prohibited from employing any child under twelve years of age more than ten hours a day, under any circumstances. In the case of fires, of explosive commodities, of contagious diseases, of immigrant passengers from infected countries, and so forth, the law vests its officers with plenary and summary powers "to save the republic from detriment."

Paley has said, that "to send an uneducated child into the world is injurious to the rest of mankind: it is little better than to turn out a mad dog or a wild beast into the streets." It is difficult to conceive why he thought it to be any "*better*," since one uneducated, vicious man may do infinitely more harm to the world than all the rabid dogs or wild beasts that ever existed. Much as we may need energetic remedies against contagious diseases, we need them against contagious vices more; and quarantine-laws in favor of moral health are the most necessary of all sanitary regulations.

But I forbear to press further considerations of this character upon the attention of the Board. I hope that the great majority of our people will rather wonder why such an argument should be deemed necessary than be disposed to question its conclusions.

Having now surveyed, somewhat at length, the various points pertaining to this subject, a brief recapitulation may not be amiss.

The basis on which it is suggested that our public school-system shall be put is carefully defined in the circular.

In some important particulars, no change is necessary, as our practice has already reached the point of theoretic excellence. Such are the unconditional rights of all children to enter the school, — or their entire exemption from rate-bills or any capitation-tax, either as a condition precedent or subsequent of their attending school, — the range of studies which may be taught, the provision for moral and religious instruction, with guaranties against its abuse, and so forth.

But, in other respects, important improvements are contemplated, — no cardinal or organic change in the system itself, but only progression in courses already begun. Such are, more befitting qualifications in teachers for the great work they undertake; the maintenance of the schools for a period of ten months in each year, instead of the present average of eight months, and, as a necessary consequence, the appropriation of moneys sufficient to sustain the prolonged school, and to pay the better-qualified teachers; and, finally, the gathering into the schools, during their entire term, of all the children in ~~the community~~ between the ages of four ~~and sixteen years~~.

From the comprehensiveness of this last condition, it is obvious that all cases of sickness, casualty, or other reasonable cause of absence, must be excepted. And equally clear is it, that when any parent or guardian prefers to educate his children at home, or in a private school, he should be allowed to do so, — the *means* of education to be left wholly optional with every one, provided assurance is given to the State that the *end* is attained.

So far as the proposed changes involve the appropriation of more money, it has been shown that the State possesses not only a sufficiency, but a redundancy of wealth for the purpose. Besides, when once in operation, the system will be found not merely a self-supporting one, but one yielding large revenues, — both saving and producing many times more than it will cost, — requiting a single expenditure by a manifold remuneration.

So far as higher mental and moral attributes in teachers will be required, reasons have been offered to show that Nature, or the common course of Providence, supplies an abundance of intellectual power and of moral capability; but that, through our present misuse or mal-administration of these noble qualities, they are either lost by neglect of culture, or diverted to less worthy pursuits. There is no more iron in the world now than there ever was; we have only discovered how to use it more advantageously, — for steamboats, for railroads, for machinery, and a thousand mechanical purposes: and thus, in point of mere pecuniary value, we have given it the first rank among the precious metals. There is no more water flowing down our streams now than there was centuries ago; but we have just found out how to make it saw timber, grind wheat, and make cloth: and already it does a thousand times more work than all our twenty millions of people could do by their own unassisted strength, should every man vie with his neighbor in the severity of his toil and in the amount of his productions. There are no more individual particles of electricity in the air or in the earth to-day than there always have been. Forever, since the creation, there has been an inconceivable host of these particles, — a multitude deriding all human power of computation, — which have careered round the earth by laws of their own, each one being as distinct from all the rest, and having as separate and independent an existence, as one wild horse upon the prairies has from another. Long ago, science learned how to catch and confine these natural racers; but it was not until our day that she discovered how to take them, — one, ten, a hundred, or a thousand, — and despatch them as messengers to distant cities; to make them the common carriers of intelligence, whom no pursuers can overtake, no bribe can corrupt, nor robbers despoil. Thus it is with the capacities of the human mind. By the bounty of Providence, they may be employed and made sufficient for the greatest work of reform. It is through our blindness and perversity that they are not yet used to achieve their sublime purposes. Like the iron, like the gravity of falling water, like the electric coursers, they, too, have the power of conferring unimaginable blessings upon the race; but as yet they have only been very partially enlisted in the highest services of humanity.

On the third point, — that which contemplates the regular attendance of *all* the children upon the school (with certain specified exceptions), and even their compulsory attendance in a class of extreme cases, — I rely upon legal precedents and analogies; upon the necessity which is imposed upon a republican government, if it means to keep itself republican; and upon the broad principle, that a parent who neglects to educate his child up to the point proposed proves that he has taken the parental relation upon himself without any corresponding idea of its solemnity, and thus, by the non-performance of his parental duties, forfeits his parental rights.

The coincidence of the results, too, to which the witnesses

have come, is, on its face, a very remarkable circumstance; but it is rendered still more remarkable by the fact, that they made their statements without any concert or comparison of views, and in entire independence of each other. The proof, therefore, is not cumulative merely; but its cogency is raised to a mathematical power equal to the number of the witnesses.

Such, then, is a condensed view or summary of the testimony given by credible and trustworthy witnesses on a subject so unspeakably important. The judicial mind cannot fail to observe that the section of country whence these results of experience have been gathered is large, embracing all the States north and east of Pennsylvania. The schools have been both public and private, in town and country; have consisted of both sexes and of all ages; and have contained children from all the States in the Union. They have embraced thousands and thousands of the youth of the land; and, commencing at a point of time now more than fifty years gone by, they reach in unbroken continuity to the present day. We have, therefore, no isolated or solitary case, illogically generalized, and made to yield an inference too broad for its premises.

Nor is it to be forgotten that each of the witnesses, in theological character, is a sincere believer in such an innate natural condition of the human heart as opposes the most formidable obstacles to success in moral training. Sovereign, indeed, must be the influences which can educe exemplary lives and a well-ordered society from a race, each one of whom could say literally, "I was shapen in iniquity, and in sin did my mother conceive me," — in a race whose alienation from the righteous law of God is supposed to antedate volition, and even consciousness, and to be mingled and inbred with the primary corpuscles of being. It was no disrespect towards the many able and eminent teachers of a different religious faith which deterred me from propounding the same questions to them, and soliciting the results of their experience; but it was because I wished to know what was deemed to be practicable by those who saw the greatest difficulties to be overcome before success could be achieved. While, therefore, their statements were solicited respecting the moral efficacy or "potentiality" of schools "*conducted on the cardinal principles of the New-England systems,*" yet it was my wish that each one should make his own theological views manifest on the face of his communication; so that governors and legislators, and all leaders of public opinion, might see how much was believed to be attainable, even while contending against the most formidable obstacles. I reasoned thus, — that if those who believe the battle-ground to be most nearly inaccessible, and the enemy's intrenchments to be most nearly impregnable, and his power to be most nearly invincible, do still believe that victory can be won, then all would say there should be no sleep in the camp until the war-cry is rung, and the hand-to-hand struggle is begun.

But I must not disguise the fact, nor in any way divert attention from it, that universality of education (either public or private) is a substantive part of the plan here proposed, and indispensable to its successful working. Indeed, I should have thought it nugatory and trifling to ask the opinion of any teacher about attainable results, had this condition been omitted from the scheme. Had it been stipulated, or supposed, as a preliminary of the plan, that one per cent only of the children might be left out of the schools, doubtless the witnesses would have made a deduction of at least five per cent in their estimate of results. They would have felt bound to make an allowance, not only for the abandoned class themselves, but for the poisonous influence of that class upon all the rest. Doubtless every advance in the qualification of teachers, and in gathering more and more of the children within the renovating influences of the schools, will yield a great reward of mental and moral benefits; but universality in the end to be accomplished demands universality in the means to be employed. If a contagious or infectious distemper were to break out in any quarter of a city, and all its victims but one were to be removed, though this removal would abate something from the malignant type of the disease, and contract the circle of its ravages, yet who would feel secure while even *one* should remain to impart its virus by contact, or radiate its noxious effluvia? In moral, no less than in physical maladies, the security of each is conditioned on the security of all. The confidence of every rational man must be impaired respecting the prospective virtue of his own children while the children of his neighbor are vicious; and, for the comprehensive meaning of the word "neighbor," Christ is our authority. I thank God that there can be no safety for any until there is safety for all. Were the sky to be opened, and a voice to address us audibly from the heavens, it could not proclaim more articulately than is done by the common course of Divine Providence, that God has made of one blood *all* nations of men to dwell on *all* the face of the earth; and that, therefore, being by the law of consanguinity one brotherhood and one body, no one member of this body can suffer but all the members must suffer with it, and no one member can be truly honored but all the members must rejoice with it. Where men are religious, therefore, this principle appeals to their religion, and enforces all its dictates; where men are not religious, but have only an enlightened selfishness, it invokes that selfishness to do good to others for the reflected benefits upon itself: and thus it leaves only those to pursue a different course who are morally selfish and intellectually blind. Hence, any system of education which does violence to this great principle of universal benevolence — which circumscribes itself within the limits of a family, a caste, a party, or a sect — is but human weakness wrestling against Divine Power; and, under whatever specious disguises it may mask itself, it is only mortal selfishness, seeking, by feigned and counterfeited compliances, to cajole Heaven out of blessings promised only to those who do unto others as they would that others should do unto them. What right has any man, or body of men, to make the second table of the law of less account than the first? or to delude themselves with the belief that they love the Lord their God with all the heart, while they do not love their neighbor as themselves? If God is our *Father*, all men must be our *brethren*.

I believe it would not be only practicable, but easy, for the legislature, at its ensuing session, now so soon to be commenced, to initiate a series of measures, which, in a very brief period, would carry us through the earlier stages of the contemplated reform, — measures which would command the ready assent of a vast majority of the citizens of Massachusetts, and would thus leave but few of those unnatural cases — of those parents who are *not* parents — to be dealt with compulsively.

In concluding this Report, I shall not attempt to heighten the effect of the evidence and the argument which have been submitted by any effort to describe the blessedness of that state of society which the universal application of this reformatory agency would usher in. Such an endeavor would be vain. He who would do this must first behold the scenes, and be thrilled by the joys, he would delineate; he must borrow the language of the Paradise he would describe. And, more than this, he must be able to depict the depth and fierceness of the pains which have been inflicted by the crimes of mankind, not only upon the guilty perpetrators themselves, but upon the innocent circles of their families and friends; the terrors of the conscience-stricken malefactor; the sorrow and shame of children bemoaning a parent's guilt; the madness of the mother at the ruin of her child; the agony which brings down a father's gray hairs with sorrow to the grave; the pangs of fraternal and sisterly affection, to which a stain upon a brother's or a sister's name is a dark spot upon the sun of life, which spreads and deepens until it eclipses all the light of existence; all the varied cries of this mingled wail of distress, which have been heard in all lands and at all times, from the death of Abel to the present hour, — all these *he* must have power to describe who would describe the blessedness of a deliverance from them.

There is one consideration, however, which I cannot forbear

to introduce, because it appeals alike to all those various and oftentimes conflicting classes of men who are endeavoring in so many different ways to ameliorate the condition of mankind. Will not a moment's reflection convince them all, that, so far as human instrumentality is concerned, education encompasses, pervades, and overrules all their efforts, grants them whatever triumphs they may achieve, and sets bounds to their successes which they cannot overpass? Why does the advocate of temperance, every time he returns upon his circuit of beneficence, find his way again blocked up with the prostrate victims of inebriation? Why so long, in both hemispheres, have the divinest appeals of the advocate of peace been drowned by the din of mustering squadrons and the clarion of war? Why does the opponent of slavery, before he can strike the fetters even from one victim, see other fetters riveted upon the limbs of many more? Why do our moral-reform societies and our home-mission societies call annually for more money and more laborers wherewith to enter the ever-enlarging fields, as they open before them, of licentiousness and of irreligion? Why do those rich and powerful associations formed for evangelizing the heathen world see the very ships which carry out the gospel and its heralds freighted also with idols, made in Christian lands, for those heathen to buy, and to worship as true gods, and laden with a liquid poison, too, which sinks its victims to such a depth of debasement as to make common heathenism enviable? Why is it that the political parties into which our country is divided, persist, year after year, in solemnly and unceasingly charging each other with heinous and premeditated offences against the fundamental principles of our government and the highest welfare of the people?—charges which, if true, must brand the accused with infamy; if untrue, the accusers. So far as the members of any one of these various parties are lovers of truth, of righteousness, and of peace, let them be asked what is the reason why they accomplish so little, and why so much ever remains to be done, and they will answer, and answer truly, that they do not fail through lack of reason

REPORT FOR 1848.

GENTLEMEN, —

. . . MASSACHUSETTS may be regarded either as a State by herself, or as a member of a mighty and yet increasing confederacy of States. In the former capacity, she has great and abiding interests, which are mainly dependent upon her own domestic or internal policy. In the latter relation, her fate depends upon the will of her partners in the association. Hence, although, in regard to all nations, the Minister for Foreign Affairs is the officer of first importance in the State, yet, in regard to our own Commonwealth, the Home Department has decided precedence.

As an individual State, the geographical extent of Massachusetts, and her civil and social interests, will remain the same; but when compared, or rather contrasted, with the vast domain, and the magnificent and overshadowing interests, of the whole Union, she is, and from year to year must be, growing relatively less and less and less. At the epoch of the Revolution, she was one of thirteen States. Now she is one of thirty. Even so late as 1790, when the first census of the United States was taken, there were but three States whose population exceeded hers. Deducting slaves, of whom she had none, there were but two. Her population at that time amounted to about one-tenth part of the population of the whole Union. It is now much below one-twentieth. At the time, too, of the adoption of the Federal Constitution, the area of Massachusetts bore some assignable and palpable proportion to that of the whole United States. The Mississippi was then the western boundary of the nation. Now our domain not only extends to the Pacific, but stretches through almost seventeen degrees of latitude upon that ocean. Florida then lay between us and the Gulf of Mexico; and, the gates of the Mississippi River being liable at any time to be closed against the Western States, their only unobstructed egress to the Atlantic was through Eastern ports. Now the Gulf is our southern boundary; and the Mississippi and its tributaries, with their more than sixteen thousand miles of waters navigable by steam, afford a channel capacious enough to drain the West of its vast productions, and then, with the refluent tide of commerce, to supply their demands for foreign merchandise. Territorially considered, the loss of Cape Cod, or of the few acres that compose the Islands of Nantucket and the Vineyard, would be greater to Massachusetts than the loss of Massachusetts would be to the Union. Our native and beloved State, indeed, seems contracting and dwindling away so fast as to suggest the idea of its more careful perambulation to see if some clandestine and rapacious neighbor has not incurred the curse of the Mosaic law by removing our landmarks inward and inward. It is only by taking Massachusetts as a unit, and comparing her area with that of other States in the Union, that we can realize how narrow and diminutive she is becoming. Ohio and Kentucky could each be divided into five States, and each of the ten would be larger than our own. New York, Pennsylvania, North Carolina, Alabama, Louisiana, Mississippi, and Tennessee would each make considerably more than six States — or the whole of them more than forty-two States — of the size of Massachusetts. Michigan, Illinois, Iowa, Wisconsin, Georgia, and Arkansas are each equal in territory to seven such States as ours, — amounting to another group of forty-two. Virginia and Florida are each equal to more than eight; Missouri is equal to nine; and Texas alone, according to the boundaries now claimed by her, would make forty-four such States. Taking an official estimate of the area of the United States, exclusive of the portion lately acquired from Mexico, it is divisible into three hundred and seventy-six such States as Massachusetts. The territory ceded by the treaty with Mexico, which was ratified on the thirtieth day of May last, exclusive of what is claimed by Texas, would make more than seventy-two States of equal dimensions. Hence it is plain that Massachusetts, territorially considered, constitutes, not exceeding, in round numbers, one four-hundred and forty-eighth part of the Union to which she belongs, or far less than the proportion which a single degree bears to the three hundred and sixty degrees of a circle. The bull's hide mentioned in Virgil's epic would nearly enclose her.*

---

* *Table exhibiting the areas of the several States and Territories of the United States in square miles and acres.*

FREE STATES.	Sq. Miles.	Acres.	SLAVE STATES.	Sq. Miles.	Acres.
Maine	35,000	22,400,000	Delaware	2,120	1,356,800
New Hampshire	8,030	5,139,200	Maryland	11,000	7,040,000
Vermont	8,000	5,120,000	Virginia	61,352	39,265,280
Massachusetts	7,250	4,640,000	North Carolina	45,500	29,120,000
Rhode Island	1,200	768,000	South Carolina	28,000	17,920,000
Connecticut	4,750	3,040,000	Georgia	58,000	37,120,000
New York	46,000	29,440,000	Kentucky	37,680	24,115,200
New Jersey	6,851	4,384,640	Tennessee	44,000	28,160,000
Pennsylvania	47,000	30,080,000	Louisiana	46,431	29,715,840
Ohio	39,964	25,576,960	Mississippi	47,147	30,174,080
Indiana	33,809	21,637,760	Alabama	50,722	32,462,080
Illinois	55,405	35,459,200	Missouri	67,380	43,123,200
Michigan	56,243	35,996,520	Arkansas	52,198	33,406,720
Iowa	50,914	32,584,960	Florida	59,268	37,931,520
Wisconsin	53,924	34,511,360	Texas (if bounded by Rio Grande)	325,520	208,332,800
			Dist't of Columbia	50	32,000
Total	454,340	290,777,600	Total	936,368	599,275,520

Territory north and west of Mississippi River, and east of the Rocky Mountains.

	Sq. Miles.	Acres.
Bounded north by 49° north latitude, east by Mississippi River, south by the State of Iowa and Platte River, and west by the Rocky Mountains	723,248	462,878,720
Indian Territory, situated west of Arkansas and Missouri, and south of Platte River	248,851	159,264,640
Carried forward	972,099	622,143,360

In other elements of national greatness, — in mineral resources, in productiveness of soil, and in natural facilities for internal intercourse, — she falls far below even this insignificant fraction. She has not an inland bay, not a navigable river; no gold is scattered among her sands; granite is her best mineral, and ice the only pearl to be found in her waters.

So far, too, as political power, founded on numbers, is concerned, Massachusetts is shrinking hardly less rapidly than in the relative compass of her borders. Out of two hundred and thirty representatives in the national Congress, she has but ten; and the next census, now so soon to be taken, will seriously reduce this meagre proportion. In the first Congress, she had eight out of sixty-five, or one in eight (and a fraction), instead of one in twenty-three, as at present, with waning prospects for the future. In the presidential election of the current year, she gives but twelve out of two hundred and ninety votes. In choosing electors, therefore; in declaring war and in making peace; and in all the mighty interests, political and moral, that depend upon war and peace; in the deep pecuniary stake which every commercial and manufacturing people have in questions of foreign commerce and domestic currency; and in all civil, military, and diplomatic appointments which require

	Sq. Miles.	Acres.
Brought forward	972,099	622,143,360
Old North-west Territory, balance remaining east of Mississippi River, and north-west of Wisconsin	22,336	14,295,040
Oregon Territory west of Rocky Mountains	341,463	218,536,320
Total of old territory not organized into States	1,335,898	854,974,720
California	448,691	287,162,240
New Mexico	77,387	49,527,680
Total	526,078	336,689,920

Grand Aggregate.

Total in Free States	454,340	290,777,600
Total in Slave States	936,368	599,275,520
Total in States	1,390,708	890,053,120
Total, old territory	1,335,898	854,974,720
Total, new territory	526,078	336,689,920
Total	3,252,684	2,081,717,760

the concurrence of the Senate, — Massachusetts is at the mercy of her sisters; and if those sisters become imperious and aggressive, as some of them give significant tokens of becoming, she must succumb and suffer, like the abused Cordelia among the haughty Gonerils and Regans of the family.

This picture is no fancy-sketch. It is drawn from the original without the exaggeration of a color or a line. We are confronted by these stern realities, these incontrovertible facts: —

	Miles.
Length of the Atlantic Coast to the mouth of St. Mary's River	1,450
From mouth of St. Mary's River to Cape of Florida	450
Gulf Coast to mouth of the Sabine River	1,200
Total	3,100

Those States where the public lands are situated are generally exclusive of lakes, ponds, &c. Marshes are estimated.

The Territories include such waters as are interior.

And no illusions of a poetic temperament, no complacent retrospection over periods of past renown, can avert or delay our impending fate. Like the foolish bird which supposes it can avoid danger by hiding its head from its pursuer, we may hide our eyes and avert our thoughts from all contemplation of the fortunes that await us; but those fortunes will nevertheless overtake us with a speed that we cannot escape from, and a resistlessness that we cannot overcome.

What, then, shall save our native and beloved State from vanishing quite away, from being unknown in the councils of the nation, and lost to the history of the world? In our domestic legislation, and in all our social relationships, what policy shall prevail, and by what spirit shall we be animated, in order to avert so deplorable a fate? Has not every patriot, every worthy son of a Pilgrim sire, an answer at hand? If Massachusetts can no longer challenge respect on account of her numbers, she must challenge it on account of her character. If she is no longer visible by her magnitude, she must become so by her light. She must be, like Hesper, "fairest of all the train of night," and compensate for the diminutiveness of her size by the intenseness of her brilliancy.

Let us reflect, then, in the first place, that Massachusetts has an absolute as well as a relative existence. She exists for her present people and for their posterity, as well as for the Union at large. Though relatively declining, when compared with the whole country, yet there is an actual and constant increase in her numbers. Within her narrow borders she will soon have a million of people; and what finite power can adequately comprehend the joys and sorrows, the hopes and fears, the honor or shame, of a million of human beings belonging to the same generation, or sum up the fearful aggregate of happiness or misery for themselves and their descendants!

Let us thank Heaven, too, that there are other standards of greatness besides vastness of territory, and other forms of wealth besides mineral deposits or agricultural exuberance. Though every hill were a Potosi, though every valley, like that of the Nile, were rank with fatness, yet might a nation be poor in the most desperate sense, — benighted in the darkness of barbarism, and judgment-stricken of Heaven for its sins. A State has local boundaries which it cannot rightfully transcend; but the realm of intelligence, the sphere of charity, the moral domain in which the soul can expand and expatiate, are illimitable, — vast and boundless as the omnipresence of the Being that created them. Worldly treasure is of that nature that rust may corrupt, or the moth destroy, or thieves steal; but even upon the earth there are mental treasures which are unapproachable by fraud, impregnable to violence, and whose value does not perish, but is redoubled with the using. A State, then, is not necessarily fated to insignificance because its dimensions are narrow, nor doomed to obscurity and powerlessness because its numbers are few. Athens was small; yet, low as were her moral aims, she lighted up the whole earth as a lamp lights up a temple. Judæa was small; but her prophets and her teachers were, and will continue to be, the guides of the world. The narrow strip of half-cultivable land that lies between her eastern and western boundaries is not Massachusetts; but her noble and incorruptible men, her pure and exalted women, the children in all her schools, whose daily lessons are the preludes and rehearsals of the great duties of life, and the prophecies of future eminence, — THESE ARE THE STATE.

Under the providence of God, our means of education are the grand machinery by which the " raw material" of human nature can be worked up into inventors and discoverers, into skilled artisans and scientific farmers, into scholars and jurists, into the founders of benevolent institutions, and the great expounders of ethical and theological science. By means of early education, those embryos of talent may be quickened which will solve the difficult problems of political and economical law; and by them, too, the genius may be kindled which will blaze forth in the poets of humanity. Our schools, far more than they have done, may supply the presidents and professors of colleges, and superintendents of public instruction, all over the land; and send, not only into our sister States, but across the Atlantic, the men of practical science to superintend the construction of the great works of art. Here, too, may those judicial powers be developed and invigorated which will make legal principles so clear and convincing as to prevent appeals to force; and, should the clouds of war ever lower over our country, some hero may be found — the nursling of our schools, and ready to become the leader of our armies, that best of all heroes — who will secure the glories of a peace, unstained by the magnificent murders of the battle-field.

The fortunes of a State depend upon antecedent causes, working with greater or less energy through longer or shorter periods of time. By virtue of this universal law, the future condition of the people of Massachusetts will be modified, and to a great extent determined, by the force of causes now put in operation. Enlightened reason discerns the connection between cause and effect; it measures the efficiency of causes; and thus, to a great extent, it is able to adopt and adapt means to the accomplishment of designed ends. Feeble and erring as is the reason of man, yet in this attribute, far more nearly than in any other, does he preserve the divine image in which he was originally formed. Supposing matter to have been first created by the fiat of the Almighty, a substantial and beautiful analogy may be traced between the methods pursued by the Creator and the creature in the formation of the works of their hands. When the fulness of time for creating the parent of the human race had arrived, we must suppose the idea or archetype of a *man* to have existed in the divine Mind as really as " the dust of the earth" from which he was to be formed existed in his hand; and that, in obedience to the sovereign volition, all the elements of which man is composed — the oxygen, the hydrogen, the nitrogen, the carbon, and all the rest — were brought together, and were arranged into his hundreds of bones and of muscles, his thousands of blood-vessels, and his millions of nerves; in fine, into his limbs, and into the manifold apparatus of his senses; into that wonderful organ, the heart; and, if any thing can surpass the heart as a miracle of creative power, into that still more wonderful organ, the brain, — we must suppose, I say, that the elements for the formation of this work were assigned, each to its appropriate place, until God saw the noble and majestic structure of the human form before him, perfect in all its parts. At a vast distance, but still in humble imitation of the divine processes, does man proceed for the completion of every work of his hands. The architect, for instance, through the medium of his senses, acquires a knowledge of all the various properties of all the substances which enter into the construction of an edifice. By his reason, he discovers the special uses and capabilities of all the materials to be employed. Then, in the solitude of his closet, or in the darkness of midnight, he revives in his mind the images of all the substances and ingredients necessary to his work; he measures and arranges and combines *the ideas* of them; he applies to them the architectural laws of fitness, proportion, and strength, until, at last, the grand conception of the edifice — whether sacred temple or human dwelling — rises in his mind, complete from foundation to turret. *He brings together and adjusts the ideas of things, just as an omnipotent arm would bring together and adjust the ponderous things themselves.* After this, he orders the materials to be collected from their respective localities, — it may be from different quarters of the globe, — the wood from the forest, the marble from the quarry, the iron from the mine, the bricks from the clay-pit, the glass, the furniture, the tapestry, and so forth, each from its place, until that ideal image which had before risen up in the silent recesses of his mind now stands forth in full and majestic proportions, embodied in visible and enduring substance, and supplying for centuries to come a fit place for the dwelling of man, or for the worship of God. So, when the Garden of Eden was planted, and when every tree that is pleasant to the sight and good for use was made to grow out of the ground, we must suppose that the Creator, proceeding upon the perfect ideas already in his mind, mingled together, in due proportion, those few chemical elements, which, in their various combinations, make up the almost infinite varieties of the vegetable world, until all of nourishment and perfume and beauty which enters into our imagination of Paradise clustered and glowed and bloomed around, and filled the air with its sweets. In like manner, the gardener, who wishes to bring together, within a narrow compass, specimens of the various plants and flowers that grow between the Equator and the Arctic, first acquires a knowledge of whatever he would cultivate; he classifies them, and arranges all the classes in his mind according to their respective natures; he encloses and prepares his grounds; and then he gathers together seed and plant and vine, indigenous and exotic: on some he pours a double portion of the sun, some he removes into the shade, others he buries in darkness to imitate the growth of caverns, and others still he surrounds with ice, to reproduce the dwarfish vegetation of the frigid zone; for some he prepares a soil dry as an Arabian desert, and for others he makes an artificial pool; until that, which at first was only a bodiless creation of fancy in the mind of the designer, becomes a utility and an embellishment, sustaining the life, and ministering to the luxury, of men.

Now, it is the especial province and function of the statesman and the lawgiver — of all those, indeed, whose influence moulds or modifies public opinion — to study out the eternal principles which conduce to the strength, wisdom, and righteousness of a community; to search for these principles as for hidden riches; to strive for them as one would strive for his life; and then to form public institutions in accordance with them. And he is not worthy to be called a statesman, he is not worthy to be a lawgiver or leader among men, who, either through the weakness of his head or the selfishness of his heart, is incapable of marshalling in his mind the great ideas of knowledge, justice, temperance, and obedience to the laws of God, — on which foundation alone the structure of human welfare can be erected; who is not capable of organizing these ideas into a system, and then of putting that system into operation, as a mechanic does a machine. This only is true statesmanship.

The chief men in society, whether they derive their pre-eminence from birth or wealth or office, or superiority in natural endowments, are mainly responsible for the institutions they leave behind them; because it is in their power to form or conform those institutions according to their own ideas of excellence. The leading spirits of one of the great nations of antiquity had no higher idea of female excellence than that of personal beauty and the attractions of voluptuousness; and hence their brightest and most boasted female ornament was a courtesan. The leading spirits of that other ancient nation, whose perpetual and disgraceful boast it was that it had conquered the whole world, were proud to trace back their ferocious lineage, through patrician and regal blood, to the wolf that suckled their founder, — a tradition, which, whether fact or fiction, is full of allegoric truth. The founders of communities contemporaneous with our own, and now component parts of this republic, filled their veins at their birth with the cancerous blood of slavery, which has now spread itself over and corrupted their whole organism; and yet the tormented sufferer contends for his disease as for his life, — fights for the devil that rends him, because, as he affirms, the exorcism of the evil spirit will be death to himself. For centuries, a leading feature in the policy of Great Britain towards Ireland was the utter abolition of all education which did not conform to the government standard of theology, and was not administered by teachers of its own choosing. None but a *Protestant* was allowed to keep a school. From 1709 to 1782, any Roman Catholic who should presume to be a schoolmaster, or assistant to a schoolmaster, *or even a tutor in a private family*, was to be transported; and if the party returned, then he was to be adjudged guilty of high treason, and to be hung, drawn, and quartered. A great portion of the present agony of starving, diseased, distracted Ireland, is directly referable to the ignorance which has resulted from those imperial interdicts against knowledge. No other acts of British oppression have been so fatal in driving sanity out of the head, and kindness out of the heart, of that maddened country, as the cruel laws by which every child in Ireland was prohibited from nourishing himself with a grain of knowledge, unless he would swallow with it a scruple of theology. These are a few specimens taken from the great storehouse of history, showing how those who enact laws and organize public institutions predetermine the fate of the masses. And are not all those who control legislation, and lead public opinion among ourselves, adjured by these admonitions of history, as well as by the voice of conscience and the precepts of Christianity, to form a model idea of a healthy, industrious, frugal, temperate, wise Christian Commonwealth, and then to exert all their faculties and all their activities in turning this idea into a living reality?

Without undervaluing any other human agency, it may be safely affirmed that the common school, improved and energized as it can easily be, may become the most effective and benignant of all the forces of civilization. Two reasons sustain this position. In the first place, there is a universality in its operation, which can be affirmed of no other institution whatever. If administered in the spirit of justice and conciliation, all the rising generation may be brought within the circle of its reformatory and elevating influences. And, in the second place, the materials upon which it operates are so pliant and ductile as to be susceptible of assuming a greater variety of forms than any other earthly work of the Creator. The inflexibility and ruggedness of the oak, when compared with the lithe sapling or the tender germ, are but feeble emblems to typify the docility of childhood when contrasted with the obduracy and intractableness of man. It is these inherent advantages of the common school, which, in our own State, have produced results so striking, from a system so imperfect, and an administration so feeble. In teaching the blind and the deaf and dumb, in kindling the latent spark of intelligence that lurks in an idiot's mind, and in the more holy work of reforming abandoned and outcast children, education has proved what it can do by glorious experiments. These wonders it has done in its infancy, and with the lights of a limited experience; but when its faculties shall be fully developed, when it shall be trained to wield its mighty energies for the protection of society against the giant vices which now invade and torment it, — against intemperance, avarice, war, slavery, bigotry, the woes of want, and the wickedness of waste, — then there will not be a height to which these enemies of the race can escape which it will not scale, nor a Titan among them all whom it will not slay.

I proceed, then, in endeavoring to show how the true business of the schoolroom connects itself, and becomes identical, with the great interests of society. The former is the infant, immature state of those interests; the latter their developed, adult state. As " the child is father to the man," so may the training of the schoolroom expand into the institutions and fortunes of the State.

PHYSICAL EDUCATION.

In the worldly prosperity of mankind, health and strength are indispensable ingredients. Reflect, for a moment, what an inroad upon the comfort of a family, and its means of support, is a case of chronic sickness or debility in a single one of its members. Should a farmer contract to support, and to continue to pay, his laborer, or a manufacturer his operative, whether able or unable to work, they would demand a serious abatement of wages as a premium for the risk. But whatever drawback a sick member would be to the pecuniary prosperity of a family, or a sick laborer to that of an employer bound to support him, just such a drawback is a sick or disabled member of the community to the financial prosperity of the State to which he belongs. The amount of loss consequent upon such sickness or disability may not be drawn out of the public treasury; but it is subtracted from the common property of the State in a way still more injurious than if the same amount of gold were taken from the public coffers by warrant of the Executive. Money so taken would be transferred to another hand. It would still exist. But the want of health and strength is a dead loss to the community; and, whenever the next valuation is taken, there will be a corresponding deficit in the aggregate of national property. Hence, every citizen, as such, is pecuniarily interested in the health and strength of all his fellow-citizens. It is right, therefore, that he should look upon them all, not only as a benevolent and Christian man would do, pitying and succoring their misfortunes; but he should look upon them, also, as a man of business, — as one who contributes, or is bound to contribute, to a reserved fund from which all the non-producing sick and valetudinary are supported.

Men see this community of interests plainly enough when sickness comes in the form of a pestilence, and decimates and redecimates a city, arresting all the currents of business, gathering the well about the sick-bed or the hearse, or scattering them abroad with fear. But in the aggregate of its periods of sickness, and in the number of its victims, the plague itself is less destructive to human life than the ordinary and stereotyped causes of mortality, which familiarity has bereft of their terrors. It is the concentration of its havoc that makes pestilence terrific. This concentration men's senses can perceive, and therefore they are affrighted. But to the eye of reason that is most alarming which is most injurious; and it is this eye with which a statesman or philosopher should look when he takes a survey of human interests.

Leaving out, then, for the present purpose, all consideration of the pains of sickness and the anguish of bereavement, the momentous truth still remains, that sickness and premature death are positive evils for the statesman and political economist to cope with. The earth, as a hospital for the diseased, would soon wear out the love of life; and, if but the half of mankind were sick, famine, from non-production, would speedily threaten the whole.

(Now, modern science has made nothing more certain than that both good and ill health are the direct result of causes mainly within our own control. In other words, the health of the race is dependent upon the conduct of the race. The health of the individual is determined primarily by his parents, secondarily by himself. The vigorous growth of the body, its strength and its activity, its powers of endurance, and its length of life, on the one hand; and dwarfishness, sluggishness, infirmity, and premature death on the other, — are all the subjects of unchangeable laws. These laws are ordained of God; but the knowledge of them is left to our diligence, and the observance of them to our free agency.) These laws are very few: they are so simple, that all can understand them; and so beautiful, that the pleasure of contemplating them, even independent of their utility, is a tenfold reward for all the labor of their acquisition. The laws, I repeat, are few. The circumstances, however, under which they are to be applied, are exceedingly various and complicated. These circumstances embrace the almost infinite varieties of our daily life, — exercise and rest; sleeping and watching; eating, drinking, and abstinence; the affections and passions; exposure to vicissitudes of temperature, to dryness and humidity, to the effluvia and exhalations of dead animal or decaying vegetable matter: in fine, they embrace all cases where excesses, indiscretions, or exposures may induce disease; or where exercise, temperance, cleanliness, and pure air may avert it. Hence it would be wholly impossible to write out any code of "rules and regulations" applicable to all cases. So, too, the occasions for applying the laws to new circumstances recur so continually, that no man can have a mentor at his side, in the form of a physician or physiologist, to direct his conduct in new emergencies. Even the most favored individual, in ninety-nine cases in a hundred, must prescribe for himself. And hence the uncompromising necessity that all children should be instructed in these laws; and not only instructed, but that they should receive such a *training* during the whole course of pupilage as to enlist the mighty forces of habit on the side of obedience; and that their judgment also should be so developed and matured, that they will be able to discriminate between different combinations of circumstances, and to adapt, in each case, the regimen to the exigency.

Looking to the various disorders and disabilities, which, as every one's experience or observation shows him, do invade and prostrate the human frame, some may be slow to believe that all men, or even the majority of them, will ever be able to administer to those which fall to their share. But, in the first place, it may be remarked that a judicious course of physical training, faithfully observed through all the years of infancy, childhood, and adolescence, will avert a vast proportion of the pains and distempers that now besiege and subdue the human system or some of its vital organs; and hence, that one may safely be ignorant of symptoms and of remedies which he will never have occasion to recognize or to use, as one who seeks a residence remote from wild beasts has no practical occasion to know how they are hunted; and in the next place, that if every one does not know, in all cases, how to prescribe for himself, yet he may always know what part of his machinery is out of order, and how necessary it is to apply promptly to a repairer. Even such a degree of anatomical knowledge as enables one to point out the suffering organ is of great value: for, doubtless, not merely children, but ignorant men, have killed themselves by giving a false location to their malady; or, which is the same kind of error, have caused their physician so to prescribe as to inflict disease on a sound organ, instead of healing a diseased one. It is not every one that can inform a dentist which tooth is the offender.

But to the objection, that all men and women cannot be physicians, the decisive answer is, that the physician must be acquainted with the laws of disease, which are countless in number, and are ever developing new symptoms. (But the sound man or woman needs to be acquainted only with the laws of health, which are few, and whose results, though acting upon different systems, are substantially uniform.] The pharmacopœia of the physician embraces nearly all minerals and all vegetables, and several of the more offensive classes of the animal kingdom, with the various mechanical or chemical combinations which can be formed from or among them. But the whole pharmacopœia of the healthy man comprises but little more than pure water and pure air, simple viands, vegetables, and bread. In quality, they are as different as in number; as different as the sweet and savory contents of store-room and larder from those acrid and mephitic substances which make the druggist's warehouse a universal conservatory of particular abominations.

Is it too much, then, to say that the leaders of society, whether makers of law, or creators of custom and fashion, are bound, by the most solemn obligations of duty as well as by interest, to curtail the ravages of sickness and untimely death, and, as far as possible, to make health and longevity the common property of men? The civil government takes cognizance of pauperism; and men of worldly substance are obliged to bear its expenses. The disabilities of ill health, and the pecuniary losses by early death, are among the leading causes of pauperism. He, therefore, who would prevent the latter, must prevent the former. The civil government exercises penal jurisdiction over crimes, and over the grosser vices; and is it not true that many of those morbid appetites and unnatural desires that seek to assuage their longings by indulgence and excess have their origin in the action of a distempered body upon the mind, rather than of the mind upon the body? Indeed, how often have pure and pious hearts encountered a relentless antagonist to their highest and most devout resolves and aspirations in the pruriences and hankerings of the body in which they were imprisoned! Many a waspish man would become amiable if he could be hung on a new set of nerves. Many a misanthropic disposition would warm into kindliness, could the acrid humors of the body be evaporated or washed away. The dyspeptic contends with evil spirits, " blue and black," against whom the eupeptic bears an invincible charm.

The civil government, too, is bound to provide for the insane, — both for the security of the sane, and for the recovery or amelioration of the insane. The diseases incident to several bodily organs give direct birth to insanity. A disease of the brain induces it at once. Indeed, insanity is often only an exacerbation of some bodily disorder. As a brook swells into a river, so the inflammation of certain organs matures into insanity. General health would greatly reduce the size of those deplorable necessities of an imperfect civilization, — hospitals for the insane.

In extraordinary emergencies, governments do not hesitate to interfere for preventing the spread of contagion, and for excluding the media through which diseases are propagated. When sudden pestilence breaks out in a city, the infected district is put under a bar of non-intercourse with the healthy. When a crew of men, or a cargo of merchandise, arrives from an infected port, a quarantine is enforced. In these cases, the civil magistracy acts under the impulse of fear. But has not government a capacity of reflection and of foresight, as well as a susceptibility to fear? Is a civilized government of modern times to be classified with those orders of existence that have propensity and appetite merely, but not reason and providence?

If not, then, surely, is the government bound to do all it can against the wastings of ill health, and the havoc of unnecessary death; and it is bound to use equal vigilance, whether these calamities invade us from abroad, or are born of home-bred ignorance and folly. And, as has been before intimated, who does not know that the aggregate suffering and loss from general and diffused causes of ill health are indefinitely greater than from the sudden irruption or outbreak of all the contagions and epidemics with which we are ever afflicted? For this greater evil, then, society is bound to provide, not a remedy, but something better than a remedy,—a preventive. Intelligence and obedience would be an antidote, sovereign in its efficacy, and universal in its applicability.

Now, it is beyond all question, that, with the rarest exceptions, every child in the Commonwealth may be endued with this intelligence, and, what is equally important, trained to conforming personal habits. Enlightened by knowledge, and impelled by the force of early and long-continued habit, he would not only see the reasonableness of adapting his regimen to his condition in the varying circumstances of life, but he would feel a personal interest in doing so, as men now feel a personal interest in procuring the gratifications of money or of power. Habit and knowledge will coincide; they will draw in the same direction; they will not be antagonists, as is now so generally the case with those adult men who acquire sound knowledge after bad habits have been enthroned,—the blind force of the latter spurning all the arguments and warnings of the former. This work may be mainly done during the period of non-age, or before children are emancipated from parental control. Let a child wash himself all over every morning for sixteen years, and he will as soon go without his breakfast as his bath. This is but a specimen of the effect of a long-continued observance of Nature's "health regulations."

Not only will a general knowledge of human physiology, or the laws of health, do much to supersede the necessity of a knowledge of pathology, or the laws of disease, but the former is as much better than the latter as prevention is better than remedy, — as much better as all the comforts and securities of an unburnt dwelling are than two-thirds of its value in money from the insurance-office. A general diffusion of physiological knowledge will save millions annually to the State. It will gradually revolutionize many of the absurd customs and usages of society, — conforming them more and more to the rules of reason and true enjoyment, and withdrawing them more and more from the equally vicious extremes of barbarism and of artificial life. It will restrain the caprices and follies of fashion in regard to dress and amusement, and subordinate its ridiculous excesses to the laws of health and decency. It will reproduce the obliterated lines that once divided day and night. It will secure cleanliness and purity, more intimate and personal than any the laundress can supply. It will teach men "to eat that they may live, instead of living that they may eat." When Satan approaches in that form in which he has hitherto been most seductive and successful, — the form of intoxicating beverages, — those who wear the talisman of this science will have an antidote against his temptations. It is a lesson of unspeakable importance to learn that nourishment, and not pleasure, is the primary object of food. God, indeed, in his benevolence, has made the reception of this food not only reparative, but pleasant. But to lose sight of the first object, in a brutish desire for the second, is voluntarily to alter our position in the scale of being, and from the rank of men to descend to the order of beasts. Physiology would reverse the ancient fable, and transform into men the swine who now sit at epicurean tables, and drink of the Circean cup. Every intelligent man deplores the almost universal condition of our dwelling-houses and public edifices, which have been built without regard to the necessities of the human system for pure air. Were physiology universally understood, no man would think of erecting a mansion without an apparatus for its thorough ventilation at all times, any more than without windows for the admission of light. Apertures and flues for the ingress and egress of air into and from sitting-rooms and sleeping-rooms are as necessary to the architectural idea of a well-finished house as nasal orifices are to the anatomical idea of a man; and a dwelling without the means of ventilation is as incomplete and as unsightly as a man without a nose. A knowledge of this science would establish a new standard of beauty,— the classic standard of the Greeks, in which strength was a primary and indispensable element; and it would demonstrate the unspeakable folly and guilt of those matrimonial alliances where hereditary disease, and even insanity itself, are wedded, and the health, mind, and happiness of a family of children are sacrificed for the mercenary object of a dowry.

But an immunity from expense, privation, pain, and bereavement, is not the only boon connected with health and longevity. Sound health is not merely the negation of ill: it is a medium through which alone we can gain access to many invaluable blessings. It enhances every pleasure, and is indispensable to the full performance of almost every duty. The elements environ us with fatal dangers, against which health is our only preserver. The vicissitudes of the climate must be encountered. We have no power to arrest the north wind that congeals by its cold, nor the south that dissolves by its heat. The humidity of one part of the year, and the aridness of another, are equally beyond human control. As our planet wheels around the sun, now turning up our hemisphere to its vertical and fervid rays, and now, by its oblique position, reducing temperature to an opposite extreme, we have no choice but to attend its circuit, and abide its changes. It is certain that nothing but health will enable us to survive exposure to these natural extremes. A thousand causes exist, too, which engender impurity in the air we breathe; we ourselves being the principal. Nothing but knowledge can enable us to eliminate the grossest of these noxious ingredients; and nothing but health, to resist the poison of those which remain. The waste constantly going on in the particles that compose our bodies lays us under an ever-recurring necessity to replenish their exhausted substance by the reception of food. And here, if the food we take is not subjected to the transforming and assimilating power of the alimentary organs, — a power which is wholly lost with the loss of health, — it will prove our destruction. Each of our organs is an avenue, through which death may invade us; and innumerable deaths — that is, innumerable agencies, each one of which has the power of causing death — hold perpetual siege at every avenue, and watch for an opportunity to enter and destroy. And yet air and nourishment, heat and cold, moisture and dryness, we must encounter, and we must have; for they are the permanent conditions of our being. How intelligible, then, and how authoritative, does the doctrine become, that high health, and high health alone, is harmony with Nature! A person without high health is just as much at war with Nature as a guilty soul is at war with the spirit of God; and the struggles of our frail bodies against the resistless might of the elements will be as unavailing as that of our souls against the retributions of Omnipotence.

The capacities of the body for resisting the force of the elements, and for appropriating and assimilating the substances around it into its own substance, is one thing; its capacities for labor are another. Let any man, who has fallen from a state of vigorous health to that of a valetudinary, compare his standard of "a day's work" in the one state with that in the other, and he can then form a better estimate of the value of the health that measures the difference between the two conditions. Sound health opens new and more lucrative employments to its possessor. Ill health often closes a career of the highest usefulness: and though the mind may have been prepared by splendid natural endowments, and by years of study and experience, to lead forward the race in the march of civilization, yet it is stricken down in the midst of its beneficence by the assaults of disease; and thus the onward movement of humanity is arrested, or becomes retrograde, and must wait through another cycle for another leader. What great works in art, in science, and in morals, have been left unfinished or unattempted by reason of the slow decays, or the sudden extinction, of health and of life! When any man of sense has an important work to perform, the first thing he does is to provide a fitting instrument — a tool, a machine, or whatever it may be — with which the work can be done. Health is the prime instrument for the performance of all the labors of life.

One more idea is inseparable from this subject. (When the religious man reflects that our bodies are God's workmanship, he sees that the laws impressed upon them can be no less than God's laws. If these laws, then, are God's laws, we are bound to recognize and obey them. We are bound to obey a law which God has impressed upon the body, on the same principle that we are bound to obey a law which he has impressed upon the soul. And here how pertinent and forcible is the great idea which has been set forth so distinctly by a late writer,* that, when we know a law to be God's law, it matters not by what means we may have arrived at the knowledge, the law becomes imperatively and equally binding upon us! Between the law of the body and the law of the soul, there may, indeed, sometimes arise what we call a conflict of duty, when the subordinate obligation of the former must yield to the supremacy of the latter; but this refers to relative importance, and not to inherent obligation.)

My general conclusion, then, under this head, is, that it is the duty of all the governing minds in society — whether in office or out of it — to diffuse a knowledge of these beautiful and beneficent laws of health and life throughout the length and breadth of the State; to popularize them; to make them, in the first place, the common acquisition of all, and, through education and custom, the common inheritance of all, so that the healthful habits naturally growing out of their observance shall be inbred in the people, exemplified in the personal regimen of each individual, incorporated into the economy of every household, observable in all private dwellings, and in all public edifices, especially in those buildings which are erected by capitalists for the residence of their work-people, or for renting to the

* Mr. George Combe.

poorer classes; obeyed, by supplying cities with pure water; by providing public baths, public walks, and public squares; by rural cemeteries; by the drainage and sewerage of populous towns, and by whatever else may promote the general salubrity of the atmosphere: in fine, by a religious observance of all those sanitary regulations with which modern science has blessed the world.

For this thorough diffusion of sanitary intelligence, the common school is the only agency. It is, however, an adequate agency. Let human physiology be introduced as an indispensable branch of study into our public schools; let no teacher be approved who is not master of its leading principles, and of their applications to the varying circumstances of life; let all the older classes in the schools be regularly and rigidly examined upon this study by the school-committees, — and a speedy change would come over our personal habits, over our domestic usages, and over the public arrangements of society. Temperance and moderation would not be such strangers at the table. Fashion, like European sovereigns, if not compelled to abdicate and fly, would be forced to compromise for the continued possession of her throne by the surrender to her subjects of many of their natural rights. A sixth order of architecture would be invented, — the hygienic, — which, without subtracting at all from the beauty of any other order, would add a new element of utility to them all. The "health-regulations" of cities would be issued in a revised code, — a code that would bear the scrutiny of science. And, as the result and reward of all, a race of men and women, loftier in stature, firmer in structure, fairer in form, and better able to perform the duties and bear the burdens of life, would revisit the earth. The minikin specimens of the race, who now go on dwindling and tapering from parent to child, would re-ascend to manhood and womanhood. Just in proportion as the laws of health and life were discovered and obeyed, would pain, disease, insanity, and untimely death, cease from among men. Consumption would remain; but it would be consumption in the active sense.

INTELLECTUAL EDUCATION AS A MEANS OF REMOVING POVERTY, AND SECURING ABUNDANCE.

Another cardinal object which the government of Massachusetts, and all the influential men in the State, should propose to themselves, is the physical well-being of all the people, — the sufficiency, comfort, competence, of every individual in regard to food, raiment, and shelter. And these necessaries and conveniences of life should be obtained by each individual for himself, or by each family for themselves, rather than accepted from the hand of charity or extorted by poor-laws. It is not averred that this most desirable result can, in all instances, be obtained; but it is, nevertheless, the end to be aimed at. True statesmanship and true political economy, not less than true philanthropy, present this perfect theory as the goal, to be more and more closely approximated by our imperfect practice. The desire to achieve such a result cannot be regarded as an unreasonable ambition; for, though all mankind were well fed, well clothed, and well housed, they might still be but half civilized.

Poverty is a public as well as a private evil. There is no physical law necessitating its existence. The earth contains abundant resources for ten times — doubtless for twenty times — its present inhabitants. Cold, hunger, and nakedness are not, like death, an inevitable lot. There are many single States in this Union which could supply an abundance of edible products for the inhabitants of the thirty States that compose it. There are single States capable of raising a sufficient quantity of cotton to clothe the whole nation; and there are other States having sufficient factories and machinery to manufacture it. The coal-fields of Pennsylvania are sufficiently abundant to keep every house in the land at the temperature of sixty-five degrees for centuries to come. Were there to be a competition, on the one hand, to supply wool for every conceivable fabric, and, on the other, to wear out these fabrics as fast as possible, the single State of New York would beat the whole country. There is, indeed, no assignable limit to the capacities of the earth for producing whatever is necessary for the sustenance, comfort, and improvement of the race. Indigence, therefore, and the miseries and degradations incident to indigence, seem to be no part of the eternal ordinances of Heaven. The bounty of God is not brought into question or suspicion by its existence; for man who suffers it might have avoided it. Even the wealth which the world now has on hand is more than sufficient to supply all the rational wants of every individual in it. Privations and sufferings exist, not from the smallness of its sum, but from the inequality of its distribution. Poverty is set over against profusion. In some, all healthy appetite is cloyed and sickened by repletion; while in others, the stomach seems to be a supernumerary organ in the system, or, like the human eye or human lungs before birth, is waiting to be transferred to some other region, where its functions may come into use. One gorgeous palace absorbs all the labor and expense that might have made a thousand hovels comfortable. That one man may ride in carriages of Oriental luxury, hundreds of other men are turned into beasts of burden. To supply a superfluous wardrobe for the gratification of one man's pride, a thousand women and children shiver with cold; and, for every flash of the diamonds that royalty wears, there is a tear of distress in the poor man's dwelling. Not one Lazarus, but a hundred, sit at the gate of Dives. Tantalus is no fiction. The ancient one might have been fabulous; but the modern ones are terrible realities. Millions are perishing in the midst of superfluities.

According to the European theory, men are divided into classes, — some to toil and earn, others to seize and enjoy. According to the Massachusetts theory, all are to have an equal chance for earning, and equal security in the enjoyment of what they earn. The latter tends to equality of condition; the former, to the grossest inequalities. Tried by any Christian standard of morals, or even by any of the better sort of heathen standards, can any one hesitate, for a moment, in declaring which of the two will produce the greater amount of human welfare, and which, therefore, is the more conformable to the divine will? The European theory is blind to what constitutes the highest glory as well as the highest duty of a State. Its advocates and admirers are forgetful of that which should be their highest ambition, and proud of that which constitutes their shame. How can any one possessed of the attributes of humanity look with satisfaction upon the splendid treasures, the golden regalia, deposited in the Tower of London or in Windsor Palace, each " an India in itself," while thousands around are dying of starvation, or have been made criminals by the combined forces of temptation and neglect? The present condition of Ireland cancels all the glories of the British crown. The brilliant conception which symbolizes the nationality of Great Britain as a superb temple, whose massive and grand proportions are upheld and.adorned by the four hundred and thirty Corinthian columns of the aristocracy, is turned into a loathing and a scorn when we behold the five millions of paupers that cower and shiver at its base. The galleries and fountains of Versailles, the Louvre of Paris, her Notre Dame, and her Madeleine, though multiplied by thousands in number and in brilliancy, would be no atonement for the hundred thousand Parisian *ouvriers* without bread and without work. The galleries of painting and of sculpture at Rome, at Munich, or at Dresden, which body forth the divinest ideals ever executed or ever conceived, are but an abomination in the sight of Heaven and of all good men, while actual, living beings — beings that have hearts to palpitate, and nerves to agonize, and affections to be crushed or corrupted — are experimenting all around them upon the capacities of human nature for suffering and for sin. Where standards like these exist, and are upheld by council and by court, by fashion and by law, *Christianity is yet to be discovered;* at least, it is yet to be applied in practice to the social condition of men.

Our ambition as a State should trace itself to a different origin, and propose to itself a different object. Its flame should be lighted at the skies. Its radiance and its warmth should reach the darkest and the coldest abodes of men. It should seek the solution of such problems as these: To what extent can competence displace pauperism? How nearly can we free ourselves from the low-minded and the vicious, not by their expatriation, but by their elevation? To what extent can the resources and powers of Nature be converted into human welfare, the peaceful arts of life be advanced, and the vast treasures of human talent and genius be developed? How much of suffering, in all its forms, can be relieved? or, what is better than relief, how much can be prevented? Cannot the classes of crimes be lessened, and the number of criminals in each class be diminished? Our exemplars, both for public and for private imitation, should be the parables of the lost sheep and of the lost piece of silver. When we have spread competence through all the abodes of poverty, when we have substituted knowledge for ignorance in the minds of the whole people, when we have reformed the vicious and reclaimed the criminal, then may we invite all neighboring nations to behold the spectacle, and say to them, in the conscious elation of virtue, "Rejoice with me," for I have found that which was lost. Until that day shall arrive, our duties will not be wholly fulfilled, and our ambition will have new honors to win.

But is it not true that Massachusetts, in some respects, instead of adhering more and more closely to her own theory, is becoming emulous of the baneful examples of Europe? The distance between the two extremes of society is lengthening, instead of being abridged. With every generation, fortunes increase on the one hand, and some new privation is added to poverty on the other. We are verging towards those extremes of opulence and of penury, each of which unhumanizes the human mind. A perpetual struggle for the bare necessaries of life, without the ability to obtain them, makes men wolfish. Avarice, on the other hand, sees, in all the victims of misery around it, not objects for pity and succor, but only crude materials to be worked up into more money.

I suppose it to be the universal sentiment of all those who mingle any ingredient of benevolence with their notions on political economy, that vast and overshadowing private fortunes are among the greatest dangers to which the happiness of the people in a republic can be subjected. Such fortunes would create a feudalism of a new kind, but one more oppressive and unrelenting than that of the middle ages. The feudal lords in England and on the Continent never held their retainers in a more abject condition of servitude than the great majority of foreign manufacturers and capitalists hold their operatives and laborers at the present day. The means employed are different; but the similarity in results is striking. What force did then, money does now. The villein of the middle ages had no spot of earth on which he could live, unless one were granted to him by his lord. The operative or laborer of the present day has no employment, and therefore no bread, unless the capitalist will accept his services. The vassal had no shelter but such as his master provided for him. Not one in five thousand of English operatives or farm-laborers is able to build or own even a hovel; and therefore they must accept such shelter as capital offers them. The baron prescribed his own terms to his retainers: those terms were peremptory, and the serf must submit or perish. The British manufacturer or farmer prescribes the rate of wages he will give to his work-people; he reduces these wages under whatever pretext he pleases; and they, too, have no alternative but submission or starvation. In some respects, indeed, the condition of the modern dependant is more forlorn than that of the corresponding serf class in former times. Some attributes of the patriarchal relation did spring up between the lord and his lieges to soften the harsh relations subsisting between them. Hence came some oversight of the condition of children, some relief in sickness, some protection and support in the decrepitude of age. But only in instances comparatively few have kindly offices smoothed the rugged relation between British capital and British labor. The children of the work-people are abandoned to their fate; and notwithstanding the privations they suffer, and the dangers they threaten, no power in the realm has yet been able to secure them an education; and when the adult laborer is prostrated by sickness, or eventually worn out by toil and age, the poor-house, which has all along been his destination, becomes his destiny.

Now, two or three things will doubtless be admitted to be true, beyond all controversy, in regard to Massachusetts. By its industrial condition, and its business operations, it is exposed, far beyond any other State in the Union, to the fatal extremes of overgrown wealth and desperate poverty. Its population is far more dense than that of any other State. It is four or five times more dense than the average of all the other States taken together; and density of population has always been one of the proximate causes of social inequality. According to population and territorial extent, there is far more capital in Massachusetts — capital which is movable, and instantaneously available — than in any other State in the Union; and probably both these qualifications respecting population and territory could be omitted without endangering the truth of the assertion. It has been recently stated in a very respectable public journal, on the authority of a writer conversant with the subject, that from the last of June, 1846, to the first of August, 1848, the amount of money invested by the citizens of Massachusetts " in manufacturing cities, railroads, and other improvements," is " fifty-seven millions of dollars, of which more than fifty has been paid in and expended." The dividends to be received by citizens of Massachusetts from June, 1848, to April, 1849, are estimated by the same writer at ten millions, and the annual increase of capital at " little short of twenty-two millions." If this be so, are we not in danger of naturalizing and domesticating among ourselves those hideous evils which are always engendered between capital and labor, when all the capital is in the hands of one class, and all the labor is thrown upon another?

Now, surely nothing but universal education can counterwork this tendency to the domination of capital and the servility of labor. If one class possesses all the wealth and the education, while the residue of society is ignorant and poor, it matters not by what name the relation between them may be called: the latter, in fact and in truth, will be the servile dependants and subjects of the former. But, if education be equably diffused, it will draw property after it by the strongest of all attractions; for such a thing never did happen, and never can happen, as that an intelligent and practical body of men should be permanently poor. Property and labor in different classes are essentially antagonistic; but property and labor in the same class are essentially fraternal. The people of Massachusetts have, in some degree, appreciated the truth, that the unexampled prosperity of the State — its comfort, its competence, its general intelligence and virtue — is attributable to the education, more or less perfect, which all its people have received: but are they sensible of a fact equally important; namely, that it is to this same education that two-thirds of the people are indebted for not being to-day the vassals of as severe a tyranny, in the form of capital, as the lower classes of Europe are bound to in the form of brute force?

(Education, then, beyond all other devices of human origin, is the great equalizer of the conditions of men, — the balance-wheel of the social machinery. I do not here mean that it so elevates the moral nature as to make men disdain and abhor the oppression of their fellow-men. This idea pertains to another of its attributes. But I mean that it gives each man the independence and the means by which he can resist the selfishness of other men. It does better than to disarm the poor of their hostility towards the rich: it prevents being poor.) Agrarianism is the revenge of poverty against wealth. The wanton destruction of the property of others — the burning of hay-ricks and corn-ricks, the demolition of machinery because it supersedes hand-labor, the sprinkling of vitriol on rich dresses — is only agrarianism run mad. Education prevents both the revenge and the madness. On the other hand, a fellow-feeling for one's class or caste is the common instinct of hearts not wholly sunk in selfish regards for person or for family. The spread of education, by enlarging the cultivated class or caste, will open a wider area over which the social feelings will expand; and, if this education should be universal and complete, it would do more than all things else to obliterate factitious distinctions in society.

The main idea set forth in the creeds of some political reformers, or revolutionizers, is, that some people are poor *because* others are rich. This idea supposes a fixed amount of property in the community, which by fraud or force, or arbitrary law, is unequally divided among men; and the problem presented for solution is, how to transfer a portion of this property from those who are supposed to have too much to those who feel and know that they have too little. At this point, both their theory and their expectation of reform stop. But the beneficent power of education would not be exhausted, even though it should peaceably abolish all the miseries that spring from the co-existence, side by side, of enormous wealth and squalid want. It has a higher function. Beyond the power of diffusing old wealth, it has the prerogative of creating new. It is a thousand times more lucrative than fraud, and adds a thousand-fold more to a nation's resources than the most successful conquests. Knaves and robbers can obtain only what was before possessed by others. But education creates or develops new treasures, — treasures not before possessed or dreamed of by any one.

Had mankind been endowed with only the instincts and faculties of the brute creation, there are hundreds of the irrational tribes to which they would have been inferior, and of which they would have been the prey. Did they, with other animals, roam a common forest, how many of their fellow-tenants of the wood would overcome them by superior force, or outstrip them by greater fleetness, or circumvent them by a sharper cunning! There are but few of the irrational tribes whose bodies are not better provided with the means of defence or attack than is the body of a man. The claws and canine teeth of the lion and of the whole tiger family, the beak and talons of the eagle and the vulture, the speed of the deer and of other timid races, are means of assault or of escape far superior to any we possess; and all the power which we have, like so many of the reptile and insect classes, of secreting a deadly venom, either for protection or for aggression, has relation to moral venom, and not to physical.

In a few lines, nowhere surpassed in philosophic strength and beauty, Pope groups together the remarkable qualities of several different races of animals, — the strength of one class, the genial covering of another, the fleetness of a third. He brings vividly to our recollection the lynx's vision of excelling keenness, the sagacity of the hound that reads a name or a sign in the last vanishing odor of a footprint, the exquisite fineness of the spider's touch, and that chemical nicety by which the bee discriminates between honey and poison in the same flower-cup. He then closes with an interrogatory, which has human reason both for its subject and its object: —

> "The powers of all subdued by thee alone:
> *Is not thy reason all these powers in one?*"

When Pope, now a little more than a century ago, mingled these beauties with his didactic strains, he had no conception, the world at that time had no conception, of other powers and properties, infinitely more energetic and more exhaustless than all which the animal races possess, to which the reason of man is an equivalent. It was not then known that God had endued the earth and the elements with energies and activities as much superior to those which animals or men possess as the bulk and frame of the earth itself exceeds their diminutive proportions. It was not then known that the earth is a great reservoir of powers, and that any man is free to use any quantity of them if he will but possess himself of the key of knowledge, — the only key, but the infallible one, by which to unlock their gates. At that time, if a philosopher wished to operate a mechanical toy, he could lift or pump a few gallons of water for a moving-power: but it was not understood that Nature, by the processes of evaporation and condensation, is constantly lifting up into the sky, and pouring back upon the earth, all the mass of waters that flow in all the rivers of the world; and that, in order to perform the work of the world, the weight of all these waters might be used again and again in each one of their perpetual circuits.* The power-press and the power-loom, the steamboat and the locomotive, the paper-machine and the telegraph, were not then known. All these instruments of human comfort and aggrandizement, and others almost innumerable, similar to them, are operated by the energies and the velocities of Nature; and, had Pope grouped together all the splendid profusion and prodigality of her powers, he might still have appealed to man, and said, —

"Is not thy reason all these powers in one?"

To the weight of waters, the velocity of winds, the expansive force of heat, and other kindred agencies, any man may go, and he may draw from them as much as he pleases without money and without price: or rather, I should say, any educated man may go; for Nature flouts and scorns, and seems to abhor, an ignorant man. She drowns him, and consumes him, and tears him in pieces, if he but ventures to profane with his touch her divinely-wrought machinery.

Now, these powers of Nature, by being enlisted in the service of man, ADD to the wealth of the world, — unlike robbery or slavery or agrarianism, which aim only at the appropriation, by one man or one class, of the wealth belonging to another man or class. One man, with a Foudrinier, will make more paper in a twelvemonth than all Egypt could have made in a hundred years during the reign of the Ptolemies. One man, with a power-press, will print books faster than a million of scribes could copy them before the invention of printing. One man, with an iron-foundery, will make more utensils or machinery than Tubal-Cain could have made had he worked

---

* The waters of the Blackstone River, which flows partly in Massachusetts, and partly in Rhode Island, are used for driving mills, twenty-five times over, in a distance of less than forty miles.

diligently till this time.* And so in all the departments of mechanical labor, in the whole circle of the useful arts. (These powers of Nature are able to give to all the inhabitants of the earth, not merely shelter, covering, and food, but all the means of refinement, embellishment, and mental improvement. In the most strict and literal sense, they are bounties which God gives for proficiency in knowledge.)

The above ideas are beginning to be pretty well understood by all men of respectable intelligence. I have adverted to them, not so much on their own account, as by way of introduction or preface to two or three considerations, which certainly are not understood, or not appreciated, as they deserve to be.

It is a remarkable fact, that human progress, even in regard to the worldly interests of the race, did not begin with those improvements which are most closely allied to material prosperity. One would have supposed, beforehand, that improvements would commence with the near rather than with the remote. Yet mankind had made great advances in astronomy, in geometry, and other mathematical sciences; in the writing of history, in oratory, and in poetry: it is supposed by many to have reached the highest point of yet attained perfection in painting and in sculpture, and in those kinds of architecture which may be called regal or religious, centuries before the great mechanical discoveries and inventions which now bless the world were brought to light. And the question has often forced itself upon reflecting minds, why there was this preposterousness, this inversion of what would appear to be the natural order of progress. Why was it, for instance, that men should have learned the courses of the stars, and the revolutions of the planets, before they found out how to make a good wagon-wheel? Why was it that they built the Parthenon and the Colosseum before they knew how to construct a comfortable, healthful

* In 1740, the whole amount of iron made in England and Wales was seventeen thousand tons; in 1840, it was more than a million tons, notwithstanding all that had been manufactured and accumulated in the intervening century. What would a Jewish or a Roman artificer have said to an annual product of a million tons of iron?

dwelling-house? Why did they construct the Roman aqueducts before they constructed a saw-mill? Or why did they achieve the noblest models in eloquence, in poetry, and in the drama, before they invented movable types? I think we have now arrived at a point where we can unriddle this enigma. *The labor of the world has been performed by ignorant men*, by classes doomed to ignorance from sire to son, by the bondmen and bond-women of the Jews, by the helots of Sparta, by the captives who passed under the Roman yoke, and by the villeins and serfs and slaves of more modern times. The masters — the aristocratic or patrician orders — not only disdained labor for themselves and their children, which was one fatal mistake, but they supposed that knowledge was of no use to a laborer, which was a mistake still more fatal. Hence, ignorance, for almost six thousand years, has gone on plying its animal muscles, and dropping its bloody sweat, and never discovered any way, nor dreamed that there was any way, by which it might accomplish many times more work with many times less labor. And yet nothing is more true than that an ignorant man will toil all his life long, moving to and fro within an inch of some great discovery, and will never see it. All the elements of a great discovery may fall into his hands, or be thrust into his face; but his eyes will be too blind to behold it. If he is a slave, what motive has he to behold it? Its greater profitableness will not redound to his benefit; for another stands ready to seize all the gain. Its abridgment of labor will not conduce to his ease; for other toils await him. But the moment an intelligent man applies himself to labor, and labors for his own benefit or for that of his family, he begins to inquire whether the same task cannot be performed with a less expenditure of strength, or a greater task with an equal expenditure. He makes his wits save his bones. He finds it to be easier to think than to work; nay, that it is easier both to think and work than to work without thinking. He foresees a prize as the reward of successful effort; and this stimulates his brain to deep contrivance, as well as his arms to rapid motion. Taking, for illustration, the result of an experiment which has been actually made, let us suppose this intelligent laborer to be employed in moving blocks of squared granite, each weighing 1080 pounds. To move such a block along the floor of a roughly-chiselled quarry requires a force equal to 758 pounds. An ignorant man, therefore, must employ and pay several assistants, or he can never move such a block an inch. But to draw the same block over a floor of planks will require a force of only 652 pounds. The expense of one assistant, therefore, might be dispensed with. Placed on a platform of wood, and drawn over the same floor, a draught of 606 pounds would be sufficient. By soaping the two surfaces of the wood, the requisite force would be reduced to 182 pounds. Placed on rollers three inches in diameter, a force equal to 34 pounds would be sufficient. Substituting a wooden for a stone floor, and the requisite force is 28 pounds. With the same rollers on a wooden platform, 22 pounds only would be required. And now, by the invention and use of locomotives and railroads, a traction or draught of between *three* and *four* pounds is found to be sufficient to move a body weighing 1080 pounds. Thus the amount of force necessary to remove the body is reduced about two hundred times. Now, take away from these steps the single element of intelligence, and each improvement would have been impossible. The ignorant man would never have discovered how nearly synonymous are freight and friction.

If a savage will learn how to swim, he can fasten a dozen pounds' weight to his back, and transport it across a narrow river or other body of water of moderate width. If he will invent an axe, or other instrument, by which to cut down a tree, he can use the tree for a float, and one of its limbs for a paddle, and can thus transport many times the former weight many times the former distance. Hollowing out his log, he will increase what may be called its tonnage, or rather its *poundage;* and, by sharpening its ends, it will cleave the water both more easily and more swiftly. Fastening several trees together, he makes a raft, and thus increases the buoyant power of his embryo water-craft. Turning up the ends of small poles, or using knees of timber instead of straight pieces, and grooving them together, or filling up the interstices between them in some other way, so as to make them water-tight, he brings his rude raft literally into *ship-shape*. Improving upon hull below and rigging above, he makes a proud merchantman, to be wafted by the winds from continent to continent. But even this does not content the adventurous naval architect. He frames iron arms for his ship; and, for oars, affixes iron wheels, capable of swift revolution, and stronger than the strong sea. Into iron-walled cavities in her bosom he puts iron organs of massive structure and strength, and of cohesion insoluble by fire. Within these he kindles a small volcano; and then, like a sentient and rational existence, this wonderful creation of his hands cleaves oceans, breasts tides, defies tempests, and bears its living and jubilant freight around the globe. Now, take away intelligence from the ship-builder, and the steamship — that miracle of human art — falls back into a floating log; the log itself is lost; and the savage swimmer, bearing his dozen pounds on his back, alone remains.

And so it is, not in one department only, but in the whole circle of human labors. The annihilation of the sun would no more certainly be followed by darkness than the extinction of human intelligence would plunge the race at once into the weakness and helplessness of barbarism. To have created such beings as we are, and to have placed them in this world without the light of the sun, would be no more cruel than for a government to suffer its laboring classes to grow up without knowledge.

In this fact, then, we find a solution of the problem that so long embarrassed inquirers. The reason why the mechanical and useful arts, — those arts which have done so much to civilize mankind, and which have given comforts and luxuries to the common laborer of the present day, such as kings and queens could not command three centuries ago, — the reason why these arts made no progress, and until recently, indeed, can hardly be said to have had any thing more than a beginning, is, that the labor of the world was performed by ignorant men. As soon as some degree of intelligence dawned upon the workman, then a corresponding degree of improvement in his work followed. At first, this intelligence was confined to a very small number, and therefore improvements were few; and they followed each other only after long intervals. They uniformly began in the nations and among the classes where there was most intelligence. The middle classes of England, and the people of Holland and Scotland, have done a hundred times more than all the Eastern hemisphere besides. What single improvement in art, or discovery in science, has ever originated in Spain, or throughout the vast empire of the Russias? But just in proportion as intelligence — that is, education — has quickened and stimulated a greater and a greater number of minds, just in the same proportion have inventions and discoveries increased in their wonderfulness, and in the rapidity of their succession. The progression has been rather geometrical than arithmetical. By the laws of Nature, it must be so. If, among ten well-educated children, the chance is that at least one of them will originate some new and useful process in the arts, or will discover some new scientific principle, or some new application of one, then, among a hundred such well-educated children, there is a moral certainty that there will be more than ten such originators or discoverers of new utilities; for the action of the mind is like the action of fire. One billet of wood will hardly burn alone, though dry as suns and north-west winds can make it, and though placed in the range of a current of air; ten such billets will burn well together; but a hundred will create a heat fifty times as intense as ten, will make a current of air to fan their own flame, and consume even greenness itself.

For the creation of wealth, then, — for the existence of a wealthy people and a wealthy nation, — intelligence is the grand condition. The number of improvers will increase as the intellectual constituency, if I may so call it, increases. In former times, and in most parts of the world even at the present day, not one man in a million has ever had such a development of mind as made it possible for him to become a contributor to art or science. Let this development precede, and contributions, numberless, and of inestimable value, will be sure to follow. That political economy, therefore, which busies itself about capital and labor, supply and demand, interest and rents, favorable and unfavorable balances of trade, but leaves out of account the element of a widespread mental development, is nought but stupendous folly. The greatest of all the arts in political economy is to change a consumer into a producer; and the next greatest is to increase the producer's producing power, — an end to be directly attained by increasing his intelligence. For mere delving, an ignorant man is but little better than a swine, whom he so much resembles in his appetites, and surpasses in his powers of mischief.

But there is a class of persons who are not unwilling to concede the advantages which education has over ignorance, both in the more rapid and perfect performance of all kinds of labor, and in the creation of all those mechanical instruments through which Nature stands ready to do the work of the world: but, while they acknowledge all this, they seem to think that the argument in favor of knowledge has lost much of its force, because mechanical ingenuity and scientific discovery must have nearly reached the outermost limit of possible advancement; that either the powers of Nature are exhausted, or human genius is in its decrepitude. The past achievements of the mind excite their admiration, but not their hope. They are regarded as the measure of what man can perform, but not as the promise of what he is yet to perform. They are accepted, not as a little earnest-money, but as full payment.

Now, the view which I am constrained to take of the history and destiny of man is exactly the contrary of this one. I hold all past achievements of the human mind to be rather in the nature of prophecy than of fulfilment, — the first-fruits of the beneficence of God in endowing us with the faculties of perception, comparison, calculation, and causality, rather than the full harvest of their eventual development. For look at the magnificent creation into which we have been brought, and at the adaptation of our faculties to understand, admire, and use it. All around us are works worthy of an infinite God; and we are led, by irresistible evidence, to believe, that, just so far as we acquire his knowledge, we shall be endued with his power. From history and from consciousness, we find ourselves capable of ever-onward improvement: and therefore it seems to be a denial of first principles — it seems no better than impiety — to suppose that we shall ever become such finished scholars, that the works of the All-wise will have no new problem for our solution, and will, therefore, be able to teach us no longer. Nor is it any less than impiety to suppose that we shall ever so completely enlist the powers of Nature in our service, that exhausted Omnipotence can reward our industry with no further bounties. This would be to suppose that we shall arrive at a period when our active and progressive natures will become passive and stationary; when we shall have nothing to do but to sit in indolent and inglorious contemplation of past achievements; and when, all aspirations having been lost in fruition, we shall have outlived the joys of hope and the rewards of effort, and no new glories will beckon us onward to new felicities.

Neither our faculties, nor their spheres of action, seem to have been projected on any such narrow plan. Ever-expanding powers are within us; eternity lies before us; and an Infinite Being, amidst his works, is the adorable object of these faculties throughout this eternity. These, no height of attainment which our powers will ever reach, and no length of duration to which the cycles of eternity shall ever have run, will enable us to exhaust or fully to comprehend. To affirm the contrary would be to affirm that our finite minds can embrace and encircle their infinite Author, as his mind embraces and encircles ours. Our relation to our Maker, then, is a moral phase of the problem of the asymptote, — a line forever approaching a point which it can never reach.

And, if we believe in our individual capacity for indefinite improvement, why should we doubt the capacity of the race for continued progress as long as it dwells upon the earth? Can man, " by searching, find out God" in a physical sense any more than in a moral one? or can all the generations of the race, by the longest and the profoundest investigations, ever fathom the depths of eternal wisdom and power as they are incorporated into this earthly frame? However far, then, science and art may push their explorations, there will always be a frontier bounding their advances; there will always be a *terra incognita* beyond the regions they have surveyed,— beyond the utmost verge of the horizon which the eye can see from the topmast pinnacle of existing discoveries. Each new adventurer can gain new trophies by penetrating still deeper into the illimitable solitudes where alone Omnipotence dwells and works. The most perfect instrument which the brightest genius of any age may ever construct will be excelled by another instrument, made after a higher ideal of perfection by the brighter genius of a succeeding age. The most rapid processes of art known to any generation will be accelerated in the generation that shall follow it, and science will be found not only a plant of perennial growth, but, in each succeeding age, it will bear blossoms of a more celestial splendor, and fruits of beneficence unknown before.

Astronomers now tell us, that the sun is not a stationary orb, fixed and immovable at one place in the heavens, as, since the days of Copernicus, it had been supposed to be, but that, in some far-off region of immensity, at a distance wholly inconceivable by us, there is a central point of attraction, around which our sun, with its attendant train of planets, is performing a magnificent revolution; just as, within their narrow orbits, the planets of our local system are revolving about the sun. They tell us, further, that the circumference of this solar orbit is so vast, that, during the six thousand years which are supposed to have elapsed since the creation of Adam, the sun has not yet travelled through so much as one of the three hundred and sixty degrees that make up its mighty circle; not through so much as one of those hundreds of astronomical spaces through which it must move before it will complete a single revolution. What number of these immense circuits the earth is destined to perform, or what part even of a single revolution it will accomplish, before it will meet with some such catastrophe as will unfit it to be the abode of a race like ours, we know not; but we have no reason to believe, even if the mighty years of the solar revolutions should equal the number of our terrestrial years since the creation of Adam, that the race will ever have exhausted the earth of all the latent capacities for ministering to the improvement and happiness of man with which God has endued it. No invention or discovery will ever be made, upon which the author can stand, and lift up his proud voice, and exclaim, "*I have found the last miracle of the miracle-working God!*"

Now, so far as these natural and yet undeveloped resources of the earth are hereafter to be brought to light, and made the ministering servants of human welfare, we suppose they are to be brought to light by the exercise of the human faculties, in the same way that all the scientific and mechanical improvements of past times have been brought to light, — that is, by education. And the greater the proportion of minds in any community which are educated, and the more thorough and complete the education which is given them, the more rapidly, through these sublime stages of progress, will that community advance in all the means of enjoyment and elevation, and the more will it outstrip and outshine its less educated neighbors. The advance-guard of education and intelligence will gather the virgin wealth of whatever region they explore, as the reward of their knowledge, just as the Portuguese reaped the great harvest of the riches of India as their reward for discovering the new route to India.

I know that it may be said, and said, too, not without a certain measure of truth, that when a more intelligent community has made a discovery in science, or devised or perfected the processes of any art, a less intelligent community by its side may adopt and copy them, and thus make the improvements their own by possession, though the invention belonged to another. After a bold navigator has opened a new channel of commerce, and while he is gathering the first-fruits of his sagacity, the stupid or the predatory may follow in his wake, and share the gains of his enterprise. Dr. Franklin may discover the uses of the lightning-rod; but when once discovered, and the manner of its use exhibited, any half-taught son of Vulcan can make and erect one by copying the given model. When a school-boy of New England has invented the cotton-gin, or perfected cotton machinery, the slaves of the South, stupid and ignorant as cattle, " according to the form of the statute in such cases made and provided," can operate them with a greater or less degree of success and profit. But there are two considerations which show how inferior the condition of the aping community must always be to that of the originating one.

(In the first place, all copying is in the nature of empiricism. The copyist operates blindly, and not on principle; and therefore he is constantly exposed to failure. In untried emergencies, he never knows what to do, for the light of example shines only in one direction; while it is the very nature of principle, like its divine Author, to circumfuse its beams, and so to leave no darkness in any direction.)

And, in the second place, even supposing the aping community to be able, after long delays and toils, to equal the originating one, still, before the period shall have elapsed which the pupil will require for studying out or copying the old lesson, his master will have studied out some new one; will have discovered some new improvement, diffusive of new utility, and radiant with new beauty: so that the distance will be kept as great as ever between him and the learner.

The slave States of this Union may buy cotton machinery made by the intelligent mechanics of the free States, and they may train their slaves to work it with more or less skill; but should they succeed ever so well, should they eventually become able to meet their entire home demand, it will nevertheless be true, that, in the mean time, the new wants and refinements generated by the progress of the age will demand some new fabric, requiring for its manufacture either more ingeniously-wrought machinery, or greater skill in the operator: and thus will the more educated community forever keep ahead of the less educated one. The progress of mankind may be compared to an ascending spiral. In moving upward along this spiral, the less intelligent community will see the more intelligent one at a point above its head. It will labor on to overtake it, and, making another toilsome circuit, will at length reach the place where the victor had been seen; but, lo! the victor is not there: he, too, has made a circuit along the ascending curve, and is still far aloft, above the head of his pursuer.

Another common idea is this: it is supposed that intelligence in workmen is relatively less important in agricultural labors than in the mechanic and manufacturing arts. The great agricultural staples of the country — corn, cotton, sugar, rice, and so forth — have been stigmatized, or at least characterized, as "coarser" products, and, therefore, requiring less skill and science for their culture and improvement than the fabrics of the loom and the workshop. This may be true; but I am by no means convinced of its truth. It seems to me that there is, as yet, no adequate proof that skill and science, if applied to agriculture, will not yield practical benefits as copious and as wonderful as any that have rewarded the mechanician or the artisan in any department of their labors. Why vegetable growths, so exquisite in their organization, animated by the mysterious principle of life, and so susceptive of all the influences of climate, whether good or ill, — why these should be called "coarser" than iron-ore or other unorganized metals, or any kind of wealth that is found in mines; or why cotton or flax, wool or leather, wood or grain, should be denominated "coarser" before they have been deprived of the principle of life than after it, and before they have lost the marvellous power of assimilating inorganic matter to their own peculiar substance, — it is not easy to perceive. May it not yet be found that a better knowledge of the laws that govern vegetable growth; a better knowledge of the properties and adaptations of different soils; a better knowledge of the conditions of fructification and germination, and of the mysterious chemistry that determines the quality of texture, color, flavor, and perfume; a better knowlof the uncombined gases, and of the effect of light, heat, electricity, and other imponderable agents, upon the size, rapidity, and variegation of vegetable growths, — in fine, a better knowledge of vegetable physiology, and of that, too, which may be called vegetable pathology, — will redeem the whole circle of agricultural occupations from the stigma of requiring less intelligent cultivators than are required for other pursuits, and thus supply a new and irresistible argument in favor of diffusing a vastly-increased amount of knowledge among our free field-laborers and our rural population generally? The marvellous improvements which have been made under the auspices of the Massachusetts Horticultural Society, in horticulture, floriculture, and pomology, already betoken such a result.*

Now, it is in these various ways that all the means of human subsistence, comfort, improvement, or what, in one word, we call wealth, are created, — additional wealth, new wealth, not another man's earnings, not another nation's treasures or lands, tricked away by fraud or wrested by force, but substantially, and for all practical purposes, knowledge-created, mind-created wealth; as much so as though we had been endued with a miraculous power of turning a granite quarry into a city at a word, or a wilderness into cultivated fields, or of commanding harvests to ripen in a day. To see a community acquiring and redoubling its wealth in this way; enriching itself with-

---

* As an illustration of the value of knowledge in agricultural pursuits, it may be mentioned, that the researches and discoveries by M. Meneville, in regard to the fly which was lately so destructive to the olive in the south of France, have increased the annual product of this fruit almost a million of dollars' worth. When would an ignorant man, or a slave, have made such a discovery?

out impoverishing others, without despoiling others, — is it not a noble spectacle? And will not the community that gains its wealth in this way, ten times faster than any robber-nation ever did by plunder, — will not such a community be a model and a pattern for the nations, a type of excellence to be admired and followed by the world? Has Massachusetts no ambition to win the palm in so glorious a rivalry?

But suppose that Massachusetts, notwithstanding her deplorable inferiority in all natural resources as compared with other States, should be content to be their equal only in the means of education, and in the development of the intelligence of her present children and her future citizens, down, down to what a despicable depth of inferiority would she suddenly plunge! Her ancient glory would become dim. No historian, no orator, no poet, would rise up among her children. Her sons would cease, as now, to fill chairs in the halls of learning in more than half the States of the Union. Her jurists would no longer expound the laws of Nature, of nations, and of States, to guide the judicial tribunals of the country. Her skilled artisans and master-mechanics would not be sought for, wherever, throughout the land, educated labor is wanted. Her ship-captains would be driven home from every ocean by more successful competitors. At home, a narrowing in the range of thought and action, a lowering of the tone of life and enterprise, a straitening in the means of living and of culture, a sinking in spirit and in all laudable and generous ambitions, the rearing of sons to obscurity and of daughters to vulgarity, would mark the incoming of a degenerate age, — an age too ignorant to know its own ignorance, too shameless to mourn its degradation, and too spiritless even to rise with recuperative energy from its guilty fall. But little less disastrous would it be to stop where we now are, instead of pressing onward with invigorated strength to a further goal. What has been done is not the fulfilment or consummation of our work. It only affords better vantage-ground from which our successors can start anew in a nobler career of improvement. And if there is any one thing for which the friends of humanity have reason to join in a universal song of thanksgiving to Heaven, it is that there is a large and an increasing body of people in Massachusetts who cannot be beguiled or persuaded into the belief that our common schools are what they may and should be; and who, with the sincerest good-will and warmest affections towards the higher institutions of learning, are yet resolved that the education of the people at large — of the sons and daughters of farmers, mechanics, tradesmen, operatives, and laborers of all kinds — shall be carried to a point of perfection indefinitely higher than it has yet reached.*

POLITICAL EDUCATION.

The necessity of general intelligence, — that is, of education (for I use the terms as substantially synonymous, because general intelligence can never exist without general education, and general education will be sure to produce general intelligence), —

* In the letter of the Hon. Abbott Lawrence, making a donation of fifty thousand dollars for the purpose of founding a scientific school at Cambridge (to which he has since added fifty thousand dollars more), the following expression occurs: "Elementary education appears to be well provided for in Massachusetts." And in the Memorial in behalf of the three colleges, — Harvard, Amherst, and Williams, — presented to the legislature in January, 1848, and signed by each of the three presidents of those institutions, it is said, "The provision [in Massachusetts] for elementary education . . . seems to be all that can be desired, or that can be advantageously done by the legislature." The average salaries of female teachers throughout the State, at the time when these declarations were made, was only $8.55 a month (exclusive of board), which, as the average length of the schools was only eight months, would give to this most faithful and meritorious class of persons but $65.40 a year. The whole value of the apparatus in all the schools of the State was but $23,826; and the whole number of volumes in their libraries was only 91,539, or an average of but twenty-five volumes for each school. In accordance with the prayer of the Memorial, the Committee on Education reported a bill, making a grant of half a million of dollars to the colleges. The House of Representatives, after maturely considering the bill, changed the destination of the money from the colleges to the common schools, and then passed it. The donation of Mr. Lawrence will be highly beneficial to the few hundreds of students who will have the direct enjoyment of his munificence; and, through them, it will also benefit the State. So, too, would the contemplated grant to the colleges. Thus far, it is believed, all liberal minds will agree. But what is needed is the universal prevalence of the further idea, that there are two hundred thousand children in the State, each one of whom would be far more than proportionally benefited by the expenditure for their improved education of one-tenth part of sums so liberal.

the necessity of general intelligence under a republican form of government, like most other very important truths, has become a very trite one. It is so trite, indeed, as to have lost much of its force by its familiarity. Almost all the champions of education seize upon this argument first of all, because it is so simple as to be understood by the ignorant, and so strong as to convince the sceptical. Nothing would be easier than to follow in the train of so many writers, and to demonstrate by logic, by history, and by the nature of the case, that a republican form of government, without intelligence in the people, must be, on a vast scale, what a mad-house, without superintendent or keepers, would be on a small one, — the despotism of a few succeeded by universal anarchy, and anarchy by despotism, with no change but from bad to worse. Want of space and time alike forbid me to attempt any full development of the merits of this theme; but yet, in the closing one of a series of reports partaking somewhat of the nature of a summary of former arguments, an omission of this topic would suggest to the comprehensive mind the idea of incompleteness.

That the affairs of a great nation or state are exceedingly complicated and momentous, no one will dispute. Nor will it be questioned that the degree of intelligence that superintends should be proportioned to the magnitude of the interests superintended. He who scoops out a wooden dish needs less skill than the maker of a steam-engine or a telescope. The dealer in small wares requires less knowledge than the merchant who exports and imports to and from all quarters of the globe. An ambassador cannot execute his functions with the stock of attainments or of talents sufficient for a parish clerk. Indeed, it is clear that the want of *adequate* intelligence — of intelligence *commensurate* with the nature of the duties to be performed — will bring ruin or disaster upon any department. A merchant loses his intelligence, and he becomes a bankrupt. A lawyer loses his intelligence, and he forfeits all the interests of his clients. Intelligence abandons a physician, and his patients die with more than the pains of natural dissolution. Should judges upon the bench be bereft of this guide, what havoc would be made of the property and the innocence of men! Let this counsellor be taken from executive officers, and the penalties due to the wicked would be visited upon the righteous, while the rewards and immunities of the righteous would be bestowed upon the guilty. And so, should intelligence desert the halls of legislation, weakness, rashness, contradiction, and error would glare out from every page of the statute-book. Now, as a republican government represents almost all interests, whether social, civil, or military, the necessity of a degree of intelligence adequate to the due administration of them all is so self-evident, that a bare statement is the best argument.

But, in the possession of this attribute of intelligence, elective legislators will never far surpass their electors. By a natural law, like that which regulates the equilibrium of fluids, elector and elected, appointer and appointee, tend to the same level. It is not more certain that a wise and enlightened constituency will refuse to invest a reckless and profligate man with office, or discard him if accidentally chosen, than it is that a foolish or immoral constituency will discard or eject a wise man. This law of assimilation between the choosers and the chosen results, not only from the fact that the voter originally selects his representative according to the affinities of good or of ill, of wisdom or of folly, which exist between them, but if the legislator enacts or favors a law which is too wise for the constituent to understand, or too just for him to approve, the next election will set him aside as certainly as if he had made open merchandise of the dearest interests of the people by perjury and for a bribe. And if the infinitely Just and Good, in giving laws to the Jews, recognized the "hardness of their hearts," how much more will an earthly ruler recognize the baseness or wickedness of the people when his heart is as hard as theirs! In a republican government, legislators are a mirror reflecting the moral countenance of their constituents. And hence it is, that the establishment of a republican government, without well-appointed and efficient means for the universal education of the people, is the most rash and fool-hardy experiment ever tried by man. Its fatal results may not be immediately developed, they may not follow as the thunder follows the lightning; for time is an element in maturing them, and the calamity is too great to be prepared in a day: but, like the slow-accumulating avalanche, they will grow more terrific by delay, and at length, though it may be at a late hour, will overwhelm with ruin whatever lies athwart their path. It may be an easy thing to make a republic; but it is a very laborious thing to make republicans; and woe to the republic that rests upon no better foundations than ignorance, selfishness, and passion! Such a republic may grow in numbers and in wealth. As an avaricious man adds acres to his lands, so its rapacious government may increase its own darkness by annexing provinces and states to its ignorant domain. Its armies may be invincible, and its fleets may strike terror into nations on the opposite sides of the globe at the same hour. Vast in its extent, and enriched with all the prodigality of Nature, it may possess every capacity and opportunity of being great and of doing good. But, if such a republic be devoid of intelligence, it will only the more closely resemble an obscene giant who has waxed strong in his youth, and grown wanton in his strength; whose brain has been developed only in the region of the appetites and passions, and not in the organs of reason and conscience; and who, therefore, is boastful of his bulk alone, and glories in the weight of his heel, and in the destruction of his arm. Such a republic, with all its noble capacities for beneficence, will rush with the speed of a whirlwind to an ignominious end; and all good men of after-times would be fain to weep over its downfall, did not their scorn and contempt at its folly and its wickedness repress all sorrow for its fate.

As the merits of this subject cannot even be sketched on the present occasion, I will confine myself to a single illustration, showing how an unenlightened people will permit, and sometimes will even require, that their government should injure their own interests.

A universal function of government — one that has pertained to every government that has ever existed, and doubtless will continue to do so while the world stands — is the collection of revenues. The government must be maintained; but it has no power of earning or of creating wealth to defray its own expenses. It must therefore be supported by revenues derived from the people.

In absolute despotisms, arbitrary exactions are made upon all the possessors of wealth, or upon all but a few excepted favorites. Where a pretence for such exactions is wanted, acts which are not crimes are declared to be criminal, so that the ruler may claim a forfeiture, or penalty, for the performance of deeds, which, before any tribunal of conscience or of justice, would be held innocent. *Ex post facto* laws are made; that is, laws which act backwards, and subject an act to punishment after the law, which was not punishable at the time it was done, — which might have been, indeed, not only guiltless, but laudable at the time of its performance.

Now, it must be obvious that such methods of raising revenue must have an almost annihilating effect upon the production of wealth; for no man will earn money beyond his immediate necessities, when the very fact of his acquisition only exposed him to pillage. When the richest men are worst plundered, poverty becomes the privilege. Intelligence, though it had been that of the Prince of Darkness, would have saved nations from this cause of poverty.

Governments less arbitrary have resorted to expedients for self-support scarcely less baneful to the general welfare. Among these are monopolies, — such as that, for instance, by which the Pacha of Egypt required all the cotton grown by his subjects to be sold to him at his own price, that he might resell it at an advanced one; or that by which the French king exercised the privilege of selling all the tobacco consumed in his kingdom, and then sold out the privilege to sell, at an enormous price. Some governments have derived a revenue from the sale of offices, even those which demand, for the fit discharge of their duties, the highest talents and the purest integrity,—such as the judicial; and so have cared every thing for the amount of the bribe, and nothing for the fitness of the incumbent. In all such cases, the most vital and enduring interests of the community have been sacrificed to the incidental benefit of revenue,—a policy vastly more ruinous than that of the incendiary who burns a house that he may steal a shilling.

Even the freest and most enlightened governments have been guilty of similar improvidences and follies. The raising of revenue from licensed lotteries furnishes a signal illustration. For every unit of gain to the public treasury, by the levy of a tax on the sale of lottery-tickets, hundreds of loss are subtracted from the public wealth. For it is obvious, in the first place, that lotteries *create* no wealth. They add nothing to the aggregate of silver and gold belonging to a community, any more than they add to the number of its houses or the extent of its lands. They can do nothing more than to transfer one man's money to another man's pocket. Then they occupy the time of many individuals, who otherwise might be usefully employed in the creation or augmentation of the public wealth. Besides this, the expenses actually incurred by agencies, brokerage, advertisements, apparatus, and so forth, is not inconsiderable. It is also true, that the poorest class of people are usually the purchasers of lottery-tickets,—on the same principle that a man must first be drowning before he will catch at a straw,—and generally with the same result. Thus all the evils of poverty are aggravated by the loss of a part of its pittance. Then adventuring in this traffic substitutes hopes of gain, founded on chance, for the certainties of regular industry. The services of a laborer or an apprentice, of a journeyman mechanic or a clerk, with an undrawn lottery-ticket in his pocket, are hardly worth half-price; for how can any one work for a few shillings a day, while hope is jingling a bag of gold in his ears to be had for nothing? But, while the earnings of a ticket-holder are less, his expenditures are greater; for why should not a man who is so soon to be rich anticipate a little the receipt of his fortune? It is on the same principle which leads a profligate heir to bind himself by post-obits. Is it said that none but a weak-minded man will be so confident of success as to be less industrious or less frugal after the purchase of a ticket than before, the answer is, that the fact of the purchase proves the weak-mindedness. A tempter of fortune may limit himself either to one or to any prescribed number of trials, and resolve, that, if unsuccessful, he will abide by the decisions of his luck, and never venture again; but such a man does not reflect that he will come out of the experiment a different man from what he was when he went into it. The state of his mind will be altered more than that of his purse; and he has no second uncorrupted will whose energies he can now use to restrain the backsliding of the first. But suppose a man to meet with the misfortune of being what he calls fortunate; suppose him to draw a prize of fifty thousand dollars; and thus, without any valid consideration, or any moral right, to pick the pockets of five thousand persons of ten dollars each (and this, too, without the dexterity or sleight of hand of a common pickpocket), — yet it is proved by data derived from the widest observation, that the chances are fifty to one, that, while his unjust gains will only injure the losers, they will ruin himself. Take all these evils into consideration, and take into consideration, also, what is far more important than all these evils united, the impositions and the frauds which accompany the whole operation, and which often bear as great a proportion to the fair dealing as the blanks bear to the prizes, — take all these pecuniary, social, and moral mischiefs into account, and how is it possible for any intelligent legislator, for the sake of a little incidental revenue, ever to legalize an institution which destroys wealth by wholesale, and cankers the morals of entire classes of the people?

And yet, until within a few years, there was not a State in this whole Union whose legislature did not stand so low, not only in the scale of morals, but of political economy, as to authorize lotteries. Sometimes they were granted for a paltry revenue to be paid into the treasury; sometimes to aid in the erection of public works, — to build a bridge, a canal, *or a church*.* Just in proportion as intelligence has advanced, petitions for lotteries have been refused, and the sale of lottery-tickets interdicted by law; until now they are driven almost exclusively into the Southern and South-western States. There they await the dawning of that general enlightenment which common schools could so rapidly give, to be banished from the country forever.

On the clearest principles of morality and political economy, the licensing of houses for the sale of intoxicating drinks, of gaming-houses, and houses of ill-fame, for the ignominious purpose of raising a revenue out of the misery and licentiousness of men, stands even on a more unsound and criminal footing than legalizing the pest of lotteries. Yet all this is done, even at the present day, by legislators who would think it an indignity if they were denied an exalted place on the roll of enlightened, patriotic, and Christian men. Great Britain, for a series of years, has derived more than one-fourth part of all her enormous revenue from the various manufactures of malt, and sale of spirituous liquors, though every pound which has gone into the treasury from this source represented some stage in the terrible process by which sanity was turned into madness, or a well man into a sick beast. France, and even some parts of our own country, have exhibited hateful specimens of the other kinds of these incarnations of evil, — these devouring monsters, who have been permitted, for a fee, by the governments which should have protected their people, to stalk through society, and to inflict upon all its interests — body, soul, and estate — direr calamities than death itself.

The multiplication of oaths is another signal illustration of the fact, how prone incompetent legislators ever are to sacrifice the greater interest to the less, the spiritual to the outward, the

---

* When a church is built by a lottery, can there be any doubt which has the best side of the bargain, the Evil Spirit, or the Good?

enduring to the temporary. Adherence to truth is so necessary among men, that even the lowest instincts of self-interest will visit the falsifier with retribution, though honor and conscience should not. But the utterance of truth, very generally speaking, is considered more in the light of an obligation between man and man than as a due to Heaven; and there are many who would not hesitate to tell a falsehood, who would tremble at the commission of perjury. But governments, for some collateral and incidental benefit, — most generally for the purpose of securing themselves against fraud in the collection of revenues, — impose an oath upon men, not merely where the oath-taker is adversely interested, but where, from the nature of the case, he cannot certainly determine the truth of the statement to which he deposes. This leads to moral laxity, and relaxes laxity itself. Hence, in mercantile communities, there has arisen a class of oaths called "custom-house oaths," — an appellation which indicates that men swear, if not to what they know to be untrue, yet, at least, to what they do not know to be true. Often the oath is administered to persons who are under the strongest temptations to perjury, and where, too, the danger of detection is small. This is PERJURY MADE EASY; for the step is a short one between swearing to a thing as true, with only a general inference or supposition that it is so, and swearing to a known untruth.

Now, can any money compensate government for contaminating public morals? Or in a republic, which is a government of the people by the people, can they afford to barter their own integrity, in order to get a little of their own money, out of their own pockets, into their own public treasury, whence it is so soon to flow back into their own pockets again? Every legislator should be a political economist, and every voter should know at least the leading elements of political economy, and be able to understand their application to the affairs of life; but, surely, that political economy is a delusion and a cheat which does not hold the morals of the community as the primal element in its prosperity; and the prayer, "Lead us not into temptation," is one which may be as appropriately addressed by a people to its rulers as by a frail and fallible mortal to his Maker.

I have now given a hasty review of a single class of errors — those pertaining to the collection of revenue — into which governments have fallen through a want of intelligence; through a want of such intelligence, it may be added, as any discreet and reflecting man would exercise in the management of his own affairs. And when will rulers be wiser than they have been? Never, until the people, to whom they are responsible, shall permit it and demand it. (Never will wisdom preside in the halls of legislation, and its profound utterances be recorded on the pages of the statute-book, until common schools — or some other agency of equal power not yet discovered — shall create a more far-seeing intelligence, and a purer morality, than has ever yet existed among communities of men. Legislators, in the execution of their high guardianship over public interests, will never secure to the State even the greatest amount of wealth while they seek to obtain it at the price of morality. It is only when the virtue of the people is supremely cared for, that they will discover the comprehensive meaning of the Scripture, that godliness is profitable unto all things.)

However elevated the moral character of a constituency may be, however well informed in matters of general science or history, yet they must, if citizens of a republic, understand something of the true nature and functions of the government under which they live. That any one, who is to participate in the government of a country when he becomes a man, should receive no instruction respecting the nature and functions of the government he is afterwards to administer, is a political solecism. In all nations, hardly excepting the most rude and barbarous, the future sovereign receives some training which is supposed to fit him for the exercise of the powers and duties of his anticipated station. Where, by force of law, the government devolves upon the heir while yet in a state of legal infancy, some regency, or other substitute, is appointed to act in his stead until his arrival at mature age; and, in the mean time, he is subjected to such a course of study and discipline as will tend to prepare him, according to the political theory of the time and the place, to assume the reins of authority at the appointed age. If in England, or in the most enlightened European monarchies, it would be a proof of restored barbarism to permit the future sovereign to grow up without any knowledge of his duties, — and who can doubt that it would be such a proof? — then, surely, it would be not less a proof of restored or of never-removed barbarism amongst us to empower any individual to use the elective franchise without preparing him for so momentous a trust. Hence the Constitution of the United States, and of our own State, should be made a study in our public schools. The partition of the powers of government into the three co-ordinate branches, — legislative, judicial, and executive, — with the duties appropriately devolving upon each; the mode of electing or of appointing all officers, with the reasons on which it was founded; and, especially, the duty of every citizen, in a government of laws, to appeal to the courts for redress in all cases of alleged wrong, instead of undertaking to vindicate his own rights by his own arm; and, in a government where the people are the acknowledged sources of power, the duty of changing laws and rulers by an appeal to the ballot, and not by rebellion, — should be taught to all the children until they are fully understood.

Had the obligations of the future citizen been sedulously inculcated upon all the children of this Republic, would the patriot have had to mourn over so many instances where the voter, not being able to accomplish his purpose by voting, has proceeded to accomplish it by violence; where, agreeing with his fellow-citizens to use the machinery of the ballot, he makes a tacit reservation, that, if that machinery does not move according to his pleasure, he will wrest or break it? If the responsibleness and value of the elective franchise were duly appreciated, the day of our state and national elections would be among the most solemn and religious days in the calendar. Men would approach them, not only with preparation and solicitude, but with the sobriety and solemnity with which discreet and religious-minded men meet the great crises of life. No man would throw away his vote through caprice or wantonness, any more than he would throw away his estate, or sell his family into bondage. No man would cast his vote through malice or revenge, any more than a good surgeon would amputate a limb, or a good navigator sail through perilous straits, under the same criminal passions.

But perhaps it will be objected, that the Constitution is subject to different readings, or that the policy of different administrations has become the subject of party strife; and, therefore, if any thing of constitutional or political law is introduced into our schools, there is danger that teachers will be chosen on account of their affinities to this or that political party, or that teachers will feign affinities which they do not feel in order that they may be chosen; and so each schoolroom will at length become a miniature political club-room, exploding with political resolves, or flaming out with political addresses, prepared by beardless boys in scarcely legible hand-writing and in worse grammar.

With the most limited exercise of discretion, all apprehensions of this kind are wholly groundless. There are different readings of the Constitution, it is true; and there are partisan topics which agitate the country from side to side: but the controverted points, compared with those about which there is no dispute, do not bear the proportion of one to a hundred. And, what is more, no man is qualified, or can be qualified, to discuss the disputable questions, unless previously and thoroughly versed in those questions about which there is no dispute. In the terms and principles common to all, and recognized by all, is to be found the only common medium of language and of idea by which the parties can become intelligible to each other; and there, too, is the only common ground whence the arguments of the disputants can be drawn.

It is obvious, on the other hand, that, if the tempest of political strife were to be let loose upon our common schools, they would be overwhelmed with sudden ruin. Let it be once understood that the schoolroom is a legitimate theatre for party politics, and with what violence will hostile partisans struggle to gain possession of the stage, and to play their parts upon it! Nor will the stage be the only scene of gladiatorial contests. These will rage in all the avenues that lead to it. A preliminary advantage, indispensable to ultimate success, will be the appointment of a teacher of the true faith. As the great majority of the schools in the State are now organized, this can be done only by electing a prudential committee, who will make what he calls political soundness paramount to all other considerations of fitness. Thus, after petty skirmishings among neighbors, the fierce encounter will begin in the district's primary assembly, — in the schoolroom itself. This contest being over, the election of the superintending or town's committee must be determined in the same way; and this will bring together the combustibles of each district, to burn with an intenser and a more devouring flame in the town-meeting. It is very possible, nay, not at all improbable, that the town may be of one political complexion, while a majority of the districts are of the opposite. Who shall moderate the fury of these conflicting elements when they rage against each other? and who shall save the dearest interests of the children from being consumed in the fierce combustion? If parents find that their children are indoctrinated into what they call political heresies, will they not withdraw them from the school? and, if they withdraw them from the school, will they not resist all appropriations to support a school from which they derive no benefit?

But, could the schools themselves survive these dangers for a single year, it would be only to encounter others still more perilous. Why should not the same infection that poisons all the relations of the schoolroom spread itself abroad, and mingle with all questions of external organization and arrangement? Why should not political hostility cause the dismemberment of districts already too small? or, what would work equal injury, prevent the union of districts whose power of usefulness would be doubled by a combination of their resources? What better could be expected than that one set of school-books should be expelled, and another introduced, as they might be supposed, however remotely, to favor one party or the other, or as the authors of the books might belong to one party or the other? And who could rely upon the reports, or even the statistics, of a committee chosen by partisan votes, goaded on by partisan impulses, and responsible to partisan domination, and this, too, without any opportunity of control or check from the minority? Nay, if the schools could survive long enough to meet the crisis, why should not any and every measure be taken, either to maintain an existing political ascendency, or to recover a lost one, in a school-district, or in a town, which has even been taken by unscrupulous politicians to maintain or to recover an ascendency at the polls? Into a district, or into a town, voters may be introduced from abroad to turn the scale. An employer may dismiss the employed for their refusal to submit to his dictation, or make the bread that is given to the poor man's children perform the double office of payment for labor to be performed, and of a bribe for principle to be surrendered. And beyond all this, if the imagination can conceive any thing more deplorable than this, what kind of political doctrines would be administered to the children amid the vicissitudes of party domination, — their alternations of triumph and defeat? This year, under the ascendency of one side, the Constitution declares one thing; and commentaries, glosses, and the authority of distinguished names, all ratify and confirm its decisions. But Victory is a fickle goddess. Next year, the vanquished triumph; and Constitution, gloss, and authority make that sound doctrine which was pestilent error before, and that false which was true. Right and wrong have changed sides. The children must now join in chorus to denounce what they had been taught to reverence before, and to reverence what they had been taught to denounce. In the mean time, those great principles, which, according to Cicero, are the same at Rome and at Athens, the same now and forever, and which, according to Hooker, have their seat in the bosom of God, become the fittest emblems of chance and change.

Long, however, before this series of calamities would exhaust itself upon our schools, these schools themselves would cease to be. The ploughshare would have turned up their foundations. Their history would have been brought to a close, — a glorious and ascending history, until struck down by the hand of political parricide; then suddenly falling with a double ruin, — with death and with ignominy.

But, to avoid such a catastrophe, shall all teaching relative to the nature of our government be banished from our schools? and shall our children be permitted to grow up in entire ignorance of the political history of their country? In the schools of a republic, shall the children be left without any distinct knowledge of the nature of a republican government, or only with such knowledge as they may pick up from angry political discussions, or from party newspapers, from caucus speeches, or Fourth-of-July orations, — the Apocrypha of Apocrypha?

Surely, between these extremes, there must be a medium not difficult to be found. And is not this the middle course, which all sensible and judicious men, all patriots, and all genuine republicans, must approve? — namely, that those articles in the creed of republicanism which are accepted by all, believed in by all, and which form the common basis of our political faith, shall be taught to all. But when the teacher, in the course of his lessons or lectures on the fundamental law, arrives at a controverted text, he is either to read it without comment or remark; or, at most, he is only to say that the passage is the subject of disputation, and that the schoolroom is neither the tribunal to adjudicate, nor the forum to discuss it.

Such being the rule established by common consent, and such the practice observed with fidelity under it, it will come to be universally understood that political proselytism is no function of the school, but that indoctrination into matters of controversy between hostile political parties is to be elsewhere sought for, and elsewhere imparted. Thus may all the children of the Commonwealth receive instruction in all the great essentials of political knowledge, — in those elementary ideas without which they will never be able to investigate more recondite and debatable questions; thus will the only practicable method be adopted for discovering new truths, and for discarding, instead of perpetuating, old errors; and thus, too, will that pernicious race of intolerant zealots, whose whole faith may be summed up in two articles, — that they themselves are always infallibly right, and that all dissenters are certainly wrong, — be extinguished, — extinguished, not by violence, nor by proscription, but by the more copious inflowing of the light of truth.

MORAL EDUCATION.

Moral education is a primal necessity of social existence. The unrestrained passions of men are not only homicidal, but suicidal; and a community without a conscience would soon extinguish itself. Even with a natural conscience, how often has evil triumphed over good! From the beginning of time, wrong has followed right, as the shadow the substance. As the relations of men became more complex, and the business of the world more extended, new opportunities and new temptations for wrong-doing have been created. With the endearing relations of parent and child came also the possibility of infanticide and parricide; and the first domestic altar that brothers ever reared was stained with fratricidal blood. Following close upon the obligations to truth came falsehood and perjury, and closer still upon the duty of obedience to the divine law came disobedience. With the existence of private relations between men came fraud; and with the existence of public relations between nations came aggression, war, and slavery. And so, just in proportion as the relations of life became more numerous, and the interests of society more various and manifold, the range of possible and of actual offences has been continually enlarging. As for every new substance there may be a new shadow, so for every new law there may be a new transgression. No form of the precious metals has ever been used which dishonest men have not counterfeited, and no kind of artificial currency has ever been legalized which rogues have not forged. The government sees the evils that come from the use of intoxicating drinks, and prohibits their sale; but unprincipled men pander to depraved appetites, and gather a harvest of dishonest profits. Instead of licensing lotteries, and deriving a revenue from the sale of tickets, the State forbids the mischievous traffic; but, while law-abiding men disdain to practise an illicit trade, knavish brokers, by means of the prohibition itself, secure a monopoly of the sales, and pocket the infamous gain. The government imposes duties on imported goods: smugglers evade the law, and bring goods into the market clandestinely; or perjurers swear to false invoices, and escape the payment of duty, and thus secure to themselves the double advantage of increased sales, and enhanced profits upon what is sold. Science prepares a new medicine to heal or alleviate the diseases of men; crime adulterates it, or prepares as a substitute some cheap poison that resembles it, and can be sold instead of it. A benefactor of the race discovers an agent which has the marvellous power to suspend consciousness, and take away the susceptibility of pain; a villain uses it to rob men or pollute women. Houses are built; the incendiary burns them, that he may purloin the smallest portion of their goods. The press is invented to spread intelligence; but libellers use it to give wings to slander. And so, throughout the infinitely complex and ramified relations of society, wherever there is a right, there may be a wrong; and wherever a law is made to repress the wrong, it may be evaded by artifice or overborne by violence. In fine, all means and laws designed to repress injustice and crime give occasion to new injustice and crime. For every lock that is made, a false key is made to pick it; and, for every Paradise that is created, there is a Satan who would scale its walls.

Nor does this view of the subject exhibit the scope and multitude of the transgressions that may be committed. To represent the range and compass of possible violations, every law that exists must be multiplied by a high power. When the whole family of mankind consisted of but two persons, there could be only two offenders. But now, when the race has increased to millions and hundreds of millions, the laws may be broken by millions and hundreds of millions, — an increased number of transgressors of an increased number of laws. The multitude, then, of possible violations of law, is terrific to the imagination: even the actual violations are sufficient to make our best civilization look but little better than barbarism.

But the above outline, whose vast circumference may be filled up by the commission of crimes against positive law, embraces not a tithe of possible transgressions. Every law in the statute-book might be obeyed, so as to leave no penalty to be awarded by the courts, or inflicted by executive officers, and yet myriads of private vices, too subtle and intangible for legislative enactments, and too undefinable to be dealt with by the tribunals of justice, might still imbitter all domestic and social relations, and leave nothing in life worth living for. Were the greater plagues of public crime and open violence to be stayed, still the lesser ones might remain; like the plagues of Egypt, they might invade every house, penetrate to every chamber, corrupt the water in the fountains and the bread in the kneading-troughs, and turn the dust into loathsome life, so that the plague of hail and the plague of darkness might seem to be blessings in the comparison. In offences against what are usually called the "minor morals," — against propriety, against decency, against the domestic relations, and against good neighborhood, as they are illustrated and enjoined by the example of Christ, the precepts of the gospel, and the perfect law of love, — here is a vast region where offences may grow, and where they do grow, thick-standing and rankly luxuriant.

Against these social vices in all ages of the world, the admonitions of good men have been directed. The moralist has exposed their deformity in his didactic page; the satirist has chastised them in his pungent verse; the dramatist has held them up to ridicule on the mimic stage; and, to some extent, the Christian minister has exhibited their gross repugnancy to the character of a disciple of Jesus. Still they continue to exist; and, to say nothing of heathen nations, the moral condition of all Christendom is, in this respect, like the physical condition of one of the nations that compose it, — that extraordinary people, I mean, whose dwellings, whose flocks, whose agriculture, whose merchandise, and who themselves, are below the level of the ocean; and against them, at all times, this ocean rages, and lifts itself up; and whenever or wherever it can find a breach, or make one, it rushes in, and overwhelms men and their possessions in one common inundation. Even so, like a weltering flood, do immoralities and crimes break over all moral barriers, destroying and profaning the securities and the sanctities of life. Now, how best shall this deluge be repelled? What mighty power or combination of powers can prevent its inrushing, or narrow the sweep of its ravages?

The race has existed long enough to try many experiments for the solution of this greatest problem ever submitted to its hands; and the race has experimented, without stint of time or circumscription of space to mar or modify legitimate results. Mankind have tried despotisms, monarchies, and republican forms of government. They have tried the extremes of anarchy and of autocracy. They have tried Draconian codes of law; and, for the lightest offences, have extinguished the life of the offender. They have established theological standards, claiming for them the sanction of divine authority, and the attributes of a perfect and infallible law; and then they have imprisoned, burnt, massacred, not individuals only, but whole communities at a time, for not bowing down to idols which ecclesiastical authority had set up. These and other great systems of measures have been adopted as barriers against error and guilt: they have been extended over empires, prolonged through centuries, and administered with terrible energy; and yet the great ocean of vice and crime overleaps every embankment, pours down upon our heads, saps the foundations under our feet, and sweeps away the securities of social order, of property, liberty, and life.

At length, these experiments have been so numerous, and all of them have terminated so disastrously, that a body of men has risen up in later times, powerful in influence, and not inconsiderable in numbers, who, if I may use a mercantile phrase, would abandon the world as a total loss; who mock at the idea of its having a benevolent or even an intelligent Author or Governor; and who, therefore, would give over the race to the dominion of chance, or to that of their own licentious passions, whose rule would be more fatal than chance.

But to all doubters, disbelievers, or despairers in human progress, it may still be said, there is one experiment which has never yet been tried. It is an experiment, which, even before its inception, offers the highest authority for its ultimate success. Its formula is intelligible to all; and it is as legible as though written in starry letters on an azure sky. It is expressed in these few and simple words: "*Train up a child in the way he should go; and, when he is old, he will not depart from it.*" This declaration is positive. If the conditions are complied with, it makes no provision for a failure. Though pertaining to morals, yet, if the terms of the direction are observed, there is no more reason to doubt the result than there would be in an optical or a chemical experiment.

But this experiment has never yet been tried. Education has never yet been brought to bear with one-hundredth part of its potential force upon the natures of children, and, through them, upon the character of men and of the race. In all the attempts to reform mankind which have hitherto been made, whether by changing the frame of government, by aggravating or softening the severity of the penal code, or by substituting a government-created for a God-created religion, — in all these attempts, the infantile and youthful mind, its amenability to influences, and the enduring and self-operating character of the influences it receives, have been almost wholly unrecognized. Here, then, is a new agency, whose powers are but just beginning to be understood, and whose mighty energies hitherto have been but feebly invoked; and yet, from our experience, limited and imperfect as it is, we do know, that, far beyond any other earthly instrumentality, it is comprehensive and decisive.

Reformatory efforts hitherto made have been mainly expended upon the oaken-fibred hardihood and incorrigibleness of adult offenders, and not upon the flexibleness and ductility of youthful tendencies. Rulers have forgotten, that though a giant's arm cannot bend a tree of a century's growth, yet the finger of an infant could have given direction to its germ. When a man has invested fifty thousand dollars in the business of importing ardent spirits into the country, it often does little more than to enrage him to point out the different results between such an investment and the investment of the same sum in whale-ships, where, besides its own permanent value, it will soon add fifty thousand dollars more to the actual wealth of the community. Show the distiller how he changes the life-sustaining fruits of the earth into a physical and moral poison, and what a deluge of destruction he is sending forth over society, and his blood will boil hardly less fiercely than his accursed caldrons: but who will be rash enough to say of any child in the land; who will be rash enough to say of any man now engaged in the business of promoting and spreading intemperance, and visiting another generation with all its calamities,— who will dare say of any of them that the nature and consequences of this direful occupation might not have been so vividly depicted to the imagination, and so clearly explained to the conscience, during the years of childhood, that any child would sooner think of getting a living by counterfeiting money than by engaging in the traffic? Would any child, on whose heart the horrors and atrocities of the slave-trade had made their natural impression before his arrival at the age of fourteen years, ever connect himself with slavery afterwards? Were a child taught the dignity, the healthfulness, and the advantages of voluntary labor, and the meanness of living upon the unrequited services of the weak and defenceless, could he ever bear to live a life of pampered indolence secured to him by a hundred lives, each as precious and as sacred in the sight of Heaven as his own, of unpaid toil and irredeemable debasement? Did genius pour out its heart as fervently to depict the calamities of war as it has done to blazon forth what is called military glory, would not children be led to abhor all unnecessary wars as much more than they abhor murder as the destruction of an army is greater than that of a single murderer? If the schools were earnestly to teach children that office and honor are not synonymous terms, and that the only value of any office consists in its opening a wider sphere for useful exertion, should we find so many men renouncing usefulness and forfeiting honor for the acquisition of office? If wealth were not forever talked of before children as among the chief prizes of life, should we see such throngs making haste to be rich, with all the attendant consequences of fraud and dishonor? Indeed, so decisive is the effect of early training upon adult habits and character, that numbers of the most able and experienced teachers — those who have had the best opportunities to become acquainted with the errors and the excellences of children, their waywardness, and their docility — have unanimously declared it to be their belief, that if all the children in the community, from the age of four years to that of sixteen, could be brought within the reformatory and elevating influences of good schools, the dark host of private vices and public crimes which now imbitter domestic peace, and stain the civilization of the age, might, in ninety-nine cases in every hundred, be banished from the world. When Christ taught his disciples to pray, " Thy kingdom come, thy will be done *on earth* as it is done in heaven," did he teach them to pray for what shall never come to pass? And, if this consummation is ever to be realized, is it to be by some mighty, sudden, instantaneous

RELIGIOUS EDUCATION.

But it will be said that this grand result in practical morals is a consummation of blessedness that can never be attained without religion, and that no community will ever be religious without a religious education. Both these propositions I regard as eternal and immutable truths. Devoid of religious principles and religious affections, the race can never fall so low but that it may sink still lower; animated and sanctified by them, it can never rise so high but that it may ascend still higher. And is it not at least as presumptuous to expect that mankind will attain to the knowledge of truth, without being instructed in truth, and without that general expansion and development of faculty which will enable them to recognize and comprehend truth in any other department of human interest as in the department of religion? No creature of God of whom we have any knowledge has such a range of moral oscillation as a human being. He may despise privileges, and turn a deaf ear to warnings and instructions such as evil spirits may never have known, and therefore be more guilty than they; or, ascending through temptation and conflict along the radiant pathway of duty, he may reach the sublimest heights of happiness, and may there experience the joys of a contrast such as ever-perfect beings can never feel. And can it be that our nature in this respect is taken out of the law that governs it in every other respect, — the law, namely, that the teachings which supply it with new views, and the training that leads it to act in conformity with those views, are ineffective and nugatory?

Indeed, the whole frame and constitution of the human soul show, that, if man be not a religious being, he is among the most deformed and monstrous of all possible existences. His propensities and passions need the fear of God as a restraint from evil; and his sentiments and affections need the love of God as a condition and preliminary to every thing worthy of the name of happiness. Without a capability or susceptibility, therefore, of knowing and reverencing his Maker and Preserver, his whole nature is a contradiction and a solecism: it is a moral absurdity, as strictly so as a triangle with but two sides, or a circle without a circumference, is a mathematical absurdity. The man, indeed, of whatever denomination or kindred or tongue he may be, who believes that the human race, or any nation, or any individual in it, can attain to happiness, or avoid misery, without religious principle and religious affections, must be ignorant of the capacities of the human soul, and of the highest attributes in the nature of man. We know, from the very structure and functions of our physical organization, that all the delights of the appetites and of the grosser instincts are evanescent and perishing. All bodily pleasures over-indulged become pains. Abstemiousness is the stern condition of prolonged enjoyment, — a condition that balks desire at the very moment when it is most craving. Did the fields teem, and the forests bend, and the streams flow, with the most exquisite delicacies, how small the proportion of our time in which we could luxuriate in their sweets without satiety and disgust! Unchastened by temperance, the richest earthly banquets stimulate, only to end in loathing. Perpetual self-restraint on the one side, or intolerable pains on the other, is the law of all our animal desires; and it may well be questioned which are the sharper sufferings, the fiercest pangs of hunger and of thirst, or the agonizing diseases that form the fearful retinue of epicurism and bacchanalian indulgence. Were the pleasures of sense the only pleasures we could enjoy, immortality might well be scoffed at as worthless, and annihilation welcomed; for if another Eden were created around us, filled with all that could gratify the appetite or regale the sense, and were the whole range and command of its embowering shades and clustering fruits bestowed upon us, still, with our present natures, we should feel intellectual longings which not all the objects of sight and of sense could appease; and luxuries would sate the palate, and beauties pall upon the eye, in the absence of objects to quicken and stimulate the sterner energies of the mind.

The delights of the intellect are of a far nobler order than those of the senses; but even these have no power to fill up the capacities of an immortal mind. The strongest intellect tires. It cannot sustain an ever-upward wing. Even in minds of Olympian vastness and vigor, there must be seasons for relaxation and repose,—intervals when the wearied faculties, mounted upon the topmast of all their achievements, must stop in their ascending career to review the distance they have traversed, and to replenish their energies for an onward flight. And although, in the far-off cycles of eternity, the stature of the intellect should become lofty as an archangel's; although its powers of comprehension should become so vast, and its intuitions so penetrating, that it could learn the history of a planet in a day, and master at a single lesson all the sciences that belong to a system of stars, — still, I repeat, that, with our present nature, we should be conscious of faculties unoccupied, and restless, yea, tormented with a sense of privation and loss, like lungs in a vacuum gasping vainly for breath, or like the eye in darkness straining to catch some glimmering of light. Without sympathy, without spiritual companionship with other beings, without some Being, all-glorious in his perfections, whom the spirit could commune with and adore, it would be a mourner and a wanderer amid all the splendors of the universe. Through the lone realms of immensity would it fly, calling for love as a mother calls for her departed first-born; but its voice would return to it in echoes of mockery. Nay, though the intellect of man should become as effulgent as the stars amid which he might walk, yet sympathetic and devout affections alone can fertilize the desolations of the heart. Love is as necessary to the human heart as knowledge is to the mind; and infinite knowledge can never supply the place of infinite good. The universe, grand, glorious, and beautiful as it is, can be truly enjoyed only through the worship as well as the knowledge of the great Being that created it. Among people where there is no true knowledge of God, the errors, superstitions, and sufferings of a false religion always rush in to fill the vacuum.

There is not a faculty nor a susceptibility in the nature of man, from the lightning-like intuitions that make him akin to the cherubim, or the fire and fervor of affection that assimilate him to seraphic beings, down to the lowest appetites and desires by which he holds brotherhood with beast and reptile and worm,—there is not one of them all that will ever be governed by its proper law, or enjoy a full measure of the gratification it was adapted to feel, without a knowledge of the true God, without a sense of acting in harmony with his will, and without spontaneous effusions of gratitude for his goodness. Convictions and sentiments such as these can alone supply the vacuity in the soul of man, and fill with significance and loveliness what would otherwise be a blank and hollow universe.

How limited and meagre, too, would be the knowledge which should know all things else, but still be ignorant of the self-existent Author of all! What is the exquisite beauty of flowers, of foliage, or of plumage, if we know nothing of the great Limner who has painted them, and blended their colors with such marvellous skill? So the profundity of all science is shallowness, if we know nothing of the eternal Mind that projected all sciences, and made their laws so exact and harmonious, that all the objects in an immensity can move onward throughout an eternity without deviation or error. Even the visible architecture of the heavens, majestic and refulgent as it is, dwindles and glooms into littleness and darkness in the presence of the great Builder, who "of old laid the foundation of the earth," and "meted out heaven with a span." Among all the objects of knowledge, the Author of knowledge is infinitely the greatest; and the microscopic animalcule, which, by a life of perseverance, has circumnavigated a drop of water, or the tiny insect which has toiled and climbed until it has at last reached the highest peak of a grain of sand, knows proportionately more of the height and depth and compass of planetary spaces than the philosopher who has circuited all other knowledge, but is still ignorant of God. In the acquisition of whatever art, or in the pursuit of whatever science, there is a painful sense of incompleteness and imperfection while we remain untaught in any great department known to belong to it. And so, in the development and culture of the human soul, we are conscious not merely of the want of symmetry, but of gross disfigurement and mutilation, when the noblest and most enduring part of an appropriate development and culture is wanting. In merely an artistical point of view, to be presented with the torso of Hercules, or with the truncated body of Minerva, when we were expecting to behold the fulness of their majestic proportions, would be less painful and shocking than a system of human culture from which religious culture should be omitted.

So, too, if the subject be viewed in relation to all the purer and loftier affections and susceptibilities of the human soul, the results are the same. If, in surveying the highest states of perfection which the character of man has ever yet reached upon earth, we select from among the whole circle of our personal or historical acquaintances those who are adorned with the purest quality and the greatest number of excellences as the objects of our most joyful admiration and love, why should not the soul be lifted into sublimer ecstasies, and into raptures proportionately more exalted and enduring, if it could be raised to the contemplation of Him whose "name alone is excellent"? If we delight in exhibitions of power, why should we pass heedlessly by the All-powerful? If human hearts are touched with deeds of mercy, there is One whose tender mercies are over all his works. If we reverence wisdom, there is such perfect wisdom on high, that that of angels becomes "folly" in its presence. If we love the sentiment of love, has not the apostle told us that God is love? There are many endearing objects upon earth from which the heart of man may be sundered; but he only is bereaved of all things who is bereaved of his Father in heaven.

I here place the argument in favor of a religious education for the young upon the most broad and general grounds, purposely leaving it to every individual to add for himself those auxiliary arguments which may result from his own peculiar views of religious truth. But such is the force of the conviction to which my own mind is brought by these general considerations, that I could not avoid regarding the man who should oppose the religious education of the young as an insane man; and, were it proposed to debate the question between us, I should desire to restore him to his reason before entering upon the discussion. If, suddenly summoned to eternity, I were able to give but one parting word of advice to my own children, or to the children of others; if I were sinking beneath the wave, and had time to utter but one articulate breath; or were wasting away upon the death-bed, and had strength to make but one exhortation more, — that dying legacy should be, "Remember thy Creator in the days of thy youth."

I can, then, confess myself second to no one in the depth and sincerity of my convictions and desires respecting the necessity and universality, both on abstract and on practical grounds, of a religious education for the young; and, if I had stronger words at command in which to embody these views, I would not fail to use them. But the question still remains, How shall so momentous an object be pursued? In the measures we adopt to give a religious education to others, shall we ourselves abide by the dictates of religion? or shall we do, as has almost universally been done ever since the unhallowed union between Church and State under Constantine, — shall we seek to educate the community religiously through the use of the most irreligious means?

On this subject I propose to speak with freedom and plainness, and more at length than I should feel required to do but for the peculiar circumstances in which I have been placed. It is matter of notoriety, that the views of the Board of Education, — and my own, perhaps, still more than those of the Board, — on the subject of religious instruction in our public schools, have been subjected to animadversion. Grave charges have been made against us, that our purpose was to exclude religion, and to exclude that, too, which is the common exponent of religion, — the Bible, — from the common schools of the

State; or, at least, to derogate from its authority, and destroy its influence in them. Whatever prevalence a suspicion of the truth of these imputations may have heretofore had, I have reason to believe that further inquiry and examination have done much to disabuse the too credulous recipients of so groundless a charge. Still, amongst a people so commendably sensitive on the subject of religion as are the people of Massachusetts, any suspicion of irreligious tendencies will greatly prejudice any cause, and, so far as any cause may otherwise have the power of doing good, will greatly impair that power.

It is known, too, that our noble system of free schools for the whole people is strenuously opposed by a few persons in our own State, and by no inconsiderable numbers in some of the other states of this Union; and that a rival system of " parochial " or " sectarian schools " is now urged upon the public by a numerous, a powerful, and a well-organized body of men. It has pleased the advocates of this rival system, in various public addresses, in reports, and through periodicals devoted to their cause, to denounce our system as irreligious and anti-Christian. They do not trouble themselves to describe what our system is, but adopt a more summary way to forestall public opinion against it by using general epithets of reproach, and signals of alarm.

In this age of the world, it seems to me that no student of history, or observer of mankind, can be hostile to the precepts and the doctrines of the Christian religion, or opposed to any institutions which expound and exemplify them; and no man who thinks, as I cannot but think, respecting the enduring elements of character, whether public or private, can be willing to have his name mentioned while he is living, or remembered when he is dead, as opposed to religious instruction and Bible instruction for the young. In making this final Report, therefore, I desire to vindicate my conduct from the charges that have been made against it; and, so far as the Board has been implicated in these charges, to leave my testimony on record for their exculpation. Indeed, on this point, the Board and myself must be justified or condemned together; for I do not believe they would have enabled me, by their annual re-elections, to carry forward any plan for excluding either the Bible or religious instruction from the schools; and, had the Board required me to execute such a purpose, I certainly should have given them the earliest opportunity to appoint my successor. I desire, also, to vindicate the system with which I have been so long and so intimately connected, not only from the aspersion, but from the suspicion, of being an irreligious or anti-Christian or an un-Christian system. I know full well, that it is unlike the systems which prevail in Great Britain, and in many of the Continental nations of Europe, where the Established Church controls the education of the young in order to keep itself established. But this is presumptive evidence in its favor, rather than against it.

All the schemes ever devised by governments to secure the prevalence and permanence of religion among the people, however variant in form they may have been, are substautially resolvable into two systems. One of these systems holds the regulation and control of the religious belief of the people to be one of the functions of government, like the command of the army or the navy, or the establishment of courts, or the collection of revenues. According to the other system, religious belief is a matter of individual and parental concern; and, while the government furnishes all practicable facilities for the independent formation of that belief, it exercises no authority to prescribe, or coercion to enforce it. The former is the system, which, with very few exceptions, has prevailed throughout Christendom for fifteen hundred years. Our own government is almost a solitary example among the nations of the earth, where freedom of opinion, and the inviolability of conscience, have been even theoretically recognized by the law.

The argument in behalf of a government-established religion, at the time when it was first used, was not without its plausibility; but the principle, once admitted, drew after it a train of the most appalling consequences. If religion is absolutely essential to the stability of the State as well as to the present and future happiness of the subject, why, it was naturally asked, should not the government enforce it? And, if government is to enforce religion, it follows, as a necessary consequence, that it must define it; for how can it enforce a duty, which, being undefined, is uncertain? And again: if government begins to define religion, it must define what it is not, as well as what it is; and, while it upholds whatever is included in the definition, it must suppress and abolish whatever is excluded from it. The definition, too, must keep pace with speculation, and must take cognizance of all outward forms and observances; for if speculation is allowed to run riot, and ceremonies and observances to spring up unrestrained, religion will soon elude control, emerge into new forms, and exercise, if it does not arrogate, a substantial independence. Both in regard to matters of form and of substance, all recusancy must be subdued, either by the deprivation of civil rights, or by positive inflictions; for the laws of man, not possessing, like the laws of God, a self-executing power, must be accompanied by some effective sanction, or they will not be obeyed. If a light penalty proves inadequate, a heavier one must follow, — the loss of civil privileges by disfranchisement, or of religious hopes by excommunication. If the non-conformist feels himself, by the aid of a higher power, to be secure against threats of future perdition, the civil magistrate has terrible resources at command in this life, — imprisonment, scourging, the rack, the fagot, death. Should it ever be said that these are excessive punishments for exercising freedom of thought, and for allowing the heart to pour forth those sentiments of adoration to God with which it believes God himself has inspired it, the answer is always ready, that nothing is so terrible as the heresy that draws after it the endless wrath of the Omnipotent; and, therefore, that Smithfield fires, and inquisitorial tortures, and *auto-da-fés*, and St. Bartholomews, are cheap offerings at the shrine of truth: nay, compared with the awful and endless consequences of a false faith, they are of less moment than the slightest puncture of a nerve. And assuming the truth of the theory, and the right of the government to secure faith by force, it surely would be better, infinitely better, that every hill-top should be lighted with the fires of Smithfield, and every day in the calendar should be a St. Bartholomew's, than that errors so fatal should go unabolished.

In the council-hall of the Inquisition at Avignon, there still is, or lately was, to be seen, a picture of the Good Samaritan painted upon the wall. The deed of mercy commemorated by this picture was supposed to be the appropriate emblem of the inquisitor's work. The humanity of pouring oil and wine into the wounds of the bleeding wayfarer who had fallen among thieves; the kindness of dismounting from his own beast, and setting the half-dead victim of violence upon it; and the generosity of purchasing comfort and restoration for him at an inn, — were held to be copied and imitated, upon an ampler and a nobler scale, by the arrest of the heretic, by the violence that tore him from home and friends, and by the excruciating tortures that at last wrenched soul and body asunder. The priests who sentenced, and the familiars that turned the wheel or lighted the fagot, or, with red-hot pincers, tore the living flesh from the quivering limbs, were but imitators of the Good Samaritan, binding up moral wounds, and seeking to take a lost traveller to a place of recovery and eternal repose. So when the news of the Massacre of St. Bartholomew's — on which occasion thirty thousand men, women, and children were butchered at the stroke of a signal-bell — reached Rome, the pope and his cardinals ordained a thanksgiving, that all true believers might rejoice together at so glorious an event, and that God might be honored for the pious hearts that designed, and the benevolent hands that executed, so Christian a deed. And, admitting their premises, surely they were right. Could communities, or even individuals, be rescued from endless perdition at the price of a massacre or an *auto-da-fé*, the men who would wield the sword, or kindle the flame, would be only nobler Samaritans; and "a picture upon the Inquisition walls at Avignon would be but an inadequate emblem of their soul-saving beneficence.

But, in all the persecutions and oppressions ever committed in the name of religion, one point has been unwarrantably assumed; namely, *that the faith of their authors was certainly and infallibly the true faith.* With the fewest exceptions, the advocates of all the myriad conflicting creeds that have ever been promulgated have held substantially the same language: "*Our* faith we know to be true. For its truth, we have the evidence of our reason and our conscience; we have the Word of God in our hands, and we have the Spirit of God in our hearts, testifying to its truth."[*] The answer to this claim is almost too obvious to be mentioned. The advocates of hundreds and thousands of hostile creeds have placed themselves upon the same ground. Each has claimed the same proof from reason and conscience, the same external revelation from God, and the same inward light of his Spirit. But if truth be *one*, and hence necessarily harmonious; if God be its author; and if the voice of God be not more dissonant than the tongues of Babel, — then, at least, all but one of the different forms of faith ever promulgated by human authority, so far as these forms conflict with each other, cannot have emanated from the Fountain of all truth. These faiths must have been more or less erroneous. The believers in them must have been more or less mistaken. Who, on an impartial survey of the whole, and a recollection of the confidence with which each one has been claimed to be infallibly true, shall dare to affirm that any one of them all is a perfect transcript of the perfect law as it exists in the Divine Mind, *and that that one is his?*

But here arises a practical distinction, which the world has lost sight of. It is this: after seeking all possible light from within, from without, and from above, each man's belief is his

---

[*] Or, as I once heard the same sentiment expressed in the pulpit, from the lips of an eminent divine, "I am right; and I know I am right; and I know I know it."

own standard of truth; *but it is not the standard for any other man.* The believer is bound to live by his belief under all circumstances, in the face of all perils, and at the cost of any sacrifice. But his standard of truth is the standard for himself alone; *never for his neighbor.* That neighbor must have his own standard, which to him must be supreme. And the fact that each man is bound to follow his own best light and guidance is an express negation of any other man's right, and of any government's right, of forcible interference. Here is the dividing-line. On one side lie personal freedom and the recognition of freedom in others; on the other side are intolerance, oppression, and all the wrongs and woes of persecution for conscience' sake. The hierarchs of the world have generally reversed this rule of duty. They have been more rigid in demanding that others should live according to their faith than in living in accordance with it themselves.

Did the history of mankind show that there has been the most of virtue and piety in those nations where religion has been most rigorously enforced by law, the advocates of ecclesiastical domination would have a powerful argument in favor of their measures of coercion; but the united and universal voice of history, observation, and experience, gives the argument to the other side. Nor is this surprising. Weak and fallible as human reason is, it was too much to expect that any mere man, even though aided by the light of a written revelation, would ever fathom the whole counsels of the Omnipotent and the Eternal. But the limitations and short-sightedness of men's reason did not constitute the only obstacle to their discovery of truth. All the passions and perversities of human nature conspired to prevent so glorious an achievement. The easily-acquired but awful power possessed by those who were acknowledged to be the chosen expounders of the divine will tempted men to set up a false claim to be the depositaries of God's purposes towards men, and the selected medium of his communication with them; and to this temptation erring mortals were fain to yield. Those who were supposed able to determine the destiny of the soul in the next world came easily to control opinion, conduct, and fortune in this. Hence they established themselves as a third power, — a power between the creature and the Creator, — not to facilitate the direct communion between man and his Maker, but to supersede it. They claimed to carry on the intercourse between heaven and earth as merchants carry on commerce between distant nations, where the parties to the interchange never meet each other. The consequence soon was, that this celestial commerce degenerated into the basest and most mercenary traffic. The favors of heaven were bought and sold like goods in the market-place. Robbery purchased pardon and impunity by bribing the judge with a portion of the wealth it had plundered. The assassin bought permission to murder, and the incendiary to burn. A price-current of crime was established, in which sins were so graduated as to meet the pecuniary ability of both rich and poor offenders. Licenses to violate the laws of God and man became luxuries, for which customers paid according to their several ability. Gold was the representative of all virtues as well as of all values. Under such a system, men lost their conscience, and women their virtue; for the right to commit all enormities was purchasable by money, and pardonable by grace, — save only the guilt of heresy; and the worst of all heresies consisted in men's worshipping the God of their fathers according to the dictates of their consciences.

Those religious exercises which consist in a communion of the soul with its Father in heaven have been beautifully compared to telegraphic communications between distant friends; where, silent as thought, and swift as the lightning, each makes known to the other his joys and his desires, his affection and his fidelity, while the busy world around may know nought of their sacred communings. But, as soon as hierarchies obtained control over men, they changed the channel of these communications between heaven and earth. An ecclesiastical bureau was established; and it was decreed that all the telegraphic wires should centre in that, so that all the communications between man and his Maker should be subject to the inspection of its chiefs, and carried on through their agency alone. Thus, whether the soul had gratitude or repentance to offer to its God, or light or forgiveness to receive from on high, the whole intercourse, in both directions, must go through the government office, and there be subject to take such form, to be added to or subtracted from, as the ministers or managers in possession of power might deem to be expedient. Considering the nature of man, one may well suppose that many of the most precious of the messages were never forwarded; that others were perverted, or forged ones put in their place; and that, in some instances at least, the reception of fees was the main inducement to keep the machinery in operation.

Among the infinite errors and enormities resulting from systems of religion devised by man, and enforced by the terrors of human government, have been those dreadful re-actions which have abjured all religion, spurned its obligations, and voted the Deity into non-existence. This extreme is, if possible, more fatal than that by which it was produced. Between these extremes, philanthropic and godly men have sought to find a medium, which should avoid both the evils of ecclesiastical tyranny and the greater evils of atheism. And this medium has at length been supposed to be found. It is promulgated in the great principle, that government should do all that it can to facilitate the acquisition of religious truth, but shall leave the decision of the question, what religious truth is, to the arbitrament, without human appeal, of each man's reason and conscience; in other words, that government shall never, by the infliction of pains and penalties, or by the privation of rights or immunities, call such decision either into pre-judgment or into review. The formula in which the constitution of Massachusetts expresses it is in these words: "All religious sects and denominations demeaning themselves peaceably and as good citizens shall be equally under the protection of law; and no subordination of one sect or denomination to another shall ever be established by law."

The great truth recognized and expressed in these few words of our constitution is one which it has cost centuries of struggle and of suffering, and the shedding of rivers of blood, to attain; and he who would relinquish or forfeit it, virtually impetrates upon his fellow-men other centuries of suffering and the shedding of other rivers of blood. Nor are we as yet entirely removed from all danger of relapse. The universal interference of government in matters of religion, for so many centuries, has hardened the public mind to its usurpations. Men have become tolerant of intolerance; and, among many nations of Christendom, the common idea of religious freedom is satisfied by an exemption from fine and imprisonment for religious belief. They have not yet reached the conception of equal privileges and franchises for all. Doubtless the time will come when any interference, either by positive infliction or by legal disability, with another man's conscience in religious concernments, so long as he molests no one by the exercise of his faith, will be regarded as the crowning and supereminent act of guilt which one human being can perpetrate against another. But this time is far from having yet arrived, and nations otherwise equally enlightened are at very different distances from this moral goal. The oppressed, on succeeding to power, are prone to become oppressors in their turn, and to forget, as victors, the lessons, which, as victims, they had learned.

The Colonial, Provincial, and State history of Massachusetts shows by what slow degrees the rigor of our own laws was relaxed, as the day-star of religious freedom slowly arose after the long, black midnight of the past. It was not, indeed, until a very recent period, that all vestige of legal penalty or coercion was obliterated from our statute-book, and all sects and denominations were placed upon a footing of absolute equality in the eye of the law. Until the ninth day of April, 1821, no person in Massachusetts was eligible to the office of governor, lieutenant-governor, or councillor, or to that of senator, or representative in the General Court, unless he would make oath to a belief in the particular form of religion adopted and sanctioned by the State. And until the eleventh day of November, 1833, every citizen was taxable, by the constitution and laws of the State, for the support of the *Protestant* religion, whether he were a Protestant, a Catholic, or a believer in any other faith. Nor was it until the tenth day of March, 1827 (St. 1826, ch. 143, § 7), that it was made unlawful to use the common schools of the State as the means of proselyting children to a belief in the doctrines of particular sects, whether their parents believed in those doctrines or not.

All know the energetic tendency of men's minds to continue in a course to which long habit has accustomed them. The same law is as true in regard to institutions administered by bodies of men as in regard to individual minds. The doctrine of momentum, or head-way, belongs to metaphysics as much as to mechanics. A statute may be enacted, and may even be executed by the courts, long before it is ratified and enforced by public opinion. Within the last few years, how many examples of this truth has the cause of temperance furnished! And such was the case in regard to the law of 1827, prohibiting sectarian instruction in our public schools. It was not easy for committees at once to withdraw or to exclude the books, nor for teachers to renounce the habits, by which this kind of instruction had been given. Hence, more than ten years subsequent to the passage of that law, at the time when I made my first educational and official circuits over the State, I found books in the schools as strictly and exclusively *doctrinal* as any on the shelves of a theological library. I heard teachers giving oral instruction as strictly and purely *doctrinal* as any ever heard from the pulpit or from the professor's chair. And more than this: I have now in my possession printed directions, given by committee-men to teachers, enjoining upon them the use of a catechism in school, which is wholly devoted to an exposition of the doctrines of one of the denominations amongst us. These directions bear date a dozen years subsequent to the prohibitory law above referred to. I purposely forbear to intimate what doctrine or what denomination was "*favored*," in the language of the law, by these means, because I desire to have this statement as impersonal as it can be.

In the first place, then, I believed these proceedings not only to be wholly unwarranted by law, but to be in plain contravention of law. And, in the next place, the legislature had made it the express duty of the Secretary, "diligently to apply himself to the object of collecting information of the condition of the public schools [throughout the State], of the fulfilment of the duties of their office by all members of the school-committees of all the towns, and the circumstances of the several school-districts in regard to all the subjects of teachers, pupils, books, apparatus, and methods of education," and so forth. I believed then, as now, that religious instruction in our schools, to the extent which the constitution and laws of the State allowed and prescribed, was indispensable to their highest welfare, and essential to the vitality of moral education. Then as now, also, I believed that sectarian books and sectarian instruction, if their encroachments were not resisted, would prove the overthrow of the schools. While, on the one hand, therefore, I deplored, in language as earnest and solemn as I was capable of commanding, the insufficiency of moral and religious instruction given in the schools; on the other hand, instead of detailing what I believed to be infractions of the law in regard to sectarian instruction, I endeavored to set forth what was supposed to be the true meaning and intent of the law. Such a general statement of legal limitations and prohibitions, instead of a specific arraignment of teachers or of committees for disregarding them, I judged to be the milder and more eligible course. Less I could not do, and discharge the duty which the law had expressly enjoined upon me. More I deemed it unadvisable to do, lest transgressors should take offence at what they might deem to be an unnecessary personal exposure. And, further, I had confidence, that when the law itself, and the reasons of equity and public policy on which it was founded.

should be better understood, all violations of it would cease. Every word of my early Reports having any reference to this subject was read in the presence of the Board, on which sat able lawyers and distinguished clergymen of different denominations; and no word of exception was ever taken to the views there presented, either on the ground that they were contrary to law, or had any sinister or objectionable tendency.

No person, then, in the whole community, could have been more surprised or grieved than myself at finding my views in regard to the extent and the limitation of religious instruction in our public schools attributed to a hostility to religion itself, or a hostility to the Scriptures, which are the "lively oracles" of the Christian's faith. As the Board was implicated with me in these charges (they never having dissented from my views, and continuing to re-elect me annually to the office of Secretary), it is well known to its earlier members that I urged the propriety of their meeting these charges with a public and explicit denial of their truth. In so grave a matter, I did not think that a refutation of the calumny would derogate from their dignity, but only evince the sensitiveness of their moral feelings, and the firmness of their moral principles. Such was the course pursued by the Board of Commissioners of Education in Ireland, composed of some of the most pious and elevated dignitaries in both communions, and at whose head was that most able and venerable prelate, Archbishop Whately. When their conduct was assailed, and their motives impugned, because they refused to turn the national schools into engines for proselyting from one sect to another, they met the charges from year to year in their Annual Reports, and finally discomfited and put to shame their bigoted assailants.

To my suggestion in regard to vindicatory measures, the reply was, that, as the charges were groundless, they probably would be temporary; and that a formal reply to the accusations might bestow an undeserved importance upon the accusers. Were it not that the opinion of the Board, at that time, did not coincide with my own, I should still think that an early, temperate, but decided refutation, by the Board itself, of the charges against them, and against the system administered by them or under their auspices, would have been greatly preventive of evil, and fruitful of good. The pre-occupancy of the public mind with error on so important a subject is an unspeakable calamity; and errors that derive their support from religious views are among the most invincible. But different counsels prevailed; and for several years, in certain quarters, suspicions continued rife. I was made to see, and deeply to feel, their disastrous and alienating influence as I travelled about the State; sometimes withdrawing the hand of needed assistance, and sometimes, when conduct extorted approval, impeaching the motives that prompted it. For no cause, not dearer to me than life itself, could I ever have persevered, amid the trials and anxieties, and against the obstacles, that beset my path. But I felt that there is a profound gratification in standing by a good cause in the hour of its adversity. I believed there must be a deeper pleasure in following truth to the scaffold than in shouting in the retinue where error triumphs. I felt, too, a religious confidence that truth would ultimately prevail; and that it was my duty to labor in the spirit of a genuine disciple, who toils on with equal diligence and alacrity, whether his cause is to be crowned with success in his own lifetime, or only at the end of a thousand years. And, as the complement of all other motives, I felt that a true education would be among the most efficient of means to prevent the re-appearance, in another generation, of such an aggressive and unscrupulous opposition as the Board and myself were suffering under in this.

After years of endurance, after suffering under misconstructions of conduct, and the imputation of motives whose edge is sharper than a knife, it was at my suggestion, and by making use of materials which I had laboriously collected, that the Board made its Eighth Annual Report,—a document said to be the ablest argument in favor of the use of the Bible in schools anywhere to be found. This Report had my full concurrence. Since its appearance, I have always referred to it as explanatory of the views of the Board, and as setting forth the law of a wise commonwealth and the policy of a Christian people. Officially and unofficially, publicly and privately, in theory and in practice, my course has always been in conformity with its doctrines. And I avail myself of this, the last opportunity which I may ever have, to say, in regard to all affirmations or intimations that I have ever attempted to exclude religious instruction from school, or to exclude the Bible from school, or to impair the force of that volume, that they are now, and always have been, without substance or semblance of truth.

But it may still be said, and it is said, that however sincere, or however religiously disposed, the advocates of our school-system may be, still the character of the system is not to be determined by the number nor by the sincerity of its defenders, but by its own inherent attributes; and that, if judged by these attributes, it is, in fact and in truth, an irreligious, an un-Christian, and an anti-Christian system. Having devoted the best part of my life to the promotion of this system, and believing it to be the only system which ought to prevail, or can permanently prevail, in any free country, I am not content to see it suffer, unrelieved, beneath the weight of imputations so grievous; nor is it right that any hostile system should be built up by so gross a misrepresentation of ours. That our public schools are not theological seminaries, is admitted. That they are debarred by law from inculcating the peculiar and distinctive doctrines of any one religious denomination amongst us, is claimed; and that they are also prohibited from ever teaching that what they do teach is the whole of religion, or all that is essential to religion or to salvation, is equally certain. But our system earnestly inculcates all Christian morals; it founds its morals on the basis of religion; it welcomes the religion of the Bible; and, in receiving the Bible, it allows it to do what it is allowed to do in no other system, —

to speak for itself. But here it stops, not because it claims to have compassed all truth, but because it disclaims to act as an umpire between hostile religious opinions.

The very terms "public school" and "common school" bear upon their face that they are schools which the children of the entire community may attend. Every man not on the pauper-list is taxed for their support; but he is not taxed to support them as special religious institutions: if he were, it would satisfy at once the largest definition of a religious establishment. But he is taxed to support them as a *preventive* means against dishonesty, against fraud, and against violence, on the same principle that he is taxed to support criminal courts as a *punitive* means against the same offences. He is taxed to support schools, on the same principle that he is taxed to support paupers,— because a child without education is poorer and more wretched than a man without bread. He is taxed to support schools, on the same principle that he would be taxed to defend the nation against foreign invasion, or against rapine committed by a foreign foe,— because the general prevalence of ignorance, superstition, and vice, will breed Goth and Vandal at home more fatal to the public well-being than any Goth or Vandal from abroad. And, finally, he is taxed to support schools, because they are the most effective means of developing and training those powers and faculties in a child, by which, when he becomes a man, he may understand what his highest interests and his highest duties are, and may be in fact, and not in name only, a free agent. The elements of a political education are not bestowed upon any school child for the purpose of making him vote with this or that political party when he becomes of age, but for the purpose of enabling him to choose for himself with which party he will vote. So the religious education which a child receives at school is not imparted to him for the purpose of making him join this or that denomination when he arrives at years of discretion, but for the purpose of enabling him to judge for himself, according to the dictates of his own reason and conscience, what his religious obligations are, and whither they lead. But if a man is taxed to support a school where religious doctrines are inculcated which he believes to be false, and which he believes that God condemns, then he is excluded from the school by the divine law, at the same time that he is compelled to support it by the human law. This is a double wrong. It is politically wrong, because, if such a man educates his children at all, he must educate them elsewhere, and thus pay two taxes, while some of his neighbors pay less than their due proportion of one; and it is religiously wrong, because he is constrained by human power to promote what he believes the divine power forbids. The principle involved in such a course is pregnant with all tyrannical consequences. It is broad enough to sustain any claim of ecclesiastical domination ever made in the darkest ages of the world. Every religious persecution since the time of Constantine may find its warrant in it, and can be legitimately defended upon it. If a man's estate may be taken from him to pay for teaching a creed which he believes to be false, his children can be taken from him to be taught the same creed; and he, too, may be punished to any extent for not voluntarily surrendering both his estate and his offspring. If his children can be compulsorily taken, and taught to believe a creed which the parent disbelieves, then the parent can be compulsorily taken, and made to subscribe the same creed. And, in regard to the extent of the penalties which may be invoked to compel conformity, there is no stopping-place between taking a penny and inflicting perdition. It is only necessary to call a man's reason and conscience and religious faith by the name of recusancy or contumacy or heresy, and so to inscribe them on the statute-book, and then the non-conformist or dissenter may be subdued by steel or cord or fire; by anathema and excommunication in this life, and the terrors of endless perdition in the next. Surely that system cannot be an irreligious, an anti-Christian, or an un-Christian one, whose first and cardinal principle it is to recognize and protect the highest and dearest of all human interests and of all human rights.

Again : it seems almost too clear for exposition, that our system, *in one of its most essential features*, is not only not an irreligious one, but that it is more strictly religious than any other which has ever yet been adopted. Every intelligent man understands what is meant by the term "jurisdiction." It is the rightful authority which one person, or one body of men, exercises over another person or persons. Every intelligent man understands that there are some things which are within the jurisdiction of government, and other things which are not within it. As Americans, we understand that there is a line dividing the jurisdiction of the State governments from the jurisdiction of the Federal government, and that it is a violation of the constitutions of both for either to invade the legitimate sphere of action which belongs to the other. We all understand, that neither any State in this Union, nor the Union itself, has any right of interference between the British sovereign and a British subject, or between the French government and a citizen of France. Let this doctrine be applied to the relations which our fellow-citizens bear to the rulers who have authority over them. Primarily, religious rights embrace the relations between the creature and the Creator, just as political rights embrace the relations between subject and sovereign, or between a free citizen and the government of his choice, and just as parental rights embrace the relation between parent and child. Rights, therefore, which are strictly religious, lie out of and beyond the jurisdiction of civil governments. They belong exclusively to the jurisdiction of the divine government. If, then, the State of Massachusetts has no right of forcible interference between an Englishman or a Frenchman, and the English or French government, still less, far less, has it any right of forcible interference between the soul of man and the King and Lord to whom that soul owes undivided and supreme allegiance. Civil society may exist, or it may cease to exist. Civil government may continue for centuries in the hands of the same dynasty, or it may change hands, by revolution, with every new moon. The man outcast and outlawed to-day, and to whom, therefore, we owe no obedience, may be rightfully installed in office to-morrow, and may then require submission to his legitimate authority. The civil governor may resign or be deposed; the framework of the government may be changed, or its laws altered; so that the duty of allegiance to a temporal sovereign may have a succession of new objects, or a succession of new definitions. But the relation of man to his Maker never changes. Its object and its obligations are immutable. The jurisdiction which God exercises over the religious obligations which his rational and accountable offspring owe to him excludes human jurisdiction. And hence it is that religious rights are inalienable rights. Hence, also, it is, that it is an infinitely greater offence to invade the special and exclusive jurisdiction which the Creator claims over the consciences and hearts of men than it would be to invade the jurisdiction which any foreign nation rightfully possesses over its own subjects or citizens. The latter would be only an offence against international law; the former is treason against the majesty of Heaven. The one violates secular and temporal rights only; the other violates sacred and eternal ones. When the British government passed its various statutes of *præmunire*, as they were called,— statutes to prevent the Roman pontiff from interfering between the British sovereign and the British subject,— it was itself constantly enacting and enforcing laws which interfered between the Sovereign of the universe and his subjects upon earth, far more directly and aggressively than any edict of the Roman see ever interfered with any allegiance due from a British subject to the self-styled defender of the faith.

It was in consequence of laws that invaded the direct and exclusive jurisdiction which our Father in heaven exercises over his children upon earth, that the Pilgrims fled from their native land to that which is the land of our nativity. They sought a residence so remote and so inaccessible, in the hope that the prerogatives of the Divine Magistrate might no longer be set at nought by the usurpations of the civil power. Was it not an irreligious and an impious act on the part of the British government to pursue our ancestors with such cruel penalties and privations as to drive them into banishment? Was it not a religious and a pious act in the Pilgrim Fathers to seek a place of refuge where the arm of earthly power could neither restrain them from worshipping God in the manner which they believed to be most acceptable to him, nor command their worship in a manner believed to be unacceptable? And if it was irreligious in the British government to violate freedom of conscience in the case of our forefathers two centuries ago, then it is more flagrantly irreligious to repeat the oppression in this more enlightened age of the world. If it was a religious act in our forefathers to escape from ecclesiastical tyranny, then it must be in the strictest conformity to religion for us to abstain from all religious oppression over others, and to oppose it wherever it is threatened. And this abstinence from religious oppression, this acknowledgment of the rights of others, this explicit recognition and avowal of the supreme and exclusive jurisdiction of Heaven, and this denial of the right of any earthly power to encroach upon that jurisdiction, is precisely what the Massachusetts school-system purports to do in theory and what it does actually in practice. Hence I infer that our system is not an irreligious one, but is in the strictest accordance with religion and its obligations.

It is still easier to prove that the Massachusetts school-system is not anti-Christian nor un-Christian. The Bible is the acknowledged expositor of Christianity. In strictness, Christianity has no other authoritative expounder. This Bible is in our common schools by common consent. Twelve years ago, it was not in all the schools. Contrary to the genius of our government, if not contrary to the express letter of the law, it had been used for sectarian purposes, — to prove one sect to be right, and others to be wrong. Hence it had been excluded from the schools of some towns by an express vote. But since the law, and the reasons on which it is founded, have been more fully explained and better understood, and since sectarian instruction has, to a great extent, ceased to be given, the Bible has been restored. I am not aware of the existence of a single town in the State in whose schools it is not now introduced, either by a direct vote of the school-committee, or by such general desire and acquiescence as supersede the necessity of a vote. In all my intercourse for twelve years, whether personal or by letter, with all the school-officers in the State, and with tens of thousands of individuals in it, I have never heard an objection made to the use of the Bible in school, except in one or two instances; and, in those cases, the objection was put upon the ground that daily familiarity with the book in school would tend to impair a reverence for it.

If the Bible, then, is the exponent of Christianity; if the Bible contains the communications, precepts, and doctrines which make up the religious system called and known as Christianity; if the Bible makes known those truths, which, according to the faith of Christians, are able to make men wise unto salvation; and if this Bible is in the schools, — how can it be said that Christianity is excluded from the schools? or how can it be said that the school-system which adopts and uses the Bible is an anti-Christian or an un-Christian system? If that which is the acknowledged exponent and basis of Christianity is in the schools, by what tergiversation in language, or paralogism in logic, can Christianity be said to be shut out from the schools? If the Old Testament were in the schools, could a Jew complain that Judaism was excluded from them? If the Koran were read regularly and reverently in the schools, could a Mahometan say that Mahometanism was excluded? Or, if the Mormon Bible were in the schools, could it be said that Mormonism was excluded from them?

Is it not, indeed, too plain to require the formality of a syllogism, that if any man's creed is to be found in the Bible, and the Bible is in the schools, then that man's creed is in the schools? This seems even plainer than the proposition, that two and two make four; that is, we can conceive of a creature so low down in the scale of intelligence, that he could not see what sum would be produced by adding two and two together, who still could not fail to see, that, if a certain system called Christianity were contained in and inseparable from a certain book called the Bible, then, wherever the Bible might go, there the system of Christianity must be.) If a vase of purest alabaster, filled with myrrh and frankincense and precious ointments, were in the school, would not their perfumes be there also? And would the beautiful vase, and the sweet aroma of spice and unguent, be any more truly there, if some concocter of odors, such as Nature never made, should insist upon saturating the air with the products of his own distillations, which, though pleasant to *his* idiosyncrasy, would be nauseous to everybody else? But if a man is conscious or suspicious that his creed is not in the Bible, but resolves that it shall be in the schools at any rate, then it is easy to see that he has a motive either to exclude the Bible from school, or to introduce some other book, or some oral interpreter in company with it, to misconstrue and override it. If the Bible is in the schools, we can see a reason why a Jew, who disbelieves in the mission of our Saviour, or a Mahometan, who believes in that of the Prophet, should desire, by oral instruction or catechism or otherwise, to foist in his own views, and thereby smother all conflicting views; but even they would not dare to say that the schools where the Bible was found were either anti-Christian or un-Christian. So far from this, if they were candid, they would acknowledge that the system of Christianity was in the schools, and that they wished to neutralize and discard it by hostile means.)

And further: our law explicitly and solemnly enjoins it upon all teachers, without any exception, " to exert their best endeavors to impress on the minds of children and youth committed to their care and instruction the principles of piety, justice, and a sacred regard to truth, love to their country, humanity, and universal benevolence, sobriety, industry, and frugality, chastity, moderation, and temperance, and those other virtues which are the ornament of human society, and the basis upon which a republican constitution is founded." Are not these virtues and graces part and parcel of Christianity? In other words, can there be Christianity without them? While these virtues and these duties towards God and man are inculcated in our schools, any one who says that the schools are anti-Christian or un-Christian expressly affirms that his own system of Christianity does not embrace any one of this radiant catalogue; that it rejects them all; that it embraces their opposites.

And further still: our system makes it the express duty of all the "resident ministers of the gospel" to bring all the children within the moral and Christian inculcations above enumerated; so that he who avers that our system is an anti-Christian or an un-Christian one avers that it is both anti-Christian and un-Christian for a "minister OF THE GOSPEL" to promote, or labor to diffuse, the moral attributes and excellences which the statute so earnestly enjoins.

So far, the argument has been of an affirmative character. Its scope and purpose show, or at least tend to show, *by direct proof*, that the school-system of Massachusetts is not an anti-Christian nor an un-Christian system. But there is still another mode of proof. The truth of a proposition may be established by showing the falsity or absurdity of all conflicting propositions. So far as this method can be applied to moral questions, its aid may safely be invoked here.

What are the other courses which the State of Massachusetts might adopt or sanction in relation to the education of its youth? They are these four:—

1. It might establish schools, but expressly exclude all religious instruction from them, making them merely schools for secular instruction.

2. It might adopt a course directly the reverse of this. It might define and prescribe a system of religion for the schools, and appoint the teachers and officers, whose duty it should be to carry out that system.

3. It might establish schools by law, and empower each

religious sect, whenever and wherever it could get a majority, to determine what religious faith should be taught in them. And,

4. It might expressly disclaim and refuse all interference with the education of the young, and abandon the whole work to the hazards of private enterprise, or to parental will, ability, or caprice.

1. A system of schools from which all religious instruction should be excluded might properly be called un-Christian, or rather non-Christian, in the same sense in which it could be called non-Jewish or non-Mahometan; that is, as having no connection with either. I do not suppose a man can be found in Massachusetts who would declare such a system to be his first choice.

2. Were the State to establish schools, and prescribe a system of religion to be taught in them, and appoint the teachers and officers to superintend it, could there be any better definition or exemplification of an ecclesiastical establishment? Such a system would create at once the most formidable and terrible hierarchy ever established upon earth. It would plunge society back into the dark ages at one precipitation. The people would be compelled to worship the image which the government, like another Nebuchadnezzar, might set up; and, for any refusal, the fiery furnace, seven times heated, would be their fate. And worse than this. The sacerdotal tyranny of the dark ages, and of more ancient as well as of more modern times, addressed its commands to *men*. Against *men* it fulminated its anathemas. On *men* its lightnings fell. But *men* had free agency. They could sometimes escape. They could always resist. They were capable of thought. They had powers of endurance. They could be upheld by a sense of duty here, and by visions of transcending rewards and glories hereafter. They could proclaim truth in the gaspings of death, — on the scaffold, in the fire, in the interludes of the rack, — and leave it as a legacy and a testimony to others. But *children* have no such resources to ward off tyranny, or to

endure its terrors. They are incapable of the same comprehensive survey of truth, of the same invincible resolve, of being inspired with an all-sustaining courage and endurance from the realities of another life. They would die under imprisonment. Affrighted at the sight of the stake, or of any of the dread machinery of torture, they would surrender their souls to be distorted into any deformity, or mutilated into any hideousness. Before the process of starvation had gone on for a day, they would swallow any belief, from Atheism to Thuggery.

For any human government, then, to attempt to coerce and predetermine the religious opinions of children by law, and contrary to the will of their parents, is unspeakably more criminal than the usurpation of such control over the opinions of men. The latter is treason against truth; but the former is sacrilege. As the worst of all crimes against chastity are those which debauch the infant victim before she knows what chastity is, so the worst of all crimes against religious truth are those which forcibly close up the avenues and bar the doors that lead to the forum of reason and conscience. The spirit of ecclesiastical domination in modern times, finding that the principles of men are too strong for it, is attempting the seduction of children. Fearing the opinions that may be developed by mature reflection, it anticipates and forestalls those opinions, and seeks to imprint upon the ignorance and receptiveness of childhood the convictions which it could never fasten upon the minds of men in their maturity. As an instance of this, the "Factories Bill," so called, which, in the year 1843, was submitted by Sir James Graham to the British Parliament, may be cited. Among other things, this bill provided that schools should be established in manufacturing districts, under the auspices of the nation, and partly at its expense. These schools were to be placed under the immediate superintendence and visitation of officers appointed by the government. No teacher was to be eligible, unless approved by a bishop or arch bishop. Any parent who hired out his child to work in a factory for half a day, unless he should go to this sectarian or government school the other half of the day, was to be fined; and, for non-payment of the fine, imprisonment was the legal consequence. So any overseer or factory proprietor, who should employ a child for half a day who did not attend school the other half, was also subject to a fine; and, of course, to imprisonment, if the fine were not paid. It did not at all alter the principle, that in a few excepted cases, owing to the peculiar nature of the work, the children were allowed to prosecute it for a whole day, or for two or three days in succession; because, just so long as they were permitted to work, just so long were they required to go to the school after the work. Nor, in the great majority of cases, was it any mitigation of the plan, that, if the parents would provide a separate school for their children at their own expense, they might send to it; because not one in ten of the operatives had either time or knowledge to found such a school, or pecuniary ability to pay its expenses if it were founded. The direct object and effect, therefore, of the proposed law, were to compel children to attend the government school, and to be taught the government religion, under the penalty of starvation or the poorhouse. Children were debarred from a morsel of bread, unless they took it saturated with the government theology.

Now, to the moral sentiments of every lover of truth, of every lover of freedom for the human soul, is there not a meanness, is there not an infamy, in such a law, compared with which the bloody statutes of Elizabeth and Mary were magnanimous and honorable? To bring the awful forces of government to bear upon and to crush such lofty and indomitable souls as those of Latimer and Cranmer, of Ridley and Rogers, one would suppose to be diabolical enough to satisfy the worst spirits in the worst regions of the universe; but for a government to doom its children to starvation unless they will say its catechism, and to imprison the parent, and compel him to hear the wailings of his own famishing offspring,—compel him to see them perish, physically by starvation, or morally by ignorance, unless he will consent that they shall be taught such religious doctrines as he believes will be a peril and a destruction to their immortal souls, — is it not the essence of all tyrannies, of all crimes, and of all baseness, concreted into one?

Such a system as this stands in the strongest possible contrast to the Massachusetts system. Will those who call our system un-Christian and anti-Christian adopt and practise this system as Christian and religious?

3. As a third method, the government might establish schools by law, and empower each religious sect, whenever and wherever it could get a majority, to determine what religious faith should be taught in them.

Under such a system, each sect would demand that its own faith should be inculcated in all the schools, and this on the clear and simple ground that such faith is the only true one. Each differing faith believed in by all the other sects, must, of course, be excluded from the schools; and this on the equally clear and simple ground that there can be but one true faith: and which that is has already been determined, and is no longer an open question. Under such a system, it will not suffice to have the Bible in the schools to speak for itself. Each sect will rise up, and virtually say, "Although the Bible from Genesis to Revelation is in the schools, yet its true meaning and doctrines are not there: Christianity is not there, unless our commentary, our creed, or our catechism, is there also. A revelation from God is not sufficient. Our commentary or our teacher must go with it to reveal what the revelation means. Our book or our teacher must be superadded to the Bible, as an appendix or an erratum is subjoined at the end of a volume to supply oversights and deficiencies, and to rectify the errors of the text. It is not sufficient that the Holy Ghost has spoken by the mouth of David; it is not sufficient that God has spoken by the mouth of all his holy prophets which have been since the world began; it is not sufficient that you have the words of one who spoke as never man spake: all this leaves you in fatal ignorance and error, unless you have our '*addenda*' and '*corrigenda*,' — our things to be supplied, and things to be corrected. Nay, we affirm, that, without our interpretation and explanation of the faith which was once delivered unto the saints, all that the Holy Ghost and God and Christ have promulgated, and taught to men, still leaves your system an un-Christian and an anti-Christian system. To accept a revelation directly from Jehovah is not enough. His revelation must pass through our hands; his infinite Mind must be measured and squared by our minds: we have sat in council over his law, his promises, and his threatenings, and have decided, definitively, unappealably, and forever, upon the only true interpretation of them all. Your schools may be like the noble Bereans, searching the Scriptures daily; but, unless the result of those searchings have our countersign and indorsement, those schools are un-Christian and anti-Christian."

Now, it is almost too obvious to be mentioned, that such a claim as the above reduces society at once to this dilemma: if one religious sect is authorized to advance it for itself, then all other sects are equally authorized to do the same thing for themselves. The right being equal among all the sects, and each sect being equally certain and equally determined, what shall be done? Will not each sect, acting under religious impulses, — which are the strongest impulses that ever animate the breast of man, — will not each sect do its utmost to establish its supremacy in all the schools? Will not the heats and animosities engendered in families and among neighbors burst forth with a devouring fire in the primary or district school-meetings? and, when the inflammable materials of all the district-meetings are gathered together in the town-meeting, what can quell or quench the flames till the zealots themselves are consumed in the conflagration they have kindled? Why would not all those machinations and oppressions be resorted to, in order to obtain the ascendency, if religious proselytism should be legalized in the schools, which would be resorted to, as I have endeavored, in a preceding part of this Report, to explain, if political proselytism were permitted in the schools? Suppose, at last, that different sects should obtain predominance in different schools, — just as is done by different religions in the different nations in Europe; so that, in one school, one system of doctrines should be taught to the children under the sanctions of law as eternal truth; and, in the neighboring schools, other and opposite systems should also be taught as eternal truth. Under such circumstances, perhaps it is not too much to suppose, that although some of the weaker sects might be crushed out of existence at once, yet that all the leading denominations, with their divisions and subdivisions, would have their representative schools. Into these, their respective catechisms or articles of faith would be introduced. And though the Bible itself might accompany them, yet, if we may judge from the history of all the religious struggles by which the world has been afflicted, the Bible would become the incident, and the catechism or articles the principal. And if these various catechisms or articles do declare, as is averred by each party, what the Bible means, and what the Christian religion is, then what a piebald, heterogeneous, and self-contradictory system does Christianity become! Suppose these schools to be brought nearer together, within hearing distance of each other, how discordant are the sounds they utter! Bring them under the same roof, remove partition, or other architectural barrier, so that they may occupy the same apartment, so that the classes may sit side by side; and does the spectacle which they now exhibit illustrate the one indivisible, all-glorious system of Christianity? or is it the return of Babel? Would such a system as this be called Christian by those who denounce our system as anti-Christian?

Is there not, on' the contrary, an unspeakable value in the fact, that, under the Massachusetts system, the Bible is allowed to speak for itself? Under a system opposite to ours, this right of speaking for itself would never be vouchsafed to it. And how narrow is the distance between those who would never allow the Bible to be read by the people at all, and those who will allow it to be read only in the presence of a government interpreter! If government and teachers really believe the Bible to be the word of God, — as strictly and literally given by his inspiration as the tables of the law which Moses brought down from the mount were written by his finger, — then they cannot deny, that, when the Bible is read, God speaks, just as literally and truly as an orator or a poet speaks when his oration or his poem is rehearsed. With this belief, it is no figure of speech to say, when the lids of the Bible are opened in school that its oracles may be uttered, that the lips of Jehovah are opened that he may commune with all his children, of whatever faith, who may be there assembled. Is that a time and an occasion for a worm of the dust, a creature of yesterday, to rush in and close the book, and silence the Eternal One, that he may substitute some form of faith of his own, — some form, either received from tradition, or reasoned out or guessed out by his fallible faculties, — and impose it upon the children as the plainer and better word of God? Or when the allotted hour for religious instruction comes, or the desire arises in the teacher's mind that the children of the school should hold communion with their heavenly Father, suppose that Father, instead of the medium of the Bible, should send an angel from his throne to make known to them his commands and his benedictions by living lips and in celestial words. Would that be a time for the chiefs of twenty different sects to rush in with their twenty different catechisms, and thrust the heavenly messenger aside, and struggle to see which could out-vociferate the rest in proclaiming what the visitant from on high was about to declare?

(I hold it, then, to be one of the excellences, one of the moral beauties, of the Massachusetts system, that there is one place in the land where the children of all the different denominations are brought together for instruction, where the Bible is allowed to speak for itself; one place where the children can kneel at a common altar, and feel that they have a common Father, and where the services of religion tend to create brothers, and not Ishmaelites.) If this be so, then it does violence to truth to call our system anti-Christian or un-Christian.

Thus far, under this head, I have supposed that the different sects, in their contests for supremacy, would keep the peace. But every page in the history of polemic struggles shows such a supposition to be delusive. In the contests for victory, success would lead to haughtiness, and defeat to revenge. Affinities and repulsions would gather men into bodies: these bodies would become battalions, and would set themselves in hostile array against each other. Weakness of argument would re-enforce itself by strength of arm; and the hostile parties would appeal from the tribunal of reason to the arbitrament of war. But after cities had been burned, and men slaughtered by thousands, and every diabolical passion in the human breast satiated, and the combatants were forced, from mere exhaustion, to rest upon their arms, it would be found, on a re-examination of the controverted grounds, that not a rule of interpretation had been altered, not the tense of a single verb in any disputed text had been changed, not a Hebrew point nor a Greek article had been added or taken away, but that every subject of dispute remained as unsettled and uncertain as before. Is any system, which, by the law of the human passions, leads to such results, either Christian or religious?

4. One other system, if it may be so called, is supposable; and this exhausts the number of those which stand in direct conflict with ours. It is this: Government might expressly disclaim and refuse all interference with the education of the young, abandoning the whole work to the hazards of private enterprise, or to parental will, ability, or caprice.

The first effect of this course would be the abandonment of a large portion of the children of every community to hopeless and inevitable ignorance. Even with all the aids, incitements, and bounties now bestowed upon education by the most enlightened States in this Union, there exists a perilous and a growing body of ignorance, animated by the soul of vice. Were government systems to be abolished, and all government

...s to be withdrawn, the number of American children, who, in the next generation, would be doomed to all the wants and woes that can come in the train of ignorance and error, would be counted by millions. This abandoned portion of the community would be left, without any of the restraints of education, to work out the infinite possibilities of human depravity. In the more favored parts of the country, the rich might educate their own children; although it is well known, even now, that, throughout extensive regions of the South and West, the best education which wealth can procure is meagre and stinted, and alloyed with much error. The "parochial" or "sectarian" system might effect something in populous places; but what could it do in rural districts, where so vast a proportion of all the inhabitants of this country reside? In speaking of the difficulties of establishing schools at the West, Miss Beecher gives an account of a single village which she found there, consisting of only four hundred inhabitants, where there were *fourteen* different denominations. "Of the most numerous portions of these," she says, "each was jealous lest another should start a church first, and draw in the rest. The result was, neither church nor Sunday school of any kind was in existence." Of another place she says, "I found two of the most influential citizens arrayed against each other, and supported by contending partisans, so that whatever school one portion patronized the other would oppose. The result was, no school could be raised large enough to support any teacher." And again: "In another large town, I was informed by one of the clergymen that no less than twenty different teachers opened schools and gave them up in about six months."

In a population of four hundred, there would be about one hundred children who *ought* to attend school; although this proportion, on an average of the whole country, is nearly threefold the number of actual attendants. One hundred children would furnish the materials for a good school, but, divided between fourteen different schools, would give only seven children and one-seventh of a child to each school. How impossible to sustain schools on such a basis! The more numerous sects, it is true, would have a larger proportion; but just so much less would be the proportion of the smaller sects, and doubtless there would be some who would be fully represented by the above-mentioned fraction of one-seventh of a child. But let us take the case of Massachusetts, where the population has a density of five times the average of the other States in the Union, and let us see how insane and suicidal would be such a course of policy even with us. Leaving out all the *cities*, there are three hundred and five *towns*, in Massachusetts; and these comprise most of the rural and sparsely-populated portion of the State. These three hundred and five towns have an average of eleven schools (wanting a very small fraction) for each. Two hundred and twenty-six of these three hundred and five towns have a population, according to the last census, of less than twenty-two hundred each. If there are twenty-two hundred inhabitants and eleven schools in a town, each school represents an average of two hundred inhabitants. Including every child who was found in *all* our public schools last year, for any part either of the summer or winter terms, they would make a mean average for those terms of only forty-eight to a school. Now, suppose these forty-eight scholars to be divided, not between "*fourteen*," but only between *four* different denominations, there would be but *twelve* to a school. Connect this result with the fact that Massachusetts has a population five times as dense as the average of the residue of the Union, and it will be seen, by intuition, that only in a few favored localities could the system of "sectarian" schools be maintained. This obstacle might be partially overcome by a union of two or more sects, between whom the repellency resulting from some punctilios in matters of form or ceremonial observance would not overcome the argument from availability; but this union, having been purchased by the sacrifice of a portion of what each holds to be absolute truth, why, when any one of the allies should become sufficiently powerful to stand alone, would it not dissolve the alliance, set up for itself, and abandon its confederates to their fate?

In making the above computation, which gives an average of forty-eight scholars to each school, it will be observed that *all* the schools in the State are included, — the numerously-attended schools of the cities as well as the small ones of the country. And although the number of districts in the two hundred and twenty-six towns whose population is less than twenty-two hundred each may be somewhat less than in the remaining seventy-nine towns, yet the fact unquestionably is, that an allowance of forty-eight scholars to a school is much too large an average for the schools in these two hundred and twenty-six, of the three hundred and five towns in the State. Of course, twelve scholars to a school would be much too large an average, if the schools were divided only between four different sects. Nor has any mention been made of the large numbers who connect themselves with no religious sect, and who, therefore, if united at all, would be united on the principle of opposition to sect. Surely the very statement of the case supersedes argument in regard to the possibility of maintaining schools for any considerable portion of the children of the country on such a basis.

The calamities necessarily resulting from so partial and limited a system as the one now under consideration would inflict retributive loss and weakness upon all classes in the community; but upon the children of the poor, the ignorant, and the unfortunate, would the blow fall with terrible severity. And what class of children ought we most assiduously to care for? Christ came to save that which would otherwise be lost. All good men, and all governments, so far as they imitate the example of Christ, strive to succor the distressed, and to reclaim the guilty; in an *intellectual* and in a *moral* sense, to feed the hungry, to clothe the naked, to visit the sick and the imprisoned; amid the priceless wealth of character, to find the lost piece of silver; and, amid the wanderings from the fold of truth, to recover the lambs. Before Heaven, it is now, today, the first duty of every government in Christendom to bring forward those unfortunate classes of the people, who, in the march of civilization, have been left in the rear. Though the van of society should stand still for a century, the rear ought to be brought up. The exterminating decree of Herod was parental and beneficent compared with the cruel sway of those rulers who dig the pit-falls of temptation along the pathway of children, and suffer them to fall, unwarned and unassisted, into the abysses of ruin. What, then, shall be said of that opposition to our system, which, should it prevail, would doom to remediless ignorance and vice a great majority of all the children in this land? Is such a system, as contradistinguished from our free system, Christian and religious?

It is a very surprising fact, but one which is authenticated by a report, made in the month of July last, by a committee of the Boston primary-schools, that, of the *ten thousand one hundred and sixty-two* children belonging to said schools, *five thousand one hundred and fifty-four* were of foreign parentage. Let sectarianism be introduced into the Boston schools, or rather let it be understood that the schools are to be carried on for the avowed purpose of building up any one of the New-England denominations, and what a vast proportion of these *five thousand one hundred and fifty-four* children would be immediately withdrawn from the schools! Their parents would as soon permit them to go to a lazar-house as to such schools; and this, too, from the sincerest of motives. The same thing would prove relatively true in regard to no inconsiderable number of the less populous cities, and of the most populous towns, in the State. Now, what would be the condition of such children at the end of twenty years? and what the condition of the communities which had thus cruelly closed the school-house-doors upon them? Would not these communities be morally responsible for all the degradation, the miseries, the vices, and the crimes consequent upon such expulsion from the school? And would such a result be one of the fruits of a Christian and a religious system?

But there would be another inseparable accompaniment of such a system. In Massachusetts, the average compensation paid to male teachers is very much larger than that which is paid in any other State in the Union. It is nearly double what is given in most of the States; and yet, even with us, the great body of ambitious and aspiring young men pass by the profession of teaching, and betake themselves to some other employment, known to be more lucrative, and falsely supposed to be more honorable. How degrading, then, must be the effect upon the general character and competency of teachers as a profession, when, on the abolition of the public schools, and the substitution of private and sectarian schools in their stead, the wages of teachers, for the poorer classes, shall be reduced to a pittance, and the collection of even this pittance shall be precarious! What will be the social rank and standing of teachers, when their customary income encourages no previous preparation for their work, doles out only a niggardly subsistence even while they are engaged in the service, and leaves no surplus for the probable wants of sickness, or the certain ones of age? And among whom shall the teacher seek his associates, when he is shunned by the learned for his want of culture, and ridiculed for his poverty by the devotees of wealth? Even in England, where the population is so dense that hardly a spot can be selected as a centre, which will not embrace, within a circumference of convenient distance, a sufficient number of children for a school, — even there, the voluntary and sectarian system leaves at least two-thirds of the agricultural and manufacturing classes in a state of the most deplorable ignorance; supplying them with teachers, so far as it supplies them with teachers at all, who fulfil the double office of perpetuating errors in school, and degrading the character of the profession out of it.

There is another fact of fearful significance, which no one who has any regard for the common interests of society can be pardoned for forgetting. It is known to all, that, in many parts of the Union, the population is so sparse, and can command so little of ready means for paying salaries, that no *resident* clergyman of any denomination is to be found throughout wide districts of country; and many of those who do devote themselves to the spiritual welfare of their fellow-men are most scantily provided for. If unmarried, they can barely live; if they have a family, there is, oftentimes, a real scantiness of the comforts and necessaries of life. They have neither books to peruse; nor leisure to read, even if they had books. They may be a pious, but they cannot be a learned clergy. At least in one respect, they are compelled to imitate St. Paul; for as he wrought at his own "craft" for a subsistence, so must they. And now, if existing means are too scanty to give a respectable support even to the ministry, how disastrous must be the effect of dividing these scanty means between the institution of the gospel and the institution of the school! Will not the vineyard of the Lord be overgrown with weeds, will not its hedges be broken down, and the wild beasts of the forest make their lair therein, if the servants who are set to tend and to dress it are so few in number, and so miserably provided for? Is not this another criterion by which to determine whether our present system is not as Christian and as religious as that which would supplant it?

(I know of but one argument, having the semblance of plausibility, that can be urged against this feature of our system. It may be said, that if questions of doctrinal religion are left to be decided by men for themselves, or by parents for their children, numerous and grievous errors will be mingled with the instruction. Doubtless the fact is so. If truth be one, and if many contradictory dogmas are taught as truth, then it is mathematically certain that all the alleged truths but one is a falsity. But, though the statement is correct, the inference which is drawn from it in favor of a government standard of faith is not legitimate; for all the religious errors which are believed in by the free mind of man, or which are taught by free parents to their children, are tolerable and covetable, compared with those which the patronage and the seductions of government can suborn men to adopt, and which the terrors of government can compel them to perpetuate. The errors of free minds are so numerous and so various, that they prevent any monster-error from acquiring the ascendency, and therefore truth has a chance to struggle forward amid the strifes of the combatants; but if the monster-error can usurp the throne of the civil power, fortify itself by prescription, defend its infallibility with all the forces of the State, sanctify its enormities under sacred names, and plead the express command of God for all its atrocities, — against such an antagonist, Truth must struggle for centuries, bleed at every pore, be wounded in every vital part, and can triumph at last, only after thousands and tens of thousands of her holiest disciples shall have fallen in the conflict.

If, then, a government would recognize and protect the rights of religious freedom, it must abstain from subjugating the capacities of its children to any legal standard of religious faith with as great fidelity as it abstains from controlling the opinions of men. It must meet the unquestionable fact, that the old spirit of religious domination is adopting new measures to accomplish its work, — measures which, if successful, will be as fatal to the liberties of mankind as those which were practised in by-gone days of violence and terror. These new measures are aimed at children instead of men. They propose to supersede the necessity of subduing free thought *in the mind of the adult*, by forestalling the development of any capacity of free thought *in the mind of the child*. They expect to find it easier to subdue the free agency of children by binding them in fetters of bigotry than to subdue the free agency of men by binding them in fetters of iron. For this purpose, some are attempting to deprive children of their right to labor, and, of course, of their daily bread, unless they will attend a government school, and receive its sectarian instruction. Some are attempting to withhold all means even of secular education from the poor, and thus punish them with ignorance, unless, with the secular knowledge which they desire, they will accept theological knowledge which they condemn. Others still are striving to break down all free public-school systems where they exist, and to prevent their establishment where they do not exist, in the hope, that, on the downfall of these, their system will succeed. The sovereign antidote against these machinations is free schools for all, and the right of every parent to determine the religious education of his children.

This topic invites far more extended exposition; but this must suffice. In bidding an official farewell to a system with which I have been so long connected, to which I have devoted my means, my strength, my health, twelve years of time, and, doubtless, twice that number of years from what might otherwise have been my term of life, I have felt bound to submit these brief views in its defence. In justice to my own name and memory; in justice to the Board of which I was originally a member, and from which I have always sought counsel and guidance; and in justice to thousands of the most wise, upright, and religious-minded men in Massachusetts, who have been my fellow-laborers in advancing the great cause of popular education, under the auspices of this system, — I have felt bound to vindicate it from the aspersions cast upon it, and to show its consonance with the eternal principles of equity and justice. I have felt bound to show, that so far from its being an irreligious, an anti-Christian, or an un-Christian system, it is a system which recognizes religious obligations in their fullest extent; that it is a system which invokes a religious spirit, and can never be fitly administered without such a spirit; that it inculcates the great commands upon which hang all the law and the prophets; that it welcomes the Bible, and therefore welcomes all the doctrines which the Bible really contains; and that it listens to these doctrines so reverently, that, for the time being, it will not suffer any rash mortal to thrust in his interpolations of their meaning, or overlay the text with any of the "many inventions" which the heart of man has sought out. It is a system, however, which leaves open all other means of instruction, — the pulpits, the Sunday schools, the Bible classes, the catechisms, of all denominations, — to be employed according to the preferences of individual parents. It is a system which restrains itself from teaching that what it does teach is all that needs to be taught, or that should be taught; but leaves this to be decided by each man for himself, according to the light of his reason and conscience, and on his responsibility to that Great Being, who, in holding him to an account for the things done in the body, will hold him to the strictest account for the manner in which he has "trained up" his children.

Such, then, in a religious point of view, is the Massachusetts system of common schools. Reverently it recognizes and affirms the sovereign rights of the Creator, sedulously and sacredly it guards the religious rights of the creature; while it seeks to remove all hinderances, and to supply all furtherances, to a filial and paternal communion between man and his Maker. In a social and political sense, it is a *free* school-system. It knows no distinction of rich and poor, of bond and free, or between those, who, in the imperfect light of this world, are seeking, through different avenues, to reach the gate of heaven. Without money and without price, it throws open its doors, and spreads the table of its bounty, for all the children of the State. Like the sun, it shines not only upon the good, but upon the evil, that they may become good; and, like the rain, its blessings descend not only upon the just, but upon the unjust, that their injustice may depart from them, and be known no more.

To the great founders of this system we look back with filial reverence and love. Amid the barrenness of the land, and in utter destitution of wealth, they coined the rude comforts, and even the necessaries, of life, into means for its generous support. Though, as laborers by day, they subdued the wilderness, and, as sentinels by night, they guarded the camp, yet they found time for the vigilant administration and oversight of the schools in the day of their infancy and weakness. But for this single institution, into which they transfused so much of their means and of their strength, and of which they have made us the inheritors, how different would our lot and our life have been! Upon us its accumulated blessings have descended. It has saved us from innumerable pains and perils that would otherwise have been our fate, — from the physical wretchedness that is impotent to work out its own relief, from the darkness of the intellect whose wanderings after light so often plunge it into deeper gloom, and from the moral debasement whose pleasures are vices and crimes. It has surrounded us with a profusion of comforts and blessings of which the most poetic imagination would never otherwise have conceived. It has found, not mythologic goddesses, but gigantic and tireless laborers, in every stream; not evil and vindictive spirits, but beneficent and helping ones, in all the elements; and, by a profounder alchemy than the schoolmen ever dreamed of, it transmutes quarries and ice-fields into gold. It has given cunning to the hand of the mechanic, keenness to the artisan's eye, and made a sterile soil grow grateful beneath the skill of the husbandman. Hence the absence of poverty among our native population; hence a competency for the whole people, the means for mental and moral improvement, and for giving embellishment and dignity to life, such as the world has never known before, and such as nowhere else can be found upon the face of the earth.

How divinely wise were our Pilgrim Fathers when they foresaw, that, if they could give knowledge and virtue to their children, they gave them all things! Wonder and admiration seize us as we reflect upon the vastness of the results which their wisdom wrought out from the scantiest of resources. They have taught us the great lesson, how the fiercest elements obey, and how the most obdurate and intractable of Nature's substances bend and melt before the power of knowledge, and the fervors of a saintly heroism. Their deeds have taught us, not only that the race is not to the swift, nor the battle to the strong, but they have taught us that the swiftness which shall win the honors of the goal, and the strength that shall triumph in the strife, are to be found in the soul, and not in the limbs, of man. But though, to this untitled yet noblest ancestry, we are bound to pay the homage of our gratitude, and to accept their benefactions with a filial love, yet neither the complacency of enjoyment, nor that of retrospection, is the frame of mind that best befits us. *We have our futurity as they had theirs,* — a futurity rapidly hastening upon us, — a futurity now fluid, — ready, as clay in the hands of the potter, to be moulded into every form of beauty and excellence; but so soon as it reaches our hands, so soon as it receives the impress of our plastic touch, whether this touch be for good or for evil, it is to be struck into the adamant of the unchanging and unchangeable past. Into whose form and likeness shall we fashion this flowing futurity, — of Mammon, of Moloch, or of Jesus? Clear, and more clear, out of the dimness of coming time, emerge to the vision of faith the myriad hosts of the generations that shall succeed us. These generations are to stand in our places, to be called by our names, and to accept the heritage of joy or of woe which we shall bequeath them. Shall they look back upon us with veneration for our wisdom and beneficent forecast, or with shame at our selfishness and degeneracy? Our ancestors were noble examples to us; shall we be ignoble examples to our posterity? They gave from their penury, and shall we withhold from our abundance? Let us not dishonor our lineage. Let us remember that generosity is not to be measured by the largeness of the sum which a man may give, but by the smallness of the sum which remains to him after his gift. Let us remember that the fortunes of our children, and of their descendants, hang upon our fidelity, just as our fortunes were suspended upon the fidelity of our fathers. Deeds survive the doers. In the highest and most philosophic sense, the asserted brevity of human life is a fiction. The act remains, though the hand that wrought it may have perished. And when our spirits shall have gone to their account, and the dust of our bodies shall be blown about by the winds, or mingled with the waves, the force which our life shall have impressed upon the machinery of things will continue its momentum, and work out its destiny upon the character and happiness of our descendants.

But not the fortunes of our children alone, or of our children's children, are dependent upon us. The influences of our conduct extend outward in space as well as onward in time. We are part of a mighty nation, which has just embarked upon the grandest experiment ever yet attempted upon earth, — the experiment of the capacity of mankind for the wise and righteous government of themselves. Fearful are the issues which hang upon the trial, but few and simple the conditions that predestine its result. The firmament, though pillared upon rottenness, shall be upheld, and the light of day shall continue to revisit the earth, though the sun be blotted out, sooner than a republic shall stand which has not knowledge and virtue for its foundations. Yet are we not braving the results of this experiment, in impious defiance of the conditions on which Heaven has decreed that the trial shall turn? Within a brief period of time, our population has spread itself westward from the Atlantic, through more than twenty degrees of longitude. It has erected thirty States, and given to each a republican frame of government. Yet, in more than one-half of these States, no provision worthy of the name is made for replenishing the common mind with knowledge, or for training the common heart to virtue. Surely, to the people of these States, a different mental and moral culture must come speedily, or it will come too late; and the sower who would scatter the elements of knowledge and virtue amongst them must press forward with gigantic strides, and cast his seed with a gigantic arm.

Nor is this all. Beyond our western frontier, another and a wider realm spreads out, as yet unorganized into governments, and uninhabited by civilized man. The western is still broader than the eastern expanse. It stretches through thirty degrees of longitude, — one-twelfth part of the circumference of the globe. Half the population of Continental Europe might be transplanted to it, find subsistence on it, and leave room to spare. It is now a waste more dreary than desolation itself; for it is filled only with savage life. Yet soon will every rood of its surface be explored by the centrifugal force of the Saxon soul; and whatever of vegetable wealth is spread upon it, or of mineral wealth is garnered beneath it, will be appropriated by the vehemence of Saxon enterprise. Shall this new empire, wider than that of the Ptolemies, and almost as extensive as that of the Cæsars, be reclaimed to humanity, to a Christian life, and a Christian history? or shall it be a receptacle where the avarice, the profligacy, and the licentiousness of a corrupt civilization shall cast its criminals and breed its monsters? If it is ever to be saved from such a perdition, the mother States of this Union, those States where the institutions of learning and religion are now honored and cherished, must send out their hallowing influences to redeem it. And if, in the benignant providence of God, the tree of Paradise is ever to be planted and to flourish in this new realm; if its branches are to spread, and its leaves to be scattered for the healing of the people, — will not the heart of every true son of Massachusetts palpitate with desire — not a low and vainglorious ambition, but such a high and holy aspiration as angels might feel — that her name may be engraved upon its youthful trunk, there to deepen and expand with its immortal growth?

AN ORATION

DELIVERED BEFORE THE AUTHORITIES OF THE CITY OF BOSTON, JULY 4, 1842.

FELLOW-CITIZENS, —

It is meet that we should assemble to mingle our congratulations in public, on the recurrence of this Anniversary. The celebration of festival days in honor of illustrious progenitors is a universal fact in human history. It therefore proves the existence of a universal sentiment in human nature, which finds its appropriate utterance in such commemorations. This is a sentiment of gratitude and reverence towards the great and good; and it is honorable both to author and object. Under the impulse of these feelings, the heroes of ancient times were deified by their descendants. To consecrate their memory, sculpture reared statues and shrines. Architecture built monuments and temples. Poetry hymned their praises. Eloquence and its responsive acclamations made the arches of heaven resound with their fame; and even the sober muse of history, dazzled by the brilliancy of their exploits, exaggerated fact into fiction, until the true was lost in the fabulous.

In our day, this sentiment is modified, but not extinguished. All modern nations celebrate the anniversary of those days, when their annals were illuminated, or their perilled fortunes rescued, by some grand historic achievement.

The universality and unbroken continuity of these observances seem prophetic of their continuance.

But it is especially worthy of remark, that these public and joyous tributes are paid only to propitious events, or magnanimous deeds, — to what is grand in conception, or glorious in achievement. No days are set apart to commemorate national disaster or ignominy for its own sake. The good only is celebrated. The base, the cowardly, whether in motive or in action, is consigned, through silence, to oblivion.

What a lesson is here, were we so teachable as to learn it! How soon will our position be changed from that of posterity to ancestors; and the strict rules by which we honor or despise predecessors, be applied to us by impartial descendants. Whatever of true, generous, or morally heroic, is wrought out by us, shall be gratefully embalmed in the memories of men; and around millions of firesides, many millions of hearts shall leap with joy at its oft-recurring narration. But what is sordid, perfidious, — a perversion of public good to private ends, — shall be scoffed and hissed at; and its happiest fate shall be an early forgetfulness.

It is, indeed, an impressive thought, — one full of the deepest significancy, — that throughout this vast country, over all its degrees of latitude and longitude, and on the seas which bind the globe in their azure and glorious cincture, — soon as the beams of this morning's sun gilded spire or mast-head, the shout of exultation and the peal of artillery arose, and sweeping onward and westward like the tidal wave, they are now circuiting the globe, in honor of those heroes and martyrs who, only sixty-six years ago, pledged "fortune, life, and sacred honor" to establish the Independence of these United States. How many times has this story been rehearsed, and yet to the patriot's ear, it never grows old. How curiously has the history of that great revolutionary epoch been investigated; and even now, if some minute of a council, — whether of war or of State, — held at midnight; some memorandum of an order given at a critical juncture; or some hitherto elusive letter, can be found among the records of our government, or pursued across the ocean and drawn from its lurking-place in British or French archives, it is published, read, and reiterated by all, and the original is prized, almost like the relic of a saint among the faithful. And all those doings and achievements were less than seventy years ago, — less than the period allotted by the Psalmist to the life of man. Nay, some of the actors in those scenes are amongst us still; and we have proof of the reality not from their lips merely, but honorable scars are their credentials — the hieroglyphs wherein the sacred history is chronicled. Not only have we the mausoleums of battlefield, but every churchyard in New England is thickly strewn with the graves of the heroic dead, whose simple inscriptions, — nobler than armorial bearings, — proclaim that they sought toil as a pleasure and rejoiced in self-sacrifice, that they might do good to us, whom they saw only with the eye of faith.

And yet, let me again say, how obvious it is that we stand in the same relation to posterity that our ancestors do to us. And, as we boldly summon our forefathers to our tribunal for adjudication upon their conduct, so will our conduct be brought into judgment by our successors. Each generation has duties of its own to perform; and our duties, though widely different from theirs, are not less important in their character, or less binding in their obligations. It was their duty to found or establish our institutions, and nobly did they perform it. It is our duty to perfect and perpetuate these institutions; and the most solemn question which can be propounded to this age, is, are we performing it nobly? Shall posterity look back upon our present rulers, as we look back upon Arnold, or as we look back upon Washington? Shall posterity look back upon us, as we look back upon the recreants who sought to make Washington Dictator, and would have turned those arms against their country, which had been put into their hands to save her? or shall posterity look back upon us with the heart-throbbings, the tears and passionate admiration, with which we regard the Saviour-like martyrs who, for our welfare, in lonely dungeons and prison-ships, breathing a noisome atmosphere, — their powerful and robust frames protracting their tortures beyond the common endurance of nature, until they slowly but literally perished by starvation, — and when the minions of power came round, day after day, and offered them life and freedom and a glad return to the upper air, if they would desert their country's cause — refused, and died?

I have said that it is our especial and appropriate duty to perfect and perpetuate the institutions we have received. I am aware that this has been said for the last fifty years, thousands of times every year. I do not reiterate the sentiment, therefore, for its originality; nor even for its importance; but for the sake of inquiring, in what manner this work is to be done? It has long seemed to me that it would be more honorable to our ancestors, to praise them, in words, less; but in deeds, to imitate them more. If from their realms of blessedness, they could address us, would they not say, "Prove the sincerity of your words, by imitating the examples you profess to admire. The inheritance we left you is worthless, unless you have inherited the spirit also by which it was acquired. The boon we would bequeath to the latest posterity, can never reach and bless them, save through your hands. In these spiritual abodes, whence all disturbing passions are excluded, where all illusions are purged from our eyes, we can neither be beguiled nor flattered by lip-service. *Deeds* are the only language we understand: and one act of self-sacrifice for the welfare of mankind is more acceptable to us than if you should make every mountain and hill-top a temple to hallow our names, and gather thither the whole generation, as worshippers."

Such is the spirit in which I believe our sainted fathers would admonish us. But, alas for the holiday patriot! it is so much easier to praise and get up jubilees than it is *to work*;—it is so much pleasanter to encore a song, than to enlist for a campaign with its privations and diseases and death;—this in-door declamation and psalm-singing so much better befit the nice and dainty sentimentalist, than to go forth into the conflict, and, year after year, to wrestle with difficulties, as with an angel of God, until Heaven yields to the importunacy of our struggles what it denied to the formality of our prayers!—all this poetic contemplation of duty is so much easier and cheaper than its stern performance, that we are in perpetual danger of degenerating from effort and self-sacrifice into ceremony and cant.

Were a stranger to come amongst us, and to hear our National

Songs, our Fourth of July Orations, and Caucus Speeches, he would say, "Verily, there never were such patriots as these since the days of Thermopylæ." But were he to remain with us, and become familiar with the spirit of ambition and self-seeking that afflicts us, if he thought any more of Thermopylæ, it would be, not of the Spartans, but of Xerxes and his plundering invaders.

Fellow-Citizens, we have sterner duties to perform than to assemble here, annually, to listen to glorifications of our great country and our great people, of our super-Ciceronian and super-Demosthenean orators, and to praise poetry and art and genius that are to be, *at sometime;* and then, after refreshing ourselves with feast and jovial song, to close the day with some gairish show, and forthwith to vote ourselves upon the pension list, for the residue of the year, in consideration of such meritorious services. The quiet seat of an honorary member in our community, is not so easily won. Trusts, responsibilities, interests, vaster in amount, more sacred in character, than ever before in the providence of God were committed to any people, have been committed to us. The great experiment of Republicanism,—of the capacity of man for self-government,—is to be tried anew, which wherever it has been tried,—in Greece, in Rome, in Italy,—has failed, through an incapacity in the people to enjoy liberty without abusing it. Another trial is to be made, whether mankind will enjoy more and suffer less, under the ambition and rapacity of an irresponsible parliament, or of irresponsible parties;—under an hereditary sovereign who must, at least, prove his right to destroy, by showing his birth, or under mobs, which are like wild beasts, that prove their right to devour by showing their teeth. A vacant continent is here to be filled up with innumerable millions of human beings, who may be happy through our wisdom, but must be miserable through our folly. Religion,—the ark of God,—which, of old times, was closed that it might not be profaned,—is here thrown open to all, whether Christian, Jew, or Pagan; and yet is to be guarded from desecration and sacrilege, lest we perish with a deeper perdition than ever befel any other people.

These are some of the interests committed to our keeping; these are some of the duties we have to discharge. These duties, too, are to be discharged by a people, who are liable to alienation from each other by all those natural jealousies which spring from sectional interests, from discordant local institutions, from differences in climate, language, and ancestry. We are exposed to the jealousies which bad men,—or which good men, whose knowledge is disproportioned to their zeal, may engender amongst us. And, on many questions of equal delicacy and magnitude, are we not already armed and marshalled against each other, rather than allied and sworn for common protection?

In this exigency, I affirm that we need far more of wisdom and rectitude than we possess. Preparations for our present condition have been so long neglected that we now have a double duty to perform. We have not only to propitiate to our aid a host of good spirits, but we have to exorcise a host of evil ones. Every aspect of our affairs, public and private, demonstrates that we need, for their successful management, a vast accession to the common stock of intelligence and virtue. But intelligence and virtue are the product of cultivation and training. They do not spring up spontaneously. As yet, all Utopias belong to fiction and not to history; and these fictions have so little verisimilitude, that ages have passed since the last one was written. We need, therefore, unexampled alacrity and energy in the application of all those influences and means, which promise the surest and readiest returns of wisdom and probity, both public and private.

This is my subject on the present occasion;—a demonstration that our existing means for the promotion of intelligence and virtue are wholly inadequate to the support of a Republican government. If the facts I have to offer should abate something from our national vain-glory and presumption, I hope they may add as much to national prudence and forethought.

The sovereignty of a great nation is surely one of the most precious of earthly trusts. The happiness or misery which a government dispenses, has dimension in two directions,—depth, as well as superficial extent. It not only reaches widely around, amongst contemporaries; but far downwards amongst posterity. Hence, as the well-being of many generations,—each of these generations consisting of many millions,—depends upon the administration of a government,—there is something sublime and awful in the mere contemplation of the interests committed to rulers; and we see the reasonableness of the requisition that they should rule in righteousness.

Without going any deeper into the philosophy of the subject than the mere consideration of these two facts,—the progressive increase of the human family, and the stationary size of the planet on which they reside,—that is, the impossibility of our pulling down and building greater, for the race, as we would to meet the wants of an enlarging household; I think we are authorized to infer that it was the design of God at the creation that men should live together in large companies or communities. As the race multiplies, and the *unenlargeable* tenement becomes crowded, mankind must obviously live together, either as social beings, or as cannibals,—for mutual improvement, or for mutual sustenance. And though the theory of the latter relation would derive much support from history, yet it seems to me clear that the former is the will of Heaven.

If then, men live together as a people or nation in a social capacity, there must obviously be some exposition or expression of the national will, in a system of laws, more or less definite, for common guidance.

But it would always be impossible that the first Legislature should foresee and provide for all future contingencies; and hence the necessity of a perpetual succession of Legislatures to supply defects, and to meet emergencies as they arise. But again; laws are general, while all the cases arising under them are particular;—and therefore, government must exercise another function,—that of expounding and applying the law. This function is Judicial, and wholly different from the Legislative. The latter declares, generally, what the rule shall be; the former, specifically, to what cases or circumstances the rule shall be applied. And once more;—the law, as it comes from the Legislature, and the decision, as it comes from the Court, have no inherent, self-executing power. The parchment on which they are written, would moulder and crumble, and leave no vestige behind, if the government had not also been vested with an Executive power,— the power of execution,— the prerogative of making things *to be*, as the Legislature and the Court have said they ought *to be*. It is obvious, then, that the simplest government has various attributes; and if Heaven has ordained the existence of human government, it must also have ordained the existence and exercise of this variety of attributes.

And further, I deem it no unauthorized assumption, to claim as a postulate, — a point to be conceded in the outset,— at least by all who are not atheists, — that, as God is a being of infinite wisdom and goodness, no part of his universe can be successfully administered except it be upon the principles of knowledge and virtue. He could neither have created nor ordained aught in violation of his own nature. He could not have created any race of intellectual and moral beings, standing in such relations to each other, that universal selfishness and false knowledge should result in the public good. And this we may affirm not only of all things which now exist, but of all things which may spring from present existences. For the goodness and wisdom of the Creator are not limited to those things which we see and understand, but they exist everywhere; — just as the beautiful rainbow of the summer shower is not confined to the bright arch which gladdens our eyes, but glows wherever sunbeam and rain-drop meet, and only needs an eye *rightly placed*, in order to be seen.

If then God made man a social being, and therefore made it necessary that he should live in a community with his fellows, and that this community should have laws binding them together, as one moral entity; he made it also necessary that these laws should be founded in wisdom and equity, and observed with fidelity; and every departure from these great principles, either in the formation or the observance of the laws, must be followed, inevitably, by a corresponding degree of loss and harm. This is as obvious, as that a machine must be operated according to the principles of its construction. The operator must have so much of the inventor's mind, as to work the machine on the inventor's plan. The application of a divergent force will at least impair its working, — of a counter-force, will destroy it. It is solely through a departure from these principles of wisdom and goodness, that mankind have suffered miseries which history cannot record nor imagination conceive. The civil tyrant has cast nations, as one man, into his fiery alembic, that from the happiness of them all, he might distil one drop to stimulate his foulest appetites; and the ecclesiastical tyrant, not content with robbing mankind of the precious blessings and joys of religion on earth, has carried his spoliations into eternity. In this western world, a portion of the race have reclaimed their freedom; but this is not a freedom to disobey the laws of our nature, or to exempt ourselves from their penalties when broken. It is simply a freedom to use our own reason in attempting to discover what those laws are, and our own free-will in obeying them; and thus to perform the conditions, under which alone, a rational and free being can fulfil his destiny.

It is impiety towards the memory of our fathers to suppose that they contended merely for the transfer of the source of misgovernment from one side of the Atlantic to the other. If we were to be governed forever by ignorance and profligacy, it mattered little whether that ignorance and profligacy should reside in King George, or in King Numbers, — only as the latter king, being much stronger than the former, and subject to the ferocity without the imbecility of madness, is capable of committing far wider havoc upon human welfare than the former. A voter may go to the polls with as light a feeling of responsibility to God and man, or with passions as vindictive, as ever actuated the British ministry when they passed the Stamp-act, or denounced Adams and Hancock as traitors, and gloated, in imagination, over their quartered bodies. No! Our fathers gave their pledge of "fortune, life, and sacred honor," and redeemed it to the letter, that here, on this broad theatre of a continent which spread around them, and with time before them, their descendants might work out that glorious destiny for mankind, — that regeneration, that deliverance from the fetters of iron which had bound the body, and from the fetters of error that had bound the soul, — which the prophets and apostles of liberty, in all ages, had desired to see, but had not seen.

I have said that all governments, even the despotic or autocratic, must exercise three distinct functions, — the Legislative, Judicial, and Executive; and that, to administer any government, fitly and according to its plan, it requires a certain amount of capacity, and responsibleness to right. And no government whatever, — Russia, Turkey, Algiers, — can be so simple as not to include these three attributes, in the last analysis.

But it is most important to observe further, that whatever adds to the complexity of any system of government increases the difficulties and hazards of administering it, and multiplies and heightens the temptations to abuse. Hence the obvious necessity, with any augmentation of difficulties and dangers, of additional wisdom and rectitude, as guaranties against failure.

To apply this remark: however simple our government may be in theory, it has proved in practice, the most complex government on earth. It is now an historical fact, that more questions for legislative interposition, and for judicial exposition and construction, have arisen under it, during the period of its existence, ten to one, than have arisen, during the same length of time, under any other form of government in Christendom. We are a Union made up of twenty-six States, a nation composed of twenty-six nations; and, even beyond the bounds of these, the Federal head is responsible for the fate of several vast territories, and of numerous Indian tribes. Amongst the component States there is the greatest variety of customs, institutions, and religions. We have the deeper, inbred differences of different ancestry and language; for our people are of the lineage of all nations. Our pursuits for gaining subsistence are various; and such is the diversity of soil and climate that they must always continue to be so. One portion is agricultural, another commercial, another manufacturing. In one section, the natural productions of the earth, in forests above the surface or in minerals beneath it, are inexhaustibly rich; while of the natural productions of another region, it has been graphically said, that they consist of "granite and ice." This region is the New England El Dorado, — whose "granite and ice," however, are turned into gold by industry and enterprise. Across the very centre of our territory a line is drawn, on one side of which all labor is voluntary; while, on the opposite side, the system of involuntary labor, or servitude, prevails. This is a fearful element of repugnance, — penetrating not only through all social, commercial, and political relations, but into natural ethics and religion.

In addition to the multitude of questions for decision is the mode of deciding them. This, indeed, is the grand distinctive feature of our government. The questions which arise for decision are submitted, not to one man, nor to a triumvirate, nor to a Council of Five Hundred, but to millions. The number of votes given at the last presidential election was nearly two millions and a half. When the appointed day for making the decision arrives, the question must be decided, whether the previous preparation which has been made for it be much, or little, or none at all. And, what is extraordinary, each voter helps to decide the question as much by not voting as by voting. If the question is so vast or complicated that any one has not time to make up his mind in relation to it; or if any one is too conscientious to act from conjecture, in cases of magnitude, and, therefore, stays from the polls, another, who has no scruples about acting ignorantly, or from caprice or malevolence, votes; and, in the absence of the former, decides the question against the right.

The founders of our government, indeed, intended to increase responsibility, by limiting the number of its depositaries in the last resort. Hence, in framing the Constitution, they gave a two years' tenure of office to the Representatives, one of six years to Senators, and of four years to the President; and in their contemporaneous expositions of that instrument, they declared that the incumbents of these offices, during their official term, should act according to their own best knowledge and ability, irrespective of the vacillations of party, or the gusts of popular clamor. Indeed, so runs the oath of office, — no provision being made, — no saving clause being inserted, — allowing a man to vote any way and all ways, according to any change among his constituents, or the bearing of his vote upon his next election.

But, through the practice of extorting pledges from a candidate before the election; through the doctrine, or right of instruction as it is called, while one continues in office; and emphatically, by the besom of destruction with which a man, who dares to act in accordance with the dictates of his own judgment and conscience, against the will or whim of his constituents, is swept into political annihilation, the theoretical independence of the Representative — Senator — President — is, to a great extent, abrogated. Instead of holding their offices for two, six, and four years, respectively, they are minute-men; and many of them examine each mail to see what their oaths mean, until the arrival of the next.

Even this representation is faint and inadequate. The most conscientious men, in one State or place, are liable to be catechised out of office, or superseded for performing their duty in it, by one party; while, in another State or place, others are subjected to the same fate, for belonging, conscientiously, to the opposite party. It actually happened, a few years since, that that great statesman and jurist, Edward Livingston, lost his election to Congress, in New Orleans, because he had honestly espoused one side of an important question; and, at the same election, John Sergeant, of Philadelphia, lost his, because he had honestly espoused the other side; — and so both were excluded from the councils of the nation. Under similar circumstances, it often happens that the places of such men are filled by some mere negation of a man, or by some political harlequin, who is ready to enter on the stage, in any dress that pit or gallery may call for. Now I would ask any sober and reflecting man, whether he would not prefer to have his own and his country's interests represented on the floor of Congress by individuals such as those above named, though widely differing from him on a particular point, rather than to have them represented by a base party chameleon, who always reflects the political complexion of the district he resides in; — or, outdoing the chameleon himself, changes to the complexion of the district he means to go to.

But it is not the legislative branch only of our government, into which the power of the people directly enters. As jurors, they decide almost all questions of fact in the judicial department. As witnesses, they are the medium for furnishing the facts themselves to which the court applies its law; and here the witness may be said to govern the court; for, accordingly as he testifies to one thing or its opposite, one legal principle or its opposite arises in the judge's mind, and is applied to the case. And again, in the absence of a standing army, the people are the only reliance of the executive power for enforcing either an act of the Legislature or a decree of the Court, which meets resistance.

I might advert to another prominent circumstance, showing the difficulties and dangers that beset our course. Our government, being representative as it regards the people, and federative as it regards the States, is new in the history of the race. It has no precedent on the file of nations. We have no experience of others, derived from similar experiments, to guide us. Hence our only resort is, to see as far as we can, to grope where we cannot see, and to plunge where we cannot grope. But I leave this fact and its natural consequences to be traced out by each one for himself.

If then every government, — even the simplest, — requires talent and probity for its successful administration; and if it demands these qualities in a higher and higher degree, in proportion to its complexity, and its newness; then does our government require this talent and probity, to an extent indefinitely beyond that of any other which ever existed. And if, in all governments, wisdom and goodness in the ruler, are indispensable to the dignity and happiness of the subject; then, in a government like our own, where all are rulers, all must be wise and good, or we must suffer the alternative of debasement and misery. It is not enough that a bare majority should be intelligent and upright, while a large minority is ignorant and corrupt. Even in such a state, we should be a house divided against itself, which, we are taught, cannot stand. Hence knowledge and virtue must penetrate society, through and through. We need general intelligence and integrity as we need our daily bread. A famine in the latter, would not be more fatal to natural health and life, than a dearth in the former to political health and life.

Two dangers then, equally fatal, impend over us;— the danger of ignorance which does not know its duty, and the danger of vice which, knowing, contemns it. To ensure prosperity, the mass of the people must be both well informed, and upright; but it is obvious that one portion of them may be honest but ignorant, while the residue are educated but fraudful.

When, therefore, we say that our government must be administered by adequate knowledge, and according to the unchangeable principles of rectitude, we mean that it must be administered by men who have acquired this knowledge, and whose conduct is guided by these principles. The knowledge and virtue we need are not abstractions, idealities, bodiless conceptions;— they must be incarnated in human form, imbodied in the living head and heart; they must glow with such fervid vitality as to burst forth spontaneously into action. Instead of our talking so much of these qualities, they must be such a matter of course as not to be talked of.

Such must have been the theory of those who achieved our Independence, and framed the organic law of our government. They did not brave the terrors of that doubtful struggle, to escape from a supposed one-headed monster on the other side of the Atlantic, into the jaws of a myriad-headed monster on this side. No! we should rob the patriots of the Revolution of their purest glory, did we not believe that the means of self-elevation and self-purification, for the whole people, was an infinitely higher object with them, than immunity from pecuniary burdens. Our fathers did not go to the British king, like a town pauper, demanding exemption from taxes; but they went, like high-priests of God, to reclaim the stolen ark of Liberty,—and to bring Dagon upon his face, again and again, till it should be restored.

With the heroes and sages and martyrs of those days, I believe in the capability of man for self-government,— my whole soul thereto most joyously consenting. Nay, if there be any heresy among men, or blasphemy against God, at which the philosopher might be allowed to forget his equanimity, and the Christian his charity,— it is the heresy and the blasphemy of believing and avowing, that the infinitely good and all-wise Author of the universe persists in creating and sustaining a race of beings, who, by a law of their nature, are forever doomed to suffer all the atrocities and agonies of misgovernment, either from the hands of others, or from their own. The doctrine of the inherent and necessary disability of mankind for self-government should be regarded not simply with denial, but with abhorrence; — not with disproof only, but with execration. To sweep so foul a creed from the precincts of truth, and utterly to consume it, rhetoric should become a whirlwind, and logic fire. Indeed, I have never known a man who desired the establishment of monarchical and aristocratical institutions amongst us, who had not a mental reservation, that, in such case, he and his family should belong to the privileged orders.

Still, if asked the broad question, whether man is capable of self-government, I must answer it conditionally. If by man, in the inquiry, is meant the Feejee Islanders; or the convicts at Botany Bay; or the people of Mexico and of some of the South American Republics (so called); or those as a class, in our own country, who can neither read nor write; or those who can read and write, and who possess talents and an education by force of which they get treasury, or post-office, or bank appointments, and then abscond with all the money they can steal; I answer unhesitatingly that *man*, or rather *such men*, are not fit for self-government. Fatuity and guilt are no more certain to ruin an individual, or a family over which they preside, than they are to destroy a government, into whose rule they enter. Politics have been beautifully defined to be *the art of making a people happy*.

Such men have no such art; but, with power in their hands, they would draw down personal, and dispense universal, misery.

But if, on the other hand, the inquiry be, whether mankind are not endowed with those germs of intelligence and those susceptibilities of goodness, by which, under a perfectly practicable system of cultivation and training they are able to avoid the evils of despotism and anarchy; and also, of those frequent changes in national policy which are but one remove from anarchy; and to hold steadfastly on their way in an endless career of improvement, — then, in the full rapture of that joy and triumph which springs from a belief in the goodness of God and the progressive happiness of man, I answer, *they are able*.

But men are not *born* in the full possession of such an ability. They do not necessarily develop any such ability, as they grow up from infancy to manhood. Competency to fill so high a sphere can be acquired only by the cultivation of natural endowments, and the subjugation of inordinate propensities. We laugh to scorn the idea of a man's being *born* a ruler or lawgiver, whether King or Peer; but men are *born* capable of making laws and being rulers, just as much in the Old World as in the New. With us, every voter is a ruler and a law-maker, and therefore it is no less absurd to say, here, that a man is fit to be a voter by right of nativity or naturalization, than it is, in the language of the British constitution, to say, that a man shall be Sovereign, or Lord, by hereditary descent. Qualification, in both cases, is something superadded to birth or citizenship; and hence, unless we take adequate means to supply this qualification to our voters, the Bishop of London or the Duke of Wellington may sneer at us for believing in the hereditary right *to vote*, with as good a grace as we can at them, for believing in the hereditary right *to rule*.

And here a fundamental question arises, — the most important question ever put in relation to this people, — whether, when our government was changed from the hereditary right to rule, to the hereditary right to vote, any corresponding measures were taken to prevent irresponsible voters from abusing their power, as irresponsible rulers had abused theirs. Government is a stewardship, always held by a comparatively small portion of those whose happiness is dependent upon its acts. Even with us, in States where the right of suffrage is most extensive, far less than a quarter part of the existing population, sway the fortunes of all the rest, — to say nothing of their power over the welfare of posterity. This precious deposit in the hands of the foreign steward had been abused; we reclaimed it from his possession, and divided it amongst thousands; but what guaranty did we obtain from the new depositaries, that our treasure should not be squandered or embezzled, as wantonly or wrongfully as before? It is more difficult to watch the million than the individual. It is a case, too, where the law of bond and suretyship does not apply; because, when the contract is broken, we have none to apply to for redress save the contractor and surety, who themselves have violated their obligation. There is but one practicable or possible insurance or gage, and that is, the capacity and conscientiousness of the fiduciary.

When the Declaration of Independence was carried into effect, and the Constitution of the United States was adopted, the civil and political relations of the generation then living and of all succeeding ones, were changed. Men were no longer the same men, but were clothed with new rights and responsibilities. Up to that period, so far as government was concerned, they might have been ignorant; indeed, it has generally been held that where a man's only duty is obedience, it is better that he should be ignorant; for why should a beast of burden be endowed with the sensibilities of a man? Up to that period, so far as government was concerned, a man might have been unprincipled and flagitious. He had no access to the statute-book to alter or repeal its provisions, so as to screen his own violations of the moral law from punishment, or to legalize the impoverishment and ruin of his fellow-beings. But with the new institutions, there came new relations, and an immense accession of powers. New trusts of inappreciable value and magnitude were devolved upon the old agents and upon their successors irrevocably.

Now the rule of common sense applicable to analogous cases,

applies emphatically here;—confide your fortunes only to the hands of a faithful and competent agent, or if, through legal limitation or restriction, they must pass into the hands of one at present unqualified to administer them; spend half, spend nine-tenths of the fortune itself, if need be, to qualify the new agent for his duty.

If, at the epoch to which I have referred, there was any class of men who believed that republican institutions contain an inherent and indestructible principle of self-preservation, or self-purification,—who believed that a Republic from the necessity of its nature is infallible and incorruptible, and, like a beautiful goddess, endowed with immortal youth and purity; or, if there is any class of men at the present day holding this faith, let me say it is as fatal an error as was ever harbored by the human mind; because it belongs to that class of errors which blind while they menace,—whose deadly shaft is unseen until it quivers in the heart. A republican government is the visible manifestation of the people's invisible soul. Through the ballot-box, the latent will bursts out into authoritative action. In a republican government the ballot-box is the urn of fate; yet no god shakes the bowl or presides over the lot. If the ballot-box is open to wisdom and patriotism and humanity, it is equally open to ignorance and treachery, to pride and envy, to contempt for the poor or hostility towards the rich. It is the loosest filter ever devised to strain out impurities. It gives equal ingress to whatever comes. No masses of selfishness or fraud, no foul aggregations of cupidity or profligacy, are so ponderous or bulky as to meet obstruction in its capacious gorge. The criteria of a right to vote respect citizenship, age, residence, tax, and, in a few cases, property; but no inquiry can be put whether the applicant is a Cato or a Catiline. To secure fidelity in the discharge of their duties, an oath is imposed on the most unimportant officers,—constables, clerks, surveyors of roads, of lumber, leather, fish,—while the just exercise of this highest function of the citizen, by which law-makers, law-expounders, and executive officers are alike created, is secured by no civil sanction. In all business transactions, especially where any doubt or distrust attaches to character, we reduce our stipulations to writing; but in conferring the right to vote, we take no promise beforehand that it shall be honestly exercised, nor do we reserve to ourselves any right of subsequent redress, should the privilege be abused.

In some States, the law provides that the *name* of every voter shall be endorsed upon the ballot he gives. Suppose, in some of our angry political contests, the *motives* of every voter were written upon his ballot, so that they should all be as legible to man, on the paper, as they are visible to God, in the heart, — what a history would they reveal! We are accustomed to quote the abominable edicts of popes and kings, and we dwell upon every line, to kindle abhorrence at human depravity; yet, as an exponent of motives, what is the verbiage of papal bulls or imperial mandates, compared with the sententious decrees which every man's ballot contains, and which go forth omnipotent to execute his will? Yet this irresponsible utterance through the ballot-box, is the inceptive process of legislation; nay, in all the most important cases, it is legislation, — the will of the people being made known here, and only passing on to legislative halls to go through certain formalities and be promulgated as law. The human imagination can picture no semblance of the destructive potency of the ballot-box in the hands of an ignorant and a corrupt people. The Roman cohorts were terrible; the Turkish Janizaries were incarnate fiends; but each was powerless as a child, for harm, compared with universal suffrage, without mental illumination and moral principle. The power of casting a vote is far more formidable than that of casting spear or javelin.

One of the foulest in the long catalogue of atrocities which necessitated the French Revolution, was the omission of *lettres de cachet*, — those secret, royal orders, by which good men, without trial and without accusation, were snatched, at midnight, from home and from all they held dear, their property confiscated, and themselves imprisoned or assassinated. Yet every vote which a bad man gives, is a secret, royal *lettre de cachet*, against the happiness and hopes of all good men, — and given equally without trial, arraignment, or accusation. The right of secret ballot is a general license to every bad man in the community, to do, on certain days, the vilest deeds he can conceive, with perfect impunity. With such, election days are the Saturnalia of all vicious desires. But evil motives will issue in evil deeds; and the deeds will be disarmed of none of their malignity because they are done in secret.

On one of these oft-recurring days, when the fate of the State or the Union is to be decided at the polls; when, over all the land, the votes are falling thick as hail, and we seem to hear them rattle like the clangor of arms; is it not enough to make the lover of his country turn pale, to reflect upon the motives under which they may be given, and the consequences to which they may lead? By the votes of a few wicked men, or even of one wicked man, honorable men may be hurled from office, and miscreants elevated to their places; useful offices abolished, and sinecures created; the public wealth, which had supported industry, squandered upon mercenaries; enterprise crippled, the hammer falling from every hand, the wheel stopping in every mill, the sail dropping to the mast on every sea, — and thus capital which had been honestly and laboriously accumulated, turned into dross; in fine, the whole policy of the government may be reversed, and the social condition of millions changed, to gratify one man's grudge, or prejudice, or revenge. In a word, if the votes, which fall so copiously into the ballot-box, on our days of election, emanate from wise counsels and a loyalty to truth, they will descend, like benedictions from Heaven, to bless the land and fill it with song and gladness, — such as have never been known upon earth since the days of Paradise; but if, on the other hand, these votes come from ignorance and crime, the fire and brimstone that were rained on Sodom and Gomorrah would be more tolerable.

So if, at the time when that almost anarchical state of things which immediately followed the Revolutionary War, subsided and took shape and character in the Republican form of our National and State constitutions; — if, at that time, there was a large class of men more wealthy and better educated than the mass, — possessing more of the adventitious distinctions of society, and conversant with an ampler range of human history, — and hence drawing auguries unfavorable to themselves and to the community, from the copious infusion of the democratic principle into all our institutions; — that class of men had one of the most solemn duties to perform ever imposed upon human beings. If they had a superior knowledge of the past, and a greater stake in the future, it was alike their duty and their interest, to stifle all considerations of person and caste, to reconcile themselves to their new condition, and to concentrate all their energies in providing some refuge from impending evils. With our change from a monarchical to a popular government, — from a government where all rule descended from "our Lord the King," to one where all rule ascended from "our Lords the People," the whole condition and relations of men were changed. It was like a change in the order of Nature. Were the poles of the earth to be now swung round ninety degrees, — to a coincidence with the equator, — it would not work a greater change in the soil and climate of all the zones than was wrought by that change of government, both in the relative and absolute conditions of men. Before this epoch, the few, by force of rank, wealth, dress, equipage, accomplishments, governed the many; after it, the many were to govern the few. Before this, birth and family were words of potent signification; but the revolution worked the most thorough attainder of all such blood; and it would have been better for a man to put on the poisoned tunic of Nessus, than to boast that a drop of aristocratical blood coursed through his veins. Before this, the deference paid to the opinions of different men, varied in the ratio of thousands to one; but after this, the vote of the veriest ignoramus or scoundrel would balance that of Franklin or Washington.

About the expediency, and especially about the *extent* of that change, a wide difference of opinion prevailed. But, the change being made, was it not the duty of its opponents to yield to the inevitable course of events, and to prepare for coming exigencies? And could not every really noble soul find an ample compensation for the loss of personal influence or family distinction, in the greater dignity and elevation of his fellow-beings? From whom should instruction come, if not from the most educated? Where should generosity towards the poor begin, if not with those whom Providence had blessed with abundance? Whence should magnanimity proceed, if not from minds expanded by culture? If there were an order of men who lost something of patrician rank by this political change, instead of holding themselves aloof from the people, they should have walked among them as Plato and Socrates did among their contemporaries, and expounded to them the nature and the vastness of the work they had undertaken to do; — nay, if need were, they should have drained the poisoned bowl to sanctify the truths which they taught. For want of that interest and sympathy in the condition of the poor and the ignorant which the new circumstances required, they and their descendants have been, and will be compelled to drink potions, more bitter than hemlock, as their daily beverage. Interest, honor, duty, alike required that no word of aspersion or contumely should be cast upon the new order of things or its supporters. Why should they laugh at the helmsman, when the ship which contained their own treasures as well as his, was in the furrows of the sea? If, as was contemptuously said by one of the most gifted men of that party, these republican institutions are " like white birch stakes whose nature it is to fail in two years;" and that " a republic wears out its morals almost as soon as the sap of a white birch rots the wood," — they should forthwith have saturated them with such a preparation of virtue and knowledge as would *kyanize** even the porous structure of birch itself, and keep the dry-rot forever from its spongiest fibres. With the change in the organic structure of our government, there should have been corresponding changes in all public measures, and institutions. For every dollar given by the wealthy, or by the State, to colleges, to cultivate the higher branches of knowledge,

---

* " *Kyanizing* " is a chemical process, by which wood is supposed to be rendered indestructible.

a hundred should have been given for primary education. For every acre of land bestowed upon an academy, a province should have been granted to Common Schools. Select schools for select children should have been discarded; and universal education joined hands with universal suffrage. It was no time for "Old Mortality" to be furbishing up the gravestones of the dead, when house, and household, and posterity were all in peril from the living. Instead of the old order of nobility, with its baubles and puerilities, a new order should have been created,— an order of Teachers, wise, benevolent, filled with Christian enthusiasm, and rewarded and honored by all; — an order looking forward to a noble line of benefactors whom they might help to rear, rather than backwards to ancestors from whom they had basely degenerated. In these schools, the first great principle of a republican government, — that of native, inborn equality, should have been practically inculcated, by their being open to all, good enough for all, and attended by all. Here too, the second great principle of a republican government should have been taught, — that all men, though natively equal, become inherently unequal the moment that one grows wiser or better than his fellow. The doctrine of "higher" and "lower" classes in society should have been retained, but with a change in its application. Those who had done the most good to mankind should have been honored as the "highest;" while those who had done no good to the race, either by the labors of the hand or by the labors of the mind, — who had lived, without requital, upon the earnings of others, and left the world no better or made it worse, than they found it, should have been thrust down in the scale of social consideration, to "low" and "lower," through all the degrees of comparison. Whatever of leisure or of knowledge was possessed by the more wealthy or educated, should have been freely expended to enlighten the laboring classes. Lectures, libraries, lyceums, mechanics' institutes, should every where have been fostered; scientific tracts gratuitously distributed; and a drowning child should not have been snatched from a watery grave with more promptness and alacrity than an ignorant or an abandoned one should have been sought out, and brought under elevating and reforming influences. The noblest public edifices, the most splendid galleries of art, theatres, gardens, monuments, should all have been deemed a reproach to any people, while there was a child amongst them without ample and improved means of education. The nature and functions of our government, the laws of political economy, the *duties* as well as the *rights* of citizens, should have been made familiar as household words. The right to vote should have been held up as the most sacred of human rights, as involving all civil and religious rights, and therefore to be constrained (*coactum*, as the Romans would have more vigorously expressed it), by all civil and religious obligations. The great truth should every where have been inculcated, by example as well as by precept, that for the dependant to vote from malice, or envy, or wantonness, involves substantially the moral guilt of treason; and for the superior to compel the dependant, through fear or bribery, to vote against his judgment, involves the baseness as well as the guilt of subornation of treason. Had this been done, our days of election would never have been, as they now so often are, days of turbulence, and bacchanalian riot, of insulting triumph or revengeful defeat; but they would have been days of thoughtfulness and of solemnity, such as befit a day whose setting sun will witness the ruin or the rescue of so much of human welfare.

Had this been done, our pioneer settlers would not have abandoned their homes, for the western wilderness, until they could have carried all the blessed influences, — the power and the spirit of education, — with them. No prospect of wealth would have tempted them to leave a land of moral culture for a moral desert. Then our civilization, as it expanded, would have been laden with blessings. We might, indeed, have subjugated less territory by the arts of industry and enterprise; but as a thousand-fold requital for this, we should have subjugated fewer aborigines by fraud and violence. Instead of the unenviable power which belongs to the sword, we should have enjoyed the godlike power which resides in beneficence.

And until all this work of improvement is done, — until this indifference of the wealthy and the educated towards the masses shall cease, and legislative bounty shall atone for past penuriousness, there can be no security for any class or description of men, nor for any interest, human or divine. With additional thousands of voters, every year crossing the line of manhood to decree the destiny of the nation, without additional knowledge and morality, things must accelerate from worse to worse. Amid increasing darkness and degeneracy, every man's rights may be invaded through legislation, — through the annulment of charters or the abrogation of remedies; — and through the corruption of jurors, or even of one juror on the panel of twelve, every man's right of redress may be denied for the grossest aggressions. As parties alternate, the rich may now be plundered of a life of gains; and now, through vindictive legislation, the arms of the laboring man struck dead by his side. And if, amid these scenes, even Washington should arise, and from the battlements of the capitol, should utter a warning voice, the mad populace would hurl him from the Tarpeian. In fine, in our government, as it present administered, or as likely to be administered, the power, even after a choice of rulers, is so far retained by the people as almost to supersede the reality of representation; and, therefore, if the whole people be not equal to the business entrusted to them, — the mass, like any individual, will assuredly ruin what they do not understand.

I have said that schools should have been established for the education of the whole people. These schools should have been of a more perfect character than any which have ever yet existed. In them the principles of morality should have been copiously intermingled with the principles of science. Cases of conscience should have alternated with lessons in the rudiments. The multiplication table should not have been more familiar nor more frequently applied, than the rule, to do to others as we would that they should do unto us. The lives of great and good men should have been held up for admiration and example; and especially the life and character of Jesus Christ, as the sublimest pattern of benevolence, of purity, of self-sacrifice, ever exhibited to mortals. In every course of studies, all the practical and preceptive parts of the Gospel should have been sacredly included; and all dogmatical theology and sectarianism sacredly excluded. In no school should the Bible have been opened to reveal the sword of the polemic, but to unloose the dove of peace.

I have thus endeavored to show, that with universal suffrage, there must be universal elevation of character, intellectual and moral, or there will be universal mismanagement and calamity.

Let us now, in the first place, inquire whether there is at present, in this country, a degree of intelligence sufficient for the wise administration of its affairs. If there is sufficient intelligence in the aggregate people, then there must be sufficient in the individual members; and, if there is not sufficient in the individual members, then there is not sufficient in the aggregate.

The last census of the United States shows the round number of five hundred and fifty thousand persons, over the age of twenty years, unable to read and write. From no inconsiderable attention devoted to this and kindred topics, I am convinced that the above number, great as it is, is far below the truth. I will state one or two of the reasons, among many, which have led me to this conclusion.

There is no part of our country where a man would not prefer to be accounted able to read and write, rather than to be written down according to the preference of Dogberry. To be supposed the possessor of power and accomplishments is a desire common to all men, whether savage, or civilized, or in the intermediate state. The deputy marshals or assistants who took the census travelled from house to house, making the shortest practicable stay at each. They received compensation, by the head, not by the day, for the work done. Considering the time to which they were limited, more was required of them than could be thoroughly and accurately performed. The most credible sources of information would be the heads of families; but as these might not always be at home, they were allowed to receive statements from persons over sixteen years of age. It must often have happened that the import of the questions proposed by them was not fully understood. Their informants were subjected to no test, — their bare word being accredited. The very question would imply disparagement, and would often be regarded as an insult, by those who saw no reason for putting it. A new source of error would exist in any want of fidelity in the agent; and who can suppose, among so many, that all were faithful? It is well known too, that no inconsiderable number of persons gave false information when inquired of by the deputies, — either through a wanton or mischievous disposition, or through a fear that the census was only a preliminary step to some tax or other requisition, to be made upon them by the government.

Let me fortify this reasoning with facts. In the annual message of Governor Campbell of Virginia, to the Legislature of that State, dated January 9th, 1839, — the year immediately preceding that in which the census was taken, — I find the following statement: —

"The importance of an efficient system of education, embracing in its comprehensive and benevolent design, the whole people, cannot be too frequently recurred to.

"The statements furnished by the clerks of five city and borough courts, and ninety-three of the county courts, in reply to the inquiries addressed to them, ascertain, that of those who applied for marriage licenses, a large number were unable to write their names. The years selected for this inquiry were those of 1817, 1827, and 1837. The statements show that the applicants for marriage licenses in 1817, amounted to four thousand six hundred and eighty-two; of whom eleven hundred and twenty-seven were unable to write; — five thousand and forty-eight in 1827, of whom the number unable to write was eleven hundred and sixty-six; — and in 1837, the applicants were four thousand six hundred and fourteen; and of these the number of one thousand and forty-seven were unable to write their names. From which it appears, there still exists a deplorable extent of ignorance, and that in truth, it is hardly less than it was twenty years ago, when the school fund was created. The statements, it will be remembered, are partial, not embracing quite all the counties, and are moreover confined to one sex. The education of females, it is to be feared, is in a condition of much greater neglect.

"There are now in the State two hundred thousand children between the ages of five and fifteen. Forty thousand of them are reported to be poor children; and of them only one-half to be attending schools. It may be safely assumed that of those possessing property, adequate to the expenses of a plain education, a large number are growing up in ignorance, for want of schools within convenient distances. Of those at school, many derive little or no instruction, owing to the incapacity of the teachers, as well as to their culpable negligence and inattention. Thus the number likely to remain uneducated and to grow up, without just perceptions of their duties, religious, social, and political, is really of appalling magnitude, and such as to appeal with affecting earnestness to a parental Legislature."

Here let the audience mark particulars. Written application was to be made for a marriage license. The rudimental or elementary education which a person obtains, usually precedes marriage. After this climacteric, people rarely go to school to learn reading and writing. The information, here given, was obtained from five city and borough, as well as from ninety-three county courts, (the whole number of counties in the State being one hundred and twenty-three;) — not, therefore, in the dark interior only, but in the blaze of city illumination. The fact was communicated by the governor of a proud State to the Legislature of the same. Each case was subjected to an infallible test, for no man who could make any scrawl in the similitude of his name, would prefer to make his mark and leave it on record. The requisition was made upon the officers of the courts, and the evidence was of a documentary or judicial character, — the highest known to the law. And what was the result? Almost one-quarter part of the men applying for marriage licenses were unable to write their names! It would be preposterous to suppose that their intended wives had gazed, from any nearer point than their husbands, at the splendors of science. Indeed, Governor Campbell clearly intimates an opinion that the women were far more ignorant than the men.

I ought to add, that an inquiry made in another part of the same State, by one of its public officers, showed that one-third of all those who had applied for a marriage license had made their marks.

Now Virginia has a free white population over 20 years of age, of 329,959. One-fourth part of this number is 82,489, which, according to the evidence presented by Governor Campbell, is the lowest possible limit, at which the minimum of adults unable to read and write, can be stated. But the census number is 58,787 only, making a difference of 23,702, or more than 40 per cent. North Carolina, with a free white population over 20 years of age of only 209,635, has the appalling number, even according to the census, of 56,609 unable to read and write; or a great deal more than one-quarter part of the whole free population, over 20 years of age, *below zero*, in the educational scale. If to this number we should add 40 per cent., as facts require us to do in the case of Virginia, we should find almost two-fifths of the whole adult population of that State in the same Cimmerian night.

I had proposed to pursue this computation in regard to Kentucky, Tennessee, South Carolina, Georgia, Alabama, etc., but the task is useless and sickening. It must suffice to state, in general terms, that the number according to the census, of persons over the age of 20, unable to read and write, is, in Virginia, 58,787, in North Carolina, 56,609, Kentucky, 40,010, Tennessee, 58,531, South Carolina, 20,615, (with a free white population over 20 years of age, of only 111,663, and with 327,038 slaves,) Georgia, 30,717, and Alabama, 22,592; and that, by the Constitution of the United States, these ignorant multitudes have the right of voting for Representatives in Congress, not only for themselves, but for their slaves, — five slaves being counted as equal to three whites. Now, if to the 550,000 free white population, over the age of 20 years, unable to read and write, as shown by the census, we should add only thirty per cent., for its undoubted underestimates, it would increase the total to more than 700,000.

I might derive another and a convincing argument, from the statistics of education given by the census, in regard to our own State, to prove their inaccuracy. The same general motives, which would lead to an under-statement in regard to the number of persons unable to read and write, would lead to an overstatement in regard to the number of those attending school. In Massachusetts, the whole number of scholars of all ages, in all our Public Schools, is annually returned by the school committees, — men highly competent to do their duty, familiar with the subject, and possessing the most ample and exact means of information. By those returns, it appears that the whole number of scholars who were in all our Public Schools, any part of the time during our school year 1840–41 (the year in which the census was taken) was but 155,041, and the average attendance was, in winter, 116,398, and in summer, 96,892;—while the number given in the census, is 158,351.

But without seeking any closer approximation to so unwelcome a truth, let us suppose, that we have but 700,000 free white persons in the United States, over the age of twenty years, unable to read and write; and further, that only one-quarter part of these are voters,—that is, we will deduct one-half for females, and allow one-half of the male moiety to be persons, either between twenty and twenty-one, or unnaturalized, (which, considering the States where the great mass of this ignorance belongs, is a most liberal allowance, because the number of ignorant immigrants is much less at the South than at the North,) and we should then have 175,000 voters, unable to read and write.

Now at the last presidential election, when every voter not absolutely in his winding sheet was carried to the polls,—when the harvest-field was so thoroughly swept that neither stubble nor tares were left for the gleaner,—at that election, the majority for the successful candidate was 146,081,—about 30,000 less than the estimated number of legal voters in the United States, unable to read and write. At this election, it is also to be remembered, a larger majority of the electoral votes was given to the successful candidate than was ever given to any other President of the United States, with the single exception of Mr. Monroe in 1820, against whom there was but one vote. Gen. Harrison's popular majority also, was undoubtedly the largest by which any President of the United States has ever been elected, with the exception above mentioned, of Mr. Monroe, and perhaps that of General Washington at his second election. And yet this majority, large as it was, was about 30,000 less than the estimated number of our legal voters, unable to read and write.

No, Fellow-Citizens, we have not for years past, and we shall not have, at least for many years to come, an election of a President, or a Congress, or a Governor of a State,—chosen under written constitutions, and to legislate and act under written constitutions, whose choice will not be dependent upon, and determinable by, *legal* voters, unable to read and write, — voters who do not know, and cannot know, whether they vote for King Log, or King Stork. The illustrious and noble band who framed the constitution of the Union, — Washington, Adams, Franklin, Jefferson, Madison, — who adjusted all the principles which it contains, by the line and the plummet, and weighed the words which describe them in scales so nice as to tremble beneath the dust of the balance, — expended the energies of their mighty minds to perfect an instrument, which, before half a century should pass away, was doomed to be administered, controlled, expounded, by men unable to read and write. The power of Congress over all the great social and economical interests of this vast country; the orbits in which the States are to move around the central body in the system; the functions of the Executive, who holds in his hands the army and the navy, manages all diplomatic relations with foreign powers, and can involve the country, at any time, in the horrors of war; and that grand poising power, the Supreme Judiciary, appointed to be the presiding intelligence over the system, to harmonize its motions and to hold its attracting and divergent tendencies in equilibrium; — all this splendid structure, the vastest and the nicest ever devised by mortals, — is under the control of men who are incapable of reading one word of the language which describes its framework, and defines its objects and its guards, — incapable of reading one word of contemporaneous exposition, of antecedent history, or of subsequent developments, and therefore ready to make it include anything, or exclude anything, as their blind passions may dictate. Phaeton was less a fool when he mounted the chariot to drive the horses of the sun, than ourselves, if we expect to reach the zenith of prosperity and happiness under such guidance!

I have spoken of those only who might as well have lived before Cadmus invented letters, as in the middle of this nineteenth century. But it is to be remembered there is no unoccupied space, — no broad line of demarcation between the totally ignorant and the competently learned. Between meridian and midnight, a dim and long twilight intervenes.

If the seven hundred thousand, who, in one particular, surpass the most learned of ancient or modern times, — because to them all written languages are alike, — if these are the most numerous class, — probably the next most numerous consists of those who know next to nothing, — and in reaching the summit of the highest intelligence, we should ascend by very easy gradations. Very many people learn to write their names for business purposes, whose attainments, at that point, become stationary; and it is one thing to be just able to read a verse in the Bible, and quite another to understand the forty thousand words in common use, among intelligent men; — there being more than a geometrical increase in the ideas which these words may be made to convey. Nay, if a few of the words, used by an intelligent man, are lost to the hearer, through his ignorance of their meaning, the whole drift and object of the speaking or writing are lost. The custom so prevalent at the West and South, of *stump-speaking*, as it is significantly but uncouthly called, had its origin in the voters' incapacity to read. How otherwise can a candidate for office communicate with ignorant voters? Should he publish his views and send them abroad, he must send an interpreter with them; but at a *barbecue*, — amid the sympathy of numbers, the excitement of visible objects, the feast, the flow, the roar, — the most abstruse points of the Constitution, the profoundest questions of national policy can all be expounded, and men and measures decided upon, to universal satisfaction!

A clear corollary is deducible from this demonstration. If the majority of a self-governing people are sober-minded, enlightened, studious of right, capable of comparing and balancing opposite interpretations of a fundamental law, or opposite views of a particular system of policy; then all appeals addressed to them in messages, speeches, pamphlets, and from the thousand-tongued newspaper press, will be calm, dispassionate, adapted at once to elucidate the subject under consideration, and to instruct and elevate the mind of the arbiters. But, on the other hand, if the people are ignorant, fickle, averse to, or incapable of, patient inquiry, prone to hasty decisions from plausible appearances, or reckless from prejudice or passion, then the demagogues who address, will adapt themselves to the dupes who hear, just as certainly, as the hunter adapts his lure to the animal he would ensnare; and flattery, imposture, falsehood, the vindication and eulogy of fellow-partisans, however wicked, and the defamation of opponents, however virtuous, will be the instruments by which a warfare, destructive in the end alike to victors and vanquished, will be waged. Let the spirit and tone of our congressional and legislative speech-makers, and the language of the political press, throughout the country, decide the question, which of the above described classes they consider themselves as addressing.

Some have thought that, in a Republic, the good and wise must necessarily maintain an ascendency over the vicious and ignorant. But whence any such moral necessity? The distinctive characteristic of a Republic is, the greater freedom and power of its members. A Republic is a political contrivance by which the popular voice is collected and uttered, as one articulate and authoritative sound. If then, the people are unrighteous, that utterance will be unrighteous. If the people, or a majority of them, withdraw their eyes from wisdom and equity, — those everlasting lights in the firmament of truth; — if they abandon themselves to party strife, where the triumph of a faction, rather than the prevalence of the right, is made the object of contest, — it becomes as certain as are the laws of omnipotence, that such a community will express and obey the baser will.

Suppose a people to be honest, but unenlightened either by study or experience; and suppose a series of questions to be submitted to them for decision, more grave and important than were ever before evolved in the history of the race. Suppose further, that many of the leading men among them, and the principal organs which hold communication with them, instead of striving to enlighten and instruct, only inflame and exasperate one portion of them against another portion, — and in this state of mind they proceed to the arbitrament. Would it not be better, like the old

Roman soothsayers, to determine the question by the flight of birds, or to learn the oracles of fate by inspecting the entrails of an animal?

When a pecuniary question, however trifling, is to be submitted to a bench of judges, composed of the most learned men in the land, the parties whose interest is at stake, employ eminent counsel, that the whole merits of the case may be developed, and conduce to a just decision. And the court will not suffer its attention to be withdrawn, or its judgment to be disturbed, by vilification of an opponent, or flattery of the tribunal, or the introduction of any other irrelevant matter, but rebukes them as a personal indignity. Now the people have questions to decide infinitely more important than are ever submitted to any court, — they may have the question of the court's existence to decide on, — and should not they, therefore, demand of all their advisers, whether elected or self-constituted, a corresponding truthfulness and gravity?

All philosophers are agreed in regard to all the great truths of astronomy, chemistry, engineering, mechanics, navigation; — if any new point arises, they address themselves most soberly and sedulously to its solution; if new instruments are wanted, they prepare them; if they are deficient in any collateral branch of information, they acquire it. And yet philosophy has no questions more difficult or important than those which are decided with us, by a major vote. Why then should we wonder that on all the great questions which, as yet, have arisen under our government, — the increase or reduction of the army and navy; peace or war; tariff or anti-tariff; internal improvements or no internal improvements; currency, bank or no bank, sub-treasury or no sub-treasury; — why should we wonder, that on all these and other vital questions, we should already have precedents and authorities on both sides, and everything as yet unsettled; — nay, even a wider diversity and a fiercer conflict of opinion, at the present time, than at the foundation of the government?

And while the present state of things exists, is it not obvious, that we can neither develop the principles of a true policy, nor enjoy the advantages of consistency even in an erroneous course? A foreigner would naturally inquire how it is, that, with such an extended country and with such predominating interests, our parties are so equally balanced, — and why it is, that power so often shifts hands amongst us, and rivals and competitors are now on this side and now on that, like partners in a country-dance. The answer is obvious. If any one party predominates, and triumphs even to the silencing of opposition, — not through any sagacity or sanity of its own, but owing to a deep undercurrent of events which bears it prosperously along, notwithstanding any follies or enormities which may be committed on the surface; it is easy to see that, in a country presenting such diversified interests as ours, and with knowledge so inadequate to a mastery of their relations, the defeated and dispersed party can rally under some new name, and avowing some new and plausible purpose, again contend for victory. And thus, in an ignorant community, the decomposition and recomposition of parties may follow each other forever. Or, suppose that each of two great parties contains a million of tried adherents, — of men who may be relied on, who will not, on the morning of battle, strike their flag and march over in a body, to the enemy's ranks; — but suppose that, in addition to this loyal million on each side, there are a hundred thousand mere mercenaries, — political Swiss, ready to fight on either side, and whose only inquiry is, which side offers greater pay and greater plunder; — is it not plain that every question will be decided by the hirelings? Foreseeing on what the fate of the day is to depend, will not each party, — at least its irresponsible members, if not its leaders, — be tempted to offer bounty and spoils, — to bid and over-bid for their services, until the venal Hessians are glutted. Is this prophecy, or is it history?

We look with a kind of contempt as well as abhorrence upon the self-styled republics of South America, which seem to be founded politically, as well as territorially, upon earthquakes. Were it not that so much of human happiness is involved in their revolutions, ridicule would overpower indignation at the spectacle they present. It is difficult to state the number of their overturns, and of late years, it has seemed hardly worth while to keep the tally, but probably the changes of party and of policy in our general government, have not been much less numerous than theirs. In some of our States certainly, the changes of party have been so frequent, that the Moon would be their most appropriate coat of arms.*

In one important particular, indeed, we have the advantage of our namesakes in the Southern hemisphere; for our revolutions of party, as yet, have been bloodless. How long they may continue so, even in New England, depends upon the measures we take to give predominance to principle over passion, in the education of the young.

To these indisputable facts respecting the general ignorance of this country, it cannot be answered, that, stationed at different points, all over its surface, with narrow intervening distances, there are a few men, who have been bred in collegiate halls, educated in all the lore of civil polity, and trained to the labors of professional life, who will be eyes to the blind, and understandings to the foolish, and will lead the ignorant in the paths of wisdom. In the first place, suppose that irreconcilable differences should arise amongst these men; — can an ignorant and stupid people decide between them, with any certainty of not deciding in favor of the erroneous? And again; the history of the world shows an ever-present desire in mankind to acquire power and privilege, and to retain them, when acquired. Knowledge is power; and the race has suffered as much from the

* In the twenty-two elections for Governor of the State of New York, which have taken place since the adoption of the Federal Constitution in 1789, the average majority has been only a little more than twelve thousand; and, omitting the election of 1822, when the opposition was only nominal, the average majority has been less than seven thousand; while, according to the census, the number of whites in that State, over 20 years of age, unable to read and write, is more than 44,000. In Pennsylvania, the majority for Governor has varied from 3,000 to 25,000. It has 33,940 whites, over 20 years of age, unable to read and write. In Ohio, the majority has varied from 2,000 (in 1828 and 1830) to 14,000 (last year). Its number of adult whites unable to read and write, is 35,394.

In the presidential election of 1836, Mr Van Buren's majority over Harrison and White was 25,000, — South Carolina choosing her electors by the Legislature. At the very next election (1840) the majority, *on the opposite side*, was 146,000.

usurpers of knowledge, as from Alexanders or Napoleons. If learning could be monopolized by a few individuals amongst us, another priesthood, Egyptian or Druidical, would speedily arise, bowing the souls of men beneath the burden of their terrible superstitions; or, if learning were more widely spread, but still confined to a privileged order, the multitude, unable to comprehend the source of the advantages it conferred, and stimulated by envy and fear, would speedily extinguish whatever there might be of light, — just as the owl and the bat and the mole, if they were promoted to the government of the solar system, would extinguish the sun, because its beams arrested their hunt for insects and vermin. No! The whole people must be instructed in the knowledge of their duties, they must be elevated to a contemplation and comprehension of those great truths on which alone a government like ours can be successfully conducted; and any hope of arresting degeneracy, or suppressing the insurgent passions of the multitude by the influence of here and there an individual, though he were wise as Solon or Solomon, would prove as fallacious as an attempt to stop the influx of malaria, by sprinkling a little chloride of lime along the creeks and shallows of the shore, if the whole ocean, in all its depths, were corrupted.

Bear with me, Fellow-Citizens, while I say, I rejoice that this emergency has burst upon us. I rejoice that power has passed irrevocably into the hands of the people, although I know it has brought imminent peril upon all public and private interests, and placed what is common and what is sacred alike in jeopardy. Century after century, mankind had groaned beneath unutterable oppressions. To pamper a few with luxuries, races had been subjected to bondage. To satiate the ambition of a tyrant, nations had been dashed against each other in battle, and millions crushed by the shock. The upward-tending, light-seeking capacities of the soul had been turned downwards into darkness and debasement. All the realms of futurity, which the far-seeing eye of the mind could penetrate, had been peopled with the spectres of superstition. The spirits of the infernal world had been subsidized, to bind all religious freedom, whether of thought or of speech, in the bondage of fear. Heaven had been sold, for money, like an earthly domicile, by those who, least of all, had any title to its mansions. In this exigency, it was the expedient of Providence, to transfer dominion from the few to the many, — from those who had abused it, to those who had suffered. The wealthy, the high-born, the privileged, had had it in their power to bless the people; but they had cursed them. Now, they and all their fortunes are in the hands of the people. The poverty which they have entailed is to command their opulence. The ignorance they have suffered to abound, is to adjudicate upon their rights. The appetites they have neglected, or which they have stimulated for their own indulgence, are to invade the sanctuary of their homes. In fine, that interest and concern for the welfare of inferiors, which should have sprung from motives of philanthropy, must now be extorted from motives of self-preservation. As famine teaches mankind to be industrious and provident, so do these great developments teach the more favored classes of society that they never can be safe while they neglect the welfare of any portion of their social inferiors. In a broad survey of the grand economy of Providence, the lesson of frugality and thrift, which is taught by the dearth of a single year, is no plainer than this grander lesson of universal benevolence, which the lapse of centuries has been evolving, and is now inculcating upon the world.

Yes, Fellow-Citizens, it is the sublimest truth which the history of the race has yet brought to light, that God has so woven the fortunes of all men into one inseparable bond of unity and fellowship, that it can be well with no class, or oligarchy, or denomination of men, who, in their own self-seeking, forget the welfare of their fellow-beings. Nature has so bound us together by the ties of brotherhood, by the endearments of sympathy and benevolence, that the doing of good to others opens deep and perennial well-springs of joy in the human soul; but if we will select the coarse gratifications of selfishness, — if we will forget our own kindred blood in whosesoever veins it may flow, then the Eternal Laws denounce, and will execute upon us, tribulation and anguish, and a fearful looking for of an earthly, as well as of a heavenly judgment.

In the first place, there is the property of the affluent, which lies outspread, diffused, scattered over land and sea, — open alike to the stealthiness of the thief, the violence of the robber, and the torch of the incendiary. If any think they hold their estates by a surer tenure, — by charters, franchises, or other muniments of property; let them know that all these, while the ballot-box which controls legislation, and the jury-box and the witnesses' stand, which control the tribunals of justice, are open; — all these are but as iron mail to protect them against lightning. Where is their security against breaches of trust, and fraudulent bankruptcies, — against stop-laws and suspension-acts, or the bolder measures of legislative repudiation? If their ultimate hope is in the protection of the laws, what shall save them, when fraud and perjury turn every legal remedy into a new instrument of aggression? And behind all these, there is an omnipotent *corps de reserve* of physical force, which mocks at the slowness of legislation and judicature, — whose decrees are irreversible deeds, — whose terrific decisions flash forth in fire, or burst out in demolition.

But houses, lands, granaries, flocks, factories, warehouses, ships, banks, are only exterior possessions, — the out-works of individual ownership. When these are carried, the assault will be made upon personal security, character and life; and, lastly, upon all the endearments and sanctities that cluster around the domestic altar, — and when these are lost, humanity has nothing more to lose.

Look at England; and is she not, at the present moment, teaching a lesson too instructive to be lost upon us? There, a landed aristocracy, by extortious rents and class-legislation, have turned every *twelfth* subject into a pauper. They have improved soils; but they have forgotten the cultivator himself, — as though the clod of the valley were worth more than the soul of the tiller. The terms offered by manufacturing capitalists, with a few most worthy exceptions, have been, absolute starvation, or work with the lowest life-sustaining pittance. Manufacturers have been most anxious about tariff laws, which merely regulate the balance of trade; but heedless of those moral laws, which determine the balance of all power in the last resort. They have been alive to all improvements in machinery, but dead to the character of the operatives who were to work it. Surely there is no such danger of spontaneous combustion in a heap of oiled cotton or wool, as there is in a mass of human ignorance and prejudice; nor can the former be so easily set on fire by a torch, as the latter by a demagogue. For years past the upper house of parliament have perseveringly and successfully resisted all measures for National Education, which they could not pervert from the bestowment of equal benefits upon all, to the support of their own monopolies. And, as a legitimate consequence of all these systematic, wholesale infractions of the great law which teaches us to do unto others as we would that they should do unto us, there are now, to-day, three millions of Chartists thundering at their palace gates, and the motto upon their banner is, "Bread or Blood."

What Paley so justly said of a parent, that "to send an uneducated child into the world is little better than to turn out a mad dog or a wild beast into the streets," is just as true when applied to parliament and hierarchy, as when applied to an individual.[*]

---

[*] For a century past, a vast portion of the wit of all English novel and dramatic literature has turned upon the ignorance and coarseness of the common people. The millions have first been shut out from the means of knowledge and good breeding, and then their cockneyisms, their provincial, outlandish pronunciation and brogue, their personal awkwardness and half-formed ideas, have been ridiculed and laughed at, by those who could afford to buy gilt-covered books, and go to Drury Lane and Covent Garden. This double injustice of withholding knowledge and good manners, and then making sport of ignorance and clownishness, has been so long pursued that some of its natural consequences are fast developing. The ignorant and debased, knowing nothing of the gratifications of intelligence and refinement, have invented a few modes of fun and merrymaking, peculiar to themselves; — such as the burning of cornstacks and hay-ricks, and the sprinkling of vitriol on magnificent dresses. Being disqualified for the use, and debarred from the dignity of the ballot-box, they betake themselves to the tinder-box. The light of blazing granaries serves them instead of brilliant ideas. In the malice of their misery, they love company too well not to reduce the diamond-studded robes of lords and prelates, to the value of their own beggarly rags. And is there not a close resemblance between these pastimes of the

But if such is the present difference between the great interests which, in this country, we have in charge, and the intelligence that superintends those interests; what is our prospect in regard to the future? I speak not of the remote future, but of that which is now opening upon our view, and which the middle-aged man may live to see. Is time sweeping us forward to a better, or to a worse condition? The answer to this depends upon the extent and the efficiency of the means now employed to educate the rising generation. Let us quicken our resolutions, or calm our fears, by looking, for one moment, at the facts of the case.

The free population of the United States in 1840, was 14,581,553. It is found that about one-fourth part of our population are between the ages of four and sixteen years. In Massachusetts it is so almost without a fraction.* Although there may be slight variations from this ratio in other States, yet undoubtedly the number *four* is an integer, by far nearer than any other that could be taken, which, when compared with unity or one, would show the ratio between the whole population of the United States, and the number of children within them, between the ages of four and sixteen years.

Now one-fourth part of the whole population, is 3,645,368, while the whole number of children *of all ages*, in the Primary and Common Schools of the Union, is only 1,845,244, which would leave 1,800,144, or almost half the children *of an age to attend school,* and far more than half the whole number, *between*

"high" and the "low?" An educated nobleman regales himself at the theatre, or in his palace, with a farce or novel, where the uncouth language and awkward manners of the poor and the neglected are made ridiculous; and, as he alights from, or re-enters his emblazoned carriage, a dexterous villain *pinks* a thousand eyelet holes through his dress of ermine, or cloth of gold, by the skilfully sprinkled contents of a vitriol bottle. The one enjoys a farce in *three* acts; the other, in *one* act. The *wit* in both instances must consist in the *incongruity*; and, as to the *humanity* of the sports, the latter seems every whit as legitimate a source of amusement as the former; or, to speak *phrenologically*, the pleasure, in both cases, is felt in the same part of the head. To a benevolent and Christian mind, how unutterably shocking are the extremes of such a state of society, and what terrible retributions follow in the train of selfish legislation!

* Whole population, 737,699;—Number between 4 and 16 (omitting three small towns), 184,392. Now 184,392 × 4 = 737,568. So far as there is any difference, the proportion of children to adults would be greatest in the new States.

four and sixteen years of age, without any of the advantages which those schools might afford.*

Nor would the result be materially altered, even should we add all the students of those institutions, called academies and grammar schools, as contradistinguished from Primary and Common Schools; for they amount, in all, only to 164,159. The difference between four and sixteen, being twelve, if we divide the number of those who neither attend any academy, grammar, common, or primary school, by twelve, it will give a quotient of 136,332 persons who belong to this uneducated class, and who are annually passing the line of majority, and coming upon the stage of life, to be the fathers and the mothers of the next generation, the depositaries of all we hold dear, — in fine, to be the electors, *or the elected*, for all our magistracy. This class alone will annually furnish a number of voters, far greater than the average popular majority by which our presidents have been chosen. And even this statement, fearfully large as it is, does not include those foreigners who are coming, thousands every week, to mingle with our people, and very soon to take part in the choice of all our officers.

It was the observation of one of the most philosophical foreigners who has ever visited this country,† that probably a majority of all the voters in the United States, were under thirty-five or thirty-six years of age. I think an examination of the last census would verify this remark. It would require then but fourteen years, — or three and a half presidential terms, — a period almost identical with that which has elapsed, since the election of Gen. Jackson, — to bring forward a numerical majority of voters who have never possessed either the intellectual or the moral advantages of a school; — and to whom the interior of a schoolroom would be as novel an object as the interior of an Egyptian pyramid, and the books and apparatus of the former as unintelligible as the hieroglyphics of the

---

* There is, of course, some *domestic* education. But this exists, but seldom, excepting in favor of those children who *also* go to school, and are therefore included in the above computation.

† George Combe, Esq.

latter. Indeed, why are not the political destinies of the country already in such hands? This class, from their profound ignorance, will necessarily be incapable of discerning principles, or of appreciating arguments; — accessible through the passions alone; creating demagogues for leaders, and then destroying them, just as naturally as a barbarian makes an idol of a stock, or a serpent, and then hews it down, or kills it, when it does not answer his ridiculous or selfish prayers. Nor will this class of men necessarily attach themselves to any one party; but they will be, like the shifting ballast of a vessel, always on the wrong side.

I have spoken only of that half of our rising population, — our future rulers, — who, from infancy to manhood, are rarely in any school of any kind. But, in no house for education is there any charm or magic, of such transforming power, as to turn an ignorant child into a capable citizen. What is the house; what the course of study and the appliances; who the teacher, and how long the attendance; become here significant questions. In regard to the moiety who, at some period of their minority, may be found in the schoolroom, look at the edifices where they assemble, which must have been first called *Temples of Science* by some bitter ironist; consider their meagre outfit of books and apparatus; reflect upon the strong tendency, in all uneducated quarters, to keep a show-school, instead of a useful one; and think, for a moment, of the character of a portion, at least, of the teachers, whose only evidence of competency is, that nothing has been made in vain, and that they have failed in everything before undertaken. It is by force of these adverse circumstances, that even in Massachusetts, although the compensation is far higher than in any other State in the Union, yet so niggardly are many teachers paid, and so little sympathy and social consideration do they receive, that young men, not unfrequently, desert the occupation of school-keeping and resort to our cities to let themselves out as servants in kitchens, or as grooms in stables; — well knowing that a kitchen, as destitute of apparatus as our common schoolrooms, is a thing unheard of, even in an alms-house; and that, if they keep their horses sleek and nimble, they will be better rewarded than if they "trained up children in the way they should go." Female teachers, too, abandon the schoolroom for the factory, for they have learned that a spinning-frame, or a power-loom, has no mother to abuse and defame them for making it work as it ought to work. And in those parts of the country where there are no Public Schools, but where a few of the wealthy procure their own teachers, how often are the private tutors and governesses treated as mere upper servants in the family, or even made the scape-goat for a child's offences; — as, in former times, it is said to have been the practice in England, when the king's son was sent to school, to send another boy with him as his companion, whose vicarious duty it was to receive all the flagellations due to the misdemeanors of his royal schoolfellow.

In looking at the last census of the United States, one might infer that, at least, something adequate to the exigencies of the times, had been done, in the higher departments of education. The census shows a list of one hundred and seventy-three universities or colleges, with more than sixteen thousand students. I rejoice in the existence of any institutions for the increase of knowledge among the people; but the honor of education is rather tarnished than brightened, by giving a President and Faculty, instead of a prudential committee man, to a district school, and then calling it a college. The census gives to Massachusetts but *four* colleges, with 769 students. What, then, are we to think of the *twelve* colleges, set down to Maryland (with less than three-sevenths of our free white population, and with almost twelve thousand over the age of 20, unable to read and write), with 813 students; — of the *thirteen* colleges, set down to Virginia, with 1,097 students; of the *ten*, in Kentucky, with 1,419 students; and of the *eighteen* in Ohio, with 1,717 students. Some of these colleges or universities, at the West and South, I know are well conducted, and embrace a competent range of studies; but whoever has visited many of the institutions bearing these high-sounding names, inquired into their course of studies, marked the ages of the students, and seen the juvenile alumni, well knows, that the amount of instruction there given bears no greater proportion to what a liberal college course of studies should be, than the narrow circuit of a mill-horse, to the vast circumference of the Hippodrome.

And what are we doing, as a people, to supply these great deficiencies? What intellectual lights are we kindling to repel the night of ignorance, whose coming on will bring, not only darkness, but chaos?

There is not a single State in this whole Union, which is doing anything at all proportionate to the exigency of the case. The most that can be said is, that there are three States out of the twenty-six, which have adopted some commendable measures for the promotion of this great work. These are Massachusetts, New York, and Michigan, — the first by sustaining her Board of Education, by her Normal Schools, and her District School Libraries; the second by her District School Libraries, her fund, and her county superintendents of schools; and the third, by her magnificent fund, and her State superintendency of education. Five years ago, Ohio entered upon the work, but after about two years, the measure was substantially abandoned. Four years ago, a new system was established in Connecticut, which was most efficiently and beneficially administered, under the auspices of one of the ablest and best of men,* but it is with unspeakable regret I am compelled to add, that within the last month, all her measures for improvement have been swept from the statute-book. New Jersey, Pennsylvania, and Kentucky may be mentioned as exhibiting signs of life on this subject, although it is a life which far more nearly resembles the imitative and feeble movements of infancy, than the independent and conscious energy of manhood.

In but few of the other States, can even a well digested system for the organization of schools be found in the statute-book; and in most of them, the meagre provisions upon the subject seem to have been inserted, only as a sort of ornamental legislation, and are disregarded or obsolete. And, what is most painful

---

* Henry Barnard, 2d, Esq.

and humiliating to reflect upon, in all the principal slave States, — Virginia, North Carolina, South Carolina, Georgia, and so forth, — the highest homage which is paid to the beneficent power of education, is the terrible homage of making it a severely punishable offence, to educate a slave!

Now, even within the narrow horizon of the politician, what is the result of this neglect of childhood, and the consequent ignorance of men? When an election is coming on, whether State or National, then the rival parties begin to play their game for the ignorant, and to purchase the salable. Mass-meetings are held. Hired speakers itinerate through the country. A thousand tireless presses are plied, day and night. Newspapers and pamphlets are scattered thick as snowflakes in a wintry storm. Reading-rooms and committee-rooms are opened, and men abandon business and family to fill them. The census is taken anew, and every man is labelled or ear-marked. As the contest approaches, fraud, intimidation, bribes, are rife. Immense sums are spent to carry the lame, to hunt up the skulking, to force the indifferent to the polls. Taxes are contributed, to qualify voters, and men are transported, at party expense, from one State to another. Couriers are despatched from county to county, or from State to State, to revive the desponding with false news of success. And after all this, even if a party chances to succeed in its choice of men, what security has it, for the fulfilment of any of its plans? Death may intervene. A "unit" cabinet may explode, and be scattered into many fragments. A party cemented together by no principle of moral cohesion, and founded upon no well-settled convictions of the intellect, may be broken in pieces, like the image of Nebuchadnezzar. Ten thousand retainers of the camp, who followed it only through hope of plundering the dead, will scent other spoils in another camp, when that hope is extinguished; and thus all the toil that was endured, and the expenditures and sacrifices that were made, will be lost.

For the last ten years, such have been the disastrous fluctuations of our National and State policy, on the single subject of the currency, that all the prodigality of nature, pouring her hundreds of millions of products, annually, into our hands, has not been able to save thousands and thousands of our people from poverty; and in many cases, economy, industry, and virtue could not rescue their possessor from want. And why? I answer, as one reason, because this question has been decided, again and again, by voters who could not read and write, — by voters to whom the simplest proposition in political economy, or in national finance, is as unintelligible as a book of Hebrew or Greek. Should such men vote right, *at any one time*, it would be for a wrong reason; and the favorable chances being exhausted, they may be relied upon to vote wrong ever afterwards. Hence, under one administration, we have had a bank, under another, a subtreasury, and the third may be commended to the benefit of its own bankrupt law.

During all this time, the course of our government, on this and other great questions of policy, has been vacillating, — enacting and repealing, advancing and receding, baffling all the plans of the wisest; — instead of imitating in some good degree, as it should do, the steadiness and force of the Divine administration.

And who are they who have suffered most under these changes which so nearly resemble anarchy? Whose property has been dissipated? Whose enterprises have been baffled? Are they not mostly those who have been, not merely neglectful, but disdainful, of the Common Schools? who have given whatever wealth they had to give, to public libraries, to colleges, and the higher seminaries of learning? who have separated their children from the mass, and gathered them into class, and clan, and sectarian schools of their own? who have opposed legislative grants and municipal taxation; and who, for their whole lives, have never countenanced, patronized, or even visited the Common School, from which their own rulers were so soon to emerge? What a remarkable fact it is in the history of this Commonwealth, that amongst all the splendid donations, — amounting in the whole to many millions of dollars, — which have been made to colleges and academies, and to theological institutions for the purpose of upholding the doctrines of some particular sect; — only one man, embracing the *whole* of the rising generation in his philanthropic plan, and acting with a high and enlightened disregard of all local, partisan, and sectarian views, has given any considerable sum to promote the prosperity of Common Schools!*

And this series of disasters, under which we are suffering, must lengthen to an interminable train; those anxieties which the wealthy and the educated now feel for their purse, they must soon feel for their characters, their persons, and their families; the whole country must be involved in wider and deeper calamities, until a more noble and Christian policy is pursued. All the newspapers that steam power can print, during the most protracted political canvass, will be no equivalent for the single book in which a child learns to read. One mind trained to thought and investigation, upon the forms of the schoolroom, will arrive at sounder truths than can ever be impressed upon it by a hired political missionary. If we would have better times, the available school teacher must be sought for, as anxiously as the available candidate for office; and efforts as energetic must be made to bring children into the schools, as are now made to bring voters to the polls. If we would have better times, we need not honor or reward the *writers* of our past history, — Sparks, Bancroft, Irving, — less; but we must honor and reward the *makers* of our future history, — the school-teachers, — more.

But I have labored to supererogation, to show both an existing and a prospective deficiency in knowledge, for managing the vast and precious interests of this great nation. I have shown, — if not an incurable, yet unless cured, — a fatal malady in the head; I must now exhibit a not less fatal malady in the heart. I tremble at the catalogue of national crimes which we are exhibiting before heaven and earth! The party rancor and vilification which rages through our newspaper press, — in utter forgetfulness or contempt of the great spiritual law, that when men pass from judgment to passion, they will soon pass from passion to violence! The fraud, falsehood, bribery, perjury, perpetrated at our elections; and the spirit of wantonness or malice, — of pride

---

* Hon. Edmund Dwight.

or envy, in which the sacred privilege of voting is exercised! The practice of double voting, like parricide in Rome, unheard of in the early days of the Republic, is becoming more and more frequent. Although, in some of the States, a property qualification, and in some even a landed qualification is necessary; yet the number of votes given at the last presidential election, equalled, almost without a fraction, one-sixth part of the whole free population in the Union. In one of the States the number of votes exceeded, by a large fraction, one-fifth of the whole population, — men, women, and children. Will it not be a new form of a Republic, — unknown alike to ancient or modern writers, when the question shall be, — not how many voters there are, but how many ballots can be printed and put surreptitiously into the ballot-box? Then, there is the fraudulent sequestration of votes, by the returning officers, because the majority is adverse to their own favorite candidates, — which has now been done, on a large scale, in three of the principal States in the Union! The scenes of violence enacted, not only *without*, but *within* the Capitol of the nation; and the halls, which should be consecrated to order, and solemnity, and a devout consultation upon the unspeakable magnitude and value of the interests of this great people, desecrated by outrage, and Billingsgate, and drunken brawls! Challenges given, and duels fought by members of Congress, in violation, or evasion, of their own lately enacted law against them; and within the space of a few days, a proud and prominent member, from a proud and prominent State, — the countryman of Washington, and Jefferson, and Madison, put under bonds *to keep the peace*, like a wild, fresh-landed Carib. In two of our legislative assemblies, one member has been murdered by another member, in open day, and during the hours of session; — in one of the cases, the deed being perpetrated by the presiding officer of the assembly, who descended from his chair, and pierced the heart of his victim with a bowie-knife, — and still goes unpunished though not unhonored. What outbreaks of violence all over the country; — the lynching of five men, at one time, at Vicksburg; — the valley of the Mississippi, from St. Louis to

New Orleans, lighted almost as with watch fires, by the burning of human beings; — the riots and demolitions, at New York, at Philadelphia, at Baltimore, at Alton, at Cincinnati; — yes, and the spectacle of our own more serene part of the heavens, crimsoned at midnight, by a conflagration of the dwelling-place of women and female children, — a deed incited and brutally executed, through prejudice, and hostility towards a sect which takes the liberty to protest against Protestants, as Protestants protested against them!

And, in addition to this barbarian force and lawlessness, are not the business relations of the community contaminated, more and more, with speculation and knavery? In mercantile honor and honesty, in the intercourse between buyer and seller, is there not a luxation of all the joints of the body, commercial and social? The number of fraudulent bankruptcies, — fraudulent in the incurring of the debts, if not in the surrender of the assets; — the rapacity of speculation; the breaches of private trust; the embezzlement of corporate funds; the abscondings with government property; the malversations of government fiduciaries, whether of a United States Bank, or of a Girard College; the repudiation of State debts; — and that other class of offences which combines the criminality both of fraud and force, — such as the shooting of a sheriff, who attempted to execute civil process, — or the burning of a bank with all its contents, by a company of debtors, in Mississippi, because their notes had been lodged in it for collection!

I trust the fact will not fail to be observed, and the motive to be appreciated, that, from this terrific array of enormities I have omitted one entire class of events; — a class which may be thought by some more ominous of ill than any I have enumerated. I refer to such facts as the late commotions in Rhode Island ensuing upon the long-delayed extension of suffrage; — the legislative declaration already made in two of the States, of an intention to disregard the apportionment law, recently passed by the general government; — the admission to a seat, in the House of Representatives of the last Congress, of the claimants from New

Jersey, against the credentials of the State authorities; — the refusal of one branch of the Tennessee Legislature to elect Senators to fill vacancies in the Senate of the United States; — the admission into the Union of Territories which had exercised, by assumption, the right of forming a constitution for themselves, without any authority from the general government, or any law prescribing the mode in which it should be done; — the armed "nullification" of South Carolina, etc. I omit all this class of cases from the catalogue, because they are, at present, implicated with strong party feelings, on one side or the other; and it is my intention, on this day, to touch no party chord; — to bring forward nothing, either of fact or of principle, which the candid men of all parties shall not acknowledge to be a compulsive reason for immediate measures of reform.

Let us look at another aspect of this case. The number of convicts at present in confinement, in the penitentiaries, and State prisons of the Union, is very nearly four thousand seven hundred and fifty; and the average duration of their imprisonment is about four years. The number under sentence *for crime*, in common jails, and houses of correction, is not less than the preceding, and the average length of their imprisonment is estimated at six months. Suppose that these culprits live, on an average, but eight years after their enlargement; and we have the appalling number of *eighty-five thousand five hundred* convicted criminals, — proved offenders against the laws of God and man, — almost universally adults, — at large, mingling in our society, and a very large portion of them competent to vote; — there being but three States in all this Union, where, by the constitution of the State, a conviction for felony, or any infamous offence, works a forfeiture of the elective franchise. YES! *voters, good and true*, — for the wrong side, and to send you and me to perdition! And I do not believe there is one State in the Union, whose elections for Governor and other high officers, have not, sometimes, been so nearly a drawn game, that its quota of this felon host, its own battalion of sin, would not have been able to decide them, by what a politician would call, a very respectable majority!

I have somewhere seen the number of atheists, of Abner Kneeland's men, in the United States, stated fearfully high; but upon what authority, or after what extent and accuracy of investigation, I am not able to say. These are all *men*, — if not all *voters*; for, thank Heaven, the female heart is untenantable by atheism. But a fact, far more important than the number of *theoretical* atheists, is the number of *practical* atheists, — of those who live without God in the world, who have neither faith nor practice, respecting the existence, the immutability, and the inevitable execution of the Divine Laws. I say the number of *practical* atheists is the question of greater importance; for who can live in this world and mingle with its people, and not be more and more deeply impressed, day by day, with the divine wisdom of the criterion, "By their fruits ye shall know them"? Actions *are* fruits, while pharisaical professions are only gilded signs or placards, hung upon thistles or thornbushes, saying: "Ho, all ye; *we* bear figs and grapes!"

In this review, I pass by those combinations of ignorance and false teaching, which lead to Mormonism, and Millerism, and Perfectionism. I pass by that reckless and flagitious spirit, which, on the Canadian border, lately came so near to involving us in a conflict with the most powerful nation on earth. I pass by our treatment of the aborigines. I pass by such an event as the Florida war, which has already cost this nation more than thirty millions of dollars; and which, as is now notorious, was instigated by desperadoes, because it promised to prove for them, as it has proved, a more lucrative business than other modes of swindling or depredation.

With irrepressible, but unspeakable joy, I pass by the hundreds of thousands of inebriates, who, so lately, lay weltering upon the sea of Intemperance; yet who, periodically, were *rafted up*, by political partisans, — as men raft up float-wood, — to drop their foul votes into the ballot-box, and elect the rulers of a self-called free and Christian people; — these do I gladly pass by, for the waters of that deluge are subsiding; and already thousands and ten thousands, yea, more than ten times ten thousand, have found an Ararat on the *terra firma* of Abstinence.

Fellow-Citizens, from this glimpse,— this mere bird's-eye view, — of our intellectual and moral condition, I do not hesitate to affirm, that our republican edifice, at this time, — in present fact and truth, — is not sustained by those columns of solid and ever-enduring adamant, — intelligence and virtue. Its various parts are only just clinging together by that remarkable cohesion, — that mutual bearing and support, which unsound portions of a structure may impart to each other; and which, as every mechanic well knows, will, for a time, hold the rotten materials of an edifice together, although not one of its timbers could support its own weight; — and unless, therefore, a new substructure can be placed beneath every buttress and angle of this boasted Temple of Liberty, it will soon totter and fall, and bury all in-dwellers in its ruins.

And what, I again ask, are we doing, to impart soundness and permanency to that which we profess so much to value and admire? We all bear witness that there is but one salvation for the State, — *the knowledge of duty and the will to do it*, among the people. But what measures are we taking, to cause that knowledge to spring up, like a new intellectual creation, in every mind; and to cause that will to be quickened into life, in every breast? We all agree, — the universal experience and history of mankind being our authority, — that, in nineteen cases out of every twenty, if the human mind ever is to be expanded by knowledge and imbued with virtuous principles, it must be done during the susceptible years of childhood and youth. But when we come to the *sine qua non*, — to the *work*, — to the point where volition must issue forth into action, or it is valueless; — when we come to the taxing, to the building, to the books, to the apparatus, to the whole system of preparatory and contemporaneous measures for carrying on, and perfecting the work of education; — where wishes and sympathy and verbal encouragement are nothing without the effective co-operation of those muscles which perform labor and transfer money; — when we come to this point, then excuses teem, and the well-wishers retire from the stage, like actors at the close of a drama. I gladly acknowledge that there are honorable exceptions, in all ranks and classes of men; and in no State in the Union, are there so many of these exceptions, as in Massachusetts; and yet even here, is it not most extensively true, that when we appeal to the different classes and occupations of men, we meet with indifference, if not with repulse? We solicit the farmer to visit the school, but he is too much engaged with the care of his stock, to look after his children. We apply to the tradesman, but his account of profit and loss must be adjusted before he can attend to the source of all profit and loss, in the mind. We call upon the physician, but he has too many patients in the arms of death, to allow him one hour for arresting the spread of a contagion by which, if neglected, hundreds of others must perish. We apply to the lawyer and the judge, but they are redressing the wrongs and avenging the violated laws of society, — they are so engaged in uncoiling the folds of a parent serpent which has wound itself round the State, that they cannot stop to crush a hundred of its young, ere they issue from the nest, to wind their folds alike around the State, and the law, and its ministers. We apply to the clergyman; he bids us God speed, — but commends us for assistance, to the first man we meet; for he and his flock are beleaguered by seven evil spirits, in the form of seven heresies, — each fatal to the souls of men. We sally forth from his doors, and the first man we meet is his clerical brother; but he, too, has seven fatal heresies to combat, and he solemnly assures us that the most dangerous leader of them all, is the man we have just left. We apply to the wealthy and the benevolent, who are carrying on vast religious enterprises abroad; but they have just shipped their cargoes of gold to Africa, to Asia, and to the uttermost isles of the sea, and can spare nothing; — never asking themselves the question, who, *in the next generation*, will support the enterprises they have begun, and retain the foothold they may acquire, if they suffer heathenism, and the idolatry of worshipping base passions, to spring up in their native land, and around their own doors. We go to those great antagonist theological institutions, which have selected high social eminences, all over the land, and entrenched themselves against each other, as warring generals fortify their camps upon the summit of confronting hills; — we implore them to send out one wise and mighty man to guide this great people through a wilderness more difficult to traverse than that which stretched between Egypt and Canaan; but each hostile sect is engaged in propagating a creed which it *knows* to be true, against the fatal delusions of those various and opposite creeds, which each of the other sects also *knows* to be true! Oh! when will men learn, that ever since the Saviour bowed his head upon the cross and said "It is finished," there has been *truth* enough in the world, to make all men wise and holy and happy. All that is wanted, — all that ever has been wanted, is, — minds that will appreciate truth. The barbarian cannot appreciate it, whether born in New Zealand, or in New England. The benighted and brutified child, whose thoughts are born of prejudice, whose actions of sensualism; whose moral sensibilities have been daily seared, from his birth, with the hot iron of vicious customs and maxims, cannot discern truth, cannot know it, will not embrace it, whether his father is called a savage or a Christian. If we say that the conceptions and desires of such minds are a transcript of Divine truth, what do we affirm the original to be! No! Two different elements are essential to the existence of truth in the soul of man; — first, the essence, or prototype of truth, as it exists in the Divine Intelligence; and secondly, a human soul, sufficiently enlightened by knowledge to conceive it, sufficiently exercised in judgment to understand it, and sufficiently free from evil to love it. The latter are every whit as essential as the former. The human mind must be so enlarged that truth can enter it, and so free from selfishness, from pride, and intolerance, that truth may be its constant and welcome resident. To give truth a passport to the souls of men, — to ensure it home and supremacy in the human heart, there must be some previous awakening and culture of the intellectual and moral nature. In this respect, it is with spiritual, as with scientific truth. The great astronomical truths which pertain to the solar system, have existed ever since the creation; — for generations past, they have been known to the learned; — and all the planets, as they move, are heralds and torch-bearers, sent round by the hand of God, revolution after revolution, and age after age, to make perpetual proclamation through all their circuits, and to light up the heavens, from side to side, with ocular and refulgent demonstration of their existence; and yet, until their elements are all laboriously taught, until our minds are opened, and made capacious for their reception, these glorious truths are a blank, and for our vision and joy, might as well never have been. And so of all truth; — there must be a mind enlarged, ennobled, purified, to embrace truth, in all its beauty, sublimity, and holiness, as well as beautiful, sublime and holy truths to be embraced. Until this is so, truth will be a light shining in darkness, and the darkness comprehending it not. But when this shall come to pass, then the awakened soul will exclaim with Jacob, "Surely the Lord was in this place, and I knew it not." Yet, — alike in all lands and for centuries past, — ninety-nine hundredths of all human efforts and expenditures have been devoted to force, upon the successive generations of the young, some special system, which happened in the particular age, to be in the ascendant; and which, in its turn, had been prejudicated by fallible men, to be infallibly true; — while scarcely anything has been done to kindle the love of truth in the human breast, and to train the intellect to strength and impartiality in all investigations after it.

Fellow-Citizens, there is one strongly developed tendency in our political affairs which I cannot pass by, on an occasion like this, without an admonitory word. Though less obvious, yet it is of more evil portent, than any in the dark catalogue I have exhibited. It leads by swift steps to proximate ruin. I refer to the practice of the different political parties, into which we are unhappily divided, of seizing upon some specious aspect of every event, giving it an exaggerated and factitious importance, and perverting it to factious profit. In common and expressive phrase, this is called *making political capital* out of a thing; and the art of making this *capital* seems now to be incorporated into the regular tactics of party leaders. But it is forged capital, and in the end, it must bring forger and accomplices to judgment and condemnation, as well as all their dupes to political and moral insolvency. In law, such practices, or rather mal-practices, are called *chicanery*; and they justly subject to infamy, the practitioner who is corrupted with them. But law deals with private interests,— politics with the vaster interests of the whole community. And why should not the trick and knavery which strike a man's name from the roll of the court, strike it also from the red-book of the nation! Look at it, Fellow-Citizens; — a great question arises in the legislative halls of the State or Nation, or springs up in any part of our country; and immediately the party leaders and the party press reflect before the eyes of all the people, — not segments or fragments, even, — but distorted and discolored images of all the truths, facts and principles, pertaining to that question, — so distorted and discolored that no impartiality or patience can reproduce any likeness to the original. So extensive has this practice become, that an honest inquirer into the merits of men or measures, in reading accounts of the same individuals or transactions, in the rival newspapers of the day, would suppose them to relate to wholly different men and different measures, were it not for the occasional identity of the proper names which are used. Must it not follow that the vast majority of the people will get mutilated and false views; and come, habitually, to decide the real question by looking at the counterfeited, until the mind itself is as perverted as the lights which shine on it. Immense responsibilities attach here to all who influence public opinion, whether they sit in the presidential, or gubernatorial, or editorial chair. The habit of ascribing, to trivial and fleeting considerations, the prominence and inviolability of eternal laws; the habit of discarding at every political crisis, the great principles which lie under the whole length of existence, and are the only possible basis of our well-being, in order to gain some temporary end; the habit, at our oft-recurring elections, of risking all future consequences, to secure present success, is high treason against the sovereignty of truth, and must be the harbinger of a speedy destruction. We can conceive of no power in the universe, that could uphold its throne, under so fatal a policy.

I do not advert to this prominent feature of our times, — worthy of far more extended consideration, — in order that one party may look into the conduct of its adversaries, to find cause of accusation; but that each may look upon its own course, and in view of it, demand and effect a speedy amendment.

Fellow-Citizens, amidst the distractions which now rend the country, let me ask you, as sober and reflecting men, what remedy do you propose for the present? what security for the future? Evils are not avoided by closing our eyes against them; — and, in which direction do you look for hope, without confronting disappointment or despair? Will the great political and financial problems which now agitate the Union, ever be rightly solved and permanently adjusted, while they are submitted, year after year, to voters who cannot even read and write? Can any additional intelligence and integrity be expected in our rulers, without additional intelligence and integrity in the constituency that elects them? Complain of President or Congress as much as we will, they are the very men whom we, the people, have chosen. If the country is an active volcano of ignorance and guilt, why should not Congress be a crater for the outgushing of its lava? Will Providence interfere to rescue us by a miracle, while we are voluntarily pursuing a course, which would make a speedier interference, and a more stupendous miracle necessary for our subsequent rescue? How much of time, of talent, and of wealth, we are annually expending, — in Legislatures, in political conventions, through newspapers, — to gain adherents to one system of policy, or its opposite, to an old party or to a new one; — but how little to rear a people with minds capable of understanding systems of policy, when developed, and of discerning between the right and the wrong, in the parties which beset and would inveigle them. What honors and emoluments are showered upon successful politicians; what penury and obscurity are the portion of those who are moulding the character of a rising generation of sovereigns! And here let not the truth be forgotten, that the weightiest obligation to foster and perfect the work of education, lies upon those States which enjoy the most, and not upon those which suffer under the least; for to whomsoever much is given, of them shall much be required.

Let us suppose that we were now overtaken by some great crisis in our national affairs, — such as we have already seen, or may soon see, — let us suppose that, in the issue of some presidential contest, for instance, not only the public interests of the nation, but the private interests of thousands of individuals, should be adroitly implicated; and that preparations should be made, and a zeal excited, corresponding to the magnitude of the occasion. War impends. Commerce, manufactures, agriculture, are at stake, or in conflict. The profits of capital, and the wages of labor, have been made to antagonize. North and South are confronted. Rich and poor, high and low, radical and conservative, bigot and latitudinarian, are marshalled for the onset. The expectants of office, — suffering under a four, perhaps an eight years' famine, are rioting on anticipated spoils. The spume of other countries and the refuse of our own are coalescing, and some Catiline is springing to the head of every ruffian band. Excitement foams through all the veins of the body politic; — in some it is fever; in others delirium; and under these auspices, or omens, the eventful day arrives.

It surely requires but little effort of the imagination to picture forth the leaders of all the party-colored bands into which our country is divided, as at the head of their respective companies, and gathering them to a mightier assembly than ever met in Grecian Areopagus or Roman Comitia. Among the vast and motley-souled hosts, which such a day would summon together, I will direct your attention to but two grand divisions; — divisions, however, of this republican army, which would be first in the field, and most contentious for the victory. I mean the legionaries of Crime and those of Ignorance.

Behold, on this side, crowding to the polls, and even candidates for the highest offices in the gift of the people, are those whose hands are red with a brother's blood, slain in private quarrel! Close pressing upon these, urges onward a haughty band glittering in wealth, — but, for every flash that gleams from jewel and diamond, a father, a mother, and helpless children, have been stolen, and sold into ransomless bondage. Invading their ranks, struggles forward a troop of assassins, rioters, lynchers, incendiaries, who have hitherto escaped the retributions of law, and would now annihilate the law whose judgments they fear; — behind these, pours on, tumultuous, the chaotic rout of atheism; — and yonder dashes forward a sea of remorseless life, — thousands and ten thousands, — all felons, convicts, condemned by the laws of God and man. In all the dread catalogue of mortal sins, there is not one, but, in that host, there are hearts which have willed, and hands which have perpetrated it. The gallows has spared its victim, the prison has released its tenants, — from dark cells where malice had brooded, where incendiarism and lust had engendered their machinations, where revenge and robbery had held their nightly rehearsals, the leprous multitude is disgorged, and comes up to the ballot-box to fore-doom the destinies of this nation. In gazing at this multitudinous throng, who emerge from their hiding-places on the days of our elections, — all flagrant with crime and infamy, — would not every man exclaim, "I did not know, I could not have thought, that all the foul kennels and stews of earth; nay, nor all the gorged avenues of hell, could regurgitate upon the world, these legions of iniquity!"

But look, again, on the other side, at that deep and dense array of Ignorance, whose limits the eye cannot discover. Its van leans against us here, its rear is beyond the distant hills. They too, in this hour of their country's peril, have come up to turn the folly of which they are unconscious, into measures which they cannot understand, by votes which they cannot read. Nay, more, and worse! for, from the ranks of crime, emissaries and bandit-leaders are sallying forth towards the ranks of ignorance, and hieing to and fro amongst them, — shouting the gibberish war-cries of faction, and flaunting banners with lying symbols.

such as cheat the eye of a mindless brain, — and thus the hosts of crime are to lead on the hosts of ignorance, in their assault upon Liberty and Law!

What, now, shall be done to save the citadel of freedom, where are treasured all the hopes of posterity? Or, if we can survive the peril of such a day, what shall be done, to prevent the next generation sending forth still more numerous hordes, — afflicted with deeper blindness and incited by darker depravity?

Are there any here, who would counsel us to save the people from themselves, by wresting from their hands this formidable right of ballot? Better for the man who would propose this remedy to an infuriate multitude, that he should stand in the lightning's path as it descends from heaven to earth. And, answer me this question; you! who would reconquer for the few, the power which has been won by the many; you! who would disfranchise the common mass of mankind, and recondemn them to become helots, and bond-men, and feudal serfs; — tell me, were they again in the power of your castes, would you not again neglect them, again oppress them, again make them the slaves to your voluptuousness, and the panders or the victims of your vices? Tell me, you royalists and hierarchs, or advocates of royalty and hierarchy! were the poor and the ignorant again in your power, to be tasked and tithed at your pleasure, would you not turn another Ireland into paupers, and colonize another Botany Bay with criminals? Would you not brutify the men of other provinces into the "*Dogs of Vendée*," and debase the noble and refined nature of woman, in other cities, into the "*Poissardes of Paris?*" Oh! better, far better, that the atheist and the blasphemer, and he who since the last setting sun, has dyed his hands in parricide, or his soul in sacrilege, should challenge equal political power with the wisest and the best; — better, that these blind Samsons, in the wantonness of their gigantic strength, should tear down the pillars of the Republic, than that the great lesson which Heaven, for six thousand years, has been teaching to the world, should be lost upon it; — the lesson that the intellectual and moral nature of man is the one thing precious in the sight of God; and therefore, until this nature is cultivated, and enlightened, and purified, neither opulence nor power, nor learning nor genius, nor domestic sanctity, nor the holiness of God's altars, can ever be safe. Until the immortal and godlike capacities of every being that comes into the world are deemed more worthy, are watched more tenderly, than any other thing, no dynasty of men, or form of government, can stand, or shall stand, upon the face of the earth; and the force or the fraud which would seek to uphold them, shall be but "as fetters of flax to bind the flame."

In all that company of felons and caitiffs, who prowl over the land, is there one man, who did not bring with him into life, the divine germ of conscience, a sensibility to right, and capacities which might have been nurtured and trained into the fear of God, and the love of man? In all this company of ignorance, which, in its insane surgery, dissects eye and brain and heart, and maims every limb of the body politic, to find the disease, which honestly, though blindly, it wishes to cure;—in all this company, is there one, who did not bring with him into life, noble faculties of thought,—capabilities of judgment, and prudence, and skill, that might have been cultivated into a knowledge, an appreciation, and a wise and loving guardianship, of all human interests and human rights? The wickedness and blindness of the subject are the judgments of heaven for the neglect of the sovereign; for, to this end and to no other, was superiority given to a few, and the souls of all men pre-adapted to pay spontaneous homage to strength and talent and exalted station, that through the benignant and attractive influence of their possessors, the whole race might be won to wisdom and virtue.

Let those, then, whose wealth is lost or jeoparded by fraud or misgovernment; let those who quake with apprehension for the fate of all they hold dear; let those who behold and lament the desecration of all that is holy; let rulers whose counsels are perplexed, whose plans are baffled, whose laws defied or evaded; —let them all know, that whatever ills they feel or fear, are but the just retributions of a righteous heaven for neglected childhood.

Remember, then, the child whose voice first lisps, to-day, before that voice shall whisper sedition in secret, or thunder treason at the head of an armed band. Remember the child whose hand, to-day, first lifts its tiny bauble, before that hand shall scatter fire-brands, arrows and death. Remember those sportive groups of youth in whose halcyon bosoms there sleeps an ocean, as yet scarcely ruffled by the passions, which soon shall heave it as with the tempest's strength. Remember, that whatever station in life you may fill, these mortals, — these immortals, are your care. Devote, expend, consecrate yourselves to the holy work of their improvement. Pour out light and truth, as God pours sunshine and rain. No longer seek knowledge as the luxury of a few, but dispense it amongst all as the bread of life. Learn only how the ignorant may learn; how the innocent may be preserved; the vicious reclaimed. Call down the astronomer from the skies; call up the geologist from his subterranean explorations; summon, if need be, the mightiest intellects from the Council Chamber of the nation; enter cloistered halls, where the scholiast muses over superfluous annotations; dissolve conclave and synod, where subtle polemics are vainly discussing their barren dogmas; — collect whatever of talent, or erudition, or eloquence, or authority, the broad land can supply, *and go forth*, AND TEACH THIS PEOPLE. For, in the name of the living God, it must be proclaimed, that licentiousness shall be the liberty; and violence and chicanery shall be the law; and superstition and craft shall be the religion; and the self-destructive indulgence of all sensual and unhallowed passions shall be the only happiness of that people who neglect the education of their children.

CPSIA information can be obtained
at www.ICGtesting.com
Printed in the USA
BVOW04s1029281017
498919BV00010BA/228/P